ARC
LIBRARY

D1602758

AMONG THE NIGHTMARE FIGHTERS

AMONG THE NIGHTMARE FIGHTERS

American Poets of World War II

DIEDERIK OOSTDIJK

The University of South Carolina Press

Published by the University of South Carolina Press
Columbia, South Carolina 29208

www.sc.edu/uscpress

Manufactured in the United States of America

20 19 18 17 16 15 14 13 12 11 10 9 8 7 6 5 4 3 2 1

Library of Congress Cataloging-in-Publication Data
Oostdijk, Diederik, 1972–
Among the nightmare fighters : American poets of World War II / Diederik Oostdijk.
p. cm.
Includes bibliographical references and index.
ISBN 978-1-57003-995-9 (cloth : alk. paper)
1. American poetry—20th century—History and criticism. 2. American poetry—Male authors—History and criticism. 3. World War, 1939–1945—United States—Literature and the war. 4. War poetry, American—History and criticism. 5. War in literature. I. Title.
PS310.W68O67 2011
811'.5209—dc22
2011004417

This book was printed on Glatfelter Natures, a recycled paper with 30 percent postconsumer waste content.

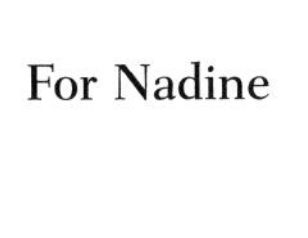

For Nadine

CONTENTS

PREFACE

One of the characters in James Dickey's novel *Alnilam* mentions that it took seventy-five men to keep one war plane in the air during World War II. Even though writing this book often felt like a solo flight with the constant fear of crashing down, I would estimate that I was levitated by roughly the same number of people when working on this project. For brevity's sake I will name only the most essential, though. A number of friends and fellow scholars offered advice from the very beginning of this project to the end. On my side of the Atlantic, Gerry Janssens read the entire typescript with a fastidious eye, correcting many mistakes. My friend Sally Clarke did the same later on, weeding out remaining errors. Another good friend, Alan Cienki, suggested many subtle changes, which taken together constituted a big help. Stef Craps taught me a few essential things about trauma theory and carefully read a chapter on Ciardi. Richard Todd astutely read the opening chapters of this book and saved me from some minor embarrassments.

I thank especially, on the other side of the Atlantic, Henry Hart for relating many revealing anecdotes about James Dickey, for his wise counsel at various stages during the writing process, and for sending American stamps. Steven Gould Axelrod supported this project in myriad ways from the very start, and he has always been a most gracious and encouraging friend. W. D. Ehrhart read the entire typescript and corrected dozens of mistakes, and asked a number of pertinent questions. Robert Phillips, the literary executor of the estate of Karl Shapiro, has encouraged my work on Shapiro for a long time, for which I am grateful, too. Richard Flynn helped in securing a crucial permission request by getting me in touch with Beatrice Garbett. Besides being an inspirational scholar on World War II, Alexander Nemerov was extremely helpful in proffering essential information about his father's career. He shared some of his father's war letters from his personal archive, and got me in touch with his mother and one of his brothers. Moreover, he also read through an earlier version of the typescript for this book and greatly improved the concept of it with his poetically insightful comments. As a writer on war poetry, I am most deeply indebted to Lorrie Goldensohn. Coteaching a course on American war poetry during her stay as a Fulbright professor at VU University in Amsterdam was an enriching experience that benefited this book in many ways. Her genuine interest, astute suggestions and questions, and unstinting support for this project made the journey so much more enjoyable and the end result so much better.

Librarians at several libraries across the United States assisted me in my search for valuable archival material that helped tell the story of the American poets of World War II. I thank especially Ruth M. Alvarez of the University of Maryland Library, who introduced me to the late Evalyn Katz, whose home-front stories during the war make up part of this book. Stephen Enniss was kind enough to grant me a Woodruff Library Research Fellowship, which allowed me to spend a month at the Manuscript, Archives & Rare Book Library (MARBL) of Emory University in Atlanta, Georgia, to study the James Dickey and Anthony Hecht papers. The Dorot Foundation granted me a fellowship in Jewish studies to study Karl Shapiro's papers at the Harry Ransom Humanities Research Center in Austin, Texas; I thank especially Pat Fox and Thomas F. Staley at that library. My own university, VU University Amsterdam, generously financed a final research trip to the Library of Congress, Yale University, Harvard University, and the New York Public Library.

Several anonymous reviewers read and commented on the book at several stages of its completion, and their questions, concerns, and critical comments really challenged me to write a better book. The Netherlands Organisation for Scientific Research (NWO) offered me a grant to finish the book manuscript, and I want to thank them for their generosity and their two anonymous reviewers for their suggestions. Theo Bögels, Mike Hannay, and Dick Schram offered advice or support when writing the grant proposal. Other colleagues, including Anita Raghunath and Kristine Steenbergh, had to work harder while I was on sabbatical. I want to express my gratitude to Suzanne Harmsen-Peraino, who taught my courses while I was away. Carmen Bohncke, a former student at VU University Amsterdam, assisted me in sorting out copyright matters. Finally, I want to thank Jim Denton at the University of South Carolina Press, who took an immediate interest in this project and shepherded it through publication.

It may seem odd for a Dutchman to have written this book on American poets of World War II, but I believe that the stories in this book are intrinsically linked to my personal history, my family's background, and my country's history. My mother was a young girl in the southwest of the Netherlands when that war started. From as long as I can remember, she has told me stories about how their town, Zierikzee, was invaded by the Germans in 1940; how she witnessed how members of the Dutch Nationalist Socialist Party looted the house of one of the town's Jewish families; how she listened in her bed to the V-1s and V-2s that flew overhead en route to England at night, and how her family was evacuated when the island on which they lived was flooded by the Germans. I grew up in another part of the Netherlands, in the city of Nijmegen, which was bombed by the American air corps, mistaking it for a German city. When cycling to school I always passed a Canadian war cemetery where soldiers were buried who had died while trying to push back the Germans in 1944 and 1945. World War II is very tangible in these regions. Immediately after the war my father, who was then a teenager, was sent to the Dutch East Indies as a private first class in the medical corps in an effort to revert Indonesia's independence. He stayed over there for three years, but never said much about that time, and I never had a chance to talk to him about it before he died in 1985. The stories my mother told me and the stories my father never told me prepared me for writing this book, and I am deeply indebted to them both. I dedicate this book to my wife, Nadine Akkerman. If not my copilot, she was at least my navigator who always made sure that I kept a steady course and could land safely.

ACKNOWLEDGMENTS

Permission was kindly granted to reprint from the following sources:

W. H. Auden, "In Memory of W. B. Yeats," © 1940 and renewed 1968 by W. H. Auden; "Shield of Achilles," © 1952 by W. H. Auden; "Homage to Clio," © 1976 by Edward Mendelson, William Meredith, and Monroe K. Spears, executors of the Estate of W. H. Auden, from *Collected Poems* by W. H. Auden. Used by permission of Random House, Inc.

John Berryman, excerpts from "Boston Common" from *Collected Poems: 1937–1971*. © 1989 by Kate Donahue Berryman. Reprinted by permission of Farrar, Straus and Giroux, LLC.

Elizabeth Bishop, excerpts from "In the Waiting Room" and "Roosters" from *The Complete Poems: 1927–1979*. © 1979, 1983 by Alice Helen Methfessel. Reprinted by permission of Farrar, Straus and Giroux, LLC.

Gwendolyn Brooks, excerpts from "Gay Chaps at the Bar" and "Negro Hero" from *Selected Poems*. Reprinted with permission of Brooks Permissions.

Hayden Carruth, "The Birds of Vietnam, from *From Snow, and Rock, From Chaos*, © 1973 by New Directions Publishing Corp. Reprinted by permission of New Directions Publishing Corp.

John Ciardi, excerpts from *The Collected Poems of John Ciardi*, edited by Edward M. Cifelli. © by John Ciardi. Reprinted with the permission of the University of Arkansas Press, www.uapress.com. Excerpts from *Lives of X* (Rutgers University Press, 1971) and unpublished letters and other archival material used by permission of John L. Ciardi, Trustee, Ciardi Trust. "Bashing the Babies," from *For Instance* by John Ciardi. © 1979 by John Ciardi. Used by permission of W. W. Norton & Company, Inc.

Malcolm Cowley, excerpt from unpublished letter used by permission of the Literary Estate of Malcolm Cowley.

James Dickey, excerpts of "The Baggage King," "The Firebombing," "Hunting Civil War Relics at Nimblewill Creek," "The Performance," "Two

Poems of Flight-Sleep," and "The Wedding" from *The Whole Motion: Collected Poems, 1945–1992.* © 1992 by James Dickey and reprinted by permission of Wesleyan University Press.

Alan Dugan, excerpts from "Speech for Aeneas," "Stentor and Mourning," "On Shields. Against World War III," and "Memories of Verdun" from *Poems Seven: New and Complete Poetry.* © 2001 by Alan Dugan. Reprinted with the permission of Seven Stories Press, www.sevenstories.com.

Anthony Hecht, "Rites and Ceremonies," "More Light! More Light," "It Our-Herods Herod. Pray You, Avoid It," "An Overview," and "The Odds," from *Collected Earlier Poems,* © 1990 by Anthony E. Hecht. "The Book of Yolek," from *Collected Later Poems,* © 2003. Used by permission of Alfred A. Knopf, a division of Random House, Inc. Quotations from the letters and papers of Anthony Hecht: © 2011 by the Estate of Anthony Hecht. Reprinted by permission of the Estate.

Richard Hugo, "Letter to Simic from Boulder," from *Making Certain It Goes On: Collected Poems of Richard Hugo.* © 1984 by the Estate of Richard Hugo. Used by permission of W. W. Norton & Company, Inc.

Randall Jarrell, excerpts from "Burning the Letters," "A Camp in the Prussian Forest," "The Death of the Ball Turret Gunner," "Eighth Air Force," "The Head of Wisdom" "Jews at Haifa," "The Lines," "Losses," "The Lost World," "A Lullaby," "Mail Call," "O My Name It Is Sam Hall," "Protocols," "Siegfried," and "The Soldier" from *The Complete Poems.* © 1969, renewed 1997 by Mary von S. Jarrell. Reprinted by permission of Farrar, Straus and Giroux, LLC. Archival material is published by permission of the Randall Jarrell Literary Estate.

Weldon Kees, permission to reprint excerpts from "June 1940" appearing in *The Collected Poems of Weldon Kees* used by permission of the University of Nebraska Press.

Lincoln Kirstein, published and unpublished writings by Lincoln Kirstein are © 2010 by the New York Public Library (Astor, Lenox and Tilden Foundations).

Robert Lowell, excerpts from "The Bomber," "The Capitalist's Meditation by the Civil War Monument," "Christmas Eve Under Hooker's Statue," "The Dead in Europe," "For the Union Dead," "Marriage," "Memories on West Street and Lepke," "My Season in Hell," "On the Eve of the Feast of the Immaculate Conception," "Our Afterlife," "Sheridan," and "Since 1939" from *Collected Poems.* © 2003 by Harriet Lowell and Sheridan Lowell. Reprinted by permission of Farrar, Straus and Giroux, LLC. Excerpts from unpublished holograph annotations, typescript/drafts of manuscript pages of poems, and letters to Karl Shapiro by Robert Lowell. © 2010 by Harriet Lowell and Sheridan Lowell. Printed by permission of Farrar, Straus and Giroux, LLC on behalf of the Robert Lowell Estate.

William Meredith, selections from the poetry of William Meredith are reprinted from *Effort at Speech: New and Selected Poems* by William Meredith, published by TriQuarterly Books / Northwestern University Press in 1997. © 1997 by William Meredith. All rights reserved; used by permission of Northwestern University Press and Richard Harteis.

Howard Nemerov, "The Afterlife," "D Day Plus Twenty Years," "Models," "Night Operations, Coastal Command RAF," "IFF," "Ultima Ratio Reagan," "The War in the Air," from *War Stories: Poems about Long Ago and Now* (University of Chicago Press, 1987); "The Air Force Museum at Dayton" from *Inside the Onion* (University of Chicago Press, 1984); and "For W___, Who Commanded Well," "I Only Am Escaped to Tell Thee," "The Language of the Tribe," "A Memory of the War," "An Old Warplane," "On Being Asked for a Peace Poem," "On Reading 'The Love and Death of Cornet Christopher Rilke,'" "Peace in Our Time," "Redeployment," "Thanksgrieving," "Thirtieth Anniversary Report," "To Clio, Muse of History," "To the Poets," and "To the Rulers," from *The Collected Poems of Howard Nemerov* (University of Chicago Press, 1977), and unpublished letters and other archival material. Used by permission of Margaret Nemerov.

Muriel Rukeyser, "To Be a Jew in the Twentieth Century" is reprinted by permission of International Creative Management, Inc. © 2005 by Muriel Rukeyser.

Karl Shapiro, excerpts from "Birthday Poem," "The Conscientious Objector," "The Gun," "He-Man," "Human Nature," "Jew," "The New Ring," "Robert Lowell," "Scyros," "Shylock," "The Soldier," "Sunday: New Guinea," "The Synagogue," "Troop Train," "University," and "V-Letter" used by permission of Harold Ober Associates, Inc. Unpublished letters and other archival material published by permission of Robert Phillips, literary executor for the Estate of Karl Shapiro.

Louis Simpson, excerpts from "Carentan O Carentan" and "The Silent Generation" from *The Owner of the House: New Collected Poems 1940–2001*. © 2003 by Louis Simpson. Reprinted with the permission of BOA Editions, Ltd., www.boaeditions.org.

W. D. Snodgrass, excerpts "Returned to Risco, 1946" from *Not for Specialists: New and Selected Poems*. © Copyright 1959, 2006 by W. D. Snodgrass. Reprinted with the permission of BOA Editions, Ltd., www.boaeditions.org.

Allen Tate, excerpts from "Ode to Our Young Pro-Consuls of the Air" and "To the Lacedemonians" from *Collected Poems: 1919–1976*. © 1977 by Allen Tate. Reprinted by permission of Farrar, Straus and Giroux, LLC. Excerpts from unpublished letters and other archival material used by permission of Helen H. Tate. Quotations from a draft of "Ode to Our Young Pro-Consuls of the Air" in the Allen Tate Papers, Manuscript Division, Department of Rare Books and Special Collections, are used by permission of Princeton University Library.

Katharine S. White, acknowledgment is made to the Estate of E. B. White for permission to reprint excerpts from the letter of Katharine S. White.

Richard Wilbur, "Place Pigalle" and "A Miltonic Sonnet for Mr. Johnson" reprinted with the permission of Richard Wilbur.

A shorter version of chapter 15 was published in *PN Review* 192 (March/April 2010). An earlier version of chapter 16 was published as "Debunking 'The Good War' Myth: Howard Nemerov War's Poetry" in Wilfried Wilms and William Rasch, eds., *Bombs Away! Representing the Air War over Europe and Japan* (Amsterdam / New York: Rodopi, 2006).

Introduction

A SILENT GENERATION?

Hidden in Howard Nemerov's archive at Washington University in St. Louis, the city where he lived the last quarter of his life, is a typescript of a poem called "D Day plus 20 years." It is a moving poem about the memory of World War II, but amazingly it was never published and lay buried in his archive for more than forty years. The first of the two stanzas offers a descriptive scene in which Nemerov sketches the awkwardness of the twentieth anniversary of D-day in Normandy in 1964. Children cannot recall the poems they had rehearsed and are supposed to declaim; veterans take pains to remember "how it would have to be"; and the wreaths end up all over the place: some are "dropped on the sand" and some "return, time after time, on the tide."

It is to the children (those who were present on Normandy beach, his own children, and perhaps all of the younger people who were not there to witness the events) that Nemerov addresses the second stanza in which he attempts to elucidate what a unique military event the invasion at Normandy was:

> Children, that immense and momentary power,
> The planning, the coordination, the fine
> June morning, and the right state of the tide,
> The maximum effort by the greatest force,
> The absolute supremacy in the air, children,
> The wreaths are spinning on the waves,
> The ones that get beyond the breakers
> Carry their messages nowhere.[1]

For a moment Nemerov lapses into grand military diction, but then catches himself and becomes decidedly solemn again. Returning once again to the wreaths, he decides that they, like his own words in his poem, "carry their messages nowhere." Both Nemerov's poem and the wreaths try to express something weighty and important that is commensurate with the suffering at Normandy. Yet they fail to relate anything close to the meaning of the events of twenty years earlier.

Nemerov is convinced that nobody will ever be able to recapture the essence of Normandy and World War II. Writing about the wreaths, but also indirectly about his own war poems, he states:

> No one will find them, no one will read
> Them, there is neither comfort nor regret
> In the drowned world of the great war
> That gives off such a silence now
> To anyone who listens.[2]

These simple but powerful lines articulate the quintessence of the poetic response to World War II. Silence seems to be the most appropriate reaction to D-day and World War II, Nemerov suggests. And yet as a poet Nemerov ironically needs words to express this. Nemerov's "D Day plus 20 years" stresses the paradox that underlies much of the poetry of World War II. Most of the poets of the era would rather have been silent about their experiences, in part because the events they witnessed or heard about were too devastating to capture in words. Yet they nevertheless were compelled to write about them.

Nemerov's poem was named after a highly publicized CBS television documentary that was broadcast on June 5, 1964, the day before the twentieth anniversary of D-day. The popular television journalist Walter Cronkite and the former general and president Dwight D. Eisenhower had revisited the beaches of Normandy for this occasion. "Eisenhower's return to Normandy drew large ratings and critical acclaim when it was broadcast," Craig Allen writes in his book *Eisenhower and the Mass Media*.[3] Nemerov's more precarious and private message about the impossibility to communicate how momentous that event was did not draw such a wide audience. Nemerov chose not to publish his poem and to keep his thoughts about the commemoration to himself.

Like Nemerov, the poets of World War II did not publicize their views about the war. Their compulsion to write about it was marked by a lack of certainty whether their message was getting through or was meaningful at all. All of the key poets discussed in this book left unpublished war poems in their archives. Some are rudimentary and perhaps not up to standard, but others, like Nemerov's "D Day plus 20 years," seem pertinent and definitely publishable. John Ciardi and James Dickey each abandoned dozens of poems that they never chose to print in magazines, journals, or books. It appears that they thought that the history of World War II was already fixed in the American imagination and that their personal musings would have no major impact.

The reticent way in which the poets of World War II wrote their poetry about the most devastating experiences of their lives influenced the way in which their poems were received. "World War II poetry did not often linger so much on overt pity or anger as the poetry of the Great War did," Janis P. Stout states, making it harder to detect the tone of the war poetry of this generation.[4] As a consequence, their contribution to the genre of war poetry has been considered negligent. In 1999 the well-known historian Douglas Brinkley devoted his commentary on National Public Radio to the question why World War II did not produce many outstanding American war poems. "What great poems emerged from World War II?" he asked before answering his own question, and providing a possible reason for this perceived lack: "Not many. It's long been my contention that the horrors of the Second World War and the Holocaust essentially silenced the poet."[5]

Brinkley voices a view that was widely held and which has persisted to a certain extent, even among literary scholars. In 2008 James Anderson Winn, for instance, claimed in *The Poetry of War* that "World War II produced far fewer poems than World War I" and that "for many poets, silence has seemed the only option."[6] Yet there are dozens of published and unpublished poems by poets like Ciardi, Dickey, and Nemerov who were in the armed forces, and many more by other American poets, both male and female, who suddenly found themselves among the nightmare fighters in the early 1940s. They were not a silent generation, but responded to the war in a quiet and undemonstrative way.

Several publications have appeared in the decade since Brinkley's remarks that show an awareness of the rich body of American poetry about World War II.[7] Foremost among these is the anthology *Poets of World War II* (2003), which was reviewed widely.[8] The editor, Harvey Shapiro, himself a poet and veteran of that war, was aware of the popular preconception that Brinkley and Winn voice: "Comparisons can be odious," he writes in the introduction to his anthology, "but common wisdom has it that the poets of World War I—Wilfred Owen, Robert Graves, Siegfried Sassoon, Edmund Blunden, Isaac Rosenberg—left us a monument and the poets of World War II did not." Shapiro's claim that the American poets of World War II "produced a body of work that has not yet been recognized for its clean and powerful eloquence" is, however, fully justified.[9]

And yet this notion of silence that both Brinkley and Winn introduce is an important consideration. How can we make sense of this strange paradox that the World War II poets are believed to have been silent, but were actually extremely prolific? Why are so few of their war poems known? Why did several poets, such as Dickey and Nemerov, wait so long to write about

World War II? Were they perceived as being silent because their audience was not inclined to listen to the poet at war's end? Was their audience really not ready to listen to them, or did the poets lack faith in their audience's ability to understand? These are questions I hope to answer in this book. Harvey Shapiro offers a tantalizing sampler of World War II poetry, but there are many more poets and poems that need to be explored and reconsidered to comprehend the indirect and variegated reaction to World War II.

Margot Norris has suggested that "the American poetry of World War II is extremely diverse both formally and thematically. As a result it defies classification and frustrates any sense of coherence."[10] There is no denying that the body of poetry of this war is extremely varied, but it is nevertheless possible to perceive clear patterns in the poets' responses when focusing on a key group of poets who began to form a generation because of the war, which was a central experience for all of them. This group principally includes John Ciardi, James Dickey, Anthony Hecht, Randall Jarrell, Lincoln Kirstein, Robert Lowell, Howard Nemerov, Karl Shapiro, Louis Simpson, and William Stafford. Yet I also discuss, more marginally, the war poems of John Berryman, Elizabeth Bishop, Gwendolyn Brooks, Hayden Carruth, Alan Dugan, Weldon Kees, Muriel Rukeyser, Richard Wilbur, and a few others. Their collective poetry shows four themes or obsessions—tradition, identity, masculinity, and afterlife—that make it possible to understand their indirect, belated, and seemingly incoherent response to the war that had engulfed them.

Most of these poets were soldier-poets and enlisted in the army, navy, or army air corps. Yet this book seeks to go beyond "the cult of the soldier-poet," as Mark W. Van Wienen calls it, and also focuses on conscientious objectors and those who were turned down for military service because they were found to be physically or mentally unfit.[11] Theirs was very much a man's world, which included some women, such as Bishop, Brooks, and Rukeyser, who also feature in this book.[12] Yet the focus of attention will be on male poets of World War II who were struggling with their own masculinity, as one part of this book explores. War had long been considered a masculine rite of passage, but the male American poets of World War II were the first generation of war poets who quietly but collectively challenged this notion.

Like many other generations of war poets, the World War II poets experienced a progression from innocence to experience. They were—like their English predecessors from the First World War—attracted to soldiering when young, but were far more conflicted about the general assumption that experience in war leads to a successful adult masculinity. Even before the war started a great number of World War II poets had stopped believing the myth that war turns boys into men. For a variety of reasons that partly stemmed from their intellectual bearings and partly from their own individual temperaments, political and religious convictions, and ethnic and national backgrounds, this ordinary equation of war and masculine development could not be wholly affirmed by the American poets of World War II.

Their unwillingness to go along with this conventional assumption, and their unwillingness to jubilantly celebrate the outcome of World War II, perhaps led to their reluctance to write, causing them to be interpreted as silent. Making them strip from their civilian clothes and forcing them to abandon their families to fight did not lead the poets of World War II to feel more mature or more manly. They were painstakingly aware of the precariousness of the human being in the face of something as overwhelming as war, and they did not consider that war had a salutary effect on anyone. Most of them did not turn against the war, however, as they realized that the alternative to fighting Nazi Germany and imperialist Japan would be even worse. Their poems thus cannot be considered simply as antiwar poems, although collectively they show that the effects of war are ultimately shattering to all individuals caught in it.

Among the Nightmare Fighters is a comprehensive but not exhaustive book on the poets of World War II. It centers on a generation of white, male, so-called academic poets who published their poems in the *Kenyon Review,* the *New Yorker,* and *Partisan Review,* and came to prominence in the 1940s and 1950s. Most of these poets knew, read, and reviewed each other, and competed for the same jobs and prizes. Despite the differences that exist between them, they should be regarded as one generation as they themselves also recognized. The focus on this tight-knit circle of poets means that I largely ignore poets of other ethnic groups, or those who wrote overtly political poetry.[13] They belong to "a very different poetry-producing and poetry-reading culture," as Van Wienen has said about American political poetry of the First World War, although they deserve to be read and discussed.[14]

It also means that I only tangentially comment on poets who belonged to earlier generations as well—for instance, T. S. Eliot or Ezra Pound—or those associated with later, experimental generations, including the Beat generation, the Black Mountain group, or the New York School poets. There is no denying that poets as diverse and accomplished as Robert Duncan, Langston Hughes, Kenneth Koch, Thomas McGrath, George Oppen, Charles Reznikoff, and Lucien Stryk have also written insightfully about their participation in World War II, but it appears that their influences or experiences were markedly different from the group of poets featured in this book. It is my belief, though, that the wide net I have cast contains many of the most important American poems published about World War II.

The prominence of Randall Jarrell will surprise few informed readers of twentieth-century American poetry. His early war poetry, including the classic "The Death of the Ball Turret Gunner," set the example of how American World War II poems would differ from their predecessors, as did his powerful reviews, articles, and personal letters, which held up a mirror to the poets of his generation, especially Robert Lowell. This book also makes a special case for the war poetry of Anthony Hecht and Nemerov, however, whose importance as World War II poets is still largely unknown. They emerged from Jarrell's shadow in the decades following the war, but their belated yet beautifully evocative responses to the war are equally successful in conveying how World War II impacted a generation of boys and men.

In the last decade articles and monographs on the "academic" generation of poets have multiplied, and several critics have made tentative efforts to define a common poetic style. This is apparent from Thomas Travisano's *Midcentury Quartet: Bishop, Lowell, Jarrell, Berryman and the Making of a Postmodern Aesthetic* (1999); Suzanne Ferguson's edited volume, *Jarrell, Bishop, Lowell & Co.: Middle-Generation Poets in Context* (2003); as well as Eric Haralson's edited collection, *Reading the Middle Generation Anew: Culture, Community, and Form in Twentieth-Century American Poetry* (2006). The names that are generally applied to this generation are notably vague and unsatisfactory as even the critics who use them realize. Travisano borrowed the word "midcentury" from Ciardi's 1950 anthology *Mid-Century American Poets*, a first attempt to take stock of what the young poets who had emerged in the 1940s had to offer. Yet the adjective "midcentury" refers only to the time period in which these poets came to prominence, not to what they all shared.

Coined by critic Bruce Bawer in 1986, the term "middle generation" has caught on the most, and it is the one I use in this book. It captures how this generation of poets is stuck in the middle between the daunting high modernists and the more vocal Beat, Black Mountain, and New York School poets. It also draws attention to their uncertain and liminal position in life and in twentieth-century American poetry, and how they remained "distant from the extremes," as Haralson has suggested.[15] Ferguson alludes to the quiet and reserved nature of the generation as well when she writes in the introduction to *Jarrell, Bishop, Lowell & Co.* that she also "fell back on Bruce Bawer's designation of the 'middle generation'" because of "the absence of manifestos by them, a suitable monarch, or overarching descriptive 'theme.'"[16] The poets themselves frequently testified that they believed they constituted a generation, but refrained from giving it a proper name.

Some two decades after the war Karl Shapiro and Louis Simpson, independent of each other, came up with another name that is a bit more revealing because it links the essence of their generation to World War II. "We all came out of the same army and joined the same generation of silence," Shapiro writes in *The Bourgeois Poet* (1964), addressing Ciardi.[17] Five years earlier Simpson had published a poem whose title, "The Silent Generation," had evoked the same concept as Shapiro's phrase. I quote Simpson's final two stanzas:

> It was my generation
> That put the Devil down
> With great enthusiasm.
> But now our occupation
> Is gone. Our education
> Is wasted on the town.
>
> We lack enthusiasm.
> Life seems a mystery;
> It's like the play a lady
> Told me about: "It's not . . .
> It doesn't have a plot,"
> She said. "It's history."[18]

The zeal of Simpson's generation is gone after the war, and they live their lives perfunctorily. The veterans do not believe that their postwar life has a clear storyline; they miss the sense of mission and purpose of the war.

Simpson seems to have taken the phrase "our occupation / Is gone" from Othello's grand farewell to arms in Shakespeare's eponymous play:

> O now for ever
> Farewell the tranquil mind, farewell content!
> Farewell the plumed troops and the big wars
> That makes ambition virtue! O farewell,
> Farewell the neighing steeds and the shrill trump,
> The spirit-stirring drum, th'ear-piercing fife,
> The royal banner, and all quality,
> Pride, pomp and circumstance of glorious war!
> And, O you mortal engines whose rude throats
> Th'immportal Jove's dread clamours counterfeit,
> Farewell: Othello's occupation's gone.[19]

The pomposity of Othello's lines and the self-pity that they exude contrast sharply with the plain, matter-of-fact style of Simpson's poem. In fact, the juxtaposition of these two texts emphasizes the understated nature of Simpson's profound message that his postwar life has lost a sense of meaning. The simplistic rhymes, unassuming diction, and prosy lines downplay the sense of tragedy that Simpson's speaker evidently feels but does not want to showcase. Whereas Othello declares this loss boisterously as is evident from the repetition of the word "Farewell" and by the many exclamation marks, Simpson whispers his privations.

Even though Simpson's poem is unmistakably about World War II, it may not be easily recognizable as a war poem. The reason for this is that it does not match the reader's expectations of what a war poem should look like. In a revealing introduction to Lincoln Kirstein's *Rhymes of a PFC* (1964), one of the most versatile poets of World War II, W. H. Auden, outlined how war poets had written in the past:

> Despite all changes in values, interests, sensibility, the basic assumptions governing the treatment of warfare in poetry remained pretty well unchanged from Homer's time down until the Napoleonic Wars. These assumptions were as follows. 1) The Warrior is a Hero, that is to say, a numinous being. 2) War is pre-eminently the sphere of public deeds of heroism by individual persons; in no other sphere can a man so clearly disclose to others who he is. 3) Since his deeds are public, the warrior himself does not have to relate them. That duty falls to the professional poet who, as the legend of Homer's blindness indicates, is not himself a combatant. 4) The poet's job is to take the known story and sing of it in a style worthy of its greatness, that is to say, in a "high" style.[20]

The English poets of the First World War changed the expectations of readers dramatically, but provided an equally strong model for the poets of World War II to engage with. After the Great War, war poets were expected to have battlefront experience and to relate the horror of war with vivid and thought-provoking details, as Wilfred Owen had done most famously.

Yet the American poets of World War II could not embrace either of these two models. They certainly could not celebrate the warrior as a hero, as previous generations of war poets had done, but the Owen model did not sit comfortably with them either. World War II was an entirely different war, without "the single traumatic focus of the Great War's trenches," as Roderick Watson has noted, making the poetry of World War II poetry more "disparate."[21] Most of the World War II poets were not in the infantry, so they did not encounter similar events that Owen, Rosenberg, and Sassoon had penned about the First World War. Many of the American poets of World War II were instead in the air corps. Not only does this fact reflect an innovation in warfare, it also means that these war poets offered, literally and figuratively, a different perspective of war. From high above, they could see what a puny creature a human being is, and how helpless they themselves were, trapped in their war machines. Those poets who were exposed to battles on land—such as Anthony Hecht and Richard Wilbur—for the most part could not or chose not to write about these experiences.[22]

Instead of opting for the usual models of the war poem, the poets of World War II present more varied and enigmatic war poems, usually approaching war from unexpected angles. They wrote poems, such as Simpson's "The Silent Generation," that are sometimes so understated and cryptic that they may not even be recognized as proper war poems. Only when expanding our ideas of what a war poem is or could be can we understand more fully what they have to say about World War II in their miniature stories.[23] "One big 'American war story' and innumerable smaller stories emerged from World War II," as Steven Gould Axelrod has written:"The big story is that American power saved the world. We might call this story the American victory narrative. The smaller stories concern the multitudinous acts, events, ideas, and feelings that circulated through the war. All of these small stories bear repeating and pondering, and they in fact dominate our poetry."[24] The American poets of World War II have left an astonishingly wide-ranging body of work, and it is important to listen to the "smaller stories" that they wrote. Yet it is equally pertinent to appreciate what they do not say, what they hesitantly and reluctantly say, and why they could not write the type of classic war poem that was expected of them.

Each of the four parts of *Among the Nightmare Fighters* is subdivided into four chapters. Each chapter explores one aspect of the theme of the part in question. This division suggests that poets were struggling with similar concerns, even though they did not subscribe to a unified vision about the war and how war poetry ought to be written. The poets of the middle generation exhibit what Ludwig Wittgenstein called "family resemblances."[25] They are members of the same poetic generation not because they often presented themselves as a group but because they share a set of overlapping features, although not all members share all features all the time.

The poetry of World War II was formed to a large degree by the poets' acute awareness of literary history. The poets of World War II are without a doubt the best read, most erudite, and most literary generation of war poets in American history. They were all college educated, and nearly all of them ended up teaching literature at universities and colleges around the country for at least some period of their lives. David K. Vaughan claims that "the English literary heritage" of the First World War "had not molded their esthetic outlook," but I argue the exact opposite.[26] When they approached war in their literary works it was often saturated with allusions to their literary forebears.

The intertextual war poem was extraordinarily rife among the poets of World War II. Ciardi, Jarrell, Lowell, Simpson, and especially Alan Dugan often allude to previous wars, war poets, and war poems in their war poetry, which appears to be a way for them to come to terms with their own perspectives on World War II as well as with their place in the tradition. The poets of the middle generation contend with more immediate literary predecessors in different ways.

Worth noting is the rapid development of Randall Jarrell, who during the war assertively and sometimes even aggressively tried to eke out a new, postmodern poetics in opposition to high modernism as symbolized by T. S. Eliot and Ezra Pound; the New Criticism as represented by Allen Tate, a personal friend of Jarrell's and a mentor of sorts; and the towering figure of W. H. Auden. The other war poets also tried to deal creatively with these influences, but they appear less resolute in searching for other forms or topics for their poetry than Jarrell was, at least not just yet. The World War II poets were clearly preoccupied with these various traditions, and they were evidently struggling to reach poetic independence. Yet the main question arises: how did absorbing or discarding these influences lead to a style that they thought could adequately describe the war and their sense of it?

The war poets were hyperconscious about their own identities during the war, and different selves manifested themselves during the war. "The problem of selfhood in the postmodern world" was a central concern for middle generation poets, as Travisano has pointed out. World War II either brought about or contributed largely to the generational sensitivity about the self.[27] The title of Ciardi's poetic autobiography, *Lives of X* (1971), draws attention to how the World War II poets believed that they did not have one self, but multiple selves that emerged through various social or personal stimuli and that cropped up during different phases of their lives. Ciardi frequently calls himself "Sgt. Ciardi" in his war poetry—for instance, in "On a Photo of Sgt. Ciardi a Year Later," a poem that is representative of the poet's search to understand how the military forced soldiers to conjure up a new self. "The sgt. stands so fluently in leather, / So poster-holstered and so newsreel-jawed" in the picture of yesteryear, but Ciardi knows that his confident, masculine pose is intended to hide his anxieties and fears.[28]

Ciardi's poem reveals a crisis of identity that was equally true for the other war poets. The extent to which the enforced uniformity of the army created the poets' concern about the self is evident, as many World War II poets moan about being confined by a homogenizing army mentality and about being stripped of their civil liberties. They almost never lapsed into rebellious behavior, which might suggest that they acquiesced that the institutional power over them is part of the human condition. Yet their poems are actually subtle protests against the overpowering force of the army and war. Other identity crises were also partly induced by World War II, for instance Lowell's manic war years and unexpected attraction to Catholicism. Anthony Hecht and Karl Shapiro came to grips with their Jewish identity during and after the war. Even though Hecht, Lowell, and Shapiro were temperamentally very different from each other and were exposed to widely dissimilar experiences between 1941 and 1945, their identity crises suggest that World War II engendered their personal predicaments.

Whereas most of the war poets explored crises of identity inwardly, Jarrell took a profound interest in imagining how other people experienced the war, fashioning identities outwardly. Speaking for a gunner after he has been blown to smithereens, a wounded veteran coming home, the mother and widow of an airman, and Jewish children at a concentration camp, Jarrell assumes the voices of both victims and aggressors all caught up in the war in various parts in the world, while he was grounded as an instructor at airfields in the United States. Jarrell was not the only poet of his generation who felt a need to conjecture how others perceived or suffered in the war, as that would develop into a trademark of this generation, but he pursued it most boldly, not eschewing the possible moral and ethical implications contained in such poems. Conflicts such as war are often "the occasion for questioning the validity of those individual and collective values and concepts of self and other," as Walter Hölbling has argued, but Jarrell and his contemporaries made it an essential part of their poetics.[29]

The middle generation came to consider the age-old concept of war as a rite of passage that separates boys from men as a shibboleth. It was a myth that still held sway earlier in their lives, and they realized that its influence on young men would not disappear easily. The profound influence of this imaginary but heartfelt test is most palpable in James Dickey's war poetry and novels. Unlike any other poet of his generation, Dickey created a myth about his war years in the Pacific that exceeded his actual accomplishments, and in his literary work he keeps yearning for the traditional war hero.

Why was Dickey so fixated on the masculine war hero, and why does the hypermasculine superman seem even more prominent in his war novels than in his poetry? It appears that Dickey's fascination with the male warrior stems from his childhood fantasy of what a man should be like and that he stuck to this childish image as the ideal incarnation of manhood. In general, the war poets obsessively traced how war—real or imagined—was an integral part of their (or their children's) childhoods. The middle generation's vicarious return to their youths is one way in which these poets differed from their modernist or New Critical predecessors. Yet it was more profoundly a way for them to analyze how the seeds of war were planted in those seemingly idyllic prewar years.

None of the war poets, not even Dickey, were particularly eager to prove their manhood by exposing themselves to danger as previous generations had done. In fact, the poets of World War II were not unhappy to be deployed on the home front or in rear echelon troops rather than on the front line. Ciardi, Nemerov, and Simpson, however, could not escape being exposed to danger almost on a daily basis. Yet they considered this their duty, which they performed reluctantly rather than as a manly test they had to pass. The recklessness with which the English war poets Keith Douglas and Wilfred Owen embraced war toward the end of their lives is conspicuously absent in the American poets of World War II. Ciardi's reasoning as described by Robert M. Cordray's foreword to *Saipan: The War Diary of John Ciardi* (1988) is typical of the poets' collective attitude to war. A former pilot on a B-29 of which Ciardi was a gunner, Cordray reminisces how he asked if Ciardi wanted to fly one more mission after Ciardi had been assigned a desk job. "'I won't volunteer,' he answered: 'That would make me responsible for my own possible death. But you order me and I'll go.'"[30]

The gung-ho fighting spirit may have been absent among the poets of World War II, but some found other ways of flaunting their manhood. Karl Shapiro, for instance, adopted an unabashedly heterosexual stance in his war poetry. Whereas the English poetry of the First World War is charged with "the homoerotic," "a sublimated (i.e., 'chaste') form of temporary homosexuality," as Paul Fussell has suggested, the American poets of World War II were decidedly more heterosexual, and generally even averse to male bonding.[31] The poets of World War II indeed reflected on wartime sexuality, and heterosexuality contributed to the construction of their masculinity and identity. The clear misogynist slant that typifies English First World War poetry is not present, but the poets' heterosexual self-image and their attitude toward women are not unproblematic. For Shapiro, the heterosexuality test seems to have replaced the bravery test to prove his masculinity to himself and to the world.

The faint misogynistic traces notwithstanding, World War II poetry can partially be defined by its embrace of the Other, as Jarrell's poetry shows most clearly. Militarized masculinity was hegemonic in the 1940s, but the poets of World War II began to comprehend that this construct, which was supposed to embody the ideal man, was neither attainable nor desirable. The poets who found themselves outside the realm of normalized masculinity—conscientious objectors and those who were declared physically or mentally unfit to fight—realized this most painfully. Yet even the poets who suffered in the army were surprisingly considerate of and compassionate toward those who were not enlisted, and they perceived both those who were rejected and themselves as victims of a war that none desired. Out of the poets' divergent experiences during the war grew their awareness that a man does not need to experience a war to be a man.

Nemerov's poem "The Afterlife," which was included in *War Stories* (1987), the penultimate volume of poetry he published during his lifetime, inspired the title of this book's fourth and final part. The poem starts off as follows:

The many of us that came through the war
Unwounded and set free in Forty-Five
Already understood the afterlife
We'd learned enough to wait for, not expect,
During the years of boredom, fear, fatigue;
And now, an hour's worth of afterlife.[32]

The afterlife commonly describes the hereafter, but Nemerov uses it to address the odd and sudden transition of soldier life to civilian life. "The Afterlife" reveals how unreal both the war and the subsequent afterlife felt for the soldier-turned-veteran. The war's afterlife felt brief and anticlimactic compared to the intensity of the war, as Simpson's "The Silent Generation" already testified. The war never left the poets of World War II, whether they had been soldiers on the front line, had remained stateside, were conscientious objectors, or had been refused for military service. "I remember almost every day that I was in the war," Dickey once mentioned, "and I think almost everything that I've done is influenced, at least to some degree, either directly or indirectly, most probably directly, by the fact that I was in the war. I write mainly from the standpoint of a survivor."[33]

Poets were affected in various and sometimes conflicting ways by World War II after it was over, and they also constructed problematic memories about it. In stark contrast to some of the most important British poets of the Second World War, such as Keith Douglas, Sidney Keyes, and Alun Lewis, all of the preeminent American poets of World War II survived the war, but they sensed that they were living on borrowed time. They had the uncomfortable luxury to mull over what had happened to them during their formative war years. Feelings of guilt and uneasiness were produced by the war long after it was over, regardless of what the poets had done during the years between 1941 and 1945. "Lucky" John Ciardi tried to reconstruct the more harrowing events that he witnessed, which continued to haunt him until his death despite his ostensibly fortunate life. The Vietnam War further aroused memories of their own war like never before, and it made them write back to the world that never learns. Nemerov subtly undermined America's collective memory of World War II in the last decades of the twentieth century, and he substituted it with his own fragile, personal stories, capturing the uneasy lives these poets lived after their army lives.

The four parts of this book trace four fixations in the works and lives of the poets of World War II that are distinct but interrelated. All reflect how parts of the poet's identity—his relationship with his literary forebears, his historical period, his nationality, his ethnic and religious background, and his masculinity—were shaken by the monumental weight of the war that overwhelmed him so early on in his life, and how his identity had to be reassembled after the war. The poems of these war poets are fragments and snippets of personal and immediate experience, written in a postwar culture that seemed to have already fixed the meaning of World War II. Their response was only ostensibly silent, but it would be more accurate to say that their response was a subdued reaction to the overpowering influence of the war on their lives. It is still possible to decode what their hesitations and reluctance to speak signify. There is a message in the oblique and uncertain poetic response to World War II, and it is worth finding out just what that message might be.

PART [1]

HAUNTING TRADITIONS

CHAPTER 1

"Im no Wilfred Owen, darling"

An unusually large number of poems written by the poets of World War II refer to earlier wars or make intertextual allusions to war poems by poets of previous generations. The most important one, which will resound throughout this book, is a line culled from a Civil War poem, "The March into Virginia," by Herman Melville, which Robert Lowell adopted in his World War II poem "Christmas Eve under Hooker's Statue." "All wars are boyish," Lowell quotes from "The March into Virginia," but he adjusts Melville's phrase by adding "but we are old."[1] The quotation that Lowell uses exemplifies his generation's awareness of writing within a tradition of war poetry, and suggests, as Lorrie Goldensohn has argued, that the World War II generation of poets looked back "in extreme self-consciousness," measuring "its own perceptions and accomplishments against that of another."[2]

The poems that this generation wrote about the war in Vietnam will be explored later, but this chapter traces which wars, war poems, and war poets from the past are alluded to by the middle generation, and it explores the reasons why so many wrote intertextual war poems. The poets of World War II were certainly not unique in their reliance on their predecessors. "In the history of poetry," as James Anderson Winn writes in *The Poetry of War,* "even the most original poems depend on past practice, building older forms and ideas into their texture."[3] Virgil's *Aeneid* consciously builds on Homer's *Iliad,* and during the First World War Edmund Blunden, for instance, quotes a line from Keats's "Ode on a Grecian Urn" in "Vlamertinghe: Passing the Chateau, July, 1917," and Owen's "Exposure" echoes the opening line of Keats's "Ode to a Nightingale." British poets of World War II—for instance, Keith Douglas, John Jarmain, and Alun Lewis—were equally aware "of a sense of tradition," as Dawn Bellamy has shown.[4] The Vietnam War poets Doug Anderson and Yusef Komunyakaa also wrote war poems inspired by Homer, but their generation of war poets was generally less allusive than their World War II predecessors.[5] What distinguishes the American poets of the Second World War is that they nearly all wrote intertextual war poems and that these poems all revolve around the poets' incapacity, unwillingness, or reluctance to take on the masculine challenge to be soldiers.

Like many other poets of the Second World War, Robert Lowell published several poems about the First World War and the Civil War, which were historically, geographically, or mentally closest to them. Lowell may have been the most historically minded poet of his generation, but Alan Dugan, who was an engine mechanic for a B-29 in the Pacific during the Second World War, wrote most significantly about other wars. Dugan also penned seemingly offhand poems about more ancient wars, drawing on Homer's *Iliad,* Virgil's *Aeneid,* and the medieval German epic poem *The Song of the Nibelungs.* In these poems Dugan relates war to masculinity and tries to make understandable why men become or stay warriors. Rather than talk directly about his own experiences during World War II as most others did, Dugan often chooses parody as a way of addressing topics that arose from his involvement in that war, as he acknowledged in an interview: "One of the things I think about constantly is the relation between the old dynasties and the nature of imperialisms, so it's given me a way to play back and forth with time. Given that historical bias, I think I can talk about modern armies accurately in terms of a Roman army or Athenian army or Spartan army. And it's very useful to me to be able to acknowledge the fact that there is a past, because in the United States of America by its nature, the past is in a constant process of destruction. Most Americans pretend there isn't a past at all."[6]

"Speech for Aeneas" is a case in point. In this short interior monologue Aeneas comments on his decision—which Virgil details in Book IV of his *Aeneid*—to leave his lover, Dido, behind in Carthage when told by the gods that he has more important civic duties to attend to. Whereas Virgil sees Aeneas's abandonment of Dido as a personally difficult but a publicly justified course of action for the greater good of the Roman Empire that he goes on to found, Dugan has his doubts. Dugan's Aeneas is not the troubled and love-smitten soldier of Virgil, but rather a coarse man who concludes that "an oecumenical society / is more important than matrimony."[7] The tone of "Speech for Aeneas" is ironic throughout. Virgil's verbose hexameters are replaced by Dugan's loose iambic pentameter with silly rhyming couplets that ridicule the ease and complacency with which Aeneas takes his decision: "so we sailed on the earliest possible tide / and she went and committed suicide."[8] The vulgar and clichéd diction that Dugan's Aeneas uses—"a roll in the hay is good for you" and "a great queen and a swell dish"—is reminiscent of the slang a soldier from the 1940s would use and a far cry from Virgil's formal and dramatic language.[9]

"Speech for Aeneas" is a parody of Virgil's epic poem, but not just for comic effect. "Parody is another way of dealing with tradition," as Winn has claimed: "By retaining some parts of the original and distorting others, the writer of parody reveals the weaknesses of the original and gains an indirect way of expressing his own views."[10] In "Speech for Aeneas" but also in "Stentor and Mourning," Dugan tries to expose a type of masculine figure that Western culture has spawned from its beginning and which has held sway well into the twentieth century. "Stentor and Mourning" is also an interior monologue spoken by a foot soldier who serves under Stentor, a Greek herald during the Trojan War as mythologized in *The Iliad,* and whom Dugan presents as the epitome of military manliness. Robert Fitzgerald—a poet of Dugan's generation—translated Homer's description of Stentor as follows: His "brazen lungs could give a battle shout / as loud as fifty soldiers."[11] While the historical and mythical backdrop of "Stentor and Mourning" is taken from *The Iliad,* Dugan's poem feels remarkably contemporary. Dugan deliberately uses several anachronisms—alluding, for instance, to "artillery over the hill" or Stentor's "captain's football voice"—that clearly do not belong to Greek antiquity.[12]

These incongruities are humorous and give "Stentor and Mourning" a light and breezy tone, but they also emphasize that Dugan's poem has a contemporary American relevance, as the football reference suggests. "Stentor and Mourning" shows by historical analogy how cultures make men out of boys and soldiers out of civilians, and indirectly how Dugan himself became a soldier during World War II. "Soldiers fear remarks / more than probably mutilation," and they fight for "good opinion" more than for "a buddy's safety" or for beautiful women like Helen of Troy.[13] Dugan's emphasis on how a cultural consensus on masculinity shapes the conduct of soldiers, and the sorrow and grief that this enforced behavior occasions, makes "Stentor and Mourning" a prototypical American poem of World War II. Like Dugan himself during the war, his speaker longs to be brave enough to rebel against society's norms of masculinity, but he does not dare to.

Dugan's reaction to the medieval German epic poem *The Song of the Nibelungs* (or Richard Wagner's adaptation of the saga) is titled "On Shields. Against World War III." This poem shows more explicitly than either "Speech for Aeneas" or "Stentor and Mourning" why Dugan wrote intertextual war poems. More abrasive than even "Speech for Aeneas," Dugan belittles this heroic saga and insults Siegfried, its principal hero:

> Ah what bastards they all were, and are,
> those heroes of the Nibelungenlied,

echt krauts, liars and fancy dressers,
robbers of the peasants for mere money
and cowards, too. Even their greatest,
strongest warrior, that Siegfried,
is afraid to fight honestly: he has
to wear a cape of invisibility and
impregnable skin-armor to win honor.
What bullshit. Worse than Hitler, a pure, lying,
murderous slob.[14]

Dugan hints at how Siegfried bathed himself in a slain dragon's blood, making him invulnerable, and how he helps Gunther defeat Brünhilde by wearing a cloak that makes him invisible.

The myth of Siegfried fascinated the American poets of World War II. William Meredith refers to it in "June: Dutch Harbor," and Jarrell used the name Siegfried in one of his war poems as well.[15] In fact, "Siegfried" is Jarrell's only war poem in which he gives one of the flyboys he describes a fictitious name; all the other airmen he dramatizes in his poems remain nameless. "Jarrell's tone," as Thomas Travisano has pointed out, "is cool, distant, sober, and dreamlike—apparently impersonal and hardly Wagnerian."[16] The insecure, vulnerable gunner in Jarrell's poem who realizes that he is "in particular dispensable / As a cartridge" is thus in no way like the unflinching Germanic warrior, making Siegfried's name highly ironic.[17] Dugan's parody, however, is direct and comical while Jarrell's take-off is less obviously connected to Wagner and more tragic.

Of Dugan's three intertextual war poems, "On Shields. Against World War III" is the only one that refers explicitly to World War II by arguing unreasonably that Siegfried and his gang are "worse than Hitler."[18] The title of Dugan's poem indicates that, like "Stentor and Mourning," this historical poem has a contemporary relevance. Veneration of heroically masculine types like Siegfried can lead to new wars, as they hold a perpetual appeal for boys and men, even to the poet himself, as the poem's last two lines concede: "That Siegfried is your hero, you cowards, / and I, too, have to acknowledge his nobility."[19] Dugan finds exalted and outstanding qualities in Siegfried, even though he hates to admit it.

John Ciardi is more explicit than Dugan in addressing his own experiences in his intertextual poem "To Lucasta, About That War." The title of Ciardi's poem alludes to Richard Lovelace's most famous poem, "To Lucasta, Going to the Wars."[20] The tone of Ciardi's poem is from the beginning much more somber than the boisterous and insolent farewell to his lover by the seventeenth-century English poet, soldier, and Royalist. Lovelace is more than glad to exchange Lucasta for "honor" on the battlefield, replacing her with "a new mistress" he is chasing: the enemy.[21] "I was mostly bored," Ciardi reports instead, voicing how many poets of World War II experienced the war, as Paul Fussell has detailed.[22]

Whereas Lovelace and his early modern contemporaries considered war a rite of passage that could distinguish a man from his peers, Ciardi and his fellow poets felt no urgency to excel as soldiers: "With reasonably-honorable and with humanly-mixed motives I did what I could of what had to be done, griped as much as everyone else while it was going on, and ran for my civilian clothes the minute I had my ruptured duck," Ciardi later reported about his years in service. He did his duty reluctantly, but was ecstatic when he got that much-coveted insignia of an eagle inside a wreath signaling to himself and the rest of the world that he was an ex-soldier: "The minute I zipped up those pleated slacks I was out of it and it was over."[23]

Ciardi does not say that he is immune from using women, however. As if he is hiding something he hardly dares to admit, Ciardi's diction becomes fairly impenetrable midway through his poem when he appears to be describing a brothel visit:

> I did, and won't
> deny several (or more) pig-blind
>
> alleys with doors, faces, dickers,
> which during, the ships slid
> over the hump where the packs hid.
> And talking voodoo and snickers
> over the edge of their welts, I did
> what I could with (they called them) knickers;
>
> and it was no goddamn good,
> and not bad either.[24]

Without specifying what was hiding in the alleyway and why he was bargaining, Ciardi's suggestive sexual diction and his indirect confession that he has wronged Lucasta, his girl on the home front, hint at his unfaithfulness. Unlike Lovelace, Ciardi has moral scruples about his "inconstancy" as he reports about it reluctantly and ambiguously.[25] His adulterous behavior was "no goddamn good" and yet "not bad either."

In the last lines Ciardi tries to account for his sexual indiscretions by addressing Lucasta directly:

> and you
> were variously, vicariously, and straight and with kinks,
> raped, fondled, and apologized to—
> which is called (as noted) war. And it stinks.[26]

Ciardi excuses himself for any wrongdoing—his infidelity was, after all, occasioned by war—but also apologizes for his behavior. Ciardi does not brag about his newly gained independence as Lovelace does, but moans about his loneliness. He does not exalt war but admits that "it stinks." Ultimately, he is not proud of his unfaithfulness and tries to understand his primal impulses and how the war may have influenced his actions.

"To Lucasta, About That War" suggests Ciardi's profound interest in the relationship between war and masculinity, which he shared with other poets of his generation. In fact, the biological, psychological, or historical connections between war and manliness were the foremost collective concern for these poets. Despite his "lifelong macho behavior and clubby, male-only attitude toward poetry," to quote Ciardi's biographer, Edward M. Cifelli, Ciardi was intrigued by the female psyche and wrote several poems from the perspectives of women, just as Jarrell did. "Poetry may have been a masculine business to John Ciardi," Cifelli continues, "but women were at the heart of his world."[27]

Jarrell himself also adapted two classic English war poems: Rupert Brooke's "The Soldier" and Alfred, Lord Tennyson's "The Charge of the Light Brigade," which are both less humoristic than those by Dugan and Ciardi. Jarrell never finished or published his "The Charge of the Light Brigade, converted." Yet his draft at the Berg Collection of the New York Public Library tells enough of how he positioned himself against Tennyson's veneration of the ill-fated British cavalry attack of October 25, 1854, during the Crimean War. The most striking difference between Tennyson's poem and Jarrell's "converted" version is that Tennyson's speaker is a faraway, upper-class commentator, someone on the home front like Tennyson himself. While mourning the deaths of those who have fallen and blaming the anonymous "someone" who has "blunder'd," Tennyson honors the unquestioning loyalty of the soldiers who obeyed the orders to attack the Russian fortification even though they were hardly protected: "Theirs not to make reply, / Theirs not to reason why, / Theirs but to do and die."[28]

Using prosopopoeia, as he often did in his war poetry, Jarrell instead speaks for one of the silent soldiers who takes part in the violent rush forward. Like the ball turret gunner, Jarrell's Crimean soldier may be speaking from the other side of life, but we do not have absolute certainty whether he is dead or whether he is one of the few survivors. Jarrell's voicing of the thoughts and feelings of one of the English soldiers of the Light Brigade gives his rudimentary draft a sense of immediacy and poignancy that Tennyson's more traditional elegiac narrative has done less forcefully, at least to a twenty-first-century reader. This emphasis on personal experience, on the vulnerability of a human being, on the single voice will prove to be characteristic of the American poets of World War II.

Jarrell's soldier is not unquestioning, but instead full of questions:

> ~~Was something won? was something cost?~~
>
> ~~Was all a fool's mistake?~~
> Was that defeat or victory?—
> A
>
> guess
>
> I cannot tell; but truly,
> We were born to die today.
> ~~I win, did I lose~~
> (I)? Did we win or lose? Was it only
>
> A mistake, as people say?
>
> Cannot tell or care.
>
> ? I can neither tell nor care. But truly,
> (I was) We were born to die today.[29]

The soldier's indecisiveness and hesitancy to draw any definitive conclusions about this battle is similar to how the middle generation wrote about World War II. Uncertainty and skepticism also distinguish Jarrell from Tennyson. In all fairness, Tennyson's speaker also asks a question about the Light Brigade, in the final stanza: "When can their glory fade?"[30] Yet considering the peremptory tone that Tennyson uses throughout, there can be no doubt that in his mind the answer should be: "Never."

Jarrell's revision of Rupert Brooke's even more patriotic "The Soldier" was one of the first war poems that he finished while he was in the army after a long spell where he could not write poetry. "Here's my *The Soldier,* to compete with Brooks' [*sic*]," Jarrell wrote home to his wife, Macky.[31] Of all poems from the First World War, Brooke's poem expresses most perfectly the sense of idealism and self-sacrifice in the face of death: "If I should die, think only this of me: / That there's some corner of a foreign field / That is for ever England."[32] Brooke died of blood poisoning a year after writing his poem and was buried on the Greek island of Scyros. Instead of Rupert Brooke's patriotic and sentimental sonnet, Jarrell offers three embittered octets in blank verse.

Jarrell replaces Brooke's nationalism with a Marxist internationalism. Soldiers do not die for their country, but so "a bank in Manchester" can ship "textiles to the blacks the Reich had taxed," Jarrell cleverly suggests."[33] Jarrell's early war poems often evince the view of the war as purely driven by economics. Malcolm Cowley, an editor at the *New Republic,* which had rejected another poem by Jarrell, lectured him about the reductiveness of viewing the war solely as a matter of profit: "This war isn't being fought for marbles or foreign trade, though there are plenty of people here who would like to make it that kind of war."[34]

Irrespective of the clear political point that he is making in "The Soldier," however, we can also detect a reason why Jarrell parodies Brooke and Tennyson. The phrase halfway through the final stanza that "our poor wits [are] sharpened with their blood" is crucial in this respect and epitomizes how Jarrell and his fellow World War II poets looked at the soldiers and poets of earlier wars. Millions of soldiers before them had "marched to die / For all the sad varieties of Good," and the poets of World War II were careful not to fall into the same masculinity or patriotism trap.[35] Jarrell eventually modified his Marxist reading of war and came to see World War II as tragic and regrettable, but also a necessary war. Yet like other members of his poetic generation, he was not keen to risk his life and limbs for brotherhood as Owen had done, or in an act of patriotic sacrifice for his country like Brooke. Unlike Ciardi and Dugan, however, Jarrell never publicized his parodies. A casual reader of Jarrell's "The Soldier" will not notice that it satirizes Brooke's poem, and Jarrell's take on the Light Brigade was until now buried in Jarrell's archive. This might indicate that Jarrell was reluctant to spoof his poetic ancestors in his own poetry.

"There was a conspicuous absence of Rupert Brooke–like verse" written by American poets during the Second World War, as Paul Fussell has claimed.[36] The World War II generation refused to glorify war and the soldier-hero. Like Jarrell, Karl Shapiro also wrote poetic replies to Brooke. His early poem "Scyros"—referring to the Greek island where Brooke was buried—was "a tribute to and an irony upon Rupert Brooke," as Shapiro noted in *The Younger Son,* and was one of his first war poems.[37] Shapiro's "The Soldier" was one of his last poems he wrote, dating probably from the mid to late 1980s. Robert Phillips included it in Shapiro's posthumous volume *Coda: Last Poems.* In it Shapiro juxtaposes a gung-ho soldier who plants "the flag upon a rock" in Iwo Jima style with another "professional soldier," most likely a conscientious objector stuck in a "night-bright cell," fighting for peace.[38] The epigraph to Shapiro's poem—"all evil shed away"—is taken from Brooke's "The Soldier," but actually applies more to Shapiro's "man of peace" than to Brooke's patriotic soldier.

This skepticism about the heroics of war may have been dominant among the World War II generation, but James Dickey's war poetry shows that it remained alluring. Dickey simply could not suppress his urge to panegyrize war, as "Hunting Civil War Relics at Nimblewill Creek" illustrates.[39] While tagging along with his brother who is scouring a former battlefield for memorabilia from that bygone war with a metal detector, Dickey not only bonds with his sibling but also senses a spiritual connection with the soldiers from the Civil War, whom he ultimately calls dramatically his "Fathers! Fathers!"[40] Dickey's narrative war poems are infused with a strong sense of lyricism and mysticism that is absent in the more self-ironic poems of his peers:

> But underfoot I feel
> The dead regroup,
> The burst metals all in place,
> The battle lines be drawn
> Anew to include us
> In Nimblewill[41]

Dickey's gesture of kinship and admiration for soldiers from this earlier war is reminiscent of Allen Tate's "Ode to the Confederate Dead," but particularly rare among the poets of World War II. Only Louis Simpson's "I Dreamed That in a City as Dark as Paris"—where the speaker talks to a statue of a soldier from the First World War and imagines they are similar—comes close. Yet Simpson feels pity for the other soldier and himself, while Dickey is in awe of the warriors of the past. Whereas previous generations of war poets always had to glorify or worship at least someone or some aspect of the war—whether it was a military or political leader, the common soldier, or the camaraderie that soldiers felt—the middle generation charily but collectively refused to accept war as an honorable and respectable enterprise. Jarrell's Crimean soldier wants none of Dickey's band-of-brothers' idea: "What cared we for those who stayed / By the wood along the wire?"[42]

Even a war poet like Walt Whitman, whose democratic principles and sorrow for all of war's victims the middle generation poets shared, reveled in brotherhood and patriotism and could not help but celebrate Abraham Lincoln as a martyr in "O Captain! My Captain!" and "When Lilacs Last in the Dooryard Bloom'd." No such poems were written by major American poets about Franklin D. Roosevelt, the third most respected president in American history (after Lincoln and Washington), who had also steered the United States through a major crisis and also died a few weeks before the end of a significant war in the nation's history.[43] Instead of "O Captain! My Captain!" Whitman's "most popular, if personally his least favorite, poem," Louis Simpson wrote "Carentan O Carentan" shortly after World War II, which seems to mimic Whitman's title, the poem's rhythm, and some of its key lines and imagery.[44] Carentan is significantly not the name of a person, but the name of a village between Juno and Omaha on Normandy beach where so many Allied soldiers died on D-day, June 6, 1944.

Whitman presents Lincoln in "O Captain! My Captain!" as heading a large ship, which represents the United States and which has become rudderless now that the captain has died. The platoon that Simpson describes in "Carentan O Carentan" is equally disorientated:

Tell me, Master-Sergeant,
The way to turn and shoot.
But the Sergeant's silent
That taught me how to do it.

O Captain, show us quickly
Our place upon the map.
But the Captain's sickly
And taking a long nap.

Lieutenant, what's my duty,
My place in the platoon?
He too's a sleeping beauty,
Charmed by that strange tune.

Carentan O Carentan
Before we met with you
We never yet had lost a man
Or known what death could do.[45]

The "Master-Sergeant," the "Captain," and the "Lieutenant" are all silent when the infantry soldier asks in which direction they should shoot, where they are on the map, and what his task now is. All of the soldier's direct superiors appear to be dead, but his naïveté or shock prevents him from accepting this truth. The childlike alternating rhyme and the short and simple iambic lines further emphasize the elementary confusion that Simpson's soldier experiences. Simpson's iambic trimeter seems to echo the rhythm and sense of confusion that Whitman uses in "O Captain! My Captain!":

My Captain does not answer, his lips are pale and still,
My father does not feel my arm, he has no pulse nor will,
The ship is anchor'd safe and sound, its voyage closed and done,
From fearful trip the victor ship comes in with object won:

Exult O shores, and ring O bells!

But I with mournful tread,
Walk the deck my Captain lies,
Fallen cold and dead.[46]

Simpson's use of apostrophe, addressing an inanimate object rather than a person as Whitman does, is ironic, but also typical for the poets of World War II. They no longer believed that they could look to leaders or heroes to guide them, but felt bitterly alone in a confusing mess of war. Heroic agency is no longer plausible.

"Carentan O Carentan" not only invites a comparison with Whitman's Civil War poem "O Captain! My Captain!" it also uses several central tropes of First World War poetry. Simpson could not help but notice that he was moving through Flanders fields with all the battle sites of the Great War when he was fighting his war. "Carentan O Carentan" is clearly about the loss of innocence, the most dominant theme of the Great War poetry. At the moment when the bullet hits him he is all but shaken out of his naïveté, just like Jarrell's ball turret gunner when hit by "black flak and the nightmare fighters."[47] Simpson also depicts "war as the ultimate anti-pastoral," to use Paul Fussell's phrase.[48] The associations of blue skies, lovers, trees, and farmers in the opening of his poem make Carentan look like an Arcadian place, lulling the speaker and his fellow soldiers into a false sense of security.

More than any other American poet of World War II, Simpson had internalized the imagery of the English poets of World War I. This is nowhere more pronounced than in Simpson's "On the Ledge," which is a simple poem in terms of diction and form but impressive because of its compelling narrative and powerful central trope. It opens evocatively with the speaker's infantry regiment waiting for a signal to attack enemy lines. The analogy to the First World War that Simpson draws is characteristic for the poets of World War II who had learned about the dire fate of the soldiers in the Great War, the thousands upon thousands of dead men at Verdun and at the Somme. Right at this moment, at the climax, Simpson interrupts his narrative by almost casually referring to a passage from Fyodor Dostoyevsky where a man is given the hypothetical choice to die or to stand forever immovable on a ledge. This interruption heightens the anxiety for the reader, as if replicating the fright of the soldiers who await their destiny. The quote that Simpson refers to is an allusion to a passage in Dostoyevsky's *Crime and Punishment* where the poor student Raskolnikov ponders about survival as the primal impulse of life:

> "Where was it," thought Raskolnikov, as he walked onward, "where was it I read about a man who's been sentenced to die, saying or thinking the hour before his death, that even if he had to live somewhere high up on a rock, and in such a tiny area that he could only just stand on it, with all around precipices, an ocean, endless murk, endless solitude and endless storms—and he had to stand there, on these two feet of space, all his life, for a thousand years, eternity—that it would be better to live like that, than to die so very soon! If only he could live, live and live! Never mind what that life was like! As long as he could live! . . . What truth is in that! Lord what truth! Man is a villain. And whoever calls him a villain because of it is one himself!"[49]

Simpson's allusion to world literature is again typical for the college-educated and book-smart poets of World War II, but the analogy is different from the other examples we have encountered so far. Rather than distancing himself from the literary works of his predecessors as Ciardi, Dugan, and Jarrell did in their intertextual war poems in terms of tone and in their skepticism of military heroism, Simpson finds comfort and solace in Dostoyevsky's passage. Dostoyevsky is an ally who helps Simpson articulate a traumatic experience.

The end of "On the Ledge" is "anticlimactic," as Janis P. Stout writes, but it provides an anticlimax that the speaker (and reader) is relieved to experience.[50] Unlike the infantry troops in the First World War, the regiment that Simpson belongs to is given a free exit. Assisted by Allied airplanes overhead that have bombed the enemy lines, they can march freely on.[51] They are off the hook, at least this time. More so than the First World War, World War II was decided in the air, as Simpson's poem suggests and many other World War II poems testify. "Air warfare originated during the First World War as an ancillary aspect of the land battle," according to military historian Michael Howard. "Only very slowly, as aircraft increased in range, speed, and armament, did it become clear that an air force which enjoyed command of the air over the battlefield might act not only as the eyes of the artillery but as a substitute for the artillery, and on a scale which might make all movement on and behind the battlefield impossible."[52] Some forty years after the experiments of Orville and Wilbur Wright with aerial flight at Kitty Hawk, North Carolina, in 1903, the aerial assistance that Simpson and his infantry colleagues got was just one hint at how aerial warfare would change the face of battle. The nuclear bombs that were dropped over Hiroshima and Nagasaki at the close of the war underline how revolutionary and destructive this change was.

This predominance of the air war during the Second World War is reflected in the large number of poems written about aerial warfare by the American poets of that war. Whereas nearly all of the famous English poets of the First World War were in the army, many of the prime American poets of World War II—Ciardi, Dickey, Dugan, Jarrell, and Nemerov among them—were in the air corps. Their poems offer, literally and figuratively speaking, a different perspective on war since "there appear to be hardly any famous poems about the air war during the 1914–18 conflict," as Peter Robinson has suggested.[53] Modern wars had become increasingly "the wars of technologists," as Howard has argued, making such heroism on the battlefields as described in *The Iliad, The Aeneid,* and *The Song of the Nibelungs* obsolete.[54] Experienced airmen like Ciardi, Dickey, and Nemerov never came face to face with their enemy, and wielded their destructive power from high above.

Yet "On the Ledge" shows another crucial difference between how the Great War and World War II were fought. Whereas the English soldier-poets of the First World War were at the start supremely innocent and were shocked by the brutality of trench warfare, the American poets of World War II (thought they) knew what was in store for them, in part from the poems of their literary predecessors. Richard Wilbur confirmed this in an interview: "My generation went into World War II in a more realistic and less crusading spirit, resolved to do what plainly had to be done; and so there was less damage to our expectations. It may be that the literature of World War I, which told of so much beastliness and stupid waste of lives, prepared us to be not altogether surprised."[55]

The title of Dugan's "Memories of Verdun" suggests the same awareness and a sense of déjà-vu similar to the one experienced in Simpson's "On the Ledge." Yet Dugan's title is slightly misleading because strictly speaking Dugan has no personal memories of the long and bloody Battle of Verdun of 1916 where an estimated quarter of a million soldiers died. Unlike Simpson, Dugan was not even stationed in Europe, but in the Pacific, and probably never even visited that town in the Lorraine region of France.

Dugan's memories echo the subtitle of Susan Gubar's book *Poetry after Auschwitz:* "remembering what one never knew."[56] Like Simpson and all intellectual soldiers of the Second World War, Dugan understood full well the lessons of Verdun through collective memory. Dugan knew most likely through the poems of Owen and Sassoon that millions of "men laughed and baaed like sheep / and marched across the flashing day / to the flashing valley."[57] Like docile sheep they are brought to the battle site where guns flare and where they are slaughtered in the "valley of death" as Tennyson called the no-man's-land between the trenches in "The Charge of the Light Brigade."[58]

The men smile because they are blissfully ignorant of what will happen. "Never such innocence again," the British poet Philip Larkin famously quipped in his poem "MCMXIV."[59] Larkin, who was about the same age as the American poets of World War II, expressed in that line the awareness that Dugan verbalizes in this poem. Dugan wonders, however, whether those who died at the Somme and Verdun were "heroically wrong" or whether he was "the proper coward."[60] Dugan admits that unlike the British soldiers of the Great War, he was not afraid of his superiors, but only "of a nothing, a death."[61] Dugan's blunt admission that he is afraid to die and his concession in an interview that he "worked on ground crews" because it was "a nice peaceful boring existence" might have been considered unmanly in the Great War and by some in World War II. Yet this candor and caution was representative for his poetic generation. When Karl Shapiro was briefly part of a mobile army surgical hospital following marines who invaded beaches when General Douglas MacArthur's notorious island-hopping or leapfrogging expeditions were taking place, Shapiro wrote to his fiancée woefully: "Im no Wilfred Owen, darling, I cant write when the bullets whistle."[62] Soon Shapiro asked for a transfer back to his old rearguard, and to his surprise and delight his request was granted.

The American poets of World War II were never naive, wanted to survive, and avoid heroics as much as possible. A "draftee in the Second World War with the education and sensibility required to become a writer was very unlikely to find himself among the combat troops," as W. H. Auden stated in his short article "Private Poet."[63] Sacrificing their lives for honor was something that belonged to the old war. In order to stress the innocence of the English poets and writers of the First World War, Paul Fussell writes in *The Great War and Modern Memory* that "it was not until eleven years after the war that Hemingway could declare in *A Farewell to Arms* that 'abstract words such as glory, honor, courage, or hallow were obscene beside the concrete names of villages, the numbers of roads, the names of rivers, the numbers of regiments and the dates.'"[64] When the poets of World War II grew up they were painstakingly aware of what a disillusionment the First World War had been for all its participants. Like Hemingway, they were more than skeptical of words like "glory," "honor," and "courage."

With his usual sense of exaggeration, Shapiro mentioned in a review of the English World War II poet Keith Douglas's *Alamein to Zem Zem* and *Collected Poems* that "like so many British poets," Douglas's "bravery was extraordinary," before adding: "American soldier-poets are never cited for heroism. The British soldier-poet, especially of the officer class, leaps into battle joyously and brilliantly."[65] Ciardi's more realistic account of his own attitude to the military and war quoted earlier—that he ran for his "civilian clothes the minute" he had his "ruptured duck"—confirms the gist of Shapiro's sweeping statement and sums up the collective spirit of his generation of war poets. Yet this less heroic attitude was not something that they felt proud about, as Dugan's "Memories of Verdun" shows. The poets of World War II were constantly grappling with internal and external expectations of wartime masculinity.

The poets of World War II measured themselves self-consciously against the tradition of war poetry because they wanted to understand how their perspective in the middle of the twentieth century on their war was different from earlier war poets writing about their wars.[66] Looking at their intertextual war poems, it becomes apparent that they realized that they could not conform to age-old masculine myths that they ought to distinguish themselves on the battlefield. They saw war "as an unpleasant obligation rather than an opportunity for individual heroism or male initiation rituals," as Walter Hölbling has mentioned.[67] The mechanized, industrialized nature of modern warfare had eroded the possibility of heroic dueling, and according to the World War II poets, heroic agency thus belonged to the past. Unlike previous generations, they did not believe that there was honor in their own deaths. The poets of World War II wanted to get the job done as quickly as possible and stay alive. Rupert Brooke's "corner of a foreign field / That is for ever England" in Scyros and Wilfred Owen's premature death a week before armistice in the Great War were frightening examples of what could happen. They were not keen to follow that tradition.

CHAPTER 2

A Little Disagreement with Some Modernists

The form of Anthony Hecht's most ambitious war poem, "Rites and Ceremonies" (1968), is strikingly different from the war poems discussed in the first chapter. Unlike nearly all World War II poems, "Rites and Ceremonies" is not a terse and mostly autobiographical poem. The content and structure of Hecht's poem are instead more suggestive of the kind of grand epic poem that several high modernist poets wrote—for instance, Ezra Pound's *The Cantos,* William Carlos Williams's *Paterson,* but especially T. S. Eliot's *The Waste Land* and *Four Quartets,* the latter of which Eliot wrote mostly after the outbreak of World War II. Hecht's poem adopts the quartet structure of *Four Quartets,* but, running over three hundred lines, "Rites and Ceremonies" resembles *The Waste Land* more in size. A more significant parallel between "Rites and Ceremonies" and *The Waste Land,* however, is that one of Hecht's parts, "The Fire Sermon," has the same name as the longest of *The Waste Land*'s five sections.

Eliot named his section after a sermon by Buddha in which the spiritual teacher encourages his followers to give up earthly passions, as symbolized by fire. "The Fire Sermon" is the segment in which Eliot introduces Tiresius, the blind Greek mythological seer, and it is mostly set near the Thames in London. Eliot depicts the river as polluted, undercutting the river's romantic associations. Eliot also describes how a "young man carbuncular," a clerk, forces himself on a weary typist.[1] The woman does not defend herself rigorously, and afterward she does not even notice when her pimply lover leaves. Toward the end of "The Fire Sermon" Eliot introduces three Thames daughters, a parody on Richard Wagner's Rhine maiden in his *Götterdämmerung,* one of the four parts of *Der Ring des Nibelungen.* The section ends with the appropriation of lines from *The Confessions of Saint Augustine* when the Carthaginian Church father thanks God that he "pluckest" him "out," which he took from a part of the saint's account where he relates his youthful life of lust. Eliot observed in a note to the poem that it was not a coincidence that representatives from Eastern and Western religions come together in this section of his poem.[2] Like Buddha and St. Augustine had done before him, Eliot seeks to expose the wanton lust and spiritual emptiness of the modern world.

The exact relationship between Eliot's "The Fire Sermon" and Hecht's version is not immediately clear. Hecht's "Rites and Ceremonies" is as fragmentary and seemingly disconnected as Eliot's *The Waste Land.* As in Eliot's section, Hecht's "The Fire Sermon" introduces various storylines, and they only very marginally overlap with the themes of Eliot's poem. The similarities are nevertheless there, however faint. Hecht, for instance, suggests that "it is barren hereabout" toward the end of "The Fire Sermon," which connects to the imagery of sterility and drought that Eliot also establishes. A more concrete connection between the two sections is contained in the allusion to St. Augustine that both poets use. Eliot quotes from the saint's jubilant address to God in Book X of his *Confessions:* "O Lord Thou pluckest me out," which underscores the ultimately hopeful and merciful Christian message of *The Waste Land* that salvation is possible, even if the quote from St. Augustine is hemmed in between the image of Carthage burning.[3] Hecht also echoes St. Augustine's words near the end of his section, but he modifies the literal words from the *Confessions* and frames them as a question: "Is there not one / Whom thou shalt pluck for love out of coals?"[4]

Hecht's adoption of the title of "The Fire Sermon" from Eliot's *The Waste Land* and his seemingly slight alteration of Eliot's St. Augustine quote are easy to miss in a long and allusive poem such as "Rites and Ceremonies." Yet they are subtle hints that reflect an internal argument Hecht was having with Eliot. This disagreement was not idiosyncratic to Hecht, but representative of his generation's preoccupation with modernist poets, especially Eliot and Ezra Pound. Not only were the World War II poets hyperconscious of the tradition of war poetry in which they wrote, as the previous chapter has shown, they were also cognizant of and alert to their immediate predecessors. World War II was the catalyst that brought their disagreements to the fore, although their differences were always counterbalanced by a tremendous respect for the erudition and mastery of the Eliot-Pound generation.

The American poets of World War II "were born under the gathering clouds of humanity's first global conflict and in the midst of modernity's opening phase," as Thomas Travisano has claimed.[5] When the new generation started writing poetry, the modernist tradition formed an impressive and inescapable presence, of which the English poets of the Great War had not been aware when they had entered their war. The legacy of the modernist poets was essentially a "polarized inheritance," as Lynn Keller has argued: "On the one hand, the poems of the great modernists are impressive models offering a body of powerful techniques that invite further development and extension. On the other hand, modernist attitudes and principles encourage the contemporary poet to reject the methods of his or her immediate predecessors, just as the modernists rejected those of the late Victorians and decadents who preceded them."[6] The poets of the middle generation "encountered modernism not as an enthusiasm still in the making," as Keller has observed, "but as something essentially made—an accomplished body of literature already part of the literary tradition they inherited."[7]

Randall Jarrell was among the first poets who realized that modernism had run its course, and he voiced this not coincidentally during World War II. In his short essay "The End of the Line" (1942) he wrote: "Poets can go back and repeat the ride; they can settle in attractive, atavistic colonies along the railroad; they can repudiate the whole system, à la Yvor Winters, for some neoclassical donkey caravan of their own. But Modernism As We Knew It—the most successful and influential body of poetry of this century is dead. . . . How can poems be written that are more violent, more disorganized, more obscure, more—supply your own adjective—than those that have already been written?"[8]

In his introduction to his section of *Five Young American Poets* (1940), his book debut with New Directions along with John Berryman and three other beginning poets, Jarrell had grappled with the same questions of tradition that emerged in "The End of the Line." Referring to events in Europe, Jarrell states that humankind has reached "one of those points in the historical process" in which the poet needs to ask himself: "'But what was it? What am I?' The *it* he asks about is the dying tradition (which dies because the world it represented is dying)."[9] The ontological questions are somewhat cryptic, but Jarrell implies that historical changes make a new kind of poetry inevitable. Imagining what the reader may think, Jarrell asks cheekily: "Does he really suppose he writes the sort of poetry that replaces modernism?" In coded terms Jarrell indicates that he would like to decline this daunting task, but then states: "But I am sorry I need to."[10] For the rest of the war, Jarrell would be "avowedly searching for a way to get beyond modernism," as Travisano has asserted.[11]

When John Crowe Ransom, the New Critic and Jarrell's former professor at Vanderbilt, reviewed *Five Young American Poets* in the *Kenyon Review* he noted Jarrell's hesitancy to classify his own poetry. Yet Ransom added significantly that while Jarrell "forbids us to say yet that he is a post-modernist," Jarrell "probably . . . will be" one. Ransom's use of the word "post-modernist" appears to be the first literary usage by an American.[12] It is noteworthy that Jarrell himself first used the word when characterizing the poetry of *Lord Weary's Castle* (1946) by his friend Robert Lowell. "Mr.

Lowell's poetry is a unique fusion of modernist and traditional poetry, and there exist side by side in it certain effects that one would have thought mutually exclusive," Jarrell asserted, "but it is essentially a post- or anti-modernist poetry, and as such is certain to be influential."[13] Jarrell's advice to Lowell in letters sent toward the end of World War II confirms that Jarrell was instrumental in bringing about this new poetics, as following sections of this book will show. What did this "post- or anti-modernist poetry" of the war poets look like in terms of how they represented the war, what "fusion" with modernism occurred, and how are these poetic developments related to the similarities and differences between Hecht's "Rites and Ceremonies" and Eliot's *The Waste Land*?

All the poets of World War II had been fascinated by modernist poets and poetry in their younger years, and initially modeled themselves on the likes of T. S. Eliot, Robert Frost, Ezra Pound, Wallace Stevens, and William Carlos Williams. Howard Nemerov has admitted in an interview that when he was an undergraduate at Harvard in the late 1930s, he was so infatuated by Eliot's first poetry recording of "Gerontion" and "The Hollow Men" that he "could imitate it even down to the scratch of the needle at the start of the record."[14] His girlfriend at the time even told Nemerov "to cut out the parson-like tone of voice" because he sounded like Eliot all the time.[15] When Nemerov started writing about the aftermath of the war shortly after returning from his air corps spell in England, he automatically used Eliot's type of diction and imagery, as is evident in "Redeployment":

> The war may be over. I know a man
> Who keeps a pleasant souvenir, he keeps
> A soldier's dead blue eyeballs that he found
> Somewhere—hard as chalk, and blue as slate.
> He clicks them in his pocket while he talks.
>
> And now there are cockroaches in the house,
> They get slightly drunk on DDT,
> Are fast, hard, shifty—can be drowned but not
> Without you hold them under quite some time.
> People say the Mexican kind can fly.[16]

Nemerov's stanzaic form may be smoother, but the debt Nemerov owed to Eliot's *The Waste Land* in terms of imagery to depict postwar urban decay is nevertheless tangible.

Around the same time Nemerov began to sound like Eliot, nineteen-year-old Robert Lowell volunteered to be adopted by Ezra Pound. "I want to come to Italy and work under you and forge my way into reality," Lowell wrote boisterously.[17] He did not visit Pound in Italy in the 1930s, but did strike up a correspondence with Pound and frequently visited him in the following decades. The roles of willing imitator and eager apprentice that Nemerov and Lowell assumed in the 1930s are fairly typical for the middle generation poets in their younger years, even though the replication and training only went so far. Lee Bartlett and Hugh Witemeyer reconstructed the complete correspondence between Ezra Pound and James Dickey, and they discovered that the poets briefly had a father-son-type relationship after a visit that Dickey made in 1955 to St. Elizabeth's, the hospital where Pound was held after being found mentally unfit to stand trial for high treason during World War II. Yet "when Pound began to demand the younger man's support for his own causes"—for instance, by trying to make Dickey "enlist in a super Ku Klux Klan"—Dickey dissociated himself from that side of Pound's personality, and the correspondence quickly ceased.[18]

As an aspiring poet Hecht was, like Nemerov, fixated on Eliot: "His influence on me was not merely formidable," Hecht told Philip Hoy in an interview, "but so strong that I had consciously to try to erase it to some extent."[19] The interview establishes clearly what Hecht's "polarized inheritance" of Eliot is. Hecht briefly praises the formal mastery of Eliot's poetry since "almost every line of Eliot's poetry seems forged of the most durable steel."[20] Still, Hecht deplores in the interview Eliot's presumed social and political views. "Rites and Ceremonies" shows the same ambivalence toward Eliot. Although the form of "Rites and Ceremonies" reflects Hecht's enduring indebtedness to Eliot, the St. Augustine passage in "The Fire Sermon" shows where Hecht departs from Eliot. As Dickey did with Pound, Hecht follows Eliot poetically in "Rites and Ceremonies," but deviates from Eliot's presumed social and political views. To understand what Hecht's modification of Eliot's "The Fire Sermon" signifies, it is important to take a closer look at the context of Hecht's section.

Like *The Waste Land,* Hecht's "The Fire Sermon" is characterized by various fragmentary storylines and perspectives taken from different historical times that are each abruptly introduced and abandoned. The opening of Hecht's section with the "small paw tracks in the snow" resembles more closely the way Eliot's "Little Gidding" starts, with an evocative scene depicting the heart of winter.[21] From this serene landscape we move to a ship lost at sea, "heavy with pepper and tea," evoking an image of seventeenth-century trade ships. The ships are doomed, and Hecht's speaker asks whether this was "a judgment."[22] In a draft of this poem, Hecht had indicated even more explicitly that he was puzzled by what the divine plan of such a disaster could possibly be:

If it was a judgment
(How could it be explained)

Some ships were found at sea laden with wares
The whole crew dead, adrift.
Bishops, priest, monks prayed and were felled.[23]

Hecht jumps in Eliotic fashion to a longer passage depicting the king of Tarsis, the ruler of a maritime country west of Palestine, who traveled to the pope in Avignon in the mid–thirteenth century to be converted to Catholicism. The plague had hit his country and had allegedly contaminated eight thousand legions of non-Christians. On his way to Avignon, however, they discovered that Christians had also succumbed to the Black Death. The king of Tharsis decided to go home immediately, but on their way back he and his train were attacked by Christians, who killed thousands of Tarsians. The king had tried to "assuage the anger of God" by traveling to the pope before the plan backfired horribly. The source for this part of "The Fire Sermon" is Henry Knighton's *Chronicle, 1337–1396,* a four-volume chronicle of the history of England and Europe written by a fourteenth-century Augustinian canon of St. Mary's Abbey in Leicester, England. In the fourth book Knighton reported on the effects of the Black Death.

One stanza is directly taken from Knighton's *Chronicle,* but put in (poetic) lines rather than (prose) sentences. Hecht interpolates Knighton's factual and (seemingly) objective record of events with more personal and subjective comments. Following two lines from Knighton how "three hundred and fifty-eight / Of the Friar Preachers died in Lent," Hecht notes wryly that "if it was judgment, it struck home in the houses of / penitence."[24] After the full paragraph from Knighton, Hecht poses this rhetorical question despondently:

How could it be a judgment,
The children in convulsions, the sweating and stink,
And not enough living to bury the dead?
The shepherd had abandoned his sheep.[25]

These tonal shifts in Hecht's poem reflect more directly the emotions behind "Rites and Ceremonies" than those Eliot uses in *The Waste Land.* Eliot's poem is certainly not as impersonal as some detractors have asserted it to be, but Eliot focuses more generally on cultural dislocation while Hecht headed toward a stricter crisis of faith.

The occurrences during the Middle Ages and Renaissance that Hecht depicts in "Rites and Ceremonies" have at least two things in common: first, the sheer brutality of the acts; and second, the absence of divine intervention. The examples that Hecht renders in "The Fire Sermon" become increasingly personal and painful, as the third and final historical disaster in this section involving Christians bears out. It focuses on the massacre of the Strasbourg Jews in 1348 and 1349. Almost two thousand Jews were put to death in the medieval Alsatian town for allegedly poisoning the wells.[26] City officials of several European cities convened, and, stirred by angry mobs, they decided that Jews would either be expelled or executed. On St. Valentine's Day, Jews were put on a wooden platform in their Strasbourg cemetery and burned alive.

Hecht's storyline here subtly but significantly twists the notions of the title of "The Fire Sermon." We forget the depressing associations of cheap carnal desire that Eliot wanted to convey, as they are substituted by Hecht's much starker image of human brutality. "The Room," the first section of "Rites and Ceremonies," centered on the Holocaust, and was partly based on Hecht's own experiences of discovering the concentration camp of Flossenbürg with his regiment in April 1945.[27] The Strasbourg slaughter of Jews presents an obvious historical parallel with the Holocaust.

Something particularly odd happens right in the middle of this excruciating narrative. Hecht unexpectedly takes a moment to admire the Strasbourg Cathedral:

The Façade, by Erwin von Steinbach,
Is justly the most admired part of the edifice
And presents a singularly happy union
Of the style of Northern France
With the perpendicular tendency
Peculiar to German cathedrals.[28]

These lines offer a bizarre, defamiliarizing aside in the agonizing climax of "The Fire Sermon." What could Hecht have meant with his strange interruption? It is possible that Hecht sought to highlight how Christian culture, how human beings, are capable of acts of extreme cruelty as well as beauty. The cathedral's design represents a unique joyous coming together of French and German styles. It is an ironic remark considering that the peoples of these rivaling regions battled out many wars from the Middle Ages to World War II. There is yet another parallel with Eliot's *The Waste Land,* though, that may further explain this peculiar passage. After introducing his exemplars of sexual lust—Sweeney and the adulterous Mrs. Porter or the "carbuncular" young man putting the moves on the apathetic typist—Eliot offers one single image in "The Fire Sermon" that counteracts the perversion of the modern world. Eliot's sketch of the interior of London's St. Magnus Martyr Church is one of the few scenes in the whole of *The Waste Land* that offers pure, unadulterated beauty.

Like the chapel in Eliot's "Little Gidding," Magnus Martyr is a place of refuge from the pressures and temptations of modern life where individuals can become reacquainted with true Christian values. King Charles I had found sanctuary in the Anglican religious community at Little Gidding during the English Civil War before it was broken up in 1647, and Eliot spiritually returns to the rebuilt chapel during World War II. The medieval Magnus Martyr Church was likewise ruined during the Great Fire of London in 1666, but magnificently restored by Christopher Wren. The chapel at Little Gidding and the Magnus Martyr Church emphasize the importance of shoring fragments against the ruin of the world—to appropriate one of Eliot's final lines of *The Waste Land*—but also reflect the splendor and values of religious faith.

The Strasbourg Cathedral in Hecht's poem, which was originally built in the eleventh century on top of a temple dedicated to the Virgin Mary, had also burned to the ground, in 1176, after the wooden framework had caught fire. Reconstructed by von Steinbach, it appears to be a symbol of renewal and Christian beauty like the houses of worship in Eliot's work. In Hecht's "The Fire Sermon," though, the cathedral is principally the site next to which almost two thousand Jews were brutally burned to death. It is within this context of barbarity instigated in part or at least ignored by the Catholic Church that Hecht alludes to St. Augustine and addresses God: "Is there not one / Whom thou shalt pluck for love out of coals?"[29] He does not thank God for plucking him out of World War II, but implores why God did not rescue a single soul from the fires.[30] Considering the vicarious dialogue with Eliot that Hecht has been engaged in, however, Hecht's question seems to be directed not only at God but also at Eliot.

Hecht was well aware of Eliot's earlier writings that could be interpreted as anti-Semitic. "Gerontion," a poem that Nemerov could recite by heart as a student, is just one example. Others include "Burbank with a Baedeker: Bleistein with a Cigar," "A Cooking Egg," and "Sweeney among the Nightingales," as well as the play *Sweeney Agonistes* (1932) and a passage from his prose work *After Strange Gods* (1934). Hecht noted in an interview that the Sweeney character is "someone of striking crassness, vulgarity and brutality," to whom Eliot gave "a distinctly Irish name." The Jews in Eliot's poems are "more plentiful and at least equally unpleasant."[31] The cantankerous old speaker in "Gerontion," for instance, complains about the "jew" who "squats on the window sill, the owner, / Spawned in some estaminet of Antwerp, Blistered in Brussels, patched and peeled in London."[32]

Eliot might be excused for these hateful lines because "Gerontion" is a dramatic monologue, and the author should not be equated with the speaker. Yet Eliot's comment in his prose work *After Strange Gods* that "reasons of race and religion combine to make any large number of free-thinking Jews undesirable" was totally his own.[33] Eliot later denied he had ever disliked Jews, saying, for instance, "that in the eyes of the Church, to be anti-Semitic is a sin."[34] Hecht clearly did not believe Eliot, and skeptically remarked about Eliot's claim that his religion prohibited anti-Semitism: "as though this were proof."[35]

It is unknown whether Nemerov, himself a "free-thinking Jew," read Eliot's words in *After Strange Gods,* and, if so, how he reacted to them. In "The Jewish Writer and the English Literary Tradition," published by *Commentary* four years after the war, Nemerov claimed that he was not personally insulted by anti-Jewish sentiments in literature, by Eliot or others: "Humanly, and in particular as a Jew, I detest and fear anti-Semitism, but do not find it especially formidable (or in any way an occasion of public action) in the writings of the authors listed in the question." Nemerov also let on that the qualities in literature he admired most were the (Eliotic) aspects of "irony, evasion, conflict, and doubt."[36] Nemerov adopted Eliot's style and sidestepped the insults. Hecht, who was equally appreciative of Eliot's poetic accomplishments, could not evade Eliot's prejudice in *After Strange Gods,* and remarked publicly: "What appalls about this is that the book appeared in 1934 (though the lectures themselves were delivered in 1933) when some of the most brutal acts against Jews in Germany were commonly reported in the public press. It took a kind of strange insensitivity and self-absorption to utter these views before an audience at the University of Virginia in those days of early Nazism without any sense of embarrassment. The embarrassment must have come later, because he forbade the book to be reprinted, and it's now a rare item."[37]

Eliot considered *After Strange Gods* to be a more sociological sequel to his literary essay "Tradition and the Individual Talent" (1919). He emphasizes in that essay the importance of following the great tradition of European literature. Yet Eliot's hankering after tradition in Christian religion and the English heritage makes him lapse into dubious comments in *After Strange Gods.* He, for instance, praises the state of Virginia and the American South for their racial homogeneity as opposed to the state of New York and the North, which are "invaded by foreign races."[38] Eliot oddly ignored the large population of African Americans in the South in his account. A year before Eliot presented his lectures at the university that Thomas Jefferson had founded, Karl Shapiro had dropped out as a student from the same university. Shapiro later reminisced in his poem "University" (1940) that "to hurt the Negro and avoid the Jew / Is the curriculum."[39] *After Strange Gods* reverses the order, however, as Eliot hurts the Jew and avoids talking about "the Negro."

Shapiro's own sense of being marginalized made him more keenly aware of the injustice done to others. He relates in his memoir, *The Younger Son,* how while he was stationed in Australia, only African American GIs were being used to build "a road to the north in case of the invasion."[40] The army was reenacting a form of slavery, Shapiro suggests, and African Americans were also deliberately kept apart from their white fellow soldiers and the Australians: "The blacks were not allowed in town, except on a few nights when whites were not allowed."[41] Lincoln Kirstein's poem "Black Joe" reflects this racial prejudice even more keenly. White American soldiers in France are kind to their black cook, but when an entire regiment of fatigued African American soldiers comes into their camp at night, the white soldiers feel that they are encroaching on their terrain: "In common against a common foe, smoulders their wrong against our right."[42]

The final line of Kirstein's poem subtly points out a racial paradox that existed in the United States. Many white Americans may have endorsed what later would be called multiculturalism as an abstract and democratic principle against Hitler's racial campaigns during the war, but they were nevertheless adamant to sustain white hegemonic norms all the same. The middle generation poets were certainly not political poets who stridently exposed racial injustice in their home country during the war, as Langston Hughes did,[43] but they did subtly hint at inequality in many of their poems.

While Eliot had ridiculed or disapproved of "free-thinking Jews" such as Sigmund Freud, Karl Marx, and Spinoza in his earlier work, Jarrell and other poets of the middle generation championed their work. In fact, these Jewish thinkers were, along with the Jewish-German refugee Hannah Arendt, some of the principal influences of Jarrell's poetry in the 1930s and 1940s. Jarrell's poems rely on psychoanalytical and psychological "concepts of the unconscious; on gestalt theories of perception; on the pre-oedipal dyad of baby and mother; on Freudian eros and thanatos; and especially on dream work," as Stephen Burt has explained.[44] Among his war poems, "Absent with Official Leave," "The Death of the Ball Turret Gunner," and "A Field Hospital" are directly influenced by Freud's *The Interpretation of Dreams,* while "Mother, Said the Child," "Protocols," and "The Truth" show Jarrell's fascination for child psychology.

Marx's influence on Jarrell's poetry was as pervasive as Freud's early on in his career, but it began to wane during the war. Yet Jarrell's frequent references to the capitalized "State" probably derive from Marx as does Jarrell's reductive economic explanation of war in early poems such as "For the Madrid Road" and "The Soldier." Spinoza, about whom Jarrell wrote a poem called "The Place of Death" during the war, was most likely behind the idea of necessity, the notion that disasters occur for no particular reason. The victims of war that Jarrell describes die for no reason; there is no explanation. "*It happens as it does because it does,*" Jarrell states in "Siegfried."[45] Mary Jarrell claimed in an unpublished letter that Arendt, whom Jarrell met soon after the war, was somewhat of a teacher to him. Jarrell instructed her about American poetry, but Arendt encouraged him to think more rigorously about European philosophers, about the European educational system as compared to the American one, and about the persecution of the Jews in Germany.[46]

Jarrell's and Shapiro's recognition of the pain and anguish of others is representative for their generation. The egalitarian spirit can be found everywhere in the writings of the middle generation, from John Berryman's story "The Imaginary Jew" to Louis Simpson's "A Story about Chicken Soup," Randall Jarrell's "Burning the Letters," "The Truth," and many more. The sense of empathy and acceptance of others that the middle generation exhibited transcended cultural, ethnic, gender, and historical boundaries, and it included African Americans, children, Jews, and women in the poems cited above. The poet and critic Edward Hirsch has suggested that these qualities set the middle generation apart from the modernist generation: "this passionate involvement and deep identification with the suffering of others, this apparently simple commitment to the humanly flawed, this way of weighting things on a subjective human scale, is radically different from the impersonal and objective standard set forth in the Pound era, by the Eliot generation. Such a credo, a textual project, carries a radically different politics, a democratic ethos, and speaks up against authoritarianism."[47] Karl Shapiro had stated something similar about thirty-five years earlier when he described his generation, "unlike our predecessors," as being "almost to a man humane humanists." His generation consisted of poets who "were democratic in politics, agnostic in religion, and baroque in literature."[48] His generation thus reversed Eliot's famous self-description that he was "classical in literature, royalist in politics, and Anglo-Catholic in religion."[49]

These two descriptions by Hirsch and Shapiro should suggest neither that racism or misogyny were completely absent in the poetry and lives of the middle generation poets, nor that modernist poets were by definition more bigoted than their poetic successors. Marianne Moore rejected racial prejudice in her poetry—for instance, in "Virginia Britannia"—and she was "deeply critical of [Pound's] racism and anti-Semitism," as Bonnie Costello has noted.[50] William Carlos Williams's "To Elsie," with its powerful claim that "the pure products of America," including Elsie, "go crazy," further shows that reductive generalizations about intolerance do not hold true for the modernist poets.[51] There are also plenty of examples to suggest that the middle generation poets were not always as accepting as they seem at first glance.[52] Yet the contrast is still significant, especially when comparing how Jews are depicted by the middle generation and by Eliot and Pound.

Whereas "Eliot's anti-Semitism was representative, and representatively mild," as critic Anthony Julius has put it, Pound's hatred for the Jews was more extreme, especially just before and during World War II.[53] "The Cantos written before 1935 are free from the ranting, paranoid antisemitism of the radio speeches" that Pound broadcast from fascist Italy between 1941 and 1943, as Wendy Stallard Flory writes.[54] Yet Pound's anti-Jewish sentiments in, for instance, *Guide to Kulchur* (1938) were already strong enough for Delmore Schwartz—who was much more sensitive to literary anti-Semitism than, for example, Nemerov—"to resign as one of your most studious and faithful admirers."[55] Pound's radio speeches rather than his poetry led to his indictment for treason in 1943 and his arrest in 1945 after the Allied forces had occupied Italy. Pound was ultimately found mentally unfit to stand trial, but was incarcerated in St. Elizabeth's Hospital near Washington, D.C. until his release in 1958.

The way in which Jews feature in the literary works of the World War II poets is the antithesis of the crude depiction in the poems of Eliot and Pound. John Berryman's short story "The Imaginary Jew," first published in the *Kenyon Review* in 1945, is probably the best example of how the middle generation poets spurned the anti-Semitism of Eliot and Pound. In this Kafkaesque story Berryman's narrator relates how he is called a Jew when he meddles in a political discussion in New York City's Union Square at the beginning of World War II. The narrator, who admits that he is "spectacularly unable to identify Jews as Jews," cannot convince the others in the park, in particular a machismo Irishman, that he is not Jewish.[56] Berryman's alter ego decides in the end that he is (like) the imaginary Jew, "as real as the imaginary Jew hunted down, on other nights and days, in a real Jew."[57] Berryman feels spiritually connected to Jews as victims and outsiders, as is also apparent from his admiration of *The Diary of Anne Frank*.[58]

Berryman's identification with Jewish suffering is similar to that of Ciardi and Jarrell, who both wrote poems from a Jewish vantage point, though neither of them was Jewish. Not only did Ciardi publish a poem, "The Gift," describing the poet Jozef Stein at Dachau, he also wrote a poem called "Sarko," which he never chose to publish, in which he speaks for a Holocaust survivor who reminisces about his days in a death camp:

> We were led to bare stalls and no soup.
> In the morning a few examples were made—
> The twisted bodies because they were twisted, a murderer
> Because he was muscular, a few at random.[59]

Even though Ciardi was (as a bombardier in the Pacific) physically and (as an Italian American man from Boston) mentally removed from the Holocaust, he nevertheless felt compelled to empathize with Jewish victims of the war, and he also chided Pound for his refusal to do so when the occasion arose a decade after the war. A decade after the war Ciardi wrote to Pound in a letter:

> I still have to feel strongly about your damned anti-semitism. I grant you Big Brother Benito didn't have gas-ovens, but his fat-ass boys were fast enough with a bottle of castor-oil, and damn them.
>
> This is not to argue with you, God knows. Who am I to think I could take your dose and still stand up? I couldn't even stand being a sgt in the goddamn Army. Still, I've got to disagree, even though it stays sweetened with admiration and with gratitudes for what I've learned from you in disagreement. And why not let a little disagreement in?[60]

Ciardi's admonishing once again shows the ambivalent stance the middle generation took to high modernism. A deep respect and admiration for Pound's accomplishments in poetry mix with a privately voiced rebuke about his racism and support for fascist Italy.

Eliot and Pound both express an insensitive attitude to Jewish suffering and at times a lack of empathy with those different from themselves. It is precisely these humane and democratic qualities that were being developed by the middle generation during and after World War II, as that war dramatized more fully than ever what bigotry and intolerance could lead to. Like many poets of his generation, Hecht gives voice to the hapless victims of war rather than focus on a "young man carbuncular" and a "bored and tired" typist. Like Ciardi, Hecht also "learned" from Eliot "in disagreement," but rather than address Eliot personally as Ciardi does with Pound, Hecht centered a poem, "Rites and Ceremonies," around their "little disagreement," which he published only after Eliot's death.

Hecht gets no answer to the question he poses to both God and Eliot: "Is there not one / Whom thou shalt pluck for love out of coals?"[61] Hecht wrote in an earlier draft of "Rites and Ceremonies" that he had "thought for twenty years about this," and "for 12 about this poem," underlining how personal, troubling, and persistent that question was to him.[62] Yet even without an answer, he struggles to come to some resolution, with both God and Eliot. The fourth and final section of "Rites and Ceremonies" is called "Words for the Day of Atonement" and is named after the Jewish holiday of repentance. Hecht asks, wishes, or implores that "the whole Congregation of the Children of Israel" as well as "the stranger dwelling in their midst" be forgiven for their sins.[63] Hecht ends his poem with a line from Psalm 72, "A Psalm for Solomon": "*He will come down like rain upon mown grass.*"[64] The psalm prophesies the kingdom of Christ when the world will be replenished and all discord between families, churches, nations, and individuals will cease to exist. The rain coming down and the earth at peace is also the image that ends Eliot's *The Waste Land,* which suggests that in the end Hecht forgivingly reaches out to Eliot.

CHAPTER 3

"Childish" Allen Tate, the New Critics, and Reaching Poetic Maturity

The poets of the middle generation all matured in the heyday of the New Criticism, that loose confederation of like-minded critics and poets, mostly from the South, who came to prominence in the 1930s. Like the practitioners of high modernism, the New Critics had a formidable influence on the World War II poets. Randall Jarrell studied under John Crowe Ransom at Vanderbilt University, where he also befriended Allen Tate, and later followed Ransom to Kenyon College. Robert Lowell famously pitched his Sears-Roebuck tent on Tate's lawn after leaving Harvard in the summer of 1937, intending to learn the trade from Tate. Lowell also went to Kenyon College because of Ransom's presence, where he met Jarrell, with whom he struck up a lifelong friendship. After graduating from Kenyon College, Lowell pursued graduate work at Louisiana State University from 1940 to 1941, with two other New Critics, Cleanth Brooks and Robert Penn Warren. Weldon Kees did not study under the New Critics, but he "considered Tate's 'Ode to the Confederate Dead' one of his favorite poems." Before the two met in New York in 1940, Tate "recommended" Kees's "For My Daughter" and several other poems to John Crowe Ransom, who published them in the *Kenyon Review.*[1] It was one of Kees's first publications in a major journal.

The slightly younger war poets were also drawn to the New Critics. As a Harvard sophomore, Howard Nemerov was mesmerized by the *Kenyon Review,* edited by Ransom. He sent Ransom a nine-page article called "A Note on Sigmund Freud," connecting Freud's psychoanalytic theory to the works of Thomas Mann and Richard Wagner. Although Ransom rejected the article, he was struck by Nemerov's mature writing style and the fecundity of his analyses, and encouraged him to submit more of his work.[2] After the war, Nemerov met Tate and dedicated a poem and a collection of essays,

Reflexions on Poetry & Poetics (1972), to him. Anthony Hecht chose to work with Ransom for a year at Kenyon College on the GI Bill, and subsequently he also worked with Tate on something similar to the poetic apprenticeship that Lowell had received a decade earlier. "The government was getting its money's worth," according to Hecht.[3] Even war poets whose work seemed unaffected by the New Critical way of writing, however, such as James Dickey and Thomas McGrath, were also trained in the New Critical mode. Dickey spent the money from his GI Bill at Vanderbilt, where, despite Ransom's departure, the English Department had continued to advance the tenets of the New Criticism, while McGrath was a student of Brooks and Warren at Louisiana State University.

The New Critics formed an unavoidable presence for this younger generation of poets. Not only did the New Critics edit some of the most prestigious journals, including the *Kenyon Review,* the *Sewanee Review,* and the *Southern Review* in the 1930s and 1940s, they had also recently theorized, in books and articles, what the logical structure and content of a successful poem should look like. The title of one of Ransom's collections of essays, *The New Criticism* (1941), became the name for this formalist approach to literature. The poets and critics who were associated with the New Criticism, at this point and later, neither formed a group or movement nor did they all agree about the principles of literary criticism. Still, their close-reading techniques revolutionized the study of poetry, a field that until then had been dominated by more impressionistic and historically minded critics. Ransom and Tate were the principal theoreticians behind the New Criticism, while Brooks and Warren popularized it through their widely accepted textbook, *Understanding Poetry* (1939).

Just before and during World War II, Allen Tate had outlined in a series of short essays the characteristics of superior and inferior poetry. Tate's critical writing of this period thus provided a blueprint or model of the kind of poem that the middle generation ought to write. In "Three Types of Poetry" (1934), Tate glorified the "kind of poetry that Shakespeare wrote," the third type, which was "complete and whole" and which he called "the creative spirit."[4] Hecht has claimed that Tate's poetry lessons taught him "about the way a poem's total design is modulated and given its energy, not by local ingredients tastefully combined, but by the richness, toughness and density of some sustaining vision of life—sustaining, at least, throughout the world of the poem and perhaps with some resonance to it after the poem is done."[5] Writing poetry should be a holistic approach where form and content, emotion and intellect, denotation and connotation, and personal and social vision merged.

Tate denounced two other types of poetry in his 1934 essay: allegorical or didactic poetry and romantic poetry. The first type included not only the moralist literature of the Middle Ages but also political or propagandistic poetry. Its "rhetoric is a forcing of the subject, which is abstractly conceived, not implicitly seized upon," Tate argues.[6] The antiwar poetry of Wilfred Owen or Thomas McGrath's critique of capitalism through his poems could not qualify as great poetry because their poems are too intent on making a point. Tate also dismissed the "inflated and emotive" style of Byron and "the romantic, disillusioned irony" of Shelley or Robinson Jeffers. Their only desire is "to revolt, pitting the individual will against all forms of order."[7] In "Tension in Poetry" (1938), Tate warned more generally against "political poetry for the sake of the cause," "didactic poetry for the sake of the parish," "picturesque poetry for the sake of the home town," "a generalized personal poetry for the sake of the reassurance and safety of numbers," and "an anonymous lyricism in which the common personality exhibits its commonness."[8] If poets followed Tate's advice, it would severely limit the range of their war poetry, a genre that often has didactic, lyrical, picturesque, and political dimensions.

It is often assumed that younger poets, of the Beat generation and the New York School, only started to rebel publicly against Tate's kind of New Critical ideas about poetry when these ideas became hegemonic in the 1950s and 1960s. Yet poets of the middle generation, such as Randall Jarrell and Karl Shapiro, were already voicing their private unease about Tate's dicta during World War II. The reason for their discomfort with Tate during the war was twofold. On the one hand, they felt frustrated because war gives rise to political and social questions as well as concerns about identity, which, according to Tate, were not the proper subject of poetry. On the other hand, Tate himself did not keep to his own rules, as much of his war poetry, including "More Sonnets at Christmas" and "Ode to the Young Pro-Consuls of the Air," was social and political. They are examples of "political poetry for the sake of the cause" and of "didactic poetry for the sake of the parish."

Hecht and Richard Wilbur, for instance, continued to write in a style that was akin to that favored by the New Critics. Yet many of the other poets, including Robert Lowell, extricated themselves from Tate's influence after the war. Tate thought that nearly all of Lowell's poems in the autobiographical, free-verse, and much-acclaimed volume *Life Studies* (1959) were "definitely bad," and he urged Lowell not "to publish them."[9] Lowell disagreed, and published them anyway, although he returned to more formal structures later on in his career, as did Karl Shapiro. Despite their occasional, mostly mild rebellion, the middle generation poets never completely got rid of Tate's teachings, although they privately concluded that Tate was too narrow about autobiographical and political material.

Randall Jarrell's relationship with Allen Tate during the war needs special attention, as Jarrell was most assertive in disentangling himself from the teachings of Tate, both in his prose and poetry.[10] Between 1942 and 1945 Jarrell reached "poetic maturity," as Suzanne Ferguson has suggested, as a result of "a series of impulses, primarily aesthetic and worldly rather than personal."[11] Jarrell used Tate (and also W. H. Auden as we will see in the next chapter) as a sparring opponent to formulate a new poetics for himself, which in time became representative for his generation. At the beginning of the war, Jarrell looked up to Tate as one of his principal mentors. Tate was instrumental in getting Jarrell his first book contract, for *Blood for a Stranger* (1941), and also invited him to give a prestigious lecture at Princeton, where Tate taught. Jarrell was genuinely grateful to Tate for these favors, realizing "that other people in [Tate's] place wouldn't have done the same thing." Not much later, however, Jarrell began to distance himself from Tate in order to be fully independent.[12]

Jarrell began to establish himself as a poetry critic just before the war, but his methodology was markedly different from that of the New Critics. Unlike Tate, Jarrell was wary of only indulging in elaborate close readings, and he excelled in the "one-line invective," as William H. Pritchard has observed.[13] This does not mean that Jarrell eschewed technique or close readings, however. Jarrell's analyses of individual poems by Robert Frost and W. H. Auden are exceptional for their brilliant precision. Jarrell also wrote magnificently on Whitman's diction and Frost's rhythms. Yet overall Jarrell was less doctrinal in his criticism than Tate. Jarrell even criticized Tate for his "odd habit of conclusively demonstrating the quality of a poet by means of a little metrical analysis: it is an idiosyncrasy that almost assumes the proportions of a vice."[14] In "Levels and Opposites," the Princeton lecture that Tate had invited him to give in 1942, Jarrell even went as far as saying that "metre, stanza-form, rhyme, alliteration, quantity" are "things any child can point at."[15] Note the slightly patronizing reference to "child," which is discussed further later on. "There are *many* different sorts of structure in poetry," Jarrell continues, "*many* possible ways of organizing a poem; and *many* of these are combined in the organization of a single poem."[16]

Whereas Ransom favored an "ontological critic" and argued that "criticism must become more scientific, or precise and systematic,"[17] Jarrell stated in 1941 that gaining "objective reliability" of "facts" in criticism is "absurd in theory and disastrous in practice."[18] Instead Jarrell argued that a good poem ought to be based on more and possibly contradictory organizing principles, creating a richer poetic structure. "Jarrell is emphasizing the importance of process, of dramatizing the mind in action, of simultaneity, of polyvocality and multiple points of view," as Thomas Travisano—who discovered "Levels and Opposites" among Jarrell's papers—has argued.[19]

More telling than his wartime critique of the New Critical approach in his lecture "Levels and Opposites" was Jarrell's negative appraisal of Tate's most famous World War II poem, "Ode to Our Young Pro-Consuls of the Air." The mocking ode opened the March/April 1943 issue of *Partisan Review*, which was widely read among intellectuals. It was the last of four satires that Tate had written since 1938.[20] As the title suggests, the poem lambastes the young, naive American airmen who rule the skies in the same way as the military commanders of the ancient Roman provinces controlled the Mediterranean world. In terse, flippant lines, "Ode to Our Young Pro-Consuls of the Air" first establishes a quick, bird's-eye view of previous wars, from the Revolutionary War to the First World War, and events leading up to the Second World War:

Toy swords, three-cornered hat
At York and Lexington—

    While *Bon-Homme* whipped at sea
    This enemy
Whose roar went flat
After George made him run;

Toy rifle, leather hat
Above the boyish beard—
    And in that Blue renown
    The Grey went down,
Down like a rat,
And the rats cheered.

In a much later age
(Europe had been in flames)
    Proud Wilson yielded ground
    To franc and pound,
Made pilgrimage
In the wake of Henry James.

Where Lou Quatorze held *fête*
For sixty thousand men,
    France took the German sword
    But later, bored,
Opened the gate
To Hitler—at Compiègne.[21]

All these wars were unnecessary, wasteful, and caused by greed or stupidity, Tate argues. He wants to expose the "facile thoughtless patriotism" that underlies them, as William Doreski has claimed.[22] The American airmen that Tate satirizes are thus symbolic for their youthful and gullible country, which has again plunged itself headlong into harm.

Tate also carped about two literary critics in his "Ode"—Archibald MacLeish and Van Wyck Brooks—who had recently become political commentators. MacLeish, also a poet and the Librarian of Congress since 1939, and Tate's friend of sorts, had accused American intellectuals in his pamphlet *The Irresponsibles* (1940) of failing to react to the rise of totalitarian regimes in Europe and of making no effort to defend democracy, freedom of speech, and other features of "the common culture of the West."[23] In *Opinions of Oliver Allston* (1941) Brooks, whom Tate disliked, had initiated a more wholesale attack on modernist literature, which he called "coterie literature" and described as "anti-literary" and "anti-vital." Brooks also lashed out at the New Critics because they "evaded the whole world of values."[24] Instead Brooks favored wholesome American authors who produced "primary literature" and who had "faith in progress."[25] Tate sarcastically praised "brave Brooks and lithe MacLeish" for whipping the derelicts into submission "with literature made Prime!"[26] In a draft of the poem, Tate had initially called MacLeish "stout," but the adjective "lithe" captures better Tate's irritation with his friend's sudden patriotic zeal and MacLeish's implicit attack on modernism.[27] MacLeish did not resent Tate for his poem. He even offered him the position of poetry consultant at the Library of Congress, which Tate accepted.

Tate reserved the last five stanzas of "Ode to the Young Pro-Consuls of the Air" for some ironic advice to the American soldiers. He coaxes them on to go "win the world / With zeal pro-consular" wherever they go—the Middle East, the Mediterranean, India, and Tibet.[28] Like Ezra Pound and Robert Lowell in their war poems, Tate represents Americans as philistines who will kill or destroy anything with historical, cultural, and mythical importance in the world.[29] Tate also explicitly charges that Americans are bent on world domination, as they look upon the earth with an "imperial eye." In earlier versions of the poem, Tate had used "a forward," "forgetting," and "unseeing eye," which all sound more innocuous.[30] The final (imaginary) scene of the poem features American soldiers who are scaling Mount Everest, the highest peak in the world, which had not been conquered yet, and who are bombing and hunting down the Dalai Lama. These scenes connect the allegedly irreverent and boorish American attitude with their supposed imperialism.

In a letter to his wife, Mackie, Jarrell mentioned that he "thought the Dalai Lama almost the only touch of imagination" of Tate's poem, but he was generally condescending about Tate's war poems, to her and to Lowell.[31] Jarrell suggested in the same letter that "one stanza" of Tate's "Ode" was "influenced by Shapiro's "Scyros" (1941). While Jarrell disliked Tate's poem, he thought that "Scyros" was "a beautifully successful *tour de force*," as he told Lowell.[32] A few years later Lowell was also "struck by the resemblance between the pro-consuls and scyros," as he mentioned to Shapiro, and added: "not to the pro-consults [*sic*] advantage!"[33] The tone, rhyme, rhythm, and stanzaic form of both poems are indeed strikingly similar, even though Shapiro modeled the poem's form on John Milton's "Nativity Ode" and Tate on Michael Drayton's "The Virginia Voyage," both early modern poems.[34] Yet, like Tate, Shapiro also painted quick scenes of the war that followed each other in rapid succession. Whereas Tate had a clear political and literary point to prove, however, Shapiro's poem mostly expresses sorrow at the escalation of the war, as the final two stanzas of the poem show:

> Hot is the sky and green
> Where Germans have been seen
> The moon leaks metal on the Atlantic fields
> Pink boys in birthday shrouds
> Loop lightly through the clouds
> Or coast the peaks of Finland on their shields
>
> That prophet year by year
> Lay still but could not hear
> Where scholars tapped to find his new remains
> Gog and Magog ate pork
> In vertical New York
> And war began next Wednesday on the Danes.[35]

Perhaps these lines indicate anger at the Nazis for invading Denmark; at God, who is nowhere to be found; or at the military or political leaders, like the ancient Gog who once attacked Israel and was crushed by Yahweh, but is now in the United States consuming plenty. Yet the message is so understated and confusing that a simple moral lesson cannot be drawn.

Tate was an admirer of Shapiro's early poetry. He had written an appreciative review of *Person, Place and Thing* in which he admitted that Shapiro "was the first poet, much younger than" him of whom he felt "a steady and disturbing envy."[36] In Shapiro's poems, Tate wrote, "there is a fine control of tone and an unpredictable rightness of observation which nobody else of [his] generation has achieved," thereby placing Shapiro ahead of Jarrell and Lowell.[37] In a personal letter, Tate gave the younger poet some avuncular advice, though. *Person, Place and Thing* had included "too many slick pieces," and he urged Shapiro to make the next book "smaller than the first one."[38] Irked by what he deemed Tate's patronizing tone, Shapiro replied boisterously that *V-Letter* "will be larger than the other" and "as fat as ever possible." "Your advice to hold my heavy guns is no go. This is now-or-never land; surely you are aware of that."[39] Shapiro's distaste for the New Criticism, as evident in *Essay on Rime* (1945), *Beyond Criticism* (1953), and *In Defense of Ignorance* (1960), was clearly budding, but he was also wary of wasting time. The "now-or-never land" of the Pacific theater propelled him to write fast and furious and to publish as much as possible.

Jarrell was no longer following Tate's advice either. In 1940 Tate had warned Jarrell that his meter was becoming faulty and his diction too prosy, but Jarrell had made a conscious choice to write more colloquial poetry: "I'd rather seem limp and prosaic than false or rhetorical, I want to be rather like speech," Jarrell replied, staunchly defending his own poetic style.[40] A month later Tate suggested that Jarrell cut a stanza from "90 North," one of his most successful early poems. Jarrell again politely declined to accept his advice, although he expressed he felt "bad about not being able to show my gratitude by taking it."[41]

By 1943 Jarrell was criticizing Tate's poetry, albeit not to his face. When Jarrell received a complimentary copy of *The Winter Sea* (1944) from Tate, he called it "the prettiest book of poems I've ever seen" and listed "the Air Corps *Ode*" and "Jubilo" among the poems he appreciated the most.[42] But to Mackie Jarrell, he called the "Ode" "poor and annoying," and called "Jubilo" and "More Sonnets at Christmas," published in the *Kenyon Review*, "childish."[43] In "More Sonnets" Tate had characterized the American citizen as spoiled, and ignorant of history, culture, and religion. Like the prisoners in Plato's cave, Americans mistake appearance for reality. "Jubilo" expresses more explicitly that Christian faith can restore the blindness of the American people. Jarrell indicated to his wife that he felt that the poems themselves were naive: "I feel so old and responsible as I read them," Jarrell claimed with his characteristic humor, but with a hint of seriousness.[44]

The tables had completely turned in Jarrell's mind. Whereas Tate used to be the mentor and Jarrell the student, Jarrell now feels the "responsible" one and Tate is deemed "childish." It is also remarkable that Jarrell's claim echoes MacLeish's claim that American intellectuals were the "*Irresponsibles*," to which Tate had reacted so furiously. Depicting Tate as immature was, for Jarrell, on a psychological level, perhaps necessary to gain his poetic maturity. In this sense, it would be no coincidence that immediately following the passage in his letter of April 5, 1943, to Mackie Jarrell in which he first criticized Tate, Jarrell writes: "I think perhaps if I ever have time I can write some good dreary poems about the army, and the war, but they won't be printable while I'm in the army, and they won't be liked by anybody until the '20's—when those return."[45] Jarrell had not written any war poetry at the time, but Tate's sullen World War II poetry convinced Jarrell that he could be more eloquent and original on the subject.

More than two years later, Jarrell further clarified his objections about Tate to Lowell, who was going through a similar struggle for independence: "I like just the parts of Allen's poems that you do, though there's a petulance and subjectivity that drops them from the rank of serious first-rate poems about such a subject as the Second World War; Allen is writing about his second war, a very different thing. Allen's great fault is a defect of sympathy in the strict sense of the word, a lack of ability to identify himself with anything that is fundamentally non-Allen."[46] While forging his bond with Lowell, Jarrell reproaches Tate for his supposed narrow egotism in using his war poetry to battle his literary opponents, but, more important, for not being able to feel for the victims of war. Jarrell's argument echoes Hecht's quarrel with T. S. Eliot, whose silence about or scorn for the less privileged people in the world disturbed him. Jarrell thought that Lowell and he, and by implication his entire generation, should write about what Tate and the older generation could clearly not write about. World War II was *their* war, not Tate's.

In his own war poetry, which he began to write after distancing himself from Tate in 1943, Jarrell empathized with all sorts of victims of the war, whether it be "bombers," "carriers," "prisoners," "children and civilians," or "soldiers," to cite the categories that he used for his *Selected Poems*.[47] Jarrell's war poetry grew at least partly from his belief that, unlike Tate, he was able "to identify himself" with many people who are "fundamentally" non-Randall. His army years had helped him to identify with the airmen who were so different from him in age, education, and intellect. That experience made him realize how sarcastic and haughty satire was, as he hinted at in a letter to Tate: "If you met your proconsuls you'd find you couldn't differentiate them from a high school team, except for the fact that half of them had gotten killed during the season. I knew a girl whose husband, a pilot, graduated from Randolph Field a day or so after Pearl Harbor; out of his class of twenty-five there are just two left alive."[48] Jarrell realized that the young airmen he helped train were not just uncultured and unworldly boys who blindly followed American propaganda the way Tate characterized them, but a group of all sorts of individuals who were also the victims of a complex historical process.

Jarrell kept an extensive notebook on William Wordsworth while he was in the army, in which he rigorously studied Wordsworth's poem "Lucy." The choice to study Wordsworth already signals a departure from Tate as the New Critic was not a fan of Romantic poetry. In his notebook Jarrell sought to extract from it a lesson that, in poetry, "'particulars' should seem so much more effective than 'universals.'" "Of course none of Tates [*sic*] or Ransoms [*sic*] particulars are really particulars," Jarrell reasoned, "but moderately high degrees of abstraction." Wordsworth's "Lucy" seems an unlikely model for Jarrell's victims of war, but Jarrell was intrigued by the way Wordsworth reflected on "the precariousness of ~~people~~ the human being." Jarrell notes that Wordsworth gives "no special reason or explanation of things happening." There is "no suggestion of tragic flaw" or of "original sin."[49]

This perspective on life fitted with Jarrell's new developing vision of the tragic events of World War II. The American proconsuls were just as precarious and vulnerable as their victims, and Jarrell disliked the abstract and general way in which Tate depicted and mocked them. How successful Jarrell was in appropriating these other identities will be explored later in this book, but it is important to stress that while Jarrell's criticism of Tate is understandable from his perspective, it is not entirely fair. Even though Tate's "Ode" is irritatingly subjective at times, Tate was capable of the compassion and understanding that Jarrell argued he was lacking.

This is not just apparent from the personal testimonies of younger poets such as Hecht who stated that Tate was a person who "let us be whatever we are, and is concerned only to discover what that might be," but also from some of his war poems.[50] "To the Lacedemonians" (1932/1936), for instance, is a moving psychological portrait of a Confederate veteran who feels out of place in the modern world, which is too densely populated and full of car noises:

The people—people of my kind, my own
People but strange with a light
In the face: the streets hard with motion
And the hard eyes that look one way.
Listen! The high whining tone
Of the motors, I hear the dull commotion:
I am come, a child in an old play.[51]

The poem, "whose title refers to a small band of doomed Spartans who preferred to die rather than surrender a pass they were defending," as Thomas A. Underwood has explained, is partly an interior monologue and partly a dramatic monologue, a genre that Jarrell took up during and after the war and made his own.[52] Although the poem has occasional end-rhyme, it is uncharacteristically inconsistent; nor is there regular meter. Tate was in his early thirties when he wrote this poem, but successfully voices the alternating fearful, angry, defiant, and nostalgic thoughts and feelings of an elderly veteran.

"To the Lacedemonians" has a clear political dimension because this anonymous veteran is symbolic for a forgotten and much-maligned generation of war veterans. Tate's poem appeared on the front-page of the *Richmond Times Dispatch* in the summer of 1932 when veterans were protesting in Washington against President Herbert Hoover's refusal to clear a $1,000 bonus that Congress had promised them. Tate had anticipated the march on Washington, as he told his friend Andrew Lytle.[53] Yet unlike "Ode to Our Young Pro-Consuls of the Air," the political message is neither obtrusive nor satirical. It offers instead a poignant portrait of the aging veteran, especially as he reminisces about the battles he fought and about his childhood. He says puzzlingly that in his youthful days, he never knew "cessation," probably meaning that he never realized that life is finite, that all things pass. The child was also too young to appreciate fully the splendor and beauty of nature: "When I was a boy the light on the hills / Was there because I could see it, not because / Some special gift of God had put it there, / Put the contraption before the accomplishment."[54] "To the Lacedemonians" proves that Tate was capable of the empathy that Jarrell said he lacked, and of writing war poetry that was universal. It is true, however, that the prematurely old Tate was perhaps not too much removed from the grumpy old veteran in his monologue.

At the end of the war Jarrell also wrote a number of interior monologues, most notably "Burning the Letters" and "The State." When juxtaposed to Tate's "To the Lacedemonians," Jarrell's monologues are clearly bolder and more experimental. "Burning the Letters" features a pilot's widow, while "The State" presents a child's view of the war. While Tate chose a persona who is still relatively close to him—an older version of himself basically—Jarrell imagined fictional characters that were most unlike himself: a grown-up, male air force instructor who remained stateside during the war. Understanding the full extent of war for Jarrell meant that one should vicariously experience it from other sides. Positioning himself against his friend and former mentor whose war poetry offered a more one-sided and reductive reading of the war helped Jarrell to achieve this.

Jarrell's falling out with Tate is representative of a process of dissociation from the New Critics that nearly all middle generation poets experienced, albeit in different degrees and at different times. The war was a first catalyst for their estrangement because poets such as Jarrell and Shapiro thought that they had a better vantage point to comprehend the war, making the teacher-mentor bond that Tate expected untenable. Yet their opposition was neither a complete repudiation of the New Critics nor a voluble protest against their teachings, but rather a "little disagreement"—to quote Ciardi's letter to Ezra Pound—voiced in private letters or hidden behind silent grudges. Jarrell's correspondence with Tate almost came to a complete standstill after the war, and they were never as close as they were before and at the beginning of World War II. Yet Jarrell (and the other middle generation poets) owed a great deal to the kind of poetry and poetics that Tate and the other New Critics promoted. A poem such as "To the Lacedemonians" precedes all of Jarrell's monologues, but it is surprisingly similar in the nostalgic tone and the theme of childhood that Jarrell presented in "The Lost World," "Thinking of the Lost World," and "Burning the Letters."

Tate never fully understood how or why Jarrell and he drifted apart. In his memoir for Jarrell, "Young Randall," written after Jarrell's death in 1965, he ponders that "for an inscrutable reason—I never understood Randall—he liked me very much for some years around 1940, but not much later on."[55] Jarrell was known to be "a proud and difficult young man" when Tate first met him, and Tate thought that "from the beginning he was his own man."[56] The irony is that Jarrell, while certainly one of a kind, was not yet "his own man" in 1940, and he needed to shun Tate in order to accomplish that. More important, Jarrell needed to disagree with Tate to find his own voice as a war poet, one that would speak for all the victims of the total war of World War II.

CHAPTER 4

Talking Back to W. H. Auden

One of the newer poems in William Meredith's volume *Partial Accounts: New and Selected Poems* (1987) is called "Talking Back (To W. H. Auden)." It reflects on what Meredith learned from one of his literary elders at a time when Meredith himself was reaching old age. "Talking Back" is a response to Auden's famous phrase from "In Memory of W. B. Yeats" (1939), which Meredith quotes as the epigraph: "for poetry makes nothing happen."[1] In three stanzas Meredith subtly and gently refutes Auden's claim by showing that poetry does make things happen, but

small things,
sometimes to some, in an area
already pretty well taken
care of by the senses.[2]

Written at a time when World War II was looming, Auden's claim was a pessimistic acknowledgment that poetry has no (political) influence or purpose. Yet Meredith concentrates on the tiny moments of insight that poetry can provide for a person who is open to new perceptions.

Meredith dwells on how reading Auden's poetry is similar to a walk in nature after a light snowfall. Carefully observing the scenery around you will make you aware of parallels that you had never observed before, just as poetry does. "Spruce needles," for instance, seem to "fix the tufts / of new snow to the twigs so the / wind cannot dislodge them."[3] Using the enjambment to full effect and exploiting both the transitive and intransitive use of the verb "to hold," Meredith continues: "They hold— / a metaphor."[4] Farther on, Meredith speaks directly to Auden, pressing home—more than a decade after Auden's death—what Auden had taught him, that "looked at carefully, nothing is sullen."[5] Meredith urges Auden not to be apologetic or harsh about his art, and to realize how important he was for the younger generation of poets:

> It is like finding on your tongue
> right words to call across the floe
> of arrogance to the wise dead,
> of health to sickness, old to young
> Across this debt, we tell you so.[6]

Throughout his poem Meredith evokes themes and techniques that Auden had also used in his own work. First, talking to or about "the wise dead," as Meredith does, is what Auden did in poems such as "In Memory of W. B. Yeats," "In Memory of Sigmund Freud," and "Musée des Beaux Arts." Second, Meredith's diction of "health," "sickness," "old," "young," and "debt" is suggestive either of the theme of a diseased society or of the Marxist imagery that Auden exercised in his early poetry. Third, Meredith applies some seemingly illogical tropes that make sense only after some time. Auden was the master of "the Incongruous" metaphor, as Jarrell argued in "Changes of Attitudes and Rhetoric in Auden's Poetry."[7] Meredith is paying a debt to Auden, but by talking back to him, he also reveals how Auden influenced the middle generation. Auden's unexpected angles, his metaphorical range, and his faith that "looked at carefully, nothing is sullen" are lessons that the middle generation poets all took to heart.

Of all the American World War II poets, Meredith knew Auden most intimately—with the possible exception of Lincoln Kirstein—and even became his joint literary executor at one point after Auden's death. Yet he was not the only member of his generation who talked back to Auden. All of them did, either publicly in published prose or poetry or in the privacy of letters or notebooks. More so than Eliot or Pound, Auden was a touchstone for younger generations of poets, both in the United States and in Great Britain.[8] Whereas modernism seemed to have reached the end of the line, as Jarrell wrote in 1942, Auden was developing constantly and churning out books of poetry faster than anyone else did when the middle generation came of age in the 1930s and 1940s. "Auden was so influential," Jarrell asserted in 1942, "because his poetry was the only novel and successful reaction away from modernism."[9] "After Eliot there is Au.," James Dickey concurred in a draft of an unpublished review of Auden's *Collected Poems,* "& thr is no escaping him."[10]

Not all of the middle generation poets were as affectionate and appreciative of Auden as Meredith in "Talking Back," though. After his declarations of independence from modernism and the New Criticism, it comes as no surprise that Jarrell took the lead in an attack on Auden that began during World War II, with his long essays "Changes of Attitude and Rhetoric in Auden's Poetry" (1941) and "Freud to Paul: The Stages of Auden's Ideology" (1945), even though his poetry up to then had been clearly influenced by Auden. Even Jarrell's invectives, however, were acknowledgments of his indebtedness to Auden as well as of his fondness. Auden must have realized this because after reading a highly critical article by Jarrell he remarked to Stephen Spender: "Jarrell is in love with me."[11] All the middle generation poets were infatuated with Auden, but nearly all of them also fell out of love with him at some point during their careers.

The sheer variety and range of Auden's poetry meant that these poets each had their own favorite Auden, but also an Auden they disliked. In an article called "'Flouting Papa': Randall Jarrell and W. H. Auden," Ian Sansom writes persuasively that Jarrell's attitude to Auden is marked by "ambivalence" in the Freudian sense, of having both "affectionate and hostile" feelings toward one person.[12] This coexistence of opposing views seems true for other middle generation poets as well. Talking back to Auden was a way for the middle generation poets to measure their own development against Auden's career, and to think critically about their own emerging poetics. What they ultimately attempted was to achieve what Auden had done so expertly himself. Auden was extremely skilled at "analyzing someone else's work, taking out what he likes, and synthesizing a new style of his own that will include this," as Jarrell claimed.[13]

This is not only true of the poets who were most obviously influenced by Auden—for example, Anthony Hecht, Randall Jarrell, and Karl Shapiro—but also of those who seem at first glance unaffected by Auden's writings, such as James Dickey and Robert Lowell. Dickey intimated in his unpublished writings that he appraised his future career in terms of how Auden wrote. Dickey wrote in a notepad from the early 1950s, for instance, that "Auden is a supremely *rational* poet," which can lead to "cleverness." "I wish to be irrational & emotional. And perhaps mystical," Dickey countered.[14] In his unpublished review of Auden's *Collected Poems* written two decades later he elaborated by stating that even though Auden is brilliant, "there is a kind of void." At the end of the review Dickey compares Auden unfavorably to Whitman: "A. gives you more to think about. But I had rather be moved."[15]

When a few years later Dickey was planning his World War II novel *Alnilam* (1987), however, he turned to Auden for inspiration. In his notes for this expansive novel Dickey wrote that he wanted to model the "mystique" of his protagonist, Joel Cahill, on "Auden's most mysterious part of 'The Orators.'"[16] The similarities between Auden's *The Orators* (1932) and Dickey's *Alnilam* do not stop there. There are in fact so many stylistic and thematic parallels between the two works that *Alnilam* seems heavily indebted to Auden's densest book, even though Dickey never acknowledged this publicly. Like *The Orators, Alnilam* revolves around the hero worship of a group of "Initiates" who yearn for their vanished "Leader." The air cadet Joel Cahill is this absent hero in Dickey's novel, and his recovered diary—full of obscure notes like the "Journal of an Airman" in Auden's book—forms the basis of their cultism. It is not surprising that of all Auden's works Dickey chose *The Orators* as a model for *Alnilam*. "*The Orators* is Auden's only published work that is virtually impenetrable without certain keys," as Edward Mendelson has claimed. This style suited the "irrational & emotional" and "mystical" mode in which Dickey sought to write.[17]

When Lowell invoked Auden in his late poem "Since 1939" he was thinking of an entirely different Auden than the inscrutable and cryptic Auden from *The Orators* that Dickey had adopted for *Alnilam*. In "Since 1939" Lowell conjures up the politically and historically minded Auden, who was perfectly attuned to write about historic developments as they occurred. Auden did this most famously in "September 1, 1939," to which Lowell's title alludes. Lowell was conscious that in this sense he was Auden's heir since Lowell's poetry was also steeped in historical consciousness. Lowell reminisces how he and his young bride, Jean Stafford, were reading Auden's volume *Poems* (1930) on their honeymoon while on a train heading west. This memory is prompted by Lowell spotting a girl who is reading Auden's *Collected Poems* some thirty-five years later. Unlike Auden who in "September 1, 1939" dolefully evoked the dark period that was up ahead, Lowell and Stafford were blissfully ignorant about what was happening back then. They "missed the declaration of war" and doze off while reading Auden, their heads "fell down / swaying with the comfortable / ungainly gait of obsolescence."[18] Lowell's innocent view of the world quickly became outdated after Germany invaded Poland.

Lowell identifies with Auden because he, too, wants to write about historic events as they occur, but also because he was just as prone to change his poetic style as was Auden. It makes him consider that he was Auden's apprentice, as an earlier version of Lowell's poem called "1938–1975" shows:

> I live in his lost urgency,
> the true apocalypse of his apprenticeship
> he learned to loathe
> with the mischievous eccentricity of age.[19]

Not only does Lowell consider himself Auden's trainee who has taken it upon himself to spell out to his fellow citizens the disasters of history taking place, Lowell also recognizes that Auden's continuous changes and his angry denunciations, which he later rescinds, are similar to his own. Like Dickey, Lowell uses Auden to define himself as a poet and a person.

Hecht, Jarrell, and Shapiro were the poets who were most fixated on Auden during the war. Hecht, who would much later write an expansive monograph on Auden, *The Hidden Law* (1993), took Auden's poetry with him while stationed in Europe and Japan. In his letters home he also occasionally refers to Auden. When trying to express to his parents his "fit of utter depression which has been blunting the edge of things" while stuck in the infantry somewhere in Germany, for example, Hecht quotes from Michael Ransom's opening soliloquy in Auden's and Christopher Isherwood's play *The Ascent of F6* (1936) without disclosing who wrote the lines or suggesting the context:[20] "Happy the foetus that miscarries, and the frozen idiot that cannot cry 'Mama.' Happy those run over in the street today, or drowned at sea, or sure of death Tomorrow from incurable diseases; they cannot be made a party to the general fiasco."[21]

Jarrell would have had no trouble identifying these words as Auden's since he knew "Auden by heart, practically," as one of the characters in Jarrell's *Pictures from an Institution* (1954) jokes about the narrator of the novel, Jarrell's alter ego.[22] Jarrell was "from the first one of Auden's warmest and most enthusiastic admirers and outright imitators," as Hecht writes in *The Hidden Law.*[23] This is especially noticeable in the poems of Jarrell's debut volume, *Blood for a Stranger* (1942), the title of which yokes together two prominent themes in Auden's work before the 1940s. "The Refugees" (1940) seems modeled on Auden's poem "Refugee Blues" (1938), as R. Clifton Spargo has pointed out, while in one of Jarrell's earliest published war poems, "The Machine Gun" (1937), written while the Spanish Civil War was going on, Jarrell also unmistakably uses Auden's motifs and diction.[24] In the first of the two stanzas Jarrell renders images of warfare in the past—"the broken blood, the hunting flame"—when our forebears hunted for prey and fought each other for survival. The diction and imagery are remarkably similar to what Auden employs in "The Hunters."[25] In the final stanza these images are juxtaposed to the omnipresent semiautomatic firearm, which symbolizes the industrialization and modernity that Jarrell, following Auden, deplores.

Shapiro was an even more explicitly Audenesque poet than Jarrell at the start of the war, but he opted to follow another specific aspect of Auden's poetry. The title of Shapiro's first commercially published book, *Person, Place, and Thing* (1942), betrays which side of Auden's poetry appealed to him the most. Shapiro's volume contained sometimes lighthearted and sometimes poignant scenes of ordinary life in middle-class America, written in colloquial diction and neat stanzaic forms. Shapiro's title was "a genuine act of homage" to Auden, Hecht suspected, since Auden had recently called the first section of his volume *Another Time* (1940) "People and Places."[26] In

Another Time, Auden also sketches poetic portraits of types of people—for instance, "The Novelist" and "The Composer"—or actual historical people like Blaise Pascal and Voltaire. In *Person, Place, and Thing* but especially his subsequent wartime volume, *V-Letter and Other Poems* (1944), Shapiro did the same, versifying about "The Communist," the "Movie Actress," and "The Puritan," or about Benjamin Franklin or Thomas Jefferson.

These Americana that Shapiro chose to write about indicate one way in which Shapiro deviates from Auden, but it is nevertheless curious how close Shapiro stayed to Auden. Shapiro was aware that his poetry leaned heavily on Auden, as he admitted to his fiancée, Evalyn Katz, in 1943. "I can't escape Auden completely yet," Shapiro wrote, but he was convinced that Auden's influence would soon seem unnoticeable: "I know that I will finally absorb Auden into my system. As it is, he isnt completely dissolved yet."[27] After the publication of *Trial of a Poet* (1947), which contains the last poems Shapiro wrote during the war, Jarrell wrote to Lowell that Shapiro had not reached that point yet. "Shapiro's new book is pretty bad," Jarrell charged, and he wondered "if he's ever going to grow up any. And stop depending on Auden."[28] Like Tate, Shapiro was, in Jarrell's estimation, still a bit childish.

Jarrell implied of course that, unlike Shapiro, *he* had fully matured as a poet, and that *he* no longer relied on Auden as much as he had at the beginning of the war. Despite the immature sense of competition that Jarrell's words espouse, it was a fair estimate to make. Compared to Shapiro, Jarrell had assimilated Auden's influence much more subtly, and Jarrell's later war poems are subsequently more truly his own than are Shapiro's. Auden was the Oedipal father who had to be murdered to attain this maturity, however, and Jarrell's two wartime articles on Auden—"Changes of Attitude and Rhetoric in Auden's Poetry" and "Freud to Paul: The Stages of Auden's Ideology"—were the daggers to accomplish the feat. Whereas he distanced himself from Tate in private letters during the war, Jarrell chose two literary quarterlies to dissociate himself from Auden's style and ideas.

Both essays are premised on Jarrell's conviction that Auden had lost the originality and mastery of his early poems. "Changes of Attitude and Rhetoric" was first published in the *Southern Review* in the fall issue of 1941, and focuses mostly on Jarrell's supposition that Auden's inventive and imaginative "language of the early poems" lapses into "the rhetoric of the late."[29] In "Freud to Paul" Jarrell distinguishes three stages in Auden's ideology, but makes it clear to the reader that "the Old Auden, the *Ur*-Auden," aka "Freud," of Stage I is to be preferred to the "Moral Auden" of Stage II, or Auden's religious phase, simply named "Paul," of Stage III.[30] "Readers of Jarrell see in these writings an Oedipal struggle or the anxiety of influence," as Stephen Burt has pointed out, but "readers of Auden remember them as attacks."[31] Jarrell's essays were nevertheless influential even to Auden critics, as John R. Boly has suggested. Jarrell's tripartite division of Auden's career up to 1945 "furnished a framework that both Auden's defenders and detractors have been obliged to accept."[32]

Jarrell's most vicious attack on Auden occurs at the end of "Freud to Paul" when he reacts furiously to a seemingly innocuous point Auden was making in a review in the *New York Times Book Review,* published on November 12, 1944, about a new translation of *Grimm's Tales.* Jarrell becomes irate after quoting the final sentences of Auden's review in which Auden quasi-seriously berates liberals for dividing the world into reductive notions of good versus evil. Jarrell not only charges Auden with "logical absurdity" but also with "moral imbecility":[33] "Such a sentence shows that its writer has saved his own soul, but has lost the whole world—has forgotten even the nature of that world: for this was written, not in 1913, but within the months that held the mass executions in the German camps, the fire raids, Warsaw and Dresden and Manila; within the months that were preparing the bombs for Hiroshima and Nagasaki; within the last twelve months of the Second World War."[34] Sansom is correct in arguing that this is a "seemingly willful misreading and misinterpretation of a remark by Auden," as Auden is harmlessly seeking to understand the forces behind the disastrous events that Jarrell sums up.[35]

It is striking that Jarrell's snipes at Auden are especially malicious when discussing either Auden's war poems or World War II. When discussing Auden's infamous hortatory plea for action during the Spanish Civil War, "Spain 1937," in a lecture at Princeton in 1951, Jarrell scoffs at Auden's lines, as when he discusses the lines "All the fun under / Liberty's masterful shadow": "(Here words fail me—few men, few women, and few children have ever written anything as shamefully silly, as *amazingly* silly, as this)—under the masterful shadow of *this* line things like *the hour of the pageant-wastes* and the *poets exploding like bombs* look like nothing but ordinary tripe; and yet really the *poets exploding like bombs* is worthy of the Stalin Prize."[36]

An example such as this one suggests that Jarrell believed that being an enlisted man in this global conflict gave him more authority on the subject of war, and gave him the self-confidence to believe that his view on war was superior to Auden's. Reviling Auden as a naive Marxist or religious moralist who did not comprehend the full moral implications of war boosted Jarrell's confidence that he could surpass the Old Master in a way that a competitor-poet like Shapiro could not. Jarrell is not wrong to dismiss "Auden's wish *to lift an affirming flame,*" as quoted from "September 1, 1939," as "sentimental idealism," and a war poem like Auden's "Spain 1937" as too premeditated and schematic.[37] Auden had indeed become programmatic and rhetorical, which may be one of the reasons why Auden suppressed the later publication of this poem. Yet Jarrell's tone in his comments on Auden (and Shapiro) also reveals a boyishly competitive edge that masks his true indebtedness to Auden.

What gets almost lost in the aggressive chastising of the Auden of Stages II and III is that Jarrell ironically built his own war poetry on the foundations of Auden's Stage I. The list of six influences on Auden's early poetry that Jarrell renders in "Changes of Attitude and Rhetoric" contains at least four that were also dominant in his own poetry during the war: "(1) Marx-Communism in general. (2) Freud and Groddeck: in general, the risky and nonscientific, but fertile and imaginative, side of modern psychology," and "(3) A cluster of related sources: the folk, the blood, intuition, religion, mysticism, fairy tales, parables, and so forth" as well as "(5) All sorts of boyish sources of value: flying, polar exploration, mountain climbing, fighting, the thrilling side of science, public-school life, sports, big-scale practical jokes, 'the spies' career,' etc."[38] Whereas the other war poets were attracted to one or two features of Auden's writings, Jarrell modeled his own poetry on a whole range of Auden themes that Auden had mostly abandoned by the 1940s.

These influences all coalesce in "Siegfried," one of Jarrell's personal favorites and one of his most Audenesque war poems. The gunner Siegfried is at first boyishly attracted to the excitement of flying in a war plane but oblivious to the lurking dangers and the suffering that goes on outside his Plexiglas turret. He experiences his missions as "a dream" in which he looks at himself: "the watcher, guiltily / Watches the him, the actor, who is innocent."[39] Like Auden's early poems, "Siegfried" revolves around Freudian ideas, especially around dreams and wish fulfillment. Siegfried gradually loses his sense of youthful invulnerability as his guilty self gets the upper hand. He wants to stay alive, but above all to be relieved of the power of life and death that he possesses: "Let it be the way it was. / Let me not matter, let nothing I do matter / To anybody, anybody. Let me be what I was."[40]

Siegfried wants to return, in other words, to the state of innocence he possessed before the war. Jarrell indicates that Siegfried's wish is only partially granted. He gets shot in the leg and is sent "home, for good now, almost as you wished," as Jarrell says with a sarcastic edge. There is a hint of Marx when Jarrell imparts how the wounded veteran is "reading of victories and sales and nations" in "sunlit papers." Only wars and commerce are newsworthy in capitalist countries, not the effects of these on individual souls like Siegfried. He survives, but he no longer matters as he had wished. Instead of being returned to his earlier state of blissful innocence, he is now terribly wise. At the end of the poem Jarrell writes that Siegfried has comprehended his "world at last: you have tasted your own blood."[41]

Jarrell writes in "Freud to Paul" that in "Auden's work the elements of *anxiety, guilt, isolation, sexuality,* and *authorities* make up a true Gestalt, a connected and meaningful whole."[42] "Siegfried" is a miniature Audenesque Gestalt that revolves around three or four of these themes: "*anxiety, guilt, isolation,*" and, to a lesser extent, "*authority.*" The turret is like a cocoon representing the solipsistic isolation in which Jarrell's airman is caught and never escapes. Even when Siegfried returns home he is painfully alone, and stared at by the other people in his town. Siegfried's guilt and anxiety are manifested in his troubled dreams, while the "whitewashed courthouse" that Siegfried passes at the end of the poem represents the antagonistic relationship that exists between the individual and the state, but also the absence of justice.[43]

The most perceptible Audenesque feature of "Siegfried" is that Jarrell lingers on that quintessential Auden word "lucky" when discussing Siegfried's dismal fate: "If you matter, it is as little, almost, as you wished. / If it has changed, still, you have had your wish / And are lucky, as you figured luck—are, truly, lucky."[44] Siegfried is "lucky" in the sense that he is only wounded, but of course his fate is not to be envied, which makes Jarrell's lines bitterly ironic. Neither Jarrell nor early Auden believed that there is a force or quality that seems to cause good things to happen to some people but not to others. By "the early 1940s," however, Auden began to use "luck" as "a synonym for grace," as Edward Mendelson has claimed, which symbolizes his change from a more secular to a more spiritual poet.[45] Jarrell continued to use "luck" as a synonym for "chance," however, since the war made him even more convinced that the universe was arbitrarily ordered, and that there is "no special reason or explanation of things happening," as he commented approvingly about Wordsworth. "*It happens as it does, it does, it does,* // But not because of you," Jarrell says to Siegfried again almost sneeringly.[46] People have no control over their own destiny in Jarrell's war poems, and there is certainly not a higher power that can be appealed to as Auden argued in his later poems—for instance, in *For the Time Being* (1942). The title of one of Jarrell's later war poems, "1945: The Death of the Gods," sums up how Jarrell thought of religion at war's end. The end of "Freud to Paul" is revealing about what he thought of Auden's conversion. After his violent attack on Auden's review of *Grimm's Tales,* Jarrell ends his essay by saying: "When the people of the world of the future—if there are people in that world—say to us—if some of us are there, 'What did you do in all those wars?' those of us left can give the old, the only answer, 'I lived through them.' But some of us will answer, 'I was saved.'"[47]

Jarrell is rightly considered to be the best and most original poetry critic of his generation, but his intense, masculine sense of competition also made him at times impolitic and misguided. Hecht realized this, and in his book on Auden, *The Hidden Law,* comes to Auden's rescue. As "an ardent liberal secularist," Jarrell felt "alienated" by Auden's conversion, Hecht senses.[48]

While praising Jarrell's "scrupulosity" when characterizing Auden's early language, Hecht asserts that Jarrell's "diatribe" is "seriously misleading":[49] "Auden's 'ideas' were neither so clear-cut nor so homogenous and neatly separable as Jarrell wants us to believe. No one was more suspicious of a doctrinaire, inflexible, unthinking position than Auden himself, and he needed no Jarrell to lecture him on this topic. Jarrell's account leaves out too much, and of what it does include, makes a tidy schematization of those themes in Auden's work which were constantly changing."[50] Hecht opens *The Hidden Law* by carefully correcting Jarrell's more blustering pronouncements, setting the tone for his own studious account of Auden's poetry, which is more evenhanded but also more labored than Jarrell's flamboyant, witty style.

Like Jarrell, Hecht criticizes Auden's war poems, including "September 1, 1939" and "Spain 1937," but he does not feel the need to ridicule Auden as Jarrell does. Hecht calls "September 1, 1939" "clearly, and perhaps seriously, flawed," and devotes several pages to why "Spain 1937" is at different times "repellent," "doctrinaire," "completely unpersuasive," and "very disturbing and possibly misleading."[51] Yet Hecht understands that Auden himself was unhappy about these poems, causing him to revise them or not to republish them. Moreover Hecht tries to find the good in poems, even if they are not successful overall. When appraising "September 1, 1939," for instance, Hecht points out how influential this poem was: "Nevertheless like many poetry readers of my generation, I continue to be enormously grateful for this poem. No one else took it upon him- or herself to address directly and unequivocally the massive crisis that was inevitably to become the Second World War. There were, in the course of time, some other war poets, some of them very good; but either they wrote about personal experience with warfare, or they wrote with a deliberate metaphoric distancing, as Eliot did in the quartets."[52]

What makes "September 1, 1939" work for Hecht is that Auden made "the crisis psychological, personal, and universal, and did so in passages that are nothing less than memorable."[53] For the American poets of World War II who were anxious to avoid imitating their literary predecessors, Auden thus offered a middle course between poems that were mostly based on personal experience like those by the English poets of the First World War and modernist poems, which to them seemed too impersonal and detached. Auden was the future of poetry as far as they were concerned.

Hecht's monograph reflects two clear influences that Auden had on the poets of World War II. First, Auden's ability in "September 1, 1939" and other poems to merge the public and the private domain had a considerable impact on Hecht's own poetry. Hecht keeps emphasizing this characteristic in *The Hidden Law,* and some of Hecht's best war poems, "It

Out-Herods Herod" and "The Odds" among them, also use this Audenesque trait. In "The Odds" Hecht juxtaposes the birth of his son in snowy New England on an April day in 1971 with "the wild strew of bodies at My Lai" during the "eleventh year of war" in Vietnam.[54] Hecht is "vaguely stunned" by the personal happiness of his family and the public nightmare of that war, and melancholically contemplates the ostensible randomness of birth and death. The "incalculable odds" that are in Hecht's and his son's favor rather than the Vietnamese people at My Lai are closer to Jarrell's "chance" than to Auden's "grace," one feels.[55]

A second Auden theme that Hecht and members of his generation kept returning to is that of the hero, or "the truly strong man" as opposed to "the truly weak man." "It is striking," Hecht writes in *The Hidden Law,* "that Auden should, from the first, have sought for some such heroic figure."[56] Hecht argues that Auden's sense of the hero progressed from his boyish enthusiasm for the spy, the explorer, and the secret agent to an admiration for the kind, patient, and unselfish conduct of the saint.[57] Auden's most inspirational poem in terms of this fascination for the male hero is, according to Hecht, "The Shield of Achilles" (1952). Hecht writes elaborately and insightfully about this poem in *The Hidden Law* and reads in it the acknowledgment that all poets of World War II eventually conceded, that "traditional heroism" in war is "a thing of the past."[58] The American poets of World War II were similarly attracted to the archetypical hero type when young, but even before they began to take part in World War II they could no longer fully believe that a superman could save the day. It is an insight that crucially separates the World War II poets from previous generations of war poets who generally took much longer to reject the heroic warrior type as a myth.

"The Shield of Achilles" is Auden's reworking of a scene from Book 18 of Homer's *The Iliad* where Hephaestos forges a shield for Achilles at the request of Thetis, Achilles' mother. Auden alternates two types of stanzas in "The Shield of Achilles." In the short-lined stanzas Thetis comments on the moral order she expects to find on the shield and which also appeared on Achilles' shield in *The Iliad.* In the long-lined stanzas, however, Auden renders scenes depicting the inane chaos that is war. Some of these longer stanzas conjure up images of the twentieth century rather than of ancient Greece; Hecht indicates that one of these "describes something like the Nuremberg rallies of Storm Troopers, and annual National Socialist Party conventions that began in 1933 and went on for many years."[59] Thetis considers war a kind of sporting event as she is keen to observe "athletes at their games," but Auden wants to have none of those classical masculine associations of war as sport. War is not a game, but an event where "girls are raped" and where "two boys knife a third."[60]

"The Shield of Achilles" makes Hecht muse about masculinity and warfare in the twentieth century as compared to antiquity: "Clearly the notion of personal heroism expressed in terms of military valor is a medieval and even Renaissance inheritance from classical models. . . . The glamor that attached to these exemplars of manly virtue was widely acknowledged for centuries; but it began to lose its luster with the invention of gunpowder and the development of firearms. And that, of course, was only the beginning."[61] Heroes once confronted each other face to face. Modern warfare is conducted so as to make such confrontations virtually impossible. Bombardiers do not see the faces of their victims, who, in general, are as likely to be women, children, and bedridden civilians as enemy troops. Hecht's insightful analysis of the relationship between masculinity and warfare—which has become increasingly technologically driven—is highly important for understanding the male poetic response to World War II. The military historian Michael Howard confirms Hecht's reasoning that by the time of World War II, wars were decided "by comparatively small numbers of military technicians wielding destructive power on an almost inconceivable scale."[62] This new development in warfare did not leave much room for brave warriors like Achilles to distinguish themselves. The poets of the middle generation would all have subscribed to Hecht's analysis, with the exception perhaps of Dickey, who continued to look for powerful masculine heroes in his war poetry and war novels throughout his life, as will be explored later in this book.

In "The Shield of Achilles," Hecht argues, "the three men who are executed and the abandoned urchin are not martyrs; they are, alas, merely victims."[63] Auden was enamored by strong male role models in his younger years—for instance, to "the heroes of medieval romance and the Wagnerian operas," as Hecht mentions.[64] And so were the poets of the middle generation, as Alan Dugan's poem "On Shields. Against World War III" shows, whose title may incidentally refer to Auden's poem.[65] Yet by 1945 the name of a Wagnerian hero like Siegfried could only be used ironically, as Jarrell and the others well understood.

It is therefore uncannily appropriate that the only war poet who literally talked to Auden at the end of World War II, Lincoln Kirstein, should do so at a Bavarian "Schloss miniature" called "Siegfriedslage."[66] It was a "mean memorial / To hero Siegfried of operatic fame," Kirstein writes in a poem of the same title that depicts their chance encounter in occupied Germany.[67] Kirstein was attached to Third Army headquarters occupied with the recovery of works of art, while Auden was an observer with the U.S. Air Force Strategic Bombing Survey, which sought to conduct an impartial study of the effects of American aerial attacks on Germany. One day Kirstein gets a surprise visit, as a fellow soldier informs him:

"Man. Get a load of this. Waiting below,
A wild man's parked, and he allows as he
Wants *you*. He must be nuts, but pronto:
Git. See for yourself. Gawd, it's just a farce—
Some stimulated Major, V.I.P.
Who does not know his silly English arse
From one damned hole in our accursed sod;
Hies here to Headquarters a lousy mess—
In *carpet*-slippers, yet! Before Gawd,
He lacks his HELMET LINER, and is clad
In uniform which Patton must suppress."[68]

Kirstein's poetic style is immediately recognizable and unlike that of any other World War II poet. He writes a highly colloquial, slangy diction yet in formally rhyming lines, and he frequently contracts words, deletes syllables or entire words, which give his poems a tremendous pace and an informal, edgy tone.

Dressed in an American uniform but with a distinct English accent and wearing "*carpet*-slippers," Auden (or actually Dunstan Morden as Kirstein calls him in this poem) is a comic sight in war-torn Germany. Auden's jeep is stashed with all sorts of goodies that he gathered along the way, "salvage or pillage," including "Wagner's profile plaque."[69] Auden has also added to his entourage a "teenage" cook and a "Wehrmacht driver," both of whom are "yesterday's P.W.s [prisoners of war]," as Kirstein writes.[70] "If at some remote future a mad film-producer risks undertaking 'The Wystan Auden Story,'" Kirstein wrote in an unpublished memoir, "his presence as an American army officer would supply a lush comic relief."[71]

Auden is not merely comical, however, but he is also the antithesis of Siegfried, the supermasculine hero that the National Socialist Party had appropriated. Richard Wagner's *Der Ring des Nibelungen* was written at the height of German nationalism in the nineteenth century and came to symbolize German nationalism, especially after World War I, with the rise of Adolf Hitler. Hitler was a fan of Wagner and adopted Wagner's music to further his ideals of Aryan superiority. Kirstein hints that Auden has selected the German "P.W.s" because they are cute or good looking. Lord of the manor at the "Siegfriedlage" and picking up German ex-soldiers, Auden seems to mock the ideal of hegemonic, German (and indeed Western), heterosexual, militarized masculinity, much to Kirstein's delight.

Despite his comical appearance, Auden does not joke about the war, however, but gives a devastating account of what World War II means to the world and what it might entail for the postwar era. It brings Kirstein down:

> I get depressed. One often gets depressed
> When pliant minds for whom the human aim
> Spell complex logic logically expressed,
> Are rendered sanguine by the basest acts,
> Discounting tragic or ironic claim,
> End up near truth with just the lyric facts,
> Yet past complaint or wisecrack cynical
> Reducing analysis to partial
> Documents of the jejune clinical,
> A poet made uncommon common-sense.[72]

Yet Kirstein realizes that he is in the presence of a great artist who can see beyond what other people can see. There is solace, despite the bleak future of the world that Auden sketches for Kirstein: "How one believes, nay, *must* believe in ART."[73] When Kirstein gets distraught by world politics, he changes the subject, and the two start gossiping about the war poets. Kirstein wants to know what Auden thinks of one "Soanso," whose "combat verse was just / Out, Pulitzer-prized, compassionate, fine / Deeply experienced, sincere; so true / It made me weep. I wished it had been mine."[74] "Soanso" is most likely Karl Shapiro, the only war poet to win a Pulitzer Prize for poetry, whose poems were also considered "deeply experienced" and "sincere," and whose name also begins with an "S" and ends with an "o."

Auden's unexpectedly terse reply is: "Thin stuff," before adding that poetry is "not in the pity. / It is in the words. What words are wide enough?"[75] Wilfred Owen had famously stated in the preface of a book of poems: "My subject is War, and the pity of War. / The poetry is in the pity."[76] Auden corrects Owen in Kirstein's account, and suggests that poetry is not the same as pity. Poetry is the verbal expression of life's experience, but Auden questions whether "words are wide enough" to encompass an event like World War II. This may help explain why Auden never directly addressed World War II as a subject or his experiences in Germany. Unlike the poets of World War II who were only perceived as being silent, Auden really was silent about the Second World War. Auden could no longer write the Audenesque poems that Shapiro was writing during the war, and he had to reinvent another style that would fit the new world and his new self. By 1960 Shapiro asserted that Auden "has been absorbed completely" "by the present generation, the poets who have begun to write since about 1940."[77]

Yet it seems fair to say that traces of Auden's former poetic selves lived on in all of them. And the same can be said of the English poets of the First World War, the modernists, and the New Critics. These traditions haunted the World War II poets. While the poets of World War II were generally too respectful to rebel openly again their poetic ancestors, they did occasionally correct them, ever so subtly most of the time, as Hecht's disagreement with Eliot's treatment of Jews for instance shows. These corrections were not just assertions of poetic maturity. They also aimed to register more accurately than their predecessors had done the "the precariousness of ~~people~~ the human being," as Jarrell wrote down tentatively in his wartime notebook.[78] Out of the absorbed traditions and their diverse, personal experiences during World War II emerged new, bewildered selves who were yet painfully aware of their own vulnerability and that of others. With their boyish years gone, the turmoil of war caused them all to reconfigure who they were.

PART [2]

EMERGING SELVES

CHAPTER 5

Caught in Amber

THE INTELLECTUAL GI AND ARMY CULTURE

Among the many characteristics of the middle generation that Edward Hirsch lists in his article "One Life, One Writing!" are the "quest for identity" and a "radical impulse to self-exposure" that these poets shared.[1] These are admittedly broad categories that might apply to general themes of all literature, but they do hint at a shared poetics despite the sometimes large personal and stylistic differences that exist between these poets. This preoccupation with the self resulted in many autobiographically tinged poems and differentiated the middle generation poets from many of their literary predecessors. It stems in part from their army years when their sense of identity was partially and temporarily taken away from them.

Stripped of their civilian clothes, the poets—like all other soldiers—were dressed in olive drab or navy blue, and were told what to do, when to eat, when to get up, when to go to bed, what continent they would be shipped to, and when they could finally go home, if they ever made it that far. "The American individualistic ethic did not lend itself to easy subordination," as Gerald F. Linderman has stated, but the military authorities deemed the "erasure of individuality" necessary to instill a sense of discipline and collectivity in the soldiers so that they could win the war: "A regime in turn intimidating, exhausting, and overpowering would shear from soldiers their idiosyncrasy and contrariness."[2]

A substantial body of American World War II poetry subtly but persistently protests the military pressure that forces the individual into submission.[3] John Ciardi's poem "On Sending Home My Civilian Clothes" is one of the most eloquent meditations on what it meant to lose one's personal identity and see it transformed into a more reductive and debased version of a self. While saying good-bye to his flashy "duds" that were "mine and mine alone," Ciardi contemplates with powerless regret that he has become a "stalker whose name is Claw."[4] Not only does Ciardi feel inept, clumsy, and ill at ease in the modern world of war, like Eliot's Prufrock who described himself as "a pair of ragged claws," his metonymic name is also an accurate reflection of his role, his identity in the army.[5] As a gunner in a B-29, Ciardi's whole identity is reduced to a "hand, a gun" that kills. Like the badges and number that he is forced to wear, the name "Claw" is only a partial reflection of his true identity. His real self is concealed or gone missing, and he mourns for it as he sends his clothes to a "foreign" and "lost address."[6] In the first entry of his war diary *Saipan,* Ciardi observed:

> It dawns on me that the Army is the last place in the world to observe human nature. The reason is, I think, that no one acts like himself: In the barracks you live mostly by whatever forty odd men may have in common—mostly dice, cards, profanity, sleep, and smuggled whiskey. Out on the town there's too much loneliness, dissociation, and whatever the word is for the compulsion of time—the feeling that all your life must be squeezed into tonight on this street under these neons over this glass in the blare of this juke box and this girl's flesh.
>
> So far the Army has been one of two things—long boring intervals of nothing to do, or long endless spells of too much to do. Neither leaves much chance for one to be himself.
>
> I find myself behaving strangely for me. I think I miss the lack of privacy. There never seems to be time to stop and think.[7]

The strictly hierarchical attitude of the army, the many senseless activities, the boredom of army life, and the sometimes unnecessary danger that they were being exposed to irritated many American soldiers during World War II, not in the least the poets of the middle generation. Before they were whisked away by the American government in the early 1940s, they had all been either still in college (James Dickey, Anthony Hecht, and Louis Simpson) or following some sort of education (Karl Shapiro), or recent college graduates (Howard Nemerov, William Meredith, and Richard Wilbur), or they had finished college some time back and were making their first forays into the job market, usually academia (Ciardi and Randall Jarrell). "The pains of arrested or interrupted domesticity" and development therefore loomed large in the wartime writings of the middle generation, as Lorrie Goldensohn has suggested.[8] "Oh, identity is a traveling-piece with some," Meredith writes nostalgically and sentimentally about his childhood home in the final couplet of his Shakespearian sonnet "Ten-Day Leave," "but here is what calls me, here what I call home." Shapiro's "Sunday: New Guinea" shares Meredith's soft-hearted craving for home, but is also representative of the tedium and intellectual deprivation that the soldier-poets resented and the idealization of home they shared:

I long for our disheveled Sundays home,
Breakfast, the comics, news of latest crimes,
Talk without reference, and palindromes,
Sleep and the Philharmonic and the ponderous *Times*

I long for lounging in the afternoons
Of clean intelligent warmth, my brother's mind,
Books and thin plates and flowers and shining spoons,
And your love's presence, snowy, beautiful, and kind.[9]

Paul Fussell writes that for the English writers of the Great War, "the opposite of experiencing moments of war is proposing moments of pastoral."[10] Domesticity is the opposite of war for the American poets of World War II. Wistful images of homely life—especially food—abound in the fantasies of the soldier speakers. One of the men in Gwendolyn Brooks's "Gay Chaps at the Bar," who complains that "no man can give me any word but Wait," admits that he is "very hungry" and holds his "honey" and stores his "bread / In little jars and cabinets" of his "will."[11] In "The Firebombing" James Dickey's protagonist frequently refers to his "half-paid for" and "well-stocked" pantry in the suburbs twenty years after the war.[12] These suburban scenes, where the speaker is overweight but "still hungry" and emotionally starved, form a telling contrast to the war memories told in flashback.[13] During and after the war, hunger becomes an appealing metaphor to describe the physical, emotional, intellectual, and sexual deprivation the soldiers felt.

Such feelings of want were felt by almost every generation of conscripted soldiers in modern times, but they were more keenly felt and expressed by the intellectual poets of the Second World War. There is a reason why the American poets of World War II felt these feelings more palpably than earlier generations. The academically schooled soldier-poets realized they were turned "into quasi-interchangeable parts" who "seemed even more anonymous and bereft of significant individual personality than their counterparts in the Great War," as Fussell has put it.[14] The poets of World War II came to feel that among the conscripted masses they did not matter as individuals, which made them cling to their sense of self even more desperately.

Despite the straightforward and sentimental feelings of homesickness that Meredith's "Ten-Day Leave" and Shapiro's "Sunday: New Guinea" voice, these poems are more problematic than they appear at first glance. Shapiro's outburst of love in the final line of his poem seems an afterthought, placed awkwardly right after the cartoons and cutlery that he also misses. The unspecific adjectives describing his fiancée make the reader suspect that he only dimly recalls what she was like. At the end of his sonnet Meredith asserts that his identity is firmly rooted in his childhood home as quoted above, but the first three stanzas of "Ten-Day Leave" contradict this idyllic image. Even though his mother and father await him eagerly in the doorway like the parents in Norman Rockwell's *Homecoming G.I.*, and even though he is happy to sleep in his boyhood bed, the soldier-speaker is also plagued by a "special dream" and feels "nothing but remorse for miles around." The soldier longs for the uncomplicated identity he had when growing up, but he has become more like the "changing dogs" who "dispute a stranger town."[15]

Most of the poets of World War II realized that they were viewed by their fellow soldiers as intellectuals, but they were not treated negatively because of their education, or so they claimed. Jarrell was pleasantly surprised that "no one quarrels with you or is impolite to you if you are at all different."[16] Nemerov reported to his friend Howard Turner that he was teased a bit at Parks Air College in East Saint Louis, Illinois: "I take a bit of hazing (chicken-shit as they call it here) about being from Harvard, but that's rather fun, and I find I have some talent for imitating FDR well enough to get by."[17] Both Jarrell and Shapiro reported that they were in hot demand to answer questions about why the United States was at war and what motivated the other nations to fight. Shapiro, for instance, filled American soldiers bound for the Pacific in "on Japanese fascism, Manchuria, the drive to the south, oil, capitalism—Too Bitter Against Big Business—and the Axis."[18] Jarrell, who was both amused and irritated by the lack of intelligence of the air cadets around him, sometimes lectured them "at some length and with great truth" about what he believed the war was about. He reported gleefully to his wife that everyone "seemed much impressed, and accepted [his] version without a murmur."[19]

The poets' identities as writers and intellectuals helped guard them remarkably against the erosion of their personal selves that the army promoted. Writing was a way to assert themselves as individuals. It was one of the few aspects of their identity that the army could not control. It also helped them come to terms (and was a reflection of their coming to terms) with their shifting identity. The act of writing itself—whether in the form of letters, diaries, or poems—helped sustain the World War II poets through the dullness and hazards of the war. Shapiro, for instance, was able "to publish four books while in uniform, while in jungles and in deserts, on ships, in cities."[20] Being prolific was important to Shapiro during the war, as was apparent in his short-tempered letter to Allen Tate in which he rejected Tate's advice not to "shoot off all [his] heavy guns now."[21] As Shapiro explained in the introduction to his Pulitzer Prize–winning volume *V-Letter,* his identity had been "reduced in size but not in meaning, like a V-Letter," and being a successful poet helped restore his sense of identity.[22]

Other poets also used the war to propel their careers as writers. Lowell revised the manuscript of his first book, *Land of Unlikeness,* in prison and started work on a long satirical poem called "Dead Briton's Vision."[23] Ciardi also tried to write and publish poems and kept a war diary as distinct efforts to express his personal self. Dickey and Hecht, who were some years younger than Ciardi, Lowell, and Shapiro, conceived of their years in service as a literary apprenticeship. Dickey ordered dozens of poetry books through his mother and studied them religiously, laying "the groundwork for his writing career," as Henry Hart has noted.[24] Hecht sought to escape the self-described "stifling, retrogressive mental atmosphere" of the army by reading everything intellectual he could put his hands on, but also by writing press releases and radio plays when he was stationed in occupied Japan.[25]

After a hesitant start Jarrell also began to write poems at a furious pace. "I, of course, haven't written any poetry," Jarrell glumly noted in a letter to his wife, Mackie, on April 25, 1943, after having been in the army for seven weeks.[26] Yet two months later he could boast that he had already finished his "thirteenth poem," which he sent to university quarterlies and major general-interest magazines.[27] Writing and publishing poetry was not only a vicarious escape from the army, as for Shapiro, but also provided Jarrell with a sense of personal identity in the homogenous, uniformed army where every GI was expendable and individual identity was shrunken.

Jarrell's sudden prolific outburst in 1943 was due to a new poetic topic or approach that he had discovered for himself and which he called his "'army' style."[28] Reporting on his breakthrough, he told his wife how his quality of life in the army had improved considerably because he had found a meaningful goal to fill his days: "I write poetry every night. Even the night we had to G.I. I rushed home, did mine immediately, and had two hours left. It makes my life much pleasanter: I think about the poetry a lot, and I have the beautiful feeling of getting something out of all this. Also I've written enough by now to have regained my beautiful old feeling that I can always write good poems—just give me the time and a subject, any subject; I'd lost it in my last year before I got in the army."[29] In 1941 Jarrell had told Parker Tyler how "a style gathers" and that you "learn to use it until it reaches its peak and does a few poems perfectly: then it dies away and gets repetitious, finally it won't work any more."[30] He had reached "the complete dead end of a style," he noted to Tyler, which was probably his "'political economy' style" influenced by Jarrell's early Marxist inclinations.[31] "The Lines," "A Lullaby," "Mail Call," and "O My Name It Is Sam Hall" are the most distinct examples of Jarrell's new style, and they are emblematic of a type of poem that nearly all the World War II poets wrote.

The "army style poem" can be defined as expressing enlisted men's frustration at being stuck in the military, curtailing their sense of privacy and their sense of freedom. It either takes the form of melancholy statements about their arrested development or their homesickness, as Ciardi's "On

Sending My Civilian Clothes Home," Meredith's "Ten-Day Leave," and Shapiro's "Sunday: New Guinea" also testify, or a variety in which the stupidity or cruelty of certain rules and people in the army are denounced in angry or indignant exposés. Such poems are "bawdy, bitchy, irreverent," as Harvey Shapiro has stated, and "do not glory in brotherhood and, as a rule, they do not find nobility in one another," as was more frequently (but certainly not always) the case in the poetry of the English Great War poets.[32] Jarrell's "army style poems" probe more deeply than those of his peers into the psychological aspects of soldiers' day-to-day existence. The soldiers find themselves caught in the homogenizing machine of the U.S. Army, or "the digestive processes of an immense worm or slug," as Jarrell called it in a letter.[33] Yet some of the other poets gave more biting and extreme examples of the resentment of army culture, nearly always drawn from their personal experiences.

"The Lines" was "the armiest army poem" that Jarrell wrote, as he told Philip Rahv in November 1945, and probably the "armiest" poem of his generation.[34] Jarrell transforms the mundane army activity of standing in lines into a metaphor of the soldiers' fate. Punning on three words—"lines," "salvage," and "things"—which are repeated over and over again to accentuate the inane process of waiting for everything, Jarrell suggests that human beings are used as mere objects by the military, GIs in the original meaning of that term, "government issue." They are "things" that "die as though they were not things."[35]

The seemingly slight lyric "A Lullaby" (1944) further exemplifies Jarrell's take on a soldier's life. Jarrell uses five similes in a mere twelve lines to show how suffocating and inhumane the soldiers' existence is. Three of the similes refer to animals, underscoring a point that Dickey made that Jarrell's tropes tend to be "homey" ones. Jarrell always compares "defeated soldiers" to "something ordinary," using much simpler and more readily accessible figures of speech than literary predecessor W. H. Auden, as "A Lullaby" shows.[36] Jarrell writes how the soldier's "dog tags ring like sheep."[37] Fussell has noted that in the lingo of World War II there were many references comparing a soldier's life to that of a dog: "An infantryman is a *dogface,* and he sleeps in a *pup-tent* (in the American Civil War, a *dog-tent*)."[38] The identity tags that the soldiers wore in World War II listing their name, number, and rank were called "dog tags" by the soldiers themselves, in ironic and self-deprecatory recognition that they were treated like animals by the authorities and that their lives were not worth more than that of a dog. The soldier is also made as docile and obedient as sheep or children, infantilized and deprived of free will. Jarrell's poem presents an indirect critique of the rite-of-passage motif. Boys are supposed to become men in the military, but they are in fact reduced to a childish state by the military authorities.

The central trope of "A Lullaby" is not a simile, however, but a thinly disguised metaphor suggesting that a soldier is similar to a fly caught in amber, as Jarrell told an audience at Pfeiffer College when introducing the poem. Amber is fossilized tree sap in which insects can get caught and are sometimes preserved for millennia. The individual soldier in World War II is equally tiny, helpless, and stuck in the great machinery of the army as the fly is in the yellowish translucent fossil resin. Sleeping "with seven men within six feet," the atmosphere inside the army barracks is about as uncomfortable and stifling for the soldier as it is for the fly, Jarrell suggests. "His life is smothered like a grave, with dirt," Jarrell posits in the final stanza, emphasizing how the soldier feels as if he is—like the fly—imprisoned or buried alive.[39]

"Mail Call" shows that through letters soldiers could still "see the world" outside the army base and glimpse at what they considered the "real world."[40] It is another short and deceptively simple lyric by Jarrell, and it derived from a daily army ritual that amused and interested him, as he wrote to his wife: "Mail call is a very pretty ceremony: everyone's wedged in at one end of the barracks, lying on beds, the tops of double decker beds, standing, sitting on the floor; there's always a big stack of letters for C.Q. (raised above the rest) to distribute. He reads the names out in a tough rapid rather charming voice: each answers *Here* or *Ho* or *Yoho* (one boy really said that) and gets the letter flung at him like a leaf out of Shelley; the letter dives under a bed or hits somebody on the head and is rapidly passed on to the owner."[41] Typical for his epistolary style during the war, Jarrell's commentary on the distribution of mail at his army base is witty and lively, but the tone of "Mail Call" is decidedly less humorous. Jarrell transforms the "very pretty ceremony" into a painful expression of the deeper psychological anxieties regarding the personal self that the soldiers were experiencing.

Mail call was the call, the lure from the real world with which they hoped to be reunited, the world they had known before the army. "Mail is really our only reminder of normal life," Louis Simpson admitted in a letter home, "and means everything."[42] "An empty hand" and "one unuttered sound" at the end of this formation, as Jarrell writes, would make the soldier feel that he is no longer remembered by the real world. Temporally and spatially removed from that world, the soldiers can only hope that what they knew in the past will also be there in the future. "The soldier," Jarrell says in the final line, "simply wishes for his name."[43] Not his rank or his serial number, the soldier needs to hear his name, so that his personal self is validated by others.

The discrepancy between the tone of Jarrell's humorous letters and his more brooding poems—even if they treat the same topic—is striking but not untypical when comparing Jarrell to his contemporaries. In fact, there are few poems about World War II that show the "gigantic slapstick of modern war," as Shapiro called it.[44] Among the "army style poems" that Jarrell published there is only one humorous one, "O My Name It Is Sam Hall." It was "the first pleasant poem I ever wrote," as Jarrell admitted to Margaret Marshall, an editor at the *Nation*.[45] "O My Name It Is Sam Hall" takes its title from a southern prison ballad of the same name, which was popularized by Carl Sandburg. Jarrell even adopted its typical four-line stanza form, rhyming *abcb*. In the original ballad a convicted murderer who is incarcerated damns everyone's eyes and promises to meet everyone in hell. Jarrell's poem features three prisoners and one prison guard in a secluded area of a military base. The prisoners are even more bored than anyone else at the base, and they listen passively to the brass band practicing and then listen to and watch how airplanes fly over. "They graze a while for scraps" and watch the "straggling grass," Jarrell says, again using an (implied) animal trope.[46]

In the final stanza of Jarrell's poem the prison guard starts singing the ballad "O My Name It Is Sam Hall," which makes the prisoners smile. It is ironic that it is the prison guard who is singing the ballad instead of the prisoners because they are actually being held captive. Yet their smiles are a tacit sign of recognition that everyone at the army base is there against their will, imprisoned like a fly in amber. Everyone in the army is doing time, even the military policeman. As Jarrell's letters show, he and many other soldiers experienced army life as being in prison, or in a hospital: "I'm in an institution, too, and I know what they're like," he wrote to his doctor friend Amy Breyer de Blasio.[47] The "Sam Hall" song is a momentary diversion from the boredom for these men and an example of subtle army humor, which helps make their war experience bearable. Jarrell's "pleasant" war poem does not present a laugh-out-loud kind of humor, but a more sardonic type, driving home the point that all soldiers are prisoners.

The subtle humor of "O My Name It Is Sam Hall" notwithstanding, Jarrell was adamant, as were most of his peers, that satire should not figure in war poetry.[48] "The evil of the universe is a poor thing to be ironic about," he noted to Mackie Jarrell about Allen Tate's "Ode to Our Young Pro-Consuls of the Air."[49] Jarrell also dissuaded Lowell from writing satirical poems, arguing that they were the "weakest sort of poem" that his friend wrote.[50] Jarrell's notion was that "the bulk of the Army [is] passively suffering, doing what it's told, not knowing why anything's happened, helplessly ignorant and determined," as he told his wife. The soldiers "needed to be treated in ways more complicated than as a satiric target for the superior poet to look down on with pity and contempt," as William Pritchard has argued.[51]

Some of the best and best-known World War II novels and a sizable number of wartime movies, however, are comedies, which makes the relative absence of satire in the poetry of the middle generation more conspicuous. Joseph Heller's *Catch-22* (1961) comes closest to characterizing "modern war" as a "gigantic slapstick"—with paranoid conscripts; glory-seeking, envious, and money-making officers; and over-the-top ineptitude all around—but Kurt Vonnegut's more heart-wrenching *Slaughterhouse-Five* (1969) and Thomas Pynchon's more complex *Gravity's Rainbow* (1973) present World War II as equally surreal and absurd. These novels were all published decades after the war when the United States was beginning to get or was fully embroiled in Vietnam, and this timing certainly influenced sarcastic content and their success. Robert Altman's movie *M*A*S*H* (1970) and the spin-off hit television series of the same name about a surgical team during the Korean War (the kind that Shapiro was part of in the Pacific) shows that the genre of literary black comedy was easily transferable to visual media as well.

In fact, *M*A*S*H* seems a more daring, irreverent, and original version of the wartime comedies and musicals, like *Caught in the Draft* (1941), *Private Buckeroo* (1942), and *They Got Me Covered* (1942). Closely monitored by the Office of War Information, these army flicks never lapsed "into a full-scale offensive against the armed forces," but they did present the military as "the favored stage for burlesques of all sorts."[52] Preston Sturges's films *The Miracle of Morgan's Creek* (1944) and *Hail the Conquering Hero* (1944) went a step further than these early war comedies and dared to poke fun at "hero worship and homefront venality" as well as holier topics, including "patriotism."[53]

This cheeky and impertinent attitude to the army resonated with most middle generation poets, but the humor about the stupidity of army life was not often found in their poetry but in letters and other prose genres, with the exception of later, retrospective poems by Alan Dugan, Lincoln Kirstein, and Howard Nemerov. In other words, the lack of comedy in World War II poetry had less to do with the temperament of the poets than with the temporal distance from the war and the medium of poetry. There is, for instance, "plenty of satiric commentary in the letters" that Jarrell wrote home, mostly about his fellow soldiers, and these letters are "tinged with more humor than bitterness," as Pritchard states.[54]

Jarrell is, for instance, amused by the "terrible mock-quarrels" that many soldiers have, "like the people on the log raft in *Huckleberry Finn*, very cute ones. All the quarrels are on a child's verbal level—astonishingly repetitive and monotonous; you hear the same insults, word for word, dozens of times in dozens of mouths."[55] Perturbed by his fellow soldiers' poor spelling and the lack of good education they received, and being caught like a fly in amber with them all, Jarrell frequently lashes out in an unmistakably superior attitude that also characterized many of his poetry reviews, but which he carefully avoided in his poems. "American education is a fine way to keep the lower classes from ever getting educated and revolting," Jarrell reported to Mackie Jarrell with Marxist vigor.[56] It should be noted, however, that his condescending attitude can partly be attributed to his frustration at being stuck in the army. Moreover it often mixes with a real affection and pity for the same soldiers, both of which feature more prominently in his war poetry.

Hecht and Nemerov had the same ambivalent attitude toward their fellow soldiers. Nemerov reminisced that his air corps "milieu" was "linguistically so barren" that he read Marcel Proust's *Remembrance of Things Past* religiously and "would now and then show up for Church Parade on a Sunday."[57] Like Jarrell, Hecht vented his frustration through humorous and flippant letters. In one letter to his parents—whom he constantly addressed as "Dear Kids"—he asked jokingly if they could send "an extra box of cocaine" if they had it handy, as he had "such a keen desire to escape completely from all features of reality."[58] Shortly after the end of the war when he was stationed in occupied Japan, Hecht found another creative outlet for his feelings of exasperation by writing two radio scripts.

Aired in weekly broadcasts of the Ninety-seventh Division on Radio Tokyo, the scripts show a breezy side of Hecht that is almost diametrically opposed to his intense and dark war poems, such as "More Light! More Light!" One of the scripts satirizes the popular notion of what the troops were fighting for. It includes not only typically American products—including "rutabagas," "Indelible ink," "roachpaste," and "cellophane"—but also foreign things, including "Scotch Tape / And Turkish Baths . . . / For Russian wolfhounds / For French dressing / And Spanish moss / For English mustard / And Persian lambs / For Canadian Club / And Dutch treats." Whether the American infantryman has succeeded in making the world free for American democracy and capitalism is not certain, Hecht ponders at the end: "Will he succeed in bringing the things he fought for to all the free peoples of the world? Will he bring jukeboxes to the valiant people of Tibet? Through his efforts are corsets finally to be brought to the long-suffering women of Madagascar? Will sanitary paper napkins be made available to all freedom-loving folk? Listen in 15 years from now, and find out—unless you can guess the answer."[59] Edward Hirsch has indicated in his article "Comedy and Hardship" that this unlikely combination of themes is one of Hecht's central motifs. Yet it is remarkable that in his poetry Hecht could not or chose not to make light of the war, as he could in his prose.[60]

Like many poets of his generation, Hecht could hardly find any aspect of army life that he truly valued. As if talking about Heller's *Catch-22,* Hecht remarked in an interview that "all the officers" he encountered "from the rank of captain on up were contemptible and often ignorant, swaggering in the full vigour of their incapacity, and this was true up to as high a level as division commander."[61] Earlier in the same interview Hecht had fumed about presumably the same commander whose obsequiousness nearly cost Hecht and his fellow soldiers their lives. As in *Catch-22,* Hecht believed that medals were awarded fairly randomly—for instance, to his company commander, who received a Silver Star for when he was in fact being treated for dysentery behind the lines. Hecht never revisited such agonizing and aggravating memories in his poetry, but some of his peers did.

W. D. Snodgrass's "Returned to Frisco, 1946" is a powerful example of this "bawdy, bitchy, irreverent" type of "army style poem." It is charged with more direct emotion and rancor than Jarrell's more meditative approach and Shapiro's and Meredith's more sentimental sort. Alan Dugan and Lincoln Kirstein were also particularly skilled in writing in this impertinent and caustic vein. The verb in the title of Snodgrass's poem—which recounts the uncomfortable homecoming at the port of San Francisco—is significantly in the passive voice. The poem deals with the soldiers' frustration that they cannot control their own fate or destiny. Even after the war they are still being held captive by their own government, as symbolized by the infamous prison of Alcatraz, situated just off the coast of San Francisco, Al Capone being its most famous inmate. Like Jarrell, Snodgrass uses animal similes to indicate the soldiers' inhumane treatment. After running "like rabbits / Up hostile beaches" in the Pacific, these marines are now leaning "like pigs along the rail" trying to catch a glimpse of their home country. While half fantasizing about being able to roam free in downtown San Francisco, they are also "dulled and shaken / By fear" because they no longer trust the authorities who have led them astray many times before.

Their fears are justified, as Snodgrass reveals in his poem's final stanza:

> Off the port side, through haze, we could discern
> Alcatraz, lavender with flowers. Barred,
> The Golden Gate, fading away astern
> Stood like the closed gate of your own backyard.[62]

They are moving away from San Francisco, as the ship is moving backward. It is likely that the soldiers will be quarantined on the ironically named Angel Island, next to the ironically situated Alcatraz Island. Shapiro went through the same ordeal and later described how he and his fellow soldiers were "prisoners with wounds and medals and crackups, and sicknesses that would never be cured, and organs blighted on Angel Island to stare at San Francisco across the Bay, and Alcatraz, their neighbor."[63] Like real prisoners, Shapiro and the others were allowed to make one phone call. Angel Island had originally been a quarantine island for the Chinese coolies, "those poor devils who had been lured to America to build the almost mythological railroad through the Sierras" who were also expendable and treated like animals.[64]

Unlike other generations of intellectuals, the poets of the middle generation did not burn their draft cards. They therefore sometimes had a hard time explaining why "they were willing to go along with the militarists," as Hayden Carruth has put it. "The irresistibility of the war, the inexorability of it" is part of the answer, Carruth has admitted.[65] But despite enlisting and participating in the American war effort, they came to resent the authoritarian aspects of military culture. They had at heart a "democratic ethos" and shared a "deep identification with the suffering of others," as Hirsch has argued, which stems at least to a certain degree from the invasive attack of the self by a uniform army culture.[66] This culture brutalized, deflated, and infantilized the soldier, according to the poets of World War II, robbing them of their boyish illusions that the army and war would teach them how to become heroic, mature, and manly. Their war poems assert their "spirit of individuality in a war which, more than any other, denied the individual identity," as Linda M. Shires has said about their British peers.[67] Poetry prevented them from becoming like Jarrell's fly caught in amber.

CHAPTER 6

"To be a Jew in the twentieth century"

In her sequence "Letters to a Front" from *Beast in View* (1944), Muriel Rukeyser opens one of her poems boldly asserting: "To be a Jew in the twentieth century / Is to be offered a gift."[1] The word "gift" suggests some kind of present or perhaps a talent, and Rukeyser probably had "the theological idea of Judaism as a gift" in mind when writing these lines, as Janet E. Kaufman has suggested.[2] Yet many contemporary readers will be struck by the incongruity of this statement when at the time when Rukeyser published her poem the Holocaust was raging in Nazi Germany. In the octave of this Petrarchan sonnet Rukeyser clarifies that the gift is essentially a choice. Twentieth-century Jews can either wish "to be invisible," which entails "death of the spirit, the stone insanity," or they can accept their Jewish heritage and be faced by possible or likely persecution as history has shown.

"The gift is torment," Rukeyser modifies her claim in the sestet, although she ends her poem on a positive and optimistic note. Only the "accepting wish" can lead to freedom, and she urges her fellow Jews to be brave enough "to live for the impossible."[3] Two Jewish American poets, Anthony Hecht and Karl Shapiro, became painfully aware of the "gift" or the "torment" that Rukeyser posited. Both poets were third-generation Jewish immigrants who had been born in cities on the eastern seaboard, although the war led them to widely divergent experiences in different parts of the world. These events shook their sense of self, as it did for the other poets of World War II, but Hecht and Shapiro underwent even more agonizing identity crises as the war and its aftermath confronted them with their Jewishness in ways they simply could not ignore.

Hecht was drafted into the army in 1943 when he was still an undergraduate at Bard College. He was accepted in the Army Specialized Training Program (ASTP) in 1944, in part because of his good command of German and French. (Hecht's parents were descendants from German Jews who had settled in New York City, and the Old World had been palpably present during Hecht's childhood.) This elite corps of army officers was supposed to help restore civilian governments in Europe after the war, but the program was disbanded later that year, partly because the army needed more regular soldiers for the liberation of Europe. Hecht was assigned to the 386th Regiment of the Ninety-seventh Infantry Division and shipped across the Atlantic in January 1945. Hecht witnessed some of the most rebarbative atrocities of the war, which he never could forget.

Hecht saw, for example, how fellow soldiers of his company machine-gunned down German women and children who were waving white flags, ready to surrender. It left Hecht "without the least vestige of patriotism or national pride," as he told Philip Hoy decades later.[4] When his division liberated the concentration camp of Flossenbürg, where thousands of mostly political prisoners had been held and executed, Hecht was assigned to translate the testimonies of the French- and German-speaking prisoners. Shortly afterward, when the war in Europe was over, Hecht wrote to his parents that he was "unscathed," but that "of course does not mean unaffected. What I have seen and heard here, in conversation with Germans, French, Czechs, & Russians—plus personal observations combines to make a story well beyond the limits of censorship regulations. You must wait till I can tell you personally of this beautiful country, and its demented people."[5] Hecht's experiences during World War II forced him to identify with the victims of the Holocaust and to investigate and understand, as Rukeyser states, the "full agonies" of the Jewish people as his own heritage.[6]

It would take Hecht two decades before he could write poetry about the Shoah and how it had affected him as a person, a belated response that is not uncommon for those who are exposed to traumatic experiences.[7] Hecht had suffered a "nervous breakdown" or what would nowadays "be styled a 'post traumatic stress disorder'" a few years after the war, as he conveyed to Philip Hoy. Even though he sought help, his "orthodox Freudian" psychologist "was not prepared to believe that [Hecht's] troubles were due wholly, or even largely, to the war, so we went ambling back together, down the rocky garden path to [his] infancy."[8] Although he had referred to the war in some earlier poems—for instance, "Christmas Is Coming," "Drinking Song," and "Japan"—Hecht's first Holocaust poems were collected in *The Hard Hours* (1967). "It Out-Herods Herod. Pray You. Avoid It," "More Light! More Light!" and especially "Rites and Ceremonies" show how Hecht tried to reflect on or work through his trauma.

Hecht was one of the most prominent members of a group of English-speaking poets of the Holocaust who emerged in the 1960s. Holocaust poetry was more prevalent and discernible in several European languages during and immediately following the war, in part because European poets had (quite literally in some cases) been closer to the fire. Both mentally (as an American Jew of German descent) and physically (as someone who helped liberate a concentration camp), Hecht was in a better position than most American poets to observe the atrocities up close, but creating art out of his gruesome insights was a different matter. "Anguish, traumatic numbing, uncomprehending shock at the surreal proportions of the horror, and a heroic resolve to rebuild a fractured life beyond the shadow of death's kingdom" are some of the general reasons that Susan Gubar gives of why people eschewed the Holocaust during the 1940s and 1950s, and they may also apply to Hecht as well.[9]

Given his determination to present World War II from all possible sides, it is no surprise that Jarrell wrote half a dozen poems about the Holocaust, including "Protocols" (1945), which was "the first poem published in America about this topic," according to Hilene Flanzbaum.[10] Among his Holocaust poems, Jarrell also published "A Camp in the Prussian Forest" (1946), an interior monologue written from the perspective of an American soldier—not unlike Hecht—who discovers a death camp. Jarrell's uncanny title is suggestive of camping out in the woods like Boy Scouts do, or of a fairy tale by the Brothers Grimm that Jarrell would later translate. The defamiliarizing title fits the eerie and unsettling discoveries that the soldier makes, however, of "load on puffed load" of "corpses, stacked like sodden wood."[11] Jarrell's uneven lines, fragmentary and unfinished thoughts, and interpolated silences aptly represent the confused mind of the American soldier. In the final stanza he begins to "laugh aloud / Again and again" since the truth is too surreal and absurd to be taken in.[12]

The central symbol of "A Camp in the Prussian Forest" is the Star of David, which the Nazis forced the Jews to wear and which is "set over Jewish graves just as the cross is set over Christian graves," as Jarrell explained in a note.[13] The soldier says that he is painting "the star I sawed from yellow pine" and puts it in the ground, which does not "refuse / Its usual Jews / Their first asylum."[14] It is a bitter comment about those nations, including the United States, that rejected Jewish refugees. Burying the yellow star is the soldier's gesture—"a kind of grief" to use the words Jarrell uses earlier in the poem—to honor those who died and give them somewhat of a proper burial. Jarrell's words are in this sense an improvised kaddish for those murdered. Earlier, in a draft of this poem, Jarrell had used the rhetorical question "and yet who grieves?" and the statement "but no one grieves" to show his anger that the victims of the Holocaust were left to their own devices and forgotten.[15] The soldier's symbolic act and the poem itself (which is also a symbolic act) are no real consolations, nor can they erase what has happened. Holocaust poetry generally does not offer "plausible reparation, explanation, or closure," as Gubar has asserted, and Jarrell's poem is representative for its acknowledgment that poetry is an inadequate token of commiseration.[16]

While Hecht was making gruesome discoveries in the Prussian forests that Jarrell described in his early war poem, Shapiro had just returned to the United States after spending two years in the Pacific. During that time, Shapiro had become fascinated with Catholicism, which coincided with a rejection of Judaism and Jewish culture. As Flanzbaum has argued, Shapiro was "thoroughly sold on the virtues of assimilation" because he rooted "his identity in the experience of an American soldier and the victory that America represents" rather than in the ethnic and religious background of his childhood.[17] His apparent distaste for everything Jewish is particularly ironic considering how Nazi Germany was at that time involved in the Final Solution, a fact of which Shapiro was aware, even though he may not have understood the full scale of the calamity. Shapiro's wish to blend in and "to be invisible," to use Rukeyser's phrase, was by no means exceptional, however. Before and during the war "the vast majority of American Jews" were more bound "by loyalty to America" than by "international ties of Jewish peoplehood."[18]

Shapiro wrote three poems that explicitly refer to his anxieties about Judaism and Jewish culture and that hint at his attraction to Catholicism: "Jew" (1943), "Shylock" (1944), and "The Synagogue" (1943). In *Person, Place, and Thing* (1942), his first commercially published book, Shapiro had made passing references to the anti-Semitism he had encountered in the United States—for instance, in "University." His point of view about the Jewish question in *Person, Place, and Thing* was only "bitter," he told his fiancée, Evalyn Katz. In these newer poems, which he considered "a different facet of the same poem," however, Shapiro was "trying by recording phases of opinion (mine) to arrive at some sounder conclusion."[19] "Jew," "Shylock," and "The Synagogue" offer a revealing portrait of the several stages of Shapiro's struggle with his faith and identity during the war, but they do not represent an objective or unproblematic view on Judaism or Jewish religion, as Shapiro had hoped.

"The Synagogue" is the longest of the three poems and the one that reflects most clearly why Shapiro wanted to separate himself from Judaism. Even though he still uses the pronouns "we," "our," and "us" to denote that Jewish culture is part of his heritage, he compares Judaism unfavorably to the Catholic Church. Shapiro presents Catholicism as a more art-minded religion with "prophets" and a clear vision for the future, while Judaism is an antiquated faith that "laments itself" and whose "scholars are afraid." Whereas the rich symbolism and splendor of the cathedral make his heart beat faster, "the synagogue dispirits the deep street," Shapiro glumly notes. The synagogue is not really a relic of a past, but rather like a piece of the desert, the Sinai, that Moses and the Israelites wandered through for forty years on their way to the Promised Land. The synagogue is as barren, uneventful, and depressing as that desert, Shapiro suggests, especially when juxtaposed to the magnificence of the cathedral.[20]

Shapiro was by no means alone in his wartime attraction to Catholicism, which gave him a sense of direction, stability, and belonging in this period of turmoil. Lowell converted to Catholicism, and Nemerov—Jewish like Hecht and Shapiro—"came close to being converted" a few years earlier when he attended Harvard. Like Shapiro, Nemerov considered Catholicism "a much more artistic and beautiful religion than Judaism (red hats and old masters, I guess)," but never pursued his enthrallment any further.[21] Shapiro had been "a convinced Marxist for eleven years" before the war, but the Nazi-Soviet pact had finally put an end to that.[22] A lady friend from the Pratt library in Baltimore where Shapiro used to work had introduced him to Catholicism and barraged him with letters and packages containing crucifixes and rosaries. For much of 1943 and 1944 Shapiro read the Bible, began to pray to the Holy Mary, and attended Catholic Church services. Shapiro came to associate Catholicism with the adoration of women like the Virgin Mary, as he admitted half-jokingly in his autobiography and insinuated more seriously in "The Synagogue." This aspect of the Catholic Church strongly appealed to him while he was stuck in the masculine culture of the army.[23]

The pull factors of Catholicism were not as strong as the push factors of Judaism, however. In "Jew," the most opaque poem of the three Jewish poems, Shapiro questions whether there is such a thing as a Jewish identity:

> The name is immortal but only the name, for the rest
> Is a nose that can change in the weathers of time or persist
> Or die out in confusion or model itself on the best.
>
> But the name is a language itself that is whispered and hissed
> Through the houses of ages, and ever a language the same,
> And ever and ever a blow on our heart like a fist.[24]

A poem in terza rima and anapestic pentameter, "Jew" seems an exercise poem not only in its form but also in its content. Shapiro is trying out a new poetic form, but is also playing with a new religious faith and identity while discarding his old ones. It is essentially a confused and therefore confusing poem. Shapiro again uses the possessive pronoun "our," but it becomes clear that he does not feel comfortable being associated with Jews and Jewish culture. The people who descended from Abraham are no longer physically similar, nor do they live in close proximity to each other, and thus they are not a people or a race. He also argues that the word "Jew" will forever connote the killer of Christ. It is unclear, however, what Shapiro's conclusion about the "Jew" is. At times it appears as if he wants to dissociate himself completely from everything Jewish, but he never follows through on this, and the ultimate message of his poem remains mystifying.

Shapiro confirmed his growing uneasiness about his Jewish identity in a letter to Evalyn Katz, relating, for instance, how he attended a rabbi's service. Shapiro believed that the rabbi—who made no mention of the situation in Europe and later quizzed Shapiro about possible jobs in California—was hypocritical. Shapiro also did not sense a connection between the Jews present: "A Jew is only a name, a negative name. I saw in each name the dispersion, not of a people, but of a single man. Each man had inherited the name Jew—that was his diaspora." Shapiro reiterated that "there is no such thing as a Jewish religion. Our religion has died. Our culture has died."[25] Shapiro's quick exchange of identities—from Marxist to Catholic—suggests the huge impact that war can have on a person's sense of self. Yet Shapiro's denial of having a Jewish identity is more disturbing than the uncertainty of self that many other war poets of his generation also experienced. Shapiro maintained that Jewish culture and religion have "died" at the moment when, in the other hemisphere, Nazi Germany tried to wipe out that culture and religion. Instead of defending or protecting his Jewish heritage, Shapiro tries to escape from it, perhaps in a vain effort to ward off what Nazi Germany was capable of doing.

The final poem of Shapiro's Jewish triptych, "Shylock," underlines this vicarious escape. Shapiro's poem zooms in on the revengeful and bitter character from William Shakespeare's *The Merchant of Venice* when Shylock is sitting alone in his house after returning from his ruinous trial. As is well known, Shylock had expected to collect a pound of Antonio's flesh, Shylock's unusual reward for lending Antonio a large sum of money that the latter could not repay. Yet in a surprising turn of events Shylock loses most of his money and is forced to convert to Christianity because he was indirectly after the life of a Venetian citizen. The scene that Shapiro paints of Shylock after the trial is his own invention and not included in the play. Whereas Shakespeare explains why Shylock has become vindictive and rancorous and leaves it open whether Shylock has learned his lesson and is remorseful for his behavior at the end of the play, Shapiro depicts Shylock in the most negative light possible.

Shylock feels totally "clear of blame," Shapiro argues. Punning on Shylock's profession of usurer, he says that Shylock's "fallen reputation would help borrow / A credit of new hate."[26] Shylock also continues to think that his daughter married a Christian "swine." Antonio does the Christian thing (more or less) by forgiving Shylock, sparing his life, and not taking all of his money, but Shapiro's Shylock does not let go. "Shylock is an attempt to record coldly and without personal judgment the normal hatred of nonjews for jews which existed in Shakespeares time and persists in ours," Shapiro wrote to Katz: "To say 'I admire Shylock' wd be the height of cynicism; I am merely trying to see him as he is, indifferent to his vileness but very vile."[27] Yet it is one thing to say that he admired Shylock and quite another to unequivocally endorse one of the most persistent and off-putting stereotypes of Jews in Western literature. Far from being an objective and dispassionate judgment about anti-Semitism as Shapiro claimed, "Shylock" is Shapiro's adoption of the Christian perspective, a flirtation with anti-Semitism, and an attempt to create a justification for his own impending conversion to Catholicism.

Hecht was equally fascinated by Shakespeare during the war. He took his copy of *Five Shakespearian Tragedies* with him to Europe, while temporarily abandoning his copies of poetry by W. H. Auden, Marianne Moore, and Karl Shapiro.[28] The longest essay that Hecht ever published was, not coincidentally, on *The Merchant of Venice*. Hecht's take on the play and on Shylock is more comprehensive and profound than Shapiro's, owing in part to the different genres that the two Jewish American poets employed, but also to temperamental and intellectual differences between the poets. Hecht's "*The Merchant of Venice*: A Venture in Hermeneutics" is a well-wrought historical analysis of Shakespeare's tragic-comedy, in which Hecht tries to explain why in Elizabethan times and in the Middle Ages the relationship between the Jewish and Christian people was so strained and hostile. Even though he does not explicitly defend Shylock for his untoward behavior, Hecht admits that Shylock presents a "convincing aspect of righteousness and aggrieved persecution" and that the "the penalties imposed upon Shylock at the end of the trial are ruthless."[29] Shakespeare used "prevailing ideas about Jews," Hecht asserts, but makes a point of stressing that they were "based largely upon ignorance."[30]

Hecht's longest and most ambitious war poem, "Rites and Ceremonies," draws on many of the topics he also addresses in his essay on *The Merchant of Venice,* most notably anti-Semitism, Judaism versus Christianity, and revenge. In this densely textured and rich poem Hecht analyzes the outbursts of violence, especially anti-Semitism, throughout European history, which are either ignored or sanctioned by the Catholic Church. Hecht's poem is a more honest, thorough, and concerted effort than Shapiro's Jewish wartime poems to understand the "hatred of nonjews for jews which existed in Shakespeares time and persists in ours."

Yet the importance of Hecht's poem goes far beyond this. By examining the eruption of hate crimes at various points in time, Hecht seeks to put the Holocaust in some kind of historical perspective and to come to a form of reconciliation for the world and for his own peace of mind. "Rites and

Ceremonies" takes the form of a confused and sprawling prayer directed at God, whom Hecht addresses with both the Christian name ("father") and Jewish name ("adonoi").[31] Hecht frequently confronts God with examples from European history where innocent people died terrible deaths, and he questions what the meaning of these atrocities was. At times it appears that Hecht is ready to stop believing in a higher power, as Jarrell does in "1945: The Death of the Gods." Yet Hecht keeps turning back to his God for answers and ultimately does not relinquish his faith.

The first section of "Rites and Ceremonies," called "The Room," is, like many World War II poems, autobiographical as it is based on Hecht's "own personal experience as an infantry rifleman in Germany."[32] Hecht relates how the speaker and his regiment enter a concentration camp and stumble upon rooms filled with valises and shoes, and one "room / The size of my livingroom filled with human hair."[33] Compared with Jarrell's "A Camp in the Prussian Forest," Hecht's descriptive passage of these dehumanizing atrocities seems almost completely devoid of artifice. Jarrell noticeably uses various poetic techniques—including alliteration, assonance, and simple end-rhymes ("hope" / "soap")—to heighten the dramatic effect of his lines or to reflect the bafflement of his speaker. Hecht's more literalist diction, however, makes an even purer and more powerful impression than Jarrell's preciosity:

> It is twenty years, now, Father. I have come home
> But in the camps, one can look through a huge square
> Window, like an aquarium, upon a room
> The size of my livingroom filled with human hair.
> Others have shoes, or valises
> Made mostly of cardboard, which once contained
> Pills, fresh diapers. This is one of the places
> Never explained.[34]

Still, as the alternately rhyming lines and the skillful positioning of the enjambment in the penultimate line reflecting the speaker's lack of comprehension indicate, Hecht does not eschew poetic techniques. He uses them, however, more sparingly and subtly than Jarrell does in his concentration camp liberation poem.

Whereas the nominally Christian Jarrell centered "A Camp in the Prussian Forest" on the Star of David, the Jewish poet Hecht centers "The Room" on the cross. The conflation of this Christian symbol and the Iron Cross, a Prussian military decoration that the Nazis adopted as their own, underlines one of the dominant themes of "Rites and Ceremonies." Hecht suggests that it was not a coincidence that a Christian society was responsible for such carnage. Hecht's poem concerns itself with the peaceful promise of that faith and the devastating crimes that are perpetrated in its name. The belt buckle that Hecht's speaker sees on a dead German soldier when he and the others enter the concentration camp is another manifestation of this phenomenon. It reads "Gott mit uns" (God with us), a translation of the name Emmanuel, which promised the birth of Jesus Christ, according to the Gospel of Matthew. The Iron Cross and the belt buckle are signs that Nazi Germany presented itself as a Christian nation, or at least used Christian imagery to further its cunning plans.

Toward the end of "The Room," Hecht connects the outrages of the concentration camps directly to the Catholic Church. After juxtaposing images of a "trainload" of "five hundred" prisoners who are "made into soap" and prisoners who were attached to carts so they can pull stones out of a quarry while being forced to sing songs, Pope Pius XII is presented as whispering: "Above all, the saving of lives."[35] Hecht's identification with the Holocaust victims here is so overwhelming that every time he prays, he becomes one of them and finds himself in a gas chamber along with the others:

> At night, Father, in the dark, when I pray.
> I am there, I am there. I am pushed through
> With the others to the strange room
> Without windows; whitewashed walls, cement floor.
> Millions, Father, millions have come to this pass,
> Which a great church has voted to "deplore."[36]

Hecht's anger in "The Room" is less directed at the Nazis, who are represented only by the dead "blond and boyish and bloody" soldier with that belt buckle—just as young and out of place as Hecht himself—than at the institution that propagated anti-Semitism for centuries and now tries to conceal the unpleasant facts of the past.[37]

Hecht wrote "Rites and Ceremonies" immediately after the proclamation of "Nostra Aetate" (1965), the Declaration on the Relation of the Church to Non-Christians. The Catholic Church denounced the hatred and persecution of Jews in the past and present. It also stated that Jewish people could not be held responsible for deicide and that since the two faiths are historically related, they can and should be able to coexist peacefully. Hecht found the Church's terminology and act of distancing infuriating. In 1998, more than three decades after "Nostre Aetate" and "Rites and Ceremonies," Hecht was still angry and thought that the official Catholic position on the Holocaust had not changed significantly. In an interview with Philip Hoy, Hecht quoted from a recently published document by the Vatican, "We Remember: A Reflection on the Shoah," which claimed that nazism "had its roots outside Christianity" and "that the people who ran the camps were essentially pagan. This, however, fails to agree with the Nazis' own view of the matter," Hecht asserted bitterly.[38]

Having lived in Rome in the early 1950s after winning the Prix de Rome, Hecht came—just like Shapiro—to admire and be fascinated by the Catholic Church, especially because of its intellectual tradition and the art and artists that it fostered. Hecht's respect for the Catholic Church is tangible in "Rites and Ceremonies," but it mixes with a lingering resentment over its support of or indifference to the persecution of the Jews throughout history. Hecht held similarly opposing attitudes toward German culture as he did to the Catholic Church.[39] This is represented by the German author Johann Wolfgang von Goethe, who occasionally features in Hecht's war poems.

The words quoted in the title of Hecht's frequently anthologized Holocaust poem "More Light! More Light!" were reportedly Goethe's final words. The poem "elaborates on a passage from *The Theory and Practice of Hell* by Eugene Kogan," as Gubar has shown, about one non-Jewish Polish prisoner and two Jewish ones at Buchenwald who are set against each other in a sinister way and who all die terrible deaths.[40] Despite Goethe's formidable influence on German and European civilization, there was no light from Goethe's "shrine at Weimar beyond the hill / Nor light from heaven appeared."[41] Neither Goethe nor God could stop this catastrophe. In "Rites and Ceremonies" Hecht twice refers to Goethe in passing, again to emphasize that German barbarism and civilization are two sides of the same coin. In both poems Hecht mentions the Catholic Church in close proximity, suggesting a correlation.

The first instance is when Hecht quotes the line "Die Vögelein schweigen im Walde" from Goethe's lullaby "Eingleiches" from *Wanderers Nachtlied* right after mentioning "The Singing Horses of Buchenwald" and criticizing Pius XII's halfhearted response to the Holocaust. Unlike the Jews who were forced to sing songs as they were being exploited and dehumanized, the birds in the Prussian forest are silent as if morally (and humanly) outraged. Yet their stillness also echoes the silence of the Catholic Church. Another Goethe reference occurs in "The Fire Sermon," and it also collates German culture with the Catholic Church. Hecht makes a seemingly offhand comment that Goethe earned his law degree in Strasbourg, the site of a massacre in 1349.

Goethe admired Erwin von Steinbach, the designer of the monumental cathedral in that Alsatian town, and even dedicated an essay on German architecture to Steinbach.[42] Steinbach's cathedral emphasizes the baffling contrast between German civilization and German cruelty, as did Goethe's literary works when juxtaposed to the Holocaust. It is (almost literally) a high point of German medieval architecture, but also the place where Jews were burned in the fourteenth century.

Jews were accused and tortured for allegedly poisoning the wells of Strasbourg in 1349. "These are the ritual murderers with ugly noses / They killed Christ and poisoned all the wells," Hecht wrote in one of the working sheets of "Rites and Ceremonies" mimicking how medieval Christians typically looked at Jews.[43] In his essay on *The Merchant of Venice* Hecht elaborated this point by arguing that those Christians reasoned that "once the Jews had crucified Jesus, they thirsted for pure and innocent blood."[44] Financial gain was partly why the wealthy Jews were attacked in Strasbourg. Just like Shylock in Shakespeare's *Merchant of Venice,* the Strasbourg Jews lost all of their money and were also forced to convert to Catholicism if they wanted their lives to be spared. Hecht's "Rites and Ceremonies" indirectly and inadvertently comments on Shapiro's wartime poem "Shylock," proposing that the money-lending Jews in medieval Europe were more often victims of Christians than the other way around.

This analysis of Hecht's quarrel with the Catholic Church should not suggest that "Rites and Ceremonies" is the testimony of an irate or fault-finding Jewish American man. On the contrary, even though Hecht's exasperation at so much injustice and savagery is at times tangible, "Rites and Ceremonies" is—unlike Shapiro's speedily written "Shylock"—a thoughtful, meditative, and well-balanced poem, composed with "prayerlike attentiveness," to use a phrase by Susan Gubar.[45] The "endless cycle of persecutions, enslavements and humiliations . . . seems to invite, or at least permit, a sense of outrage," Hecht told an audience at Yom Kippur when introducing "Rites and Ceremonies" before uttering a warning:

> But righteous indignation is an easy and convenient emotion, and not altogether uncomfortable, either. It contrives smoothly to divide the world into two neat and distinguishable camps: the Good and the Bad. And, of course, the person entertaining the emotion enjoys with unthinking satisfaction his own swift positioning of himself on the side of the Good. But aside from the fact that he may not be entitled to quite so easy an assumption, serious meditation would tell him, as the Scriptures have often told him, that the world itself is not so obviously divided into two camps; neither is his own soul to be neatly purified without God's grace and without serious meditation and penitence.[46]

"Rites and Ceremonies" is Hecht's most ambitious attempt to comprehend the cataclysm that he saw taking place in Flossenbürg, but he resists easy emotions, reductive binary oppositions, and ultimate judgment.[47] The final section, "Words for the Day of Atonement," contains hopeful and forgiving words from both the Bible and the Talmud, which is suggestive of Hecht's admirable, fair-minded conclusion.

Shapiro did not convert to Catholicism in the end. When he approached the army chaplain in New Guinea to discuss it, Shapiro was crushed that the chaplain was in a hurry to go on his furlough.[48] The Bollingen affair, which erupted when Ezra Pound's *The Cantos* was given a federal prize a few years after the war, when Pound was still at St. Elizabeth's, forced Shapiro's struggle with his Jewish identity to a visible crisis. As a fellow of American letters and former poetry consultant, Shapiro was selected as one the jury members, as was Pound's friend Eliot. Shapiro initially acquiesced to the jury's decision to grant the award to Pound, but soon reversed his opinion. Feeling that, as a Jew, he could not honor an alleged fascist and anti-Semite, Shapiro sent the Librarian of Congress a note in which he explained that, to him, Pound's "moral and political philosophy ultimately vitiated the *Cantos* and lowered the literary quality of the work."[49] His wavering position made Shapiro appear confused to most observers, on both sides of the debate, as he of course was.[50]

The Bollingen affair opened Shapiro's eyes to the fact that he could not escape being a Jew. By the 1950s Shapiro began to identify himself and present himself explicitly as Jewish, culminating in *Poems of a Jew* (1958), in which he collected all of his poems that dealt directly or obliquely with his Jewish identity. The collection contains his three Jewish war poems as well as newer poems—for instance, "The Phenomenon" (1953) about the Holocaust, squeezed uncomfortably in between "The Synagogue" and "University," with its radically divergent claims. Whereas Hecht found "a kind of grief" (to use Jarrell's words) by writing "Rites and Ceremonies," Shapiro appeared to be still tormented by the special gift of being a Jew in the twentieth century.

CHAPTER 7

Robert Lowell's Ideological Vacillations

When Robert Lowell was an eighteen-year-old high school senior at St. Mark's in 1935, he published a short article in the student magazine the *Vindex,* which he called "War: A Justification." It was a particularly bold and ambitious piece of writing that stood out for the author's seriousness and self-assurance. Lowell argued that war was not only necessary in offering great nations, such as Germany, Italy, and Japan, the *Lebensraum* they needed and deserved, but also suggested that it was beneficial to all men: "It unites mankind, for it shows that greatness is to be achieved, not by individualism, but by coöperation. It is democratic, for rich and poor, plebeian and aristocrat, are called upon, equally. It is edifying, for cowards and thieves are given a chance to gain self-respect and honor. It is idealistic, for mercy, constancy, magnanimity, pity, personal courage—indeed, all that is noble in man comes to the surface."[1] Lowell's early views on war—his social Darwinian defense of it, his disdain for pacifists, and his belief that war is an egalitarian force that helps men to distinguish themselves as individuals—are remarkable. Not only do they sound outdated after the mass slaughter of the first mechanized world war; they also contrast sharply with the poet's later public persona as a conscientious objector during World War II and a voluble protester of the Vietnam War.

Yet the decade between 1935 and the end of World War II was a disorienting period, especially for young men coming of age. The ideological beliefs of many emerging poets shifted noticeably during those years, partly because of personal reasons and partly because of events in the world—for instance, the Great Depression and the Spanish Civil War. Shapiro's initial attraction to Marxism, his subsequent fling with Catholicism, and the dilemmas that he faced with his Jewish identity throughout this period appear to be typical for Shapiro's capricious character. Yet many more poets were troubled by ideological uncertainties in the prewar period. These doubts were exacerbated when they had to make a choice as to how they stood in relation to World War II. Who were they individually, religiously, politically, and patriotically?

Lowell's decision to declare himself a conscientious objector was made suddenly. He had volunteered for the navy and army several times in 1942 and 1943, but was found unfit because of his myopia six times. In August 1943 he reported to his parents that he would finally be inducted early in September, and made no mention of his objection to the way the United States fought the war.[2] On the first of that month Lowell's wife, Jean Stafford, wrote a letter to Eleanor and Peter Taylor in which she stated that Lowell was "to be inducted on the 8th, a week from today."[3] Yet less than a week later, on September 7, 1943, Lowell wrote his now famous letter to President Roosevelt, including his "Declaration of Personal Responsibility" in which he stated that he could not "honorably participate in a war whose prosecution, as far as I can judge, constitutes a betrayal of my country."[4] Lowell had come to believe that the United States had, after the bombing of Hamburg, become engaged in a wantonly destructive rather than a necessary war.

Only 1 percent of the total number of men drafted became conscientious objectors during World War II, approximately forty-three thousand in total.[5] Among these conscientious objectors, Lowell was a clear minority. Most of the noncombatants during World War II came from the three historic peace churches in the United States, had family members who were pacifists, had been involved in the interwar peace movement, or had been influenced by the "classical prophets of pacifism and civil disobedience—Tolstoy, Emerson and Thoreau" as well as more recent ones, such as Erich Maria Remarque and Mahatma Gandhi.[6] None of these motivations apply to Lowell. Many conscientious objectors believed that their pacifism was "native to their personalities," but this does not accurately describe Lowell's character or behavior either. Lowell was known to have an irascible and belligerent side, even during this time period.[7]

Lowell was also a different kind of conscientious objector than fellow poet William Stafford. Unlike Lowell, Stafford was "a pacifist from the beginning," being taught the ethical values of nonviolence by his mother as he recalled in his poem "Religious Training and Belief."[8] Stafford was three years Lowell's junior and fought forest fires and planted trees in Arkansas and California for the Civilian Public Service during the war. Stafford's entire life was dedicated to nonviolence, and he was weary of the public celebration of dissent that Lowell and others engaged in, believing that "the true pacifist . . . seeks peace in both the short- and the long term, not stridency now for vague future ends."[9] Stafford, for instance, never spanked his children nor was he ever provoked into violence, as Lowell was on occasion.

Many detailed accounts exist that analyze Lowell's troubled war years, with each biographer and critic taking a slightly different stance when explaining Lowell's sudden decision to become a conscientious objector. As Philip Metres writes in *Behind the Lines,* Ian Hamilton's biography "directly conflates Lowell's objection to the war with his manic-depression," while another biographer, Paul Mariani, frames "the objection within the poet's Catholic period."[10] While living in Baton Rouge, Louisiana, after graduating from Kenyon College in 1941, Lowell had unexpectedly become a Catholic. Like his objection to the war, his conversion came out of the blue, and was painful to his parents. He was a descendant of Puritan, Unitarian, and Episcopalian clergy, and had shown no previous signs of being interested in Catholicism; on occasion he had even ridiculed the Catholic faith.[11] By comparing Lowell to other conscientious objectors during World War II, such as William Everson and William Stafford, Metres himself portrays Lowell as less principled and more skeptical than most war resistance writers, although he believes that Lowell made a rational and well-balanced decision when he wrote to President Roosevelt.

All of these views are plausible and contribute to our understanding of what happened to Lowell during these years. Yet the differences in these interpretations are also testimony to how difficult it is to evaluate Lowell's momentous decision from a distance of decades. Lowell himself admitted that his Catholicism and his bipolar disease affected his decision to become a conscientious objector, claiming in his autobiographical poem "Memories of West Street and Lepke," written in the 1950s: "I was a fire-breathing Catholic C.O., / and made my manic statement, / telling off the state and president."[12]

An earlier typescript version of the same poem at the Houghton Library of Harvard University suggests that rebellion against his family was also part of the bargain: "My conscientious objector statement meant to blow the lid off / The United States, Roosevelt and my parents."[13] Lowell's relationship with his mother and father was notoriously troubled, as his masterful story or memoir "91 Revere Street" makes clear. Religious, political, familial, and mental reasons thus all conspired for Lowell to make his remarkable decision.

And yet Lowell may have been partly also genuinely outraged by the bombings of civilian populations in Germany. Seen in the context of the experiences and writings of his poetic peers who signed up for the military, Lowell's position seems less idiosyncratic and odd than might seem apparent at first glance. Richard Wilbur has stated in an interview that he "was inclined toward pacifism, for religious reasons" and that he was also "a potential war resister on political grounds." If the Allied "cause" had "been more dubious," he "might have ended as a C.O."[14] Howard Nemerov's wartime letters also evidence his absorption with religious issues, and, like Lowell, he also contemplated opting for jail rather than the military, as he admitted to his friend Howard Turner from Parks Air College in East St. Louis: "I have been wondering, in the last few days, about putting it squarely up to the draft board (in the event that I wash out here) and saying: 'I have no means of proving that I do not belong in the army, but quite honestly, if it is allowed, I should prefer going to jail.' Of course there is the question of the family, who would all be shamed—but I think of it quite seriously. In jail I might feel more responsible, though this may be difficult to understand, for anyone but myself."[15]

Nemerov did wash out, but decided to try another training course, in the Royal Canadian Air Force, rather than refuse to enter the services. Even though he had contemplated the same daunting decision as Lowell, Nemerov eventually became a decorated fighter pilot rather than a conscientious objector. One senses that he might also have made a radically different choice, which would have altered the course of his life dramatically. Lowell's ideological wavering was perhaps more extreme than that of his peers, but they battled with many of the same anxieties and pressures.[16]

Lowell's early war poems also appear to set him apart from the other war poets of his generation. His diction and intertextual references to Greek and Roman mythology as well as to Christian imagery differentiate his poems from the early war poems of Ciardi, Jarrell, Shapiro, and Wilbur, which were more accessible, even in their allusions. Lowell's models in the early 1940s were not W. H. Auden or Robert Frost, but Gerard Manley Hopkins and the religious verse of seventeenth-century poets, such as John Donne and George Herbert, and the bitter sarcasm of Ezra Pound's and Allen Tate's war poems. With the help of Randall Jarrell, however, Lowell found a poetic voice and a vision of World War II that closely resembles Jarrell's and is also more in line with that of the other war poets of his generation. The poems of *Land of Unlikeness* (1944) were written when Lowell was severely struggling with his identity and his poetics, while the poems of his Pulitzer Prize–winning *Lord Weary's Castle* (1946) show hints of him gaining more control over his art and his own selfhood.

Lowell wrote the poems of *Land of Unlikeness* in roughly two years. The publication of Jarrell's *Blood for a Stranger* had prompted him to start writing poetry again in December 1941, and he was proofreading the galleys of *Land of Unlikeness* in jail in December 1943.[17] *Land of Unlikeness* contains twenty poems of which five—"The Boston Nativity," "The Bomber," "Christmas Eve in Time of War," "Cistercians in Germany," and "On the Eve of the Feast of the Immaculate Conception"—deal explicitly with World War II, while others refer to the war more obliquely. His notebooks for *Land of Unlikeness,* held at the Houghton Library of Harvard University, also contain dozens of drafts for poems that Lowell never published. He salvaged a number of lines from *Land of Unlikeness* and revised some poems for *Lord Weary's Castle,* but consciously let the poems of *Land of Unlikeness* go out of print.[18] None of the poems from *Land of Unlikeness* are well known, and they are not among Lowell's best work, but these early war poems and their copious drafts offer an opportunity to understand Lowell's ideological vacillations during the war, and to trace his development before *Lord Weary's Castle.*

The poems of *Land of Unlikeness* have "three related themes," as Steven Gould Axelrod has indicated: "history, current events, and God" and share an anger about agnostic America.[19] In a letter to Gertrude Buckman, Lowell once mentioned that during his manic periods he began to act and feel like "a prophet and everything was a symbol . . . religion and antics" and this accurately sums up the tone and rhetoric of his first collection of poems.[20] "On the Eve" was one of the first poems of *Land of Unlikeness* that he wrote. In this carefully constructed and perhaps schematic poem, Lowell uses nineteen different rhymes and an intricate stanza structure to boot. Each of the three stanzas consists of eight lines rhyming *aabbcdcd.* Lines 1, 2, 4, 5, and 6 correspond roughly with tetrameters; lines 3, 7, and 8 are much shorter and are mostly iambic dimeters. We can find references to the Bible and Christianity (Mary, Cain, Nimrod, Satan, Jesus Christ, the serpent), to Greek and Roman history and mythology (Bellona, Mars, Plato), and to contemporary history (Eisenhower, Burma, and Bizerta). The many intellectual allusions make the poem less immediately accessible than the poetry of the other middle generation poets.

Addressed to the Catholic icon the Holy Mary and written on the occasion of the feast of the Immaculate Conception—December 8—it fits in a long tradition of English religious verse. Yet it "takes the form of a blasphemous prayer," as Margot Norris has indicated.[21] Like John Donne's Holy Sonnets, the tone of the poem is angry and confused instead of reverential and obedient. Posing questions and hoping for answers, Lowell's speaker is at times disrespectful—for instance, addressing the Holy Mary as a "Celestial Hoyden," a heavenly tomboy. Lowell describes the Holy Mary in masculine rather than in feminine terms, which is not particularly flattering. Lowell's anger and frustration are functional, as he tries to juxtapose the promise of Mary's miracles with her silence in this latter-day world crisis. When Jesus Christ died, Mary "shook a sword / From his torn side," but now she does not seem to react to the world in turmoil.[22] Mary is challenged by Bellona, the goddess of war, who threatens to take over, and Lowell is anxiously waiting for Mary's response. From the Asian battleground of Birma to the Tunisian port of Bizerta, and from the North Pole to the South Pole, the world is in disarray, and Lowell wants to snap Mary out of her passivity.

Ian Hamilton is not far from the truth when he writes that Lowell's poems contain "a high fever, a driven, almost deranged belligerence in both the voice and the vocabulary, as if poems had become hurled thunderbolts, instruments of grisly retribution"—for instance, to avenge his enemies.[23] "On the Eve" shows Lowell's indignation at the political and military leaders of the United States, whom he accuses of belligerence and imperialism. Oddly enough, Lowell does not blame Germany or Japan for their warmongering and expansionism. "Freedom and Eisenhower have won / Significant laurels where the Hun / and Roman kneel / To lick the dust from Mars' bootheel," Lowell observes sarcastically.[24] Eisenhower purports to fight for freedom, but he is merely a vain minion of the Roman god of war who crushes the Germans and Italians. This is the only example from *Land of Unlikeness* or *Lord Weary's Castle* where Lowell engages in a direct attack on actual people, as he generally favored detached symbolism in his early poetry. Interestingly, such attacks do occur frequently in his drafts.

One long fragment provisionally called "To the President of the United States Who, on the Verge of War Desires the Blessings of the Churches" is such a scathing poem. Unlike his ancestor James Russell Lowell, who also used satire in the first series of *The Biglow Papers* to mock the ambitions of politicians in the wake of the Mexican-American War, Lowell's drafts are rancorous and not particularly humorous. Lacking such fictional characters as Hosea Biglow, Wilbur Homer, and Birdofredum Sawin, at whom the author can also poke fun of, the younger Lowell's attack on Roosevelt feels cold and offensive, which might be the reason why Lowell ultimately suppressed it. The United States was a "gluttonous Leviathan" and Roosevelt was a "mammon–mammothed" man, an alliterative phrase that expresses America's and Roosevelt's size and greed. This draft shows a disturbing fascination for Roosevelt, which is also dimly felt in his public letter to the president. In his draft Lowell calls Roosevelt a "subverted superhuman, superman," and he seems strangely attracted to Roosevelt's sense of power, even if he ridicules and violently opposes it.[25]

Randall Jarrell, who became Lowell's most important influence during the war and who called Lowell "the only writer" he felt "much in common with," disliked such satirical poems.[26] In a candid letter, Jarrell wrote to Lowell in November 1945:

> I think your biggest limitations right now are (1) not putting enough about people in the poems—they are more about the actions of you, God, the sea, and the cemeteries than they are about the "actions of men"; (2) being too harsh and severe—but this is already changing, very much for the better too, I think. Contemporary satires (which you don't seem to write any more) are your weakest sort of poem,

> and are not really worth wasting your time on; your worst tendency is to do too-mannered, mechanical, wonderfully contrived, exercise poems; but these you don't do much when you feel enough about the subject or start from a real point of departure in contemporary real life.[27]

Jarrell persuaded Lowell not to use "On the Eve" in *Lord Weary's Castle,* as it was too much like Tate's "Ode to Our Young Pro-Consuls of the Air," while some phrases, including his "Celestial Hoyden," were "pure Hopkins."[28] Lowell's "The Bomber" was even more similar to Tate's "Ode," as both are satirical denunciations of American aircrew wreaking their destruction from above. Whereas Jarrell is both critical of and sympathetic to the young bombers he helped train, Lowell is, like Tate, coldly dismissive of the airmen.

The inspiration for "The Bomber" was the Latin poem "Dies Irae," which is recited at Catholic masses on All Souls' Day and during funeral masses.[29] Lowell had scribbled the first stanza of the poem in his first draft, from which he adopted the idea that "David and Sybil's bluff" foretold how the world will be reduced to ashes after Judgment Day. The bombers, who are sarcastically likened to God as they have the power to choose who lives or dies, make fun of David and Sybil's prediction that the world will burn down like ashes. Yet they will soon be chastised by God, as "the Master has had enough / Of your trial flights and your cops / And robbers and blind-man's buff," as Lowell awkwardly threatens.[30]

While the first stanza uses Christian imagery, the second uses Greek mythology, most notably the myth of Phaeton. This son of the sun-god Helios convinced his father to let him drive the sun's chariot across the heavens for one day. Helios consented, but the horses were too powerful for Phaeton to contain, and they ran off course. When Zeus realized that they were about to burn and destroy the earth, he sent out a thunderbolt, killing Phaeton. Like the Icarus myth, the Phaeton myth stresses youthful ambition and folly. The bombers of the fledgling nation move rapidly and forcefully, like Phaeton's horses, until they come close to destroying the world. Lowell emphasizes the blind and wild enthusiasm of the American bombers with their "frail wings," but expects that God will destroy them for their supercilious recklessness.[31] Even though "The Bomber" is already overloaded with references to the Bible and Greek and Roman mythology, Lowell's drafts contain many more. Most were taken out in his final version.

In an earlier draft of the poem Lowell used the words "Pilate" and its homophone "Pilot" instead of "Bombers," a reference to Pontius Pilate, which Jarrell later also uses in his "Eighth Air Force." Stephen Burt has suggested that "Eighth Air Force" "mediat[es] between the unsophisticated airmen and the angry, educated Lowell all of whom in different ways [are] too young, too committed to a single perspective, to be able to judge."[32] In this sense, "Eighth Air Force" can be read as a response to "The Bomber" as well as to "Ode to Our Young Pro-Consuls of the Air," which are both "too harsh and severe" about the American bombers, as Jarrell said about Lowell's style in general. Jarrell instead described American conscripts as victims in their own right. Jarrell portrays the airmen in "Eighth Air Force" as both "murderers" and "saviour[s]," but they have unmistakable human sides.[33]

Jarrell's airmen are boys and men who play ball, dream, and are afraid that their next sortie may be their last. "The Bomber" does not describe "the 'actions of men,'" as Jarrell does in "Eighth Air Force." The "goggled pilots" or bombers are symbols of agnostic America, but they are not real or credible people.[34] Like "On the Eve," "The Bomber" is too much a "too-mannered, mechanical, wonderfully contrived, exercise poem." In both poems, Lowell uses similar lines—for instance, about Christ giving up the ghost—and contrived rhyming words such as "bluff" and "blindman's buff."[35] Lowell seems more intrigued by showing off his erudition and his technical acuity than the accuracy of his argument.

Yet Lowell was growing as a poet, as Jarrell realized when penning his letter to Lowell. He was dropping the overly satirical poems, lost much of his angry tone, and made a conscious effort to use his own experiences as departing points for his poems, as is evident from "Christmas Eve under Hooker's Statue" and "The Dead in Europe" from *Lord Weary's Castle*. There are three published versions of "Christmas Eve under Hooker's Statue," and each in succession becomes less preachy and more personal. Lowell had earlier published "The Capitalist's Meditation by the Civil War Monument, Christmas, 1942" in *Partisan Review* in 1943 and "Christmas Eve in the Time of War: A Capitalist Meditates by a Civil War Monument" in *Land of Unlikeness*.[36] Even the titles of these former versions express how Lowell initially wanted to make foremost a political statement. Lowell deleted the word "Capitalist" from the title and used colloquial lines, such as "Tonight a blackout. Twenty years ago / I hung my stocking on the tree" instead of the more didactic lines "Tonight the blackout. Twenty years ago / The playboys starred a neon tree."[37] Jarrell encouraged and applauded these changes.[38]

Susceptible to Jarrell's suggestions, Lowell was also moving closer to the kind of war poetry that Jarrell was writing. This is especially clear in "The Dead in Europe," which is in a sense an amalgamation of "On the Eve" and "The Bomber," since it deals with Judgment Day, the Virgin Mary, and the bombing war in Europe. Yet Lowell has also incorporated Jarrell's vision of the war. Jarrell approved of "The Dead in Europe" as "an *awfully* good poem and wonderfully strong and brilliant too."[39] Written later than the two poems from *Land of Unlikeness,* this poem is devoid of the manic personal attacks on Roosevelt and Eisenhower and refrains from using heavy-handed allusions to Greek and Roman mythology. Even though the references to Mary and Judgment Day remain, they are more subtle, playful, and made in passing. They no longer dominate the poem. Lowell's technical virtuosity is again on display, especially his original, unusual diction and his use of assonance. Yet these features are less obtrusive and more functional. The words "hugger-mugger," "curse," "rubble," "bundle," and "blockbusters" create a subtle unity between the stanzas, but these rhymes are less forced and farfetched than in "The Bomber" and "On the Eve" and more precisely handled.[40]

Yet the biggest change in Lowell's poetics is in content, as "The Dead in Europe" deplores all casualties in Europe; instead of chastising the aggressors as he did in "The Bomber," Lowell now empathizes with all the victims, the bombers and the bombed:

> After the planes unloaded, we fell down
> Buried together, unmarried men and women;
> Not crown of thorns, not iron, not Lombard crown,
> Not grilled and spindle spires pointing to heaven
> Could save us. Raise us, Mother, we fell down
> Here hugger-mugger in the jellied fire:
> Our sacred earth in our day was our curse.[41]

Although the poem is not entirely unambiguous, the plural pronoun "we" seems to refer to the bombers who crashed and were "buried together" with those they bombed. This interpretation would link the poem with Jarrell's "Losses," in which the speaker states ruefully: "our bodies lay among / The people we had killed and never seen."[42] Whereas Lowell vents his slightly sanctimonious and snobbish superiority in "The Bomber," "The Dead in Europe" is more subdued and melancholic.

When commenting on a draft of this poem, Jarrell suggested only a few changes, including that Lowell tone down the more heavily rhetorical lines. In the first three lines of the poem's last stanza Lowell had stated: "Mother, my bones are trembling and I hear / Global reverberations and the trumpet / Bruit upon my tombstone." Jarrell ridiculed these lines as having "that terrible Wallace Clare Boothe Luce sound," referring to the politician's first speech in the House of Representatives in 1943. She had famously ridiculed Vice President Henry Wallace's ambitious plans for the postwar world as "globaloney." Jarrell added in a less flippant note that these lines would strike many readers as "a little on the pedantic 'over-learned' side."[43] Whether by mockery or by being brutally honest, Jarrell helped Lowell lose his bombastic and pompous tendencies. Lowell faithfully amended many of the lines that Jarrell objected to, and Jarrell's critique helped Lowell in finding a more mature poetic voice as well as a less furious view of the atrocities of World War II. Lowell would later frequently thank Jarrell for the "many spurs and reviews in the past," and claimed that he "couldn't have gone on . . . without them." In fact, more than a decade later, when writing the poems for *Life Studies,* which included "Memories of West Street and Lepke," he again turned to Jarrell for advice, remembering how successfully Jarrell had helped him.[44]

By the time that *Lord Weary's Castle* was published in 1946, World War II was finally over. Around the same time Lowell also stopped being a practicing Catholic. His attraction to Catholicism and his opposition to the war were over as quickly as they had begun. While his actions may have seemed erratic and opportunistic, Lowell's behavior reflects the great internal confusion that many poets of his generation felt about who they were and about which position they should take. Neither his wartime conversion to Catholicism nor his opposition to the war is abnormal when you compare him to his peers. Shapiro came close to converting to Catholicism too, but that attraction also faded. Jarrell's views about the bombing of German cities did not differ too much from Lowell's either. Other poets also had reservations about or strong objections to the total war in which the United States was engaged.

What makes Lowell unique is the abruptness and public nature of his declaration that he was a conscientious objector after his past history as a defender of war, rather than the convictions themselves. Fueled by his mental instability and familial pressures, Lowell channeled his confusion into a steadfast conviction that his Catholicism and objection to the war were correct and everybody else was wrong. This led to the angry and rebellious war poetry of *Land of Unlikeness,* which is nevertheless intriguing in terms of his poetic apprenticeship and as a reflection of his bewildered worldview at the time. The new war poems of *Lord Weary's Castle* offer intimations of the more open-minded Lowell, who was too magnanimous for resentment and who closely resembles Jarrell as a war poet.

CHAPTER 8

Randall Jarrell's Secondhand Reality

James Dickey's review-article of Randall Jarrell's *Selected Poems* (1956) still stands out as one of the most creative and thought-provoking essays on Jarrell, exposing Jarrell's weaknesses but also expressing his brilliance. In some ways Jarrell was to Dickey what W. H. Auden or Allen Tate represented for Jarrell: slightly older poets whose work formed an inspiration and a yardstick for his own, but whose influence needed to be overcome in order to be a fully independent poet in his own right. The ambivalent stance that these contrary motives created resulted in the unusual style of Dickey's review, which contains two voices, one appreciative of Jarrell, voice "A," and the other disparaging him, voice "B." Dickey may well have borrowed the idea for his review from Auden, who had used a similar form on W. B. Yeats when surveying the Irish poet's oeuvre in *Partisan Review* in 1939.[1] Like Auden, who acted as both a "Public Prosecutor" and "the Counsel for the Defense," Dickey in turns attacks and defends Jarrell, thereby also showing two sides of his personality or two selves.

Dickey's detracting voice B is most detailed when critiquing Jarrell's acclaimed war poems, as B charges that Jarrell does not really feel compassion for specific human beings, but rather for generic soldiers and victims of war in general: "I am disturbed, though, that despite all the pity he shows, none of it is actually brought to bear on any*one*. Did Jarrell never love any *person* in the service with him? Did he just pity himself and all the Others, in a kind of monstrous, abstract, complacent, and inhuman Compassion? I don't think there are really any *people* in the war poems. There are just collective Objects, or Attitudes, or Killable Puppets. You care very little what happens to them and that is terrible."[2]

These emphatic words sound ironically similar to Jarrell's own comment back in 1945 rebuking Lowell that he was "not putting enough about people in the poems."[3] The titles of some of Jarrell's poems—"The Death of the

Ball Turret Gunner," "The Dead Wingman," "A Pilot from the Carrier"—reflect the anonymity of Jarrell's airmen as opposed to, for instance, Richard Eberhart in "The Fury of Aerial Bombardment" who names them—"Of Van Wettering I speak, and Averill"—although he admits that he does "not recall" the "faces."[4]

Even though voice A counters that Jarrell's anonymity is a consequence of his attempt to show "the impersonal side of war" that was fought "almost entirely by machines," voice B's comments linger throughout the article as a sustained critique of Jarrell's poetry at midcareer.[5] "Jarrell's second-hand Reality simply does not do enough," voice B concludes with the same devastating finality that Jarrell had used to sneer at Auden and for which Jarrell was a feared poetry critic.[6] In fact, Dickey seems to try to outdo Jarrell in this essay in clever witticisms and one-liners, which betrays the same kind of devotion that Jarrell had shown for Auden even when exposing his flaws most cruelly. Only someone who is so dedicated to another's person's work is able to lay bare with such brutal honestly the shortcomings of that work. In some way Dickey was in love with Jarrell, just as much as Jarrell was in love with Auden.

Dickey's critique goes to the heart of a new poetics that Jarrell was quickly developing during the war, but the question arises as to how fair Dickey is. Most readers would agree that in "The Death of the Ball Turret Gunner," Jarrell is able to present a convincing psychological sketch of the young and tiny airman who experiences an epiphany in his dying seconds. Yet some of Jarrell's other flyers remain hollow types rather than real, believable people. Jarrell tried to create a type of poetry that was guided neither by an overarching belief—whether communism, fascism, or religion—nor by a prescribed set of technical dicta. The new poetics that Jarrell was envisaging also reflected his move away from Auden, the New Critics, and the high modernists. Auden writes in "Private Poet" that a war poet "can only deal with events of which he has first-hand knowledge," as "invention, however imaginative, is bound to be fake."[7] Jarrell, however, ignored such edicts. Jarrell's new protean poetics entailed that he wrote the majority of his war poems from the perspectives of speakers radically different from himself, which made him unique among the World War II poets.

Beyond poetic independence, Jarrell also aimed to reflect adequately the total war that had broken out all around him. In a sense Jarrell built on Walt Whitman's achievement during the Civil War, to show that "the living remain'd and suffer'd—the mother suffer'd / And the wife and the child, and the musing comrade suffer'd / And the armies that remain'd suffer'd," as Whitman wrote in "When Lilacs Last in the Dooryard Bloom'd."[8] Yet the international scope of World War II and new developments in how wars were fought, especially aerial warfare, meant that even more people around the globe were directly affected by warfare. Like Whitman, though, Jarrell aimed to create a type of democratic poetry that reflected the reality of people's daily lives, mostly as victims of forces they could neither change nor fully understand, written in a language that was immediately accessible: "It is better to have the child in the chimney-corner moved by what happens in the poem, in spite of his ignorance of its real meaning, than to have the poem a puzzle to which that meaning is the only key," Jarrell wrote—hinting at William Blake's "The Chimney Sweeper"—in *Mid-Century American Poets,* the anthology in which editor John Ciardi attempted to define Jarrell's poetic generation for the first time.[9]

"A Camp in the Prussian Forest," the poem that features an American soldier who discovers a concentration camp, serves as a good example of Jarrell's new poetics. Most war poems by poets of his generation were at least semi-autobiographical, but Jarrell took a chance to imagine how other people around the world experienced this total war.[10] Such secondhand reality allowed Jarrell to present the war from the points of view of women ("Burning the Letters" and "Second Air Force"), children ("Mother Said the Child," "The Truth," and "Protocols"), and air force crew ("Siegfried" and "A Pilot from the Carrier"), which collectively show a unique poetic portrait of the impact of that global conflict. W. D. Snodgrass's tour-de-force *The Fuehrer Bunker* (1995) contains more poems from the perspectives of other people who reflect on World War II than Jarrell ever wrote, but he focuses on the leaders of the Nazi government and their families, and his monologues are thus less broadly ranging than Jarrell's poetry.

Jarrell's poems in *Blood for a Stranger* (1942), *Little Friend, Little Friend* (1945), and *Losses* (1948); his notes and working sheets; and various published articles from that time show how he labored during the war to bring about a new kind of postmodern poetry, which influenced other poets of his generation. Dickey's jarring observation that Jarrell failed early on to write war poems that rose above the commonplace and that spoke to and about real people rather than in abstractions is correct. Yet as a poet and as a person Jarrell experienced a remarkable transformation during the war, and in his best war poems he was able (in the words of Anthony Hecht paraphrasing Matthew Arnold on William Shakespeare) "to imagine an infinite variety of humanity and to endow each with convincing life."[11]

Jarrell's transformation is especially noticeable when comparing his longest and most ambitious poem from *Blood for a Stranger,* "For an Emigrant," with his later war poems. This allegorical poem tracks, in the first part, the early life of a generic European Jew and in the second part reflects on his journey to the United States in the wake of World War II. Like his later war poem "Jews at Haifa," "For an Emigrant" shows Jarrell's interest in the fate of displaced people, but this early poem is spoken by an omniscient narrator—presumably Jarrell himself—rather than the emigrant himself. A first crucial difference between "For an Emigrant" and Jarrell's later poems is that Jarrell talks to (and in some ways talks down to) the helpless victims of historical and international disasters rather than for them. This creates a distance and a sense of superiority that prevent Jarrell from communicating the empathy that characterizes so many of his more successful war poems:

Summer is ending.
The storms plunge from the tree of winter, death
Moves like an impulse over Europe. Child,
What man is just or free?—but fortunate,
Warm in time's hand, turning and trusting to his face;
And that face changes.
Time is a man for men, and He is willing
For many a new life, for others death.[12]

Not only is the use of pathetic fallacy bothersome and the conventional metaphor of the changing seasons to indicate the dark times up ahead trite, but the tone is also decidedly paternalistic, demonstrating one of Dickey's points. Addressing the emigrant as a child while asking him a question that Jarrell knows the answer to (unlike the naive emigrant) is just the type of superior posturing that Jarrell resented in Tate's war poetry.

Other early war poems confirm Jarrell's superior air. Like "For an Emigrant," "The Head of Wisdom" (1941) shows that Jarrell is concerned about the underprivileged, the less fortunate, and the more vulnerable people of this planet, including children. "The Head of Wisdom" is an ambivalent ode to Katharine Louise Lyle Star, the daughter of Jarrell's friends, who was born on May 16, 1940, a week after the Netherlands, Belgium, Luxembourg, and Denmark fell to Nazi Germany. Similar to Weldon Kees's sinister ode "For My Daughter," Jarrell foresees a dark future for Katharine, but rather than foregrounding his compassion for this infant, Jarrell uses his poem to emphasize his Marxist point that the "State," the "King, priest, philosopher," and "the lean professors" keep the masses ignorant.[13] "The Head of Wisdom" is a far cry from the much more effective and compassionate poem "Protocols," written four years later, in which he lets the children do the talking.

A second difference between "For an Emigrant" and the later war poems is a question of scope. Jarrell's principal interest in this poem is not the fate of a specific emigrant, but rather the United States and its supposedly democratic and Christian values of freedom, innocence, and forgiveness. Throughout "For an Emigrant" Jarrell deconstructs the notion of freedom, at a time when President Roosevelt had just explained to the American public how "Four Freedoms"—the freedom of speech, the freedom of religion, the freedom from want, the freedom from fear—were at the heart of why the United States should be involved in World War II. In contrast, Jarrell lectures the emigrant that freedom is not a guarantee for happiness. Predicting the emigrant's future, Jarrell foresees that he will be "free to be homeless, to be friendless, to be nameless."[14] Jarrell also attacks America's convenient neutrality in the early 1940s and its presumed innocence by stating that "existence is guilt / enough."[15] In his powerful but highly rhetorical conclusion Jarrell negates the Christian notion of forgiveness, and he replaces it with Marx's notion of show and tell: "Forgive, forgive? Forgive no one. / Understand and blame."[16]

In hindsight Jarrell's "For an Emigrant" comes across as just as self-righteous and ill-fated as "Spain 1937," the poem by Auden that Jarrell criticized so harshly. Admonishing a stereotypical Jewish emigrant that the United States is not the promised land at a time when millions wanted to flee Nazi-occupied Europe sounds in retrospect not only pedantic but also morally dubious. Jarrell must also have realized that such examples of "rhetorical excess" and "rhetorical extravagance," as R. Clifton Spargo has called them, harmed his poetry.[17] Even before the war was over he heavily revised "For an Emigrant," replacing it with a much shorter and expunged version called "To the New World," which made it into his *Selected Poems* and *The Complete Poems*.[18] Unlike Lowell, Jarrell rarely revised his poems, which indicates what an embarrassment "For an Emigrant" must have been to him. The author's copy of *Blood for a Stranger* at the Berg Collection of the New York Public Library shows that Jarrell violently crossed out large sections of "For an Emigrant" with pen and pencil while rewriting it, especially his bold ending. Jarrell struck through all lines of the final stanza, and put a big cross through the whole stanza to boot, illustrating that he was through with the tenor of his argument.

On the last page of his copy of *Blood for a Stranger* Jarrell wrote an entirely new final stanza, which was published as the ending of "To the New World." The new ending was more benign than the end of "For an Emigrant," even though the blessings of the new continent remain ambiguous at best. Jarrell had become milder about the United States, realizing—probably through friends like the Jewish immigrant Hannah Arendt—that his home country was often welcoming to immigrants who could in turn provide a valuable contribution to American education and culture. In his new poem Jarrell sketches an American nation that looks ambivalently at foreigners, both accusatory and accepting.

Arendt was not the only influence Jarrell embraced to replace Auden and Tate; equally important were William Wordsworth, about whom Jarrell kept a notebook at Davis-Monthan Field, and war correspondent Ernie Pyle. Jarrell recognized in Pyle a kindred spirit whose compassion for ordinary soldiers he admired and emulated. Like Jarrell, Pyle was "skilled at turning their tales into miniature narratives," as James Tobin has observed.[19] Jarrell and Pyle were both outsiders because they were observers rather than active participants during this war, although Pyle went to combat zones, which also caused his death. Yet Jarrell and Pyle also thought alike about style: "You don't have to be smart-alecky or pseudo-funny," Pyle once told fellow reporters in a memo: "Be human. Try to write like people talk." Pyle's words inadvertently capture Jarrell's wartime transformation. Jarrell was "smart-alecky" and "pseudo-funny" in "For an Emigrant," but tried to become more compassionate. While he was more intellectual than Pyle, Jarrell sought to write in his "plain, transparent, but oddly personal style," to achieve the same kind of "sympathy and understanding and affection."[20] Always weary of political approaches to the war, Pyle was interested in "the unexpected human emotion in the story," as he noted in that memo before the war, and Jarrell thought that war poets should do the same.[21] Both Pyle and Wordsworth taught Jarrell to emphasize the particular rather than the general, the human story rather than the political message.

His late war poem "Jews at Haifa" (1947) is, for a number of reasons, revealing about Jarrell's changing poetics. First, like "For an Emigrant," "Jews at Haifa" is about displaced Jews, but this time the speaker is one of them rather than a superior observer. "Jews at Haifa" dramatizes the fate of the thousands of Jewish Holocaust survivors who tried to enter Palestine illegally between 1945 and 1947, but were instead put in detainment camps on Cyprus by the British government, which still had control over Palestine. Jarrell's poem had a clear political point, but it focuses on the personal experiences of a single observer who speaks directly to us. The British policy on Cyprus became an international scandal when three Jewish emigrants were killed and many more injured on board the *Exodus 1947*, after they opposed being taken to Haifa by the British navy. The navy subsequently held the refugees on board for weeks amid appalling conditions before forcing them back to Germany.[22] Jarrell seemed to have the *Exodus 1947* in mind when writing this poem. Although he does not refer explicitly to it in the published version of the poem, in a draft he writes: "The dying and the dead / Were taken from us, the ship turned, we slept / tonight, and woke a day."[23]

It is testimony to Jarrell's development that he no longer pointed his finger at a government or a state. "Jews at Haifa" is not primarily a political indictment, but rather a melancholy rumination about how people treated each other in the twentieth century. It expresses mostly a sense of disbelief that "men with our faces" are capable of such demeaning acts to other people.[24] The speaker, who watches the "hundreds at the rail" of a "freighter, gay with rust," is indeed faceless as Dickey suggested, and may be more a reflection of an attitude rather than a real person. Yet Jarrell allows us to vicariously experience the grim fate of these refugees. They are trying to convince themselves that they are still alive and that pity and compassion have not just vanished from the face of the earth:

We believe: truly, we are not dead;
It seems to us that hope
Is possible—that even mercy is permitted
To men on this earth,
To Jews on this earth . . . . But on Cyprus, the red earth,[25]

Jarrell's many caesuras in these few lines express the bewilderment of those held captive in Cyprus. Halfway between what looked like certain death in Europe and hopefully a future life in the Promised Land of Israel, they feel like "ghosts" as Jarrell wrote in a draft, as if they are hovering in limbo, a sort of purgatory.[26]

"Jews at Haifa" also shows the technical transformation Jarrell experienced during the war, a second major change. Whereas "For an Emigrant" was written in fairly regular blank verse, "Jews at Haifa" has a looser and more imaginative structure despite its six regular stanzas of six lines. The rhyme and meter are conspicuously irregular. The working sheets of this poem indicate that Jarrell was highly aware of rhyme, meter, and the length of his lines, as he occasionally scanned them or indicated the number of stresses or syllables in the margins of his text. Similar to Shapiro's style, Jarrell wanted his poems to be "irregular" to convey "a more or less conscious dramatic irony," as he wrote down in a notebook that he kept during the war.[27]

When placing "Jews at Haifa" and Jarrell's other Holocaust poems in a historical context, it becomes clear how daring and innovative Jarrell's new approach was. Jarrell wrote his Shoah poems—"A Camp in the Prussian Forest," "In the Camp There Was One Alive," "Jews at Haifa," and "Protocols"—immediately after the war, before all other poets of the English language broached this painful subject matter. Holocaust verse was scarcely written by Americans until the 1960s. Not only was Jarrell one of the few who dared to speak out, he also contributed to the development of an important genre of Holocaust poetry, which Gubar calls "proxy-witnessing." She defines it as "a way to testify for those (such as children, or animals, or the dead) who cannot testify for themselves."[28]

Jarrell's most remarkable example of proxy-witnessing is "Protocols." It is spoken by two children, illustrating Jarrell's (and, in fact, most of his contemporaries') fascination with exploring the lives of war-torn children. The siblings are taken from Odessa in what is now the Ukraine to a death camp in Poland. "Protocols" presents an eerie perspective of one of the cruelest aspects of World War II, the wanton murder of children. What distinguishes

"Jews at Haifa" from "Protocols" is that those held captive at the incarceration camps in Cyprus could have told their tales themselves. The gassed children from "Protocols," however, could not, and needed someone else to bear witness for them.

Jarrell appropriated the voices of others—even those of the dead—without any apparent moral scruples. Gubar writes that proxy-witnessing poets "often acknowledge their belated dependence on after-the-fact accounts of extremities never within their purview" to "avoid any confusion between victims in the vulnerability of 'then' and poets or readers in the safety of 'now.'" This does not apply to Jarrell.[29] As Shakespeare did with his plays, Jarrell used whatever historical evidence was available to him to shape his war poems. He did not make known his sources when endowing his stories "with convincing life," and it appears that he was not heavily dependent on those sources either. Other poets who would write about the Shoah, such as John Ciardi, Anthony Hecht, and Charles Reznikoff, depended more on exterior sources than on their imagination, and were more anxious about the authority and sensitivities involved when assuming the voices of others.

The Holocaust poetry of Ciardi, Hecht, and Reznikoff leans more to "documentary verse," as Gubar has categorized it.[30] Reznikoff's volume *Holocaust* (1975) consists, for instance, entirely of quotations from actual testimonies made by prisoners, while Hecht's "The Book of Yolek" and "More Light! More Light!" adopt stories of Holocaust victims, although he does not quote from them literally. Both poets condense the real accounts, remove the contextual framework, and directly mold them into poems before offering them to the reader. Hecht has a tendency to be verbose and intellectual, but in these poems he relates the events as simply and factually as he can.

In "More Light! More Light!" Hecht relates a brutal incident based on a passage from *The Theory and Practice of Hell,* by Eugen Kogan, a survivor of the Buchenwald concentration camp, involving two Jews and one non-Jewish Pole. They are ordered to dig a hole, which will be their own grave. When the hole is big enough, the Jews are asked to lie in it. The Polish man is told to bury the two Jews alive by piling sand on them. When the Pole refuses, presumably out of moral compunction, the executioner cynically tells them to change places as punishment for the Pole's insolence. In the end, all three die. Hecht's diction is deliberately lucid, stark, and almost purely descriptive when depicting this gruesome scene. Like Jarrell, Hecht attempts to let the reader face the facts as directly as possible within the linguistic confines of the genre of poetry. "We move now to outside a German wood," Hecht writes in "More Light! More Light!" taking the reader by the hand before illuminating this one horrific event that encapsulates the horror of Nazi Germany's cruelty.[31]

In his virtuosic sestina "The Book of Yolek," Hecht succeeds perhaps even better in relating the fate of the individual victim of the Holocaust. Hecht's speaker initially treats us to either his or the imagined reader's childhood memory of a summer camp before shockingly connecting it to a forgotten victim of World War II. Hecht uses various denotations and connotations of the six repeated words that a sestina requires to involve the reader directly in his half-imagined and half-factual account of Yolek, an orphan who was taken from "The Home / For Jewish Children" to quite another camp. Hecht uses the form of the sestina so perfectly and unexpectedly that Jarrell's unadulterated praise of Auden comes to mind: "He is thoroughly old-fashioned in his ability to write to order, in his ability to do exactly what this particular work calls for *just here*. . . . (My hearers may feel: 'But what work ever demanded such a sestina as this?' Well, Auden's works often do.)"[32]

And so does Hecht's sestina. Hecht has related how he found Yolek's name in Hanna Mortkowicz-Olczakowa's narrative of the Polish educator Yanosz Korczak, who was head of an orphanage and "refused to part from them, and went with them to their deaths."[33] Hecht endows Yolek with a life after his relatively anonymous death, and imposes that life on the reader:

Whether on a silent, solitary walk
Or among crowds, far off or safe at home,
You will remember, helplessly, that day,
And the smell of smoke, and the loudspeakers of the camp
Wherever you are, Yolek will be there, too.
His unuttered name will interrupt your meal.

Prepare to receive him in your home some day.
Though they killed him in the camp they sent him to.
He will walk in as you're sitting down to a meal.[34]

"The Book of Yolek" has the same powerful and haunting quality as Jarrell's "Protocols" and "The Death of the Ball Turret Gunner," even though, unlike Jarrell, Hecht does not speak *as* those victims, but *for* one of them. It is a pity that "The Book of Yolek" is often left out of anthologies of war poetry because it certainly is one of the most outstanding war poems of World War II, and not just because of Hecht's dexterity.[35] Yolek's startling presence at the dinner table will make a deep and lasting impression on many contemporary readers, bringing home the long-gone war quite literally.

Hecht confirmed how concerned he was about the issue of ethics and appropriation in war poetry in a letter to the editor of *Poetry* magazine in 2003, a year before his death. While acknowledging the contributions made, in prose and poetry, by noncombatants like Stephen Crane, Emily Dickinson,

Thomas Hardy, A. E. Housman, Andrew Marvell, Herman Melville, William Shakespeare, Walt Whitman, and W. B. Yeats, Hecht ventured: "Some experiences are so devastating or traumatizing that we feel they ought to be spoken by those who have experienced them first hand, who have earned the right to speak by the forfeiture of enormous suffering; and that anyone else is simply exploiting their horror for personal literary advantage."[36]

Hecht does not explicitly mention which "experiences" he considers off limits. Yet since he mentions Sylvia Plath as someone who transgresses the boundaries of propriety in "Daddy" and excuses James Dickey's milder peccadillo of lying or exaggerating about his war record in his poetry, it appears that Hecht believes that the Holocaust is taboo for those who have not witnessed the events themselves. Having been among the American soldiers who discovered a concentration camp, Hecht grants himself a bit more authority to speak for the victims. "The Book of Yolek" indicates how far he allows himself to go. Considering Jarrell's reputation as the foremost American poet of World War II and his poems about the Holocaust, it is remarkable that Hecht does not mention Jarrell, who, after all, transgresses a similar imaginary boundary as Plath, though he does not use Jewish suffering as background to illustrate his own personal problems, while Plath does.

Among John Ciardi's papers at the Library of Congress, there is one unpublished holograph poem, the remarkable and strange poem called "Sarko." Ciardi speaks as and for a Holocaust survivor in this poem.[37] Sarko remembers that those in the death camp who volunteered "to dig the graves / Were given a can of sardines." Those who brazenly rushed to volunteer, though, were "clubbed / For disorderliness." Nicknamed "Szardina" by the guards, Sarko survives, partly because he digs graves diligently and partly because the guards "bet on how long" he will "last." Yet his shameful but provoked contribution to the demise of his fellow inmates continues to haunt him. Spiritually he considers himself already dead: "for the grave I have always been in."[38] Like "More Light! More Light!" "Sarko" is a moving and complex poem about the Holocaust, espousing different conflicting emotions. It looks finished, but Ciardi nevertheless chose not to publish it, begging the question why he censored himself. It is possible that, unlike Jarrell, he felt a moral compunction about writing about such tragic events he had not witnessed firsthand, but there is no definitive proof for this.

Even though Jarrell's Holocaust poems are historically significant, it is important that they are part of a series of war poems in which Jarrell viewed the total war of World War II from every conceivable angle. War was no longer "a matter for the feudal ruling class or a small group of professionals, but one for the people as a whole," as historian Michael Howard has argued about wars in the twentieth century.[39] Jarrell's war poetry reflects this new fact. Equally remarkable as his Holocaust poems are his two war poems from the perspectives of women, "Burning the Letters" and "Second Air Force." Like the victims of the Holocaust, these imaginary women were physically and mentally far removed from this stateside instructor of air cadets. It is one of the remarkable features of Jarrell's career and testimony to his self-proclaimed "semifeminine mind" that some of his most successful poems were spoken by women.[40]

In the interior monologue "Burning the Letters" the anger of the wife of a pilot killed in the Pacific mixes with acquiescence and is credible and moving. Note the "talky stuttery style," as Stephen Burt has called Jarrell's vernacular phrasings:[41]

> Here in my head, the home that is left for you
> You have not changed; the flames rise from the sea
> And the sea changes: the carrier, torn in two,
> Sinks to its planes—the corpses of the carrier
> Are strewn like ashes on the star-reflecting sea;
> Are gathered, sewn with weights, are sunk.
> The gatherers disperse.[42]

The imagery of burning connects the two related narratives of the woman burning the pilot's letters and the pilot dying in the flames of his plane's crash. The woman's mind is "the home that is left for" the pilot. He has no proper grave, as he was cremated alive instantaneously, with his remains scattered over the Pacific Ocean. The pilot only dwells in her memory and in her imagination. While her head is full of Christian imagery, she can no longer be a true believer, as Jarrell indicates in a note that precedes the poem. As colloquial as Pyle and as particular as Wordsworth, Jarrell's miniature narrative reflects an unexplored, human side of war. In cultures of war where the suffering of men tends to be foregrounded and the suffering of women takes the backseat, "Second Air Force" and "Burning the Letters" are extraordinary poems.

Jarrell's poetic cross-gender identification in war poems is rare but not unique. Walt Whitman did it in his Civil War poem "Come up from the Fields Father," where he focuses on a mourning mother, and more cursorily elsewhere.[43] Robert Frost did it in "Not to Keep" about World War I. In her interior monologue "Negro Hero" and in part of her sonnet sequence "Gay Chaps at the Bar," Gwendolyn Brooks speaks for African American men caught in World War II in the way that Jarrell speaks for white women who are affected by that war. "Few literary women besides Gwendolyn Brooks took on the persona of a male soldier in order to write Second World War poetry," as Susan Schweik has claimed, and Brooks was at least as audacious as Jarrell in imagining and voicing the thoughts and feelings of others.[44] Whereas Jarrell's empathetic identification seems mostly focused on exposing how everyone suffers in war, Brooks engages more fully in issues of racial and gender difference.

Despite this dissimilarity, however, Brooks's poems about World War II also share remarkable similarities with the male war poets. Many critics have rightfully emphasized how Brooks's two war poems give a voice to the marginalized African American soldier and that the importance of these poems mainly resides in their treatment of race—for instance, in the sonnet "the white troops had their order / but the Negroes looked like men" of "Gay Chaps at the Bar." Part of Brooks's objective is "to present the injustices of the Black warriors' situation, and reasonable doubts about what they might be fighting for," as Henry Taylor suggests.[45] Both poems center on the conflicted national and racial identities these African American soldiers feel in a desegregated American army. Yet Brooks's poems also echo many of the male soldier-poets' anxieties about their identity, masculinity, and future lives after the war, showing her keen awareness of how the pressures of World War II affected American men in general, regardless of color. Brooks's and Jarrell's willingness and ability to understand the Other during a war are especially praiseworthy because war always accentuates the differences between the sexes, as Paul Fussell has written.[46]

It would be cynical to say of Jarrell or Brooks that they exploited the "horror" of others "for personal literary advantage" as Hecht said of Plath, even though Jarrell was fiercely competitive at this point in his career. What he aimed for was something that he claimed Pyle had achieved in his famous column "Beloved Captain": to create the illusion "that we are no longer separated from the actual event by anything at all," to make believe that we are experiencing the tragedies of war firsthand. According to Jarrell, Pyle's empathy with the American soldiers went so far that he became "unconscious of himself" and arrived at "a steady humility and self-forgetfulness."[47] Jarrell was also trying to achieve this. He wrote his war poetry "as if in spite of himself," as Hayden Carruth has suggested.[48] As Dickey's more gentle self, who has the last word about Jarrell in his remarkable dialogue, admits, Jarrell ultimately achieved what Pyle had also done: "He gives you, as all great or good writers do, a foothold in a realm where literature itself is inessential." Jarrell gives us "humanity in the twentieth century."[49]

Jarrell's peers agreed with Dickey's voice A and suggested that Jarrell was the greatest war poet of their generation. Carruth praised Jarrell for describing "the suffering of all its victims, Americans, Germans, Japanese—Jarrell wrote it down with equal understanding, equal sympathy. And he wrote it then, there, at that time and in those places, with power, spontaneity, and perfect conviction."[50] In "From the Tombs to Danbury," an excised part of what became "Memories of West Street and Lepke," Lowell asserted something similar. Reminiscing about his ride in a police car with two Puerto

Rican draft dodgers to the Connecticut prison where he would be held for refusing to serve in the army, Lowell thinks of Jarrell and asserts that it was he who wrote about and understood the essence of World War II:

> your verse
> Shows us for mirrors of ourselves: the child,
> The Jew, the kenneled German and that mild
> And open-handed bomber in his void
> Of vision—the destroyer, the destroyed.[51]

Jarrell's self-effacing invention of overlooked war victims and his audacity to endow them with convincing life seem the opposite of the more self-obsessed struggle of Lowell and Shapiro to become Catholics during the war. Yet the actions of these poets are essentially different manifestations of the same emotion. The army and war threatened their sense of personal self and forced them into a straitjacket of normalized and uniformed behavior. Unlike earlier American war poets from the twentieth century—for instance, Alan Seeger and Edwin Rolfe—they did not revel in the joys of "high fellowship" or "comradeship" with other soldiers, but mourned the loss of their individuality.[52] They mostly accepted the hegemonic wartime norms and dolefully waited until the nightmare was over, as Ciardi, Hecht, and Nemerov did. Yet they also responded by vicariously escaping from that pressure and adopting different selves, in real life, as Lowell and Shapiro did, or in their poetry, as Jarrell did. Shapiro, in fact, continually wavered back and forth between his personal self and his propagandized GI Joe self. His struggle with various emerging selves was more extreme than that of others, but represents the tensions that all of them experienced.

The one aspect of their identity that was most violently thrown into disarray, however, was their sense of manhood. From boyhood onward they knew the age-old expectations of how men should react to war. It was supposed to be the maturing crown of masculine experience, but they had also learned from the disillusionment of Herman Melville, Wilfred Owen, and W. H. Auden. "All wars are boyish," Melville had written during the time of the Civil War, "but we are old" Lowell realized in his World War II poem "Christmas Eve under Hooker's Statue."[53] How did the poets of World War II respond to this ancient test of manhood when they were no longer so naive and young to understand that the test was really a fiction, a fabrication, "another lie about our life," as Nemerov would write in "To Clio, Muse of History"?[54]

PART

[3]

CONFUSED MASCULINITIES

CHAPTER 9

James Dickey's Hypermasculinity

In the summer of 1958, thirteen years after the war, James Dickey published a poem titled "Joel Cahill Dead" in the *Beloit Poetry Journal.* It was a short but moving lyric about an air force cadet who crashes his plane near a farm and succumbs to his injuries in the farmer's house. Reminiscent of Randall Jarrell's "Losses," which cites similar training accidents, the poem was partly based on a real-life event in 1943. Dickey experienced a ruinous landing in aviation school in Camden, South Carolina, and "expected St. Peter to greet [him] at the Pearly Gates."[1] He survived the near crash, but in his poem "Joel Cahill Dead" he imagines the sights and sounds as well as the emotions of the bystanders when a cadet actually crashes his plane and dies. The drafts for the poem "equate Dickey and Joel more obviously" than the published version of the poem itself, as Henry Hart has indicated.[2] Dickey initially focused on Joel Cahill on "his first solo flight," singing and laughing to ward off his fears, while his fellow cadets watch how he disappears from the sky.[3] Later drafts shift the perspective to the farmer and his wife, making Joel and his crash more mysterious.

Dickey never republished "Joel Cahill Dead." He held on to the idea of the young air force cadet crashing, however, and worked it into his plans for a novel, which he started to write in the early 1970s right after finishing his best seller *Deliverance.* The novel became Dickey's sprawling but critically and commercially unsuccessful *Alnilam* (1987) about a blind, middle-aged man, Frank Cahill, in search of his son, Joel. Like the character in the poem, Joel had crashed his plane. Yet instead of dying in the farmer's house, he flees from the farm and disappears. Frank Cahill, who had been estranged from his son, discovers that Joel had been an enigmatic ringleader for a cultish group of cadets at his air force base in Peckover, North Carolina, who were antiauthoritarian and antimachine. A charismatic cadet in life, Joel Cahill becomes a mythical hero in death, sharing more with Jesus Christ than just his initials. Whereas the Joel from the poem is a regrettable casualty of a war whose life has not even started properly, the Joel of the novel is a dauntless and hypermasculine superhero whose legend will never die.

"Joel Cahill Dead" and *Alnilam* are representative of all of Dickey's war poetry and war novels. It is remarkable that the protagonists of Dickey's poetry reflect more sensitively and truthfully the emotions that Dickey must have felt during World War II, while the novels present protagonists who are like the public persona that Dickey tried to invent: the hypermasculine male, the "all American heterosexual superman," as Hart has called that persona.[4] Unlike the other poets of World War II, Dickey bragged about his war record in interviews and often heroicized acts of war in his prose. Like Ernest Hemingway and William Faulkner had done before him, Dickey changed his military experience into a heroic myth. Dickey, for instance, claimed in interviews that he was a pilot rather than a radar observer, that he had crashed down in the Pacific Ocean, and that he had flown over Nagasaki when the second nuclear bomb was dropped, none of which was true. The mere fact of Dickey's prevarication is less interesting than the psychological reasons behind his lies and what it tells us about the genres of war poetry and prose. Each of these media partly conditioned his act of representing war. For Dickey, the genre of war poetry lent itself more easily to truthful introspection than the genre of the war novel, which allowed him to fantasize.

Dickey published more than two dozen war poems, but wrote several dozen more that he never chose to show to the world. Two of the three novels Dickey published during his lifetime, *Alnilam* and *To the White Sea* (1993), are set during World War II.[5] Like Joel Cahill in *Alnilam*, Sergeant Muldrow, the hero of *To the White Sea*, is an intrepid and skillful airman, much admired by his peers. A day before the Tokyo firebombing starts on March 10, 1943, this tail gunner is forced to parachute from his burning B-29 to land in the enemy's capital. While hundreds of B-29s unleashed thousands of tons of explosives over Tokyo, Muldrow starts his journey from Honshu to Japan's arctic, northern island of Hokkaido, killing twelve Japanese along the way. Born in a log cabin and "raised in the wilderness of Alaska," Muldrow is "a frontier American," as Dickey jotted down in his notes for *To the White Sea*, not unlike Daniel Boone and the fictional Natty Bumppo in James Fenimore Cooper's *The Pioneers*.[6] Muldrow's physical strength and bravery, heterosexuality, suppression of vulnerable emotions, independence, and control over other men make him a prime example of hegemonic masculinity or even hypermasculinity.

Most of these characteristics are established when Dickey juxtaposes Muldrow with other, more marginal characters in *To the White Sea*. Since Muldrow is a loner and does not speak Japanese, such opportunities are rare, but

Dickey seizes them all to establish Muldrow's superiority. When preparing for a mission early in the novel, for instance, Muldrow meets two rookie replacements who react hostilely when he offers them some friendly advice. Muldrow subsequently challenges the gruffest one to a pull-up contest to prove "that I'm stronger than you are."[7] The more experienced Alaskan tailgunner wins easily, which causes the rookies' aggression to make way for admiration, especially when they hear that Muldrow has shot seven Japanese planes from the sky. It does not bother him to kill other people, he confidently charges: "That's what I'm here for."[8]

Later in the novel Muldrow has an odd chance encounter with an American Buddhist monk who has lived in Japan since 1939. The effeminate monk, who keeps touching the tailgunner, is the opposite of manly Muldrow. Dickey wrote in his notes to the novel that there should be "a suspicion that the American monk is homosexual, but this must not be emphasized."[9] Muldrow is intrigued by the monk's philosophizing about dreams, time, and nothingness and lets his "ever-present guard down."[10] The monk offers him a place to sleep, which Muldrow accepts, but when he wakes up he has been betrayed by the monk, and he is being held captive by the Japanese army. The monk may think he is beyond time and politics, but plays the game all the same. Muldrow miraculously overcomes the Japanese guards, however, killing all of them.

During his voyage through Japan, Muldrow proves that he has the physical courage, endurance, strength, and skill of the true warrior, traits that have traditionally been "central component[s] of manhood, forged by male initiation rites worldwide."[11] But Dickey's manifestation of Muldrow's masculinity is so exaggerated and exalted at times that he becomes a caricature rather than a character. As Nelson Hathcock has mentioned, Muldrow's solitary campaign against the enemy seems remarkably similar to Sylvester Stallone's Rambo, the hero of a blockbuster movie trilogy in the 1980s.[12] Hathcock sees in Muldrow's solitary and heroic adventures a return to a typical American war story that had become almost anachronistic after World War II. *To the White Sea* relishes in "a purer field of battle on which one can feel the dying breath of one's enemy," Hathcock mentions.[13] Yet, as Anthony Hecht wrote in his monograph about Auden, "modern warfare" had made "such confrontations virtually impossible."[14] Dickey was the only poet of his generation who kept hankering after the ideal of the warrior hero.

Frank and Joel Cahill in *Alnilam* are only slightly less hypermasculine than Muldrow. Despite being middle-aged and blind, Frank Cahill is sexually aggressive toward the few women near the Peckover air force base, and he likes to impress other men by arm wrestling or bragging about how much he can bench-press. Like Muldrow, Cahill is a lone hero: "I don't need nobody but myself."[15] His son, Joel, is more social and mysterious than either

Cahill or Muldrow. He is idolized by his peers and highly regarded by, if not the envy of, his instructors. Civilian Instructor McClintock McCaig, for example, is one of many who regarded Joel as a future fighter-pilot ace and was clearly in awe of him: "He looked like he belonged there, doin' what he was doin'. He just went right with it. He could'a been in a Spitfire in North Africa, with fifteen thousand hours behind him. I was interested in him right off, because he had a good chance of ending up in combat."[16] An adroit daredevil in the sky, Joel acted out the fantasies that many boys, such as Ciardi, Dickey, and Nemerov, had growing up in the 1920s and 1930s, inspired by the legendary pilots of the First World War.

Yet Joel was more than just a talented cadet. Lieutenant Spigner observed that he was "full of some strange kind of enthusiasm, some kind of energy."[17] Joel was, unlike Muldrow, also precocious, widely read, and fascinated by numerology, astronomy, and celestial navigation. Joel was "able to formulate these weird, strange, provocative, evocative notions," Dickey explained in an interview with Ernest Suarez, and those ideas seize the interest of other young men at the air force base.[18] Dickey inserted these obscure and puzzling concepts more or less randomly into his novel: "Aim for aphorisms: the half-wisdom, half nonsense of Ern Malley," Dickey wrote in his notes, referring to the greatest literary hoax of the twentieth century.[19] Concocted by two Australian soldiers who tried to expose modernist poetry, Malley was a fictitious poet who had allegedly died and left a body of work. Some of the verse was published in respected journals.

After his crash and mysterious disappearance, Joel's followers are resolved to carry out his vague ideas and plans. Applying Joel's cryptic diary—which states that "when the father comes, Orion will leap free"—they intend to destroy all aircraft at the Peckover air force base when Frank Cahill is present and when the stars are in a particular alignment.[20] Joel's disciples do not completely understand him, but his mastery in the air combined with his "own masculine mystique" played upon "the insecurities of young men not so talented as himself," as Casey Clabough has suggested.[21] It makes them look up to Joel as their leader, even after his disappearance and presumed death. Like Muldrow, Joel is larger than life, a fearless superhero.

Joel is also a tragic, legendary figure—much like Hemingway's carefree, reckless heroes—whose promises are nipped in the bud. In the interview with Suarez, Dickey compared Joel's appeal to "Alexander the Great, Caesar, Frederick II, Napoleon, Hitler, [and] John F. Kennedy," who all satisfied "some deep hunger in people that somebody has got hold of a truth and a way of life that they themselves cannot command."[22] None of the other poets of World War II shared Dickey's need to explore or venerate hypermasculine warriors such as Muldrow, or intrepid heroic leaders such as Joel Cahill. Robert Lowell was from childhood onward intrigued by strong leaders such as Caesar, Napoleon, Hitler, and later Kennedy, especially during Lowell's manic phases, but Dickey never grew out of his fixation.

Like Dickey, John Ciardi had "dreams of being a pilot," as he admitted to Studs Terkel in *"The Good War."*[23] So did Howard Nemerov, who succeeded in becoming a fighter pilot where Dickey had failed. Dickey maintained to Nemerov that he, too, had been a pilot instead of a radar observer, and on occasion they shared stories about their flying days in the war.[24] Nemerov could not stomach the prose and characters of *Alnilam,* however, who talked and acted "like he-man," as he jotted down in a note to novelist Mary Hood.[25] Fresh out of the army, Karl Shapiro wrote a poem with that very title. Shapiro published "He-Man" in the *New Yorker,* but the poem was never reprinted. In his sharply ironic style that is so characteristic of his early poetry, Shapiro exposes the hypermasculine type in a series of quick, vivid images:

> The whiskey shivers when he laughs, the lion
> Speeding toward him crashes at his feet,
> A perfect rug. He is the world's Orion
> Who shoots to prove virility in sport,
> In war, in literature, in love. Complete
> With beard he yachts into the cheering port.[26]

While many poets of his generation had grown weary of the supermasculine man, however, Dickey continued to admire this type and sought to recreate him in his prose.

Both Muldrow and Joel Cahill exhibit traditional traits of militarized masculinity, despite their differences. They show courage, strength, and hardness. Yet they are too rebellious and headstrong to accept "the collectivist masculinity of World War II," to use Joshua S. Goldstein's phrase, which was "based on teamwork and self-sacrifice."[27] They are too autonomous for the army—which confines soldiers' independence and checks individual freedom—and therefore they both break away from it. As one of *Alnilam*'s characters, Whitehall, paradoxically says of Joel: "military life was not for him, though. It was not military enough."[28] In their ultimate rejection of army culture, Dickey presents hypermasculine heroes who belong to "a peculiarly post-Vietnam, pre–Gulf War type of American militarized male."[29] Joel Cahill is not unlike Lieutenant Pete Mitchell (Tom Cruise) in *Top Gun* (1986), while Muldrow is not much different from John J. Rambo (Sylvester Stallone) in the *First Blood–Rambo* trilogy (1982–1988), all prototypes of this particular type of manhood.

In terms of masculinity, the contrast between Dickey's war prose and his war poetry is striking, however. His war poems present more vulnerable males who disclose their uncertainties and anxieties more freely—for instance, in

"Joel Cahill Dead," "Two Poems of Flight Sleep," and "The Wedding." Joel Cahill of the poetry drafts and his namesake, the novel's hero, illustrate the distinction between the two types of masculinity perfectly. Whereas the Joel Cahill of *Alnilam* is an audacious and masterful pilot, the Joel Cahill of the poem is so afraid during his first solo flight and moments before his tragic crash that "in the core of panic" he laughs and sings out loud in an attempt to assuage his fears.[30] The first part of "Two Poems of Flight-Sleep," "Camden Town" (1970), shows an equally nervous cadet on a solo flight in a Stearman. This young man does not crash his plane, but wants "to (get away) escape // From the Air Force," as Dickey penned in a note on the typescript of the fair copy of this poem.[31] Taking off in the Stearman feels "like stealing two hundred and twenty horses / Of escape from the Air Corps," Dickey says referring to the plane's horsepower.[32]

"Camden Town" is all about gaining and losing control. At first the cadet seems to be in command:

The altimeter made me
At six thousand feet. We were stable: myself, the plane,
The earth everywhere
Small in its things with cold
But vast beneath.[33]

The young airman tries to stabilize the plane and himself, but realizes that things are happening outside of his influence. Dickey has a distinct style—unique among the middle generation poets—of using the full width of the page and sporadic empty spaces. They function as caesuras, creating in the reader an uneasy sensation that mirrors the pilot's nervousness. All of a sudden "a banner like World War One" tears at the cadet's head, which he tries to remove from his helmet.[34] This streamer is probably an actual relic from the previous war, but it is also a metaphor. The collective memory of the First World War makes the pilot aware of his slim chances of surviving the war now that he is "in Death's baby machine, that led to the fighters and bombers."[35] In *Alnilam* Dickey would also use this powerful image of "Death's baby machine" to describe the Stearman, which guides the trainee airmen to the real, murderous warplanes, the nightmare fighters.

Dickey's cadet in "Camden Town" tries to flee "the war," "the Cadet Program," and his "peanut-faced Instructor and his maps."[36] Several critics have correctly interpreted the recruit's westward flight as a variation on Sigmund Freud's death wish. Dickey's Freudian themes in "Camden Town" establish once again how influential Freudian theory was for this generation of war poets. According to Ronald Baughman, flying to the west is "an image of peaceful death," while Henry Hart takes the pilot's "fetal position" to mean that the cadet is reduced "to a trembling infant in the cockpit" who wants to return to (the womb) from where he came, like Jarrell's ball turret gunner.[37]

Dickey also intersperses the cadet's flight with images of the mythology of the West, however. This young man goes west to escape authority and is lighting out for the territory, as many have done before him. Escaping the war, as Dickey's speaker attempts to do, is not a manly thing to do, but it is a natural emotion, as any sane human being confronted with the possibility of battle "instinctually wants to run away, or hunker down and freeze up," as Joshua S. Goldstein has argued.[38] At the end of the poem the cadet swings east and returns to his base, despite his urge for freedom or his fear of what might happen in the war. Yet "Camden Town" does not glorify flight or celebrate the imperviousness of a male hero, but emphasizes rather the trainee's loneliness and uncertainties.

The airman's anguish is also explored in "The Wedding" (1960), which is representative of a more anecdotal war poem that Dickey wrote but did not frequently publish. At the heart of such accessible and descriptive poems—a type of poem that Ciardi and Nemerov also frequently wrote—is a seemingly trifling war incident or story. These accounts, often autobiographical in nature, offer insights into aspects of war that are seldom related in other media. Yet Ciardi's and Nemerov's autobiographical poems are usually more self-ironic, whereas Dickey's war poems are more lyrically and emotionally charged. "The Wedding," for instance, focuses on the art, craft, and handiwork that the aircrew engage in while they are not flying. One airman is sewing "a tiger's gold head" onto "the scarred leather breast of his jacket," while another is pounding a silver "Dutch coin" into "a ring for his wife."[39] The story is told in hindsight, and Dickey's speaker, a veteran himself, recollects these activities with affection. It moves him that "during that long time, in those places," airmen were trying to make "good before the dark missions."[40] It is remarkable that the activities that these hardened men are occupied with counter the stereotypes of militarized masculinity. Sewing a shirt is considered a woman's job, while making a ring is a romantic gesture that is untypical for a rough, tough soldier. It fits the pattern of Dickey's war poetry, however, that his protagonists are more gentle and sensitive than Muldrow and Joel Cahill, the protagonists of his prose.

"The Wedding" borders on the sentimentally patriotic. In the sixth stanza Dickey says: "All of them turn into heroes," and he is glad that "they are / to history also, / Heroes as well."[41] The poem itself does not prove this, and just stating a patriotic claim so blatantly does not mean the reader will accept it either. Other parts of the poem are more convincing, however. The airmen fly their mission with

their silver rings upon
Their gloved, sprung little fingers,
So precious had they become,
So full of the thought of their wives
That the scratched, tired, beaten-out shining
Was more
Humanly constant
Than they.[42]

This is an unexpectedly tender image that Dickey presents to his readers. The makeshift, improvisatory rings are "more / Humanly constant," Dickey suggests, than the soldiers themselves. The ring reflects a more human and humane side of the aircrew than they can really afford to show during a war.

When Dickey's war poems do occasionally feature hypermasculine males, he usually undercuts their invulnerability, or presents their idealized masculine image as a pose. "The Baggage King" and "The Performance" are good examples of Dickey's more ambivalent stance toward the unflinching and indomitable American military man. Like "The Wedding," "The Baggage King" is an anecdotal war poem in which a veteran is reminiscing about the war. The memory involves a freighter dropping soldiers as well as their luggage, in all forms and sizes, on New Guinea. The large variety of baggage reflects the diversity of boys and men that land on New Guinea. These "recruits, / The never-failing replacements" are young and naive and have no idea of what will happen to them.[43] The fact that replacements are necessary suggests that many soldiers have probably died or are severely injured, as personified by the trucks that come to collect the troops, which are "moaning like the wounded."[44]

Dickey's speaker in "The Baggage King" is too fresh, hardheaded, and boisterously optimistic to fully realize this yet. At first he seems slightly distressed that his luggage with his personal belongings will get lost or crushed. The weight of the luggage makes the pile sink on the beach, a disconcerting image that appears to the speaker "like the hill of a dead king / Beleaguered by mosquitoes and flies / Losing their way in the dark."[45] The king is dead, long live the king, Dickey's immature speaker thinks, and he starts climbing on top of the pile. It is a highly meaningful act. First, it reflects a juvenile playfulness normally expected of children, but not of serious and dedicated soldiers who are sent to get a job done. Second, it suggests his misapprehension that he will somehow sidestep or overcome the misery and mishap that have befallen his predecessors on these beaches. The diction describing the soldier's climb onto the mound is tinged with irony at the arrogance of youth:

And not caring, not at all,
But only knowing that I was there,
Drenched in sweat, my shirt open down to my balls,
Nineteen years old, commanding the beach
Where life and death had striven, but safe
At the top of the heap, in the dark
Where no lights came through
From the water, and nothing yet struck.[46]

By commenting on his cocksure younger self, the speaker signals a significant gap between him and the boyish soldier he used to be. The wise older man mocks the youthful naïveté of his previous self and his glorious, boyish fantasy of "commanding the beach."

Even though Dickey's war poems proffer a less hypermasculine militarized male than his war novels, the speakers of his poems nevertheless feel compelled to glorify either themselves or their fellow soldiers, as "The Wedding" and "The Baggage King" show. Dickey's assertion in "The Wedding" that the airmen "are / to history also, / Heroes" is an attempt to valorize their actions as courageous and gallant, while the nineteen-year-old replacement in "The Baggage King" also needs to assert himself as a paragon of force and fearlessness by climbing on the luggage mound. Also in this sense, Dickey was an exception among the poets of his generation. The poets of World War II, in particular Jarrell and Nemerov, followed the general pattern of twentieth-century war poetry "looking to dismantle glory," as Lorrie Goldensohn has indicated.[47] Dickey harks back to what Goldensohn has described as "earlier positions, the persistent eruption on modern poems of old styles of sensation and focus, assenting not only to war's necessity, but to its terrible grandeurs."[48] The focus and setting of Dickey's poems are usually vivid and original in their indirect approach to the war—focusing on a makeshift ring or a heap of luggage—but the tendency to celebrate "terrible grandeurs" is undeniably present.

One of Dickey's best-known war poems, his powerfully evocative "The Performance" (1959) about a pilot, Donald Armstrong, who is captured by the Japanese and decapitated, confirms this urge to glorify. The beheading, which is loosely based on an actual occurrence in the Pacific theater and which also surfaces in *To the White Sea,* made a lasting impression on the poet. Dickey changed significant details about the incident, both for poetic effect and because he sought to mythologize the event, creating "a parallel of fanciful alternative," as Goldensohn calls it.[49] It was not pilot Donald Armstrong who was murdered by his Japanese captors, as Hart has shown, but his radar observer, James J. Lally. Armstrong had died instantly when their plane crashed.[50] Like Joel Cahill, Armstrong was "a risk-taking, fun-loving man," and someone "who had succeeded where Dickey had failed; he had become a pilot."[51] Dickey "idolized" Armstrong in the same way that the speaker of "The Performance" does.[52]

In the final two stanzas of the poem the speaker conjures up an image of what he thinks or wants to think happened just before Armstrong was beheaded. He fantasizes that Armstrong tried to amuse or distract his captors by standing on his hands, as Dickey himself was apt to do, showing off his athletic body and his strong forearms, just as Muldrow does in *To the White Sea.* Armstrong's fellow airman then fancies, even more implausibly, that "the headsman" who is about to decapitate Armstrong "broke down / In a blaze of tears" because of Armstrong's act.[53] The executioner proposes to cut off Armstrong's feet instead of his head, but Armstrong declines the offer and nobly "knelt down in himself" and accepts his full punishment.[54] Dickey's speaker thus transforms Armstrong's ignominious death into a heroic and honorable act. Dickey refuses to see Armstrong as a victim, but presents him as someone who controlled his own destiny until the bitter end.

The admiration for Armstrong's manly physique as expressed in "The Performance" may have homosexual overtones, but it expresses even more Dickey's illusory belief in the infallibility and perfection of the American male body. During World War II the American government, military, and general populace were ardent to present "powerful, hypermasculinized male bodies in public images," as Christina S. Jarvis has argued, because they reflected "the United States' rising status as a world power."[55] Dickey was equally captivated by the ideal male body, as is evident from *To the White Sea* and the second part of his unpublished "Two Poems on the Survival of the Male Body," entitled "For Jules Bacon." The sprawling poem of fourteen pages is dedicated and addressed to bodybuilder Jules Bacon, who became Mr. America in 1943 and who was featured three times on the cover of *Strength and Health* between 1941 and 1944. Dickey picked up the magazines while stationed in the Pacific. Bacon "saved my life," Dickey wrote dramatically.[56]

"For Jules Bacon" explains why Dickey was so fixated on the male body during the war. Moreover it helps us to understand the psychological reasons Dickey was so attracted to hypermasculine superheroes, and sometimes pretended that he was one himself. The pictures of Jules Bacon in *Strength and Health* provided Dickey with a model of physical perfection, which in turn provided a sense of purpose during the boring breaks in between missions. Around this time Dickey began to show "a fondness for the beautiful male body by manicuring his face and toning his biceps," to quote Hart.[57] Yet fine-tuning his own body also had a talismanic function for him, as Bacon "would help [Dickey] get the body that would rise / And live that would outlive / The night . . . ."[58] A body like Jules Bacon's would exert a protective influence over the owner, or so Dickey believed.

There is something naive and childish about Dickey's conviction that a perfect body would save him from harm. In fact, it seems to have been taken straight from the comic book *Superman* that was becoming increasingly popular at the time. Jarvis's argument that wartime "representations of the American male body were not directly rooted in the classical Greek tradition, but in the more contemporary ideals of bodybuilding, 1930s representations of brawny workers, and, most especially, comic book superheroes" supports such a reading.[59] Yet airmen often had "to play tricks with [themselves] to keep going," as John Ciardi admitted in his war diary *Saipan:* "It produces all sorts of rationalization, and plain intellectual dishonesty."[60] Dickey assures us that his fellow airmen were not weirded out by his narcissistic bodybuilding:

Nobody thought anything
Of it Jules; everyone (body) in the squadron was insane (crazy)
For survival; everyone had his own guarantee
For life, practiced, some in secret,
Maybe a vice. Making a ring from Australian coins,
Flying kites, playing softball or volleyball,
Studying calculus or civil engineering
Or Greek (or learning Greek), or reading up
On Robert E. Lee's lieutenants.

Jules Bacon has become Dickey's imaginary friend, his home-front double to whom he can confide his insecurities while creating his impervious and unyielding body.

The carefully crafted hypermasculine pose and body that Dickey created for himself—and for his prose characters—were thus designed to hide the fears and anxieties of his true emotions. Whereas the novel was a medium in which Dickey chose to sensationalize the most exhilarating and thrilling aspects of war, the poem was a medium in which he allowed for a level of honesty and introspection that he rarely expressed elsewhere. It is similar to what Elizabeth Bishop had noticed about her own work: "it's almost impossible not to tell the truth in poetry, I think, but in prose it keeps eluding me in the funniest way."[61]

Dickey's war poems often feature protagonists who are eager to mythologize and glorify soldiers and war, but they also present a more gentle, sensitive, and caring alternative to Dickey's rather one-dimensional hypermasculine men of his novels. Although Dickey conceived of Joel Cahill as a "kind of Rimbaud of the air,"[62] he and Muldrow are more a kind of Rambo of the air, or flat characters of comic-book proportions. The other World

War II poets were equally attracted to strong, masculine war heroes when young, as the next chapter shows. Yet while his contemporaries outgrew their youthful fantasies about war, Dickey held on to them throughout his lifetime. Dickey stayed true to the Platonic image of himself from the age of six when he described his future life as a fighter pilot to the author in old age who invented Joel Cahill and Muldrow.

CHAPTER 10

"All wars are boyish"

The poets of the middle generation have rightfully been credited with reopening the subject of childhood as a viable theme for serious poetry. It was "a subject largely dismissed from the impersonal ideology of modernist poetry for its associations with romantic sentimentality," as Thomas Travisano stated in *Midcentury Quartet.*[1] The modernist poets generally did not explore their own childhood in their poetry, although T. S. Eliot briefly and obliquely reminisced about his boyhood. However, with the exception of Eliot's *Old Possum's Book of Practical Cats,* none of them wrote for children. One of John Crowe Ransom's most famous poems, "Bells for John Whiteside's Daughter," deals with a child's death, but emotions are kept at bay in this understated elegy, and the restrained speaker is unmistakably a rational adult. Ransom asserted tellingly that writing and reading poetry should be the "act of an adult mind" and not the "act of a child."[2]

The succeeding generation of poets disagreed with Ransom. John Ciardi, James Dickey, Randall Jarrell, William Jay Smith, and Richard Wilbur all published children's poetry or stories, and many more probed issues relating to their own youth in their poems. Poets such as John Berryman and Elizabeth Bishop, as well as Jarrell and Lowell, saw childhood as "a ripe field for serious poetic reexploration" and helped "construct a new poetry and poetics of childhood," as Travisano has asserted.[3] The personal, autobiographical, and lyrical poem written from the perspective of a child may seem "commonplace, even exhausted" to our contemporary ears, as Richard Flynn has claimed, but it was a quiet revolution instigated by middle generation poets in the 1940s.[4]

The return to childhood was in some ways a return to the legacy of romanticism. Like the Romantics, the middle generation poets showed an interest in both "the life of the actual child and that of the residual child within the adult," as Flynn has observed when referring to Jarrell.[5] Their approach differed, however, from the more dreamy and wistful revisitings of youth in William Blake's *Songs of Experience* and William Wordsworth's *The Prelude*. When approaching the topic of childhood the poets of the middle generation were "resistant to the utopian manifestations of Romantic subjectivity," as Flynn has also argued.[6] Influenced by Freud's interpretation of a person's psychological development from infancy, the middle generation poets reveal a darker and more traumatic dimension, caused by their awareness of the subconscious and repression.[7] Romantic childhood suggests the infinite human potential, but when the war poets looked back at their boyhoods they mostly saw the dark clouds of war hanging over those years. Retrospectively, they realized the tragically shrunken possibilities for a young American male in the first decades of the twentieth century, who was being culturally prepared for war and instructed to follow the traditional heroic model of masculinity.

Why did the middle generation poets feel so duty bound to reexamine their boyhoods through their poetry, and how is this search linked with war and their own sense of masculinity? Revisiting their own boyhoods is an extension of the poets' preoccupation with their selves and identities. The poets probe deep into their past to recover and understand the moments when their lives changed forever, when they lost their childhood innocence, or when they received an epiphany that shaped their adult identities. The poets present a kind of "infant sight," as Flynn argues, borrowing the phrase from Bishop's poem "Over 2,000 Illustrations and a Complete Concordance."[8] This representation reflects how the child looks at the world, but this view is "mediated both through the artistic process and through an experiential state, adulthood," which is thus "temporally and emotionally distanced from the original experience."[9]

War is a pervasive underlying theme in the childhood writings of the middle generation poets. This is hardly surprising since they were all born slightly before, during, or just after the First World War. Sometimes their fathers were in the military—as was the case with Lowell and Smith—while, for others, the tragedy of war and the general atmosphere of violence, peril, and doom hit home in another way. War is often indirectly but significantly present as a menacing backdrop to the personally involved, autobiographical narratives. The final lines of Bishop's "In the Waiting Room" present perhaps the most famous example of how the public encroaches on the private, and how the realm of the child is invaded by grown-up concerns:

The War was on. Outside,
in Worcester, Massachusetts,
were night and slush and cold,

and it was still the fifth
of February, 1918.[10]

It is not a coincidence that the almost seven-year-old girl's realization of selfhood ("you are an *I* / you are an *Elizabeth,* / you are one of *them*") coincides with an awareness of war.[11]

Personal and public calamities conspired to usher in an unstable period in Bishop's life during the First World War. Unable to cope with the death of her husband, Bishop's mother experienced a nervous breakdown and was hospitalized in 1916, as recalled in Bishop's story "In the Village." Sandra Barry has indicated that Bishop's mother imagined that she was "going to die for her country" and that she was "the cause of war," confirming how the world of war infringes on the private self.[12] Even though it was thousands of miles away, World War I also took its toll on their small town of Great Village, Nova Scotia, in more direct ways: twenty-one of the seventy young men who enlisted died. Meanwhile Bishop—who would never see her mother again—was sent to live with her maternal grandparents until September 1917, when she was taken "unconsulted and against [her] wishes" to her paternal grandparents' house in Worcester, Massachusetts, where "In the Waiting Room" is set.[13] The abrupt end to Bishop's childhood innocence (as well as the devastation of the First World War, which robbed humanity of much of its innocence) is symbolized in Bishop's short story by a "scream." It is the "scream" or "the echo of a scream" of her mother when she goes mad, and it continues to "hang over that Nova Scotian village."[14]

Much of the middle generation's "best work," Travisano has argued, "would explore the world of the threatened child or the traumatic emotional aftermath for those expelled too quickly from the protected realm of childhood innocence."[15] Jarrell's "The State" and "The Rising Sun" relate such childhood traumas directly to war. A cause for this preoccupation seems to be that World War I filled the precocious children with intimations of tragedy and catastrophe. Four-year-old Randall Jarrell had a nightmarish dream about a fighter plane, a "poor two-seater being attacked by four / Triplanes" during the last year of the First World War, as he remembered in "The Lost World."[16] He had spotted the aircraft on the front of the *Literary Digest,* and it had slipped into his subconscious mind, but in his surreal dream a camel comes to the plane's rescue. While hugging his teddy bear, he reassures himself: "I am not afraid."[17] And yet the faraway war impacts Jarrell's boy all the same, as it did Bishop's girl in "In the Waiting Room."

As the oldest son of a corporal in the Sixth Infantry Band, William Jay Smith grew up in and around Jefferson Barracks in Missouri between the two world wars. Smith came of age "in the eye of the hurricane," as he called the interbellum, but in his ambivalent memoir about his youth, *Army*

Brat (1980), he shows that his boyhood was anything but idyllic. Smith's father was a gambler and a heavy drinker turned bootlegger, and not the strong and upstanding role model one might expect of a military man. At one point, when Smith was the same age as Jarrell's child, his father disappeared after payday. Smith's mother, his little brother, and he go look for him at all the seedy places near the army base. When they return home their house is "riddled with bullet holes." The father is "sprawled on the living room floor" with "money, piles of bills, all the green of the gambling tables coming home to roost" scattered all around the room. As in Bishop's story "In the Village," "there was a scream: it felt as if it came right up through the floor on which I stood, rising within me and fountaining out, spreading in every direction like the green ooze on the floor."[18] Smith's father is soon nursed back to life, but Smith's childhood innocence dies. As Bishop writes, with the scream, "the child vanishes."[19]

Despite these pervasive traumatizing experiences, the boys and poets-to-be were not just afraid of war and the military. They were likewise drawn to warfare in search of powerful role models or as a form of empowerment for the vulnerable male child. In "Negro Hero" Gwendolyn Brooks speaks for Dorie Miller, the African American mess attendant who became a hero when he got hold of a machine gun and shot down at least two Japanese airplanes. Brooks writes that ever since childhood, Miller had a "boy itch to get at the gun" when he seized his opportunity for glory: "Of course all the delicate rehearsal shots of my childhood massed / In mirage before me."[20] Miller's pent-up aggression that is released at Pearl Harbor may have been caused by his sense of patriotism, as the War Department tried to prove when they depicted him on a poster in his navy uniform bearing his navy cross with the text "above and beyond the call of duty" printed above. This belated public recognition of his heroism was ironic, as Jennifer C. James has pointed out, because the military "initially denied him public accolade."[21] Brooks's monologue allows for such an interpretation, as her speaker admits that "their white-gowned democracy" was his "fair lady" whom he tried to protect.[22]

Yet Brooks also suggests that Miller's impulsive act at Pearl Harbor was at least partly rooted in a restless boyhood desire to prove himself through violence. This craving may have been related to his underprivileged upbringing, but writings by the white male poets of World War II intimate that this yearning may be also be gendered. "Negro Hero" presents "the soldier-as-really-a-child, whose ferocious combat urges seem half-feral and half-spoon fed," as Susan Schweik argues.[23] This nature/nurture debate consumed many of the male poets of World War II as well. Many of their writings implicitly question why they (and their sons) were beguiled by toy soldiers, guns, war planes, and war itself when young. They also explore how that childhood fascination was related to their involvement in the war years later.

Dickey, Shapiro, Lowell, and Nemerov are among the poets who were captivated by warfare when young. At the age of six Dickey wrote a make-belief biography entitled *The Life of James Dickey* in which he describes his imagined future life as an air force ace, along with "crayon drawings of airplanes."[24] Shapiro reminisces in *The Bourgeois Poet* how after the Great War he and other "boys play soldier with real weapons," meaning pineapples for hand grenades and "dark-brown wood for rifles." Shapiro and his neighborhood friends indulge in these fantasies of war despite being acquainted with a "shell-shocked newsman." This veteran from the First World War is randomly "shouting commands and thumping his truncheon-stick on the ground," but the boys pay no heed that this should serve as a warning of what a real war can do to people.[25]

As a child Lowell was infatuated with toy soldiers. In fact, people were to him "valueless except as chances for increasing [his] armies of soldiers."[26] War figures, like Lowell's toy soldiers, "offer boys the concrete, powerful models that they are seeking," Joshua S. Goldstein has argued. They have also been interpreted as "opportunities to express the possible anger and frustration" that boys may experience. Yet they also serve as "alternative models to their nurturing mothers."[27] All three reasons may help to explain why young Lowell is so infatuated with his toy soldiers in his memoir "91 Revere Street." Like Smith in *Army Brat,* Lowell desperately searches for an adequate male role model in "91 Revere Street," but also to counterbalance his overbearing mother.

Lowell's father was second-in-command at the Charlestown Naval Shipyard, but Lowell is "quite without hero worship" for his weak father.[28] The camaraderie in the navy was the one thing that kept his father "from being completely emasculated by his wife," as Paul Mariani has put it.[29] When she forces him to retire from the navy in 1927, he loses all his credibility in the eyes of his son. Lowell can only find two strong male role models at 91 Revere Street. The first is a rowdy colleague of his father, Commander Billy, who became "a vice-admiral and hero in World War II." Unlike Lowell's father, he dares to stand up to Lowell's mother. The second is Lowell's Jewish ancestor Mordecai Myers, whose picture hangs in the dining room.[30] Just like the exotic Myers in his war uniform, Lowell is an outsider in his own family, and destined to become a kind of Wandering Jew.

"91 Revere Street" climaxes when Lowell, who is becoming increasingly erratic and belligerent, bloodies the nose of a school bully in Boston's Public Garden, right underneath the statue of George Washington, and is expelled from the garden by a policeman, who is "forced to put his foot down."[31] This eruption of violence—later echoed by Lowell hitting his father—is as symbolic as it is effective. Lowell rebels against everything that the Boston elite stands for, as symbolized by the Public Garden with its "polite, landscaped walks," and especially against his mother's dominance.[32] Yet Lowell's aggressively masculine behavior ensures that he put his foot down, where his father did not. Lowell's fixation on militarized masculinity as a model for his own developing identity—whether in the form of Commander Billy, a photograph of Mordecai Myers, his toy soldiers, or his beloved Napoleon books, which he dragged with him everywhere—is striking. It evidences how influential the armed forces and toys were in providing a model for this generation of boys to conceptualize their budding sense of manhood.

Howard Nemerov's childhood was similarly protected and privileged as that of Lowell. Whereas Lowell was the progeny of Boston Brahmins, however, the Nemerov-Russek family of New York City was prototypical nouveau riche. Nemerov's mother, Gertrude Russek, was the daughter of the cofounder of Russeks fashionable department store, which her husband, David Nemerov, the son of less affluent Jewish immigrants, helped run. As their only son, Howard was destined to take over the prosperous family business, but he decided as a teenager that he wanted to pursue a career in writing, much to his father's dismay. His childhood seems to have been less marked by the traumatic experiences that Bishop, Lowell, and Smith chronicled in their work. With characteristic understatement, he downplays whatever hardship there was in "Thanksgrieving":

Infant mortality didn't, as they say, claim me
(though it damn near did), so I grew what they call up.
To the childhood illnesses routine for those times
I added only para-typhoid on my own.
Was never starved, nor did my parents
Whip me or leave me chained to the bed;
Nor did I get born, a Jew, in Germany,
Plus I went to their war and didn't die of it.[33]

Nemerov is often portrayed as a poet mainly concerned with metaphysical subjects. Yet like the other middle generation poets, he also reexplores his own childhood in his poems, albeit more sporadically and more covertly than do some of the others.

Reminiscent of the autobiographical childhood poetry of Bishop, Jarrell, and Lowell, Nemerov's poem "Models" is the most impressive of these revisitings. In three interrelated snapshots spanning Nemerov's childhood and adulthood, we are offered, as if in a time lapse, glimpses of Nemerov's early fascination for aviation leading to his first day at an airbase in England. In the first part, a twelve-year-old boy is constructing a model airplane out of balsa wood to reenact a battle between a Fokker and a Spad from the First World War:

That primitive, original war in the air
He made in miniature and flew by hand
In clumsy combat, simulated buzz:
A decade away from being there himself.[34]

The "primitive, original war in the air"—later modified to the "avant-garde war in the air"—holds a strong elementary attraction over the boy. It is significant that the German Fokker is as dear to him as the French Spad, just as Manfred von Richthofen, the "Red Baron," is as much a formidable favorite as America's ace of aces Eddie Rickenbacker. The boy has not yet learned to politicize the war, nor does he realize the horror that is involved in war; he is still completely immersed in what the English novelist E. M. Forster called "the Romance of the Air—war's last beauty parlor."[35] There is a causal connection between the physical, aerodynamic splendor of (model) airplanes and the speaker's attraction to war. As the colon in the third line of this quotation indicates, the visual and aural beauty of the aircraft as experienced by the boy explains the young man's entry into war ten years down the road.

The title of "Models" is significant in two ways. In the final section of "Models" Nemerov suggests that the recollection of war makes one see it on a model scale:

And memory, that makes things miniature
And far away, and fit size for the mind,
Returned to him in the form of images
The size of flies, his doings in those days[36]

Thinking back to his war past is like looking through a bombsight the way Nemerov described in another late war poem, "The Air Force Museum at Dayton": "miniature and quaint."[37] From a distance, the past (as well as the world down below) looks smaller, so one should get a better view. Yet what that vision presents is so selective, distorted, and miniature that this outlook is also inaccurate. Both the innocent boy playing with his model airplanes and daydreaming about participating in the war in the air and the experienced old man who cannot get the images of the war out of his head have an impaired vision and incomplete perspective on the war.

Second, the poem reflects on role models, which is a key motif. Charles Lindbergh—the aviator who William Jay Smith had spotted at Jefferson Barracks right after Lindbergh's pioneering intercontinental flight—had been Nemerov's childhood hero, too, despite the flyer's anti-Semitic sympathies. Nemerov also enjoyed reading the air-war pulps of the 1930s, such as *Sky Fighters* or *Wings: Fighting Aces of War Skies,* "on the subway coming home from school."[38] Like Lowell's toy soldiers, the air force aces that Nemerov played with or pretended to be offered him "clearly defined male models" with which he could identify, as war toys often do, perhaps as a substitute for his father, as is the case with Lowell in "91 Revere Street."[39] When Nemerov himself became a fighter pilot, his colleagues were not moral paragons, incidentally. In real life they turned out to be "cruel-mouthed and harsh" and looked down on Nemerov as "not worth their welcome, as unlike to last," as Nemerov explains at the end of "Models."[40]

Nemerov's relationship with his father was troubled. A workaholic who spent "fourteen hours a day" at the office, David Nemerov "showed little warmth or interest in his children."[41] He was adamant, however, that his son follow in his footsteps, but Nemerov was more fascinated by his grandfather, a scholar of the Torah and Old Testament, who shared his love of words. When Nemerov announced after the war that he wanted to be a writer, his father was "bitterly disappointed."[42] Enlisting in the air force after graduating from Harvard had also been "a fierce gesture of independence against his father, a way of testing himself," as Patricia Bosworth, the biographer of Diane Arbus, Nemerov's sister, has noted.[43] During the war Nemerov's father tried to persuade fellow poet Archibald MacLeish to give Nemerov a job at Washington's Office of Facts and Figures, which MacLeish directed. MacLeish replied, however, that "your son had better take his chances with the others," which Nemerov did, and "had meant to do anyhow."[44]

Lincoln Kirstein was also searching for models of (militarized) masculinity in his early days. He was, however, in W. H. Auden's words, "an intellectual aesthete who in childhood was, or believed himself to be, a sissy." As a consequence, Kirstein's idealized male other, his "Lame Shadow, half worshipped, half despised," as Auden writes, was "a gentile inarticulate warrior-athlete."[45] Among Kirstein's papers at the New York Public Library is his World War I scrapbook, from when he was eight years old. It confirms Auden's musings on Kirstein as it is clearly young Lincoln's ode to the military, masculine hero. An aggressive-looking American Eagle with the motto "E Pluribus Unum" is displayed on the cover of the scrapbook, and it opens with a clipping of a partisan poem written by Percy MacKaye called "To Marshal Foch," the French soldier-hero from the Great War.[46] Many more clippings celebrating General Pershing and the victorious airman follow in what is the first book Kirstein ever compiled.

One of the cartoons in the scrapbook is called "The First Dive" and features a young boy who stands frozen on the springboard while other kids yell "Jump" and "C'mon." The cartoon is oddly similar to Kirstein's first poem in *Rhymes of a PFC* (1964). Kirstein's highly symbolic poem "Fall In" describes the rite of passage from boyhood to adolescence when the young speaker's uncle teaches him how to swim. Kirstein's revealing title describes a literal fall in the water of a pool, but also refers to the military term for standing in line, and to the falling in with the crowd of men whom he both worships and despises. It is an uncomfortable and frightening experience to the young speaker, as he feels as if he is being tested and realizes that he has failed. Being given a chance to join the "big-boys' club" ought to be a "mystic privilege," but Kirstein's speaker does not value it as such. He feels "condemned" and sentenced to this society of men, where he has been taken against his will, and where he senses he does not belong. The others are much hairier and older than he is, and it makes him feel genderless: "No boy, no man, a neuter in-between, / One hairless silly, neither he nor she."[47]

"Fall In" seems at first unrelated to the army and war, which is characteristic of the oblique way with which these poets approached their war. Yet the final stanza establishes the connection between the swimming pool incident and a fighting army. With his powerful iambs, Kirstein suggests very eloquently in the final stanza why "all wars are boyish," why armies need boys to fight society's wars, and what motivates soldiers to fight:

> The rage of armies is the shame of boys;
>   A hero's panic or a coward's whim
> Is triggered by nerve or nervousness.
>   We wish to sink. We do not choose to swim.[48]

Soldiers do not particularly want to fight, in the same way that Kirstein's young protagonist does not want to swim. Yet peer pressure shames them to take part and not to be different from the others. "Shame is the glue that holds the man-making process together," as Goldstein knows: "Males who fail tests of manhood are publicly shamed, are humiliated, and become a negative example for others."[49] There are no born heroes or cowards, Kirstein suggests. Both act impulsively and are motivated by panic. Decisions are "triggered by nerve or nervousness" and moral doubt, and the poets of World War II spent the rest of their lives thinking about their earlier choices involving childhood, war, and masculinity.

Nemerov reflected on his decision to "fall in" after a bizarre news story transpired in the early 1960s. Several statues of Etruscan warriors at the Metropolitan Museum of Art in New York City had been discovered to be modern forgeries. Nemerov's poem "To Clio, Muse of History" (1962) refers to a famous scam when two Italian artists, Riccardo Riccardi and Alfredo Fioravanti, conceived of a plan in the years between 1910 and 1920 to create three warriors in terra cotta and pretend they were ancient statues. A purchasing agent for the museum in Italy acted as middleman, and the "Etruscan warriors" were bought for many thousands of dollars, and displayed for the first time in 1933, when Nemerov was thirteen years old. Nemerov grew up just a few blocks away from the Metropolitan Museum, and remembers how he visited the museum. Together with other "children," he "stared" at the combatant, "learning from him / Unspeakable things about war that weren't in the books."[50]

Having learned that the statue is a fake, he is compelled to reconfigure his own boyhood in light of this new falsehood:

My childhood in the glare of that giant form
Corrupts with history, for I too fought in the War.

He, great male beauty
That stood for the sexual thrust of power,
His target eyes inviting the universal victim
To fatal seduction, the crested and greaved
Survivor long after shield and sword are dust
Has now become another lie about our life.[51]

The boy was so much attracted to this commanding and seductive warrior that the statue conspired with history to tempt him into battle, in the same way that the model airplanes did. Like the myth of "the Romance of the Air," however, the warrior is one big fabrication, "another lie about our life." The statue can be destroyed and erased from the (art) history books, but it is impossible to wipe out the influence it had on the young boy who grew up to be an adult warrior. Nemerov therefore instructs Clio, the muse of history, to stop putting spells on young people: "no more / Enchantments, Clio."[52] "To Clio, Muse of History" is not devoid of a comic undertone, but it is primarily serious. Nemerov's poem derives its poignancy from the guilt and anger Nemerov feels for having gullibly fallen for the hypermasculine but fake warrior. Another muse, Calliope of poetry, can be said to have helped him understand and rationalize the sources of these emotions, and even to joke about the whole affair.

The guiding theory of history that Nemerov explores in "To Clio, Muse of History" is Socrates' notion of anamnesis, which Plato wrote about in Meno. Socrates believed that the soul is immortal and is reincarnated, that when we are born the shock of birth temporarily erases that knowledge, but what we actually do when we learn during the course of our lives is try to regain the knowledge we once had. The childhood poetry of Nemerov and the other middle generation poets is essentially a modified version of anamnesis without the reincarnation: a process of trying to regain lost knowledge, to paraphrase the title of Marcel Proust's *Remembrance of Things Past,* the French novelist's masterpiece of which Jarrell and Nemerov were especially fond.[53] It is a confrontational and never-ending process, as the past can never be reproduced accurately. Reexploring their childhoods was a generational preoccupation in attempting to comprehend the (gender) expectations and pressures of society, but also to understand the compulsions of one's younger self. Nemerov is intrigued why as a child he was drawn to and why he "too fought in the War."

When Dickey and Lowell each fathered one or more sons, they were especially struck by their sons' war play and aggression, which indirectly made them reexamine their own boyhoods as well. In "Child in Armor" (1953) Dickey stares at his son who is playing while dressed up in a Roman gladiator outfit, the kind of uniform that young Randall Jarrell was also wearing in the "Children's Arms" section in "The Lost World." The actions of the son in Dickey's poem remind the speaker of himself, but there is also something more mysterious going on; it is as if his son is acting out some deep-seated or primal warrior instinct, of which remnants are to be found in all men.[54] Scientists generally agree that there are indeed "modest biological tendencies towards males' higher average war capability," as Goldstein puts it. And these differences are exacerbated by gender roles that society imposes—for instance, by "systematically rewarding and punishing, by indoctrinating youth, creating role models to be emulated, and honoring those who perform well."[55]

Whereas Dickey hints in this poem at biological reasons to explain his son's (and his own) fascination for battle, Nemerov is looking for cultural reasons to fathom why he was attracted to war, as "Models" and "To Clio, Muse of History" indicate. When, during the war in Vietnam, two of Nemerov's sons started to become inordinately attracted to GI Joe dolls, he could only try to make light of the situation. In a letter sent to the *New York Times* that was never published, Nemerov realizes that he will not be able to talk his prepubescent sons out of wanting those twelve-inch poseable fighting-man toys. Yet he cannot help but poke fun at the fact that the male dolls are not fully equipped:

> Dear Sir:
>
> As a far-sighted, or television, parent, I know even this early on that come Christmas my two youngest sons are going to receive two soldier-dolls called G I Joes, ingeniously realistic figures that can be equipped with much in the way of uniforms, weapons, and so on.
>
> It is not the warlike aspect of these toys in the hands of children that so startles me—for the word *infantry* means exactly what it says—but the fact that the full military equipment of the G I Joe does not include genitals. My boys are five and three years old and normally observant. I write to ask if some wiser parent can advise me as to my best line of response if questioned. Possibly I am suffering from an unresolved Military-Industrial Complex?[56]

As was the case with "To Clio, Muse of History," Nemerov's humor only veils a serious point he is also making. Nemerov was in a very real sense suffering from a "Military-Industrial Complex," and not in the sense that President Eisenhower had used the phrase when leaving the Oval Office in 1961. World War II had remained an obsession that had not yet been satisfactorily dealt with. His letter to the *New York Times*—at a time when his eldest son ran a real risk of being drafted—was a faint protest against the war in Vietnam, and an equally futile attempt to emasculate, to render impotent the war toys that had done him in.[57]

In "Marriage" Lowell notes that his six-year-old son, Sheridan—born to his British wife, Caroline Blackwood—is particularly attracted to guns and violence:

> This summer, he is a soldier—
> unlike father or mother,
> or anyone he knows,
> he can choose both sides:
> Redcoat, Minuteman, or George the Third . . .
> the ambivalence of the Revolution that made him
> half-British, half-American.[58]

Lowell deliberately chose not to be a soldier during World War II, and none of the other people in Sheridan's circles were soldiers, so Lowell is at a loss how to account for his son's predilection for soldiering. To Stanley Kunitz, Lowell wrote that Sheridan seemed "a microcosm of James Dickey, but on the wagon," referring to Dickey's aggression, bulky size, and alcoholism.[59] In "Sheridan" his son prances around underneath a "Nazi helmet" and calls his father "Mr. Loser" for losing "*weir* guns," as he says in his Kentish accent.[60] In an earlier draft of this poem, Sheridan was wearing a "knight's helmet," but Lowell probably wanted to accentuate the extremity of his son's behavior.[61] In both "Marriage" and "Sheridan" Lowell's son's soldiery absorption is mentioned in passing, but these two poems are important steps in Lowell's investigation into his own past, trying to understand his own childhood and marriage.

Part of the reason the middle generation poets were so keen to reexplore their childhood through poetry was that the roots of their reaction to World War II were planted there. Herman Melville's famous line in "The March into Virginia" that "all wars are boyish, and are fought by boys" accurately sums up how the middle generation poets experienced the crossing from childhood to adulthood, from innocence to experience, from peacetime war play to the real thing.[62] "War must rely on the young, for only they have the two things fighting requires: physical stamina and innocence about their own mortality," as Paul Fussell has claimed: "The young are proud of their athleticism, and because their sense of honor has not yet suffered compromise, they make the most useful material for manning the sharp end of war."[63] Kirstein and Nemerov became fully aware of this fact, and realized that the idea of war as a masculine rite of passage had had a significant effect on them.

William Stafford also used his poetry to explore his own childhood, but he ironically found that his opposition to World War II and war in general had its roots in those Kansas years. "Learning" (1992) relates one of Stafford's earliest childhood memories when he was a toddler and when the United States was involved in the Great War. Young Stafford hears the sounds of a piccolo, a small, shrill flute, which is followed by a drum at a parade. He is inclined to follow the piccolo player like the rats and children who followed the Pied Piper of Hamelin in Brothers Grimm's famous fairy tale. Yet his mother tells him not to:

> My mother said, "Don't run—
> the army is after someone
> other than us. If you stay
> you'll learn our enemy."
>
> Then he came, the speaker. He stood
> in the square. He told us who
> to hate. I watched my mother's face,
> it's quiet. "That's him," she said.[64]

The poem is called "Learning" because this episode taught Stafford not to follow his sensual instincts and be taken in by the sound of the piccolo and the drum and the sight of the horse, but to think about what is happening in front of him.

The plain language and carefully avoided adornments of Stafford's poem, which are so typical for his style (and so different from a poet such as Anthony Hecht), may suggest that "Learning" is a simple poem. It may appear as if Stafford's mother is just as opinionated as the jingoistic speaker in the square, telling her young son what to think and dividing the world up into binary oppositions of friends who are against the war and "enemies" who are in favor of war. It may seem that Stafford thus became a conscientious objector because of peer pressure, which influenced Nemerov to stay in the military. Yet "Learning" provides a more subtle example about learning than that. The boy finds out that "the speaker," the man who "stood in the square," is the "enemy" because paradoxically "he told us who to hate." Stafford's mother points out the "enemy" to her son, but other than that she is "quiet." She does not tell him what to think, but to think for himself why the man could be the "enemy." "Learning" was published a year before

Stafford's death, and it seems as if he needed a lifetime to resolve his mother's puzzle. Stafford's poem is likewise a puzzle that is meant to challenge his readers. He is careful, however, not to solve it completely for them. Yet like his mother, Stafford must have come to the conclusion that the "enemy" can only be someone who suggests that one's identity as an American and as a man is based on the hatred one can feel for someone else.

Lowell adopted Melville's line—"all wars are boyish"— in "Christmas Eve under Hooker's Statue" (1946) early on in his career. As "Marriage" and "Sheridan" show, he remained troubled by the relationship between boyhood and war even in the final years of his life. In "Christmas Eve under Hooker's Statue" Lowell talks about a serpent that hides an apple in a Christmas stocking that will "sting the child with knowledge."[65] It is a telling image that reflects his entire generation's belief that their childhood innocence was corrupted by war. Sooner rather than later all the poets of World War II became wise beyond their years. One of the quickest to wise up was Jarrell, the poet who wrote most consistently about the relationship between childhood and war, even while the Second World War was still in progress.

It is therefore no coincidence that Jarrell's "The Death of the Ball Turret Gunner," the most famous American poem about World War II, addresses the theme of childhood innocence, diminished possibility, and the nightmare of war in the most succinct and eloquent way imaginable. Jarrell's ball turret gunner is also "expelled too quickly from the protected realm of childhood innocence," to adopt Travisano's phrase. The ball turret gunner wakes up to "black flak and the nightmare fighters" just before he dies, and after his body is unceremoniously removed from the plane "with a hose."[66] The poets of World War II had more time than the ill-fated ball turret gunner to reflect on their childhood and "the dream of life," and they did so repeatedly.

CHAPTER 11

Karl Shapiro's Sexual Appetite

Karl Shapiro and his fiancée, Evalyn Katz, were to all appearances poetry's version of GI Joe and Rosie the Riveter, the upbeat American icons of World War II. Shapiro had met Katz shortly before he was drafted into the army. When Shapiro had sailed off to Australia on the *Queen Mary* in February 1942, his twenty-three-year-old girlfriend moved from their hometown of Baltimore to New York, the hub of American publishing. From her one-bedroom apartment and the office of a Park Avenue physician where she worked as a secretary, Katz directed Shapiro's career while he was overseas. She ensured that his poems wound up in major magazines, such as the *New Yorker, Poetry,* and *Partisan Review,* and convinced Reynal & Hitchcock—a small but respected publishing house in New York—to print three of Shapiro's books during World War II. She was instrumental in getting Shapiro a Guggenheim Fellowship and compiled and arranged Shapiro's poems in *Person, Place and Thing* (1942) and *V-Letter* (1944) in consultation with Reynal & Hitchcock's editor Albert Erskine and Shapiro himself. "SOLDIER'S GIRL KEEPS BUSY MAKING HIS POEMS FAMOUS" headlined the *World-Telegram* in a typical feature on the unusual partnership between the two lovers, featuring Evalyn Katz as a regular 1940s pin-up girl.

The air of romance and patriotism that clung to Shapiro and Katz also partly explains Shapiro's popularity during the war, along with the accessibility and topicality of his poems. With a heavy dose of sarcasm, Jarrell suggested to Lowell that his Bostonian friend should stop being "a special-case neo-17th-century poet" and be more like "a fine clean upstanding American one à la Shapiro."[1] Jarrell's gibe suggests that he saw Shapiro as a middlebrow poet-propagandist. Yet this assessment is not entirely accurate: a number of Shapiro's poems are intensely critical of the United States, and Shapiro was certainly not as spotless or unsoiled as his image was at the time.[2]

While he gained the reputation for being a clean-cut and patriotic American soldier-poet as opposed to his more moody contemporaries, Shapiro's wartime poems and letters show a darker and more confused picture of his war years. With the exception of Lincoln Kirstein, Shapiro was the most sexually explicit American poet of World War II, and of his generation. Few mainstream poets of the postwar era treated sexuality so bluntly and directly as Shapiro did—for instance, in his poems "The First Time" from *Poems of a Jew* (1958) or "Fucking" in *The Old Horsefly* (1992). In the two parts of his autobiography, *The Younger Son* and *Reports of My Death,* Shapiro is also remarkably explicit and detailed about his sexuality, before, during, and after the war.

This chapter explores how Shapiro and other poets reflected on wartime sexuality, how they depicted women, and why Shapiro wrote about these subjects while other poets of the Second World War did not. Soldiers are perennially obsessed with sex in any war, Joshua S. Goldstein and others have argued.[3] The huge popularity of pin-up girls like Betty Grable, Rita Hayworth, and Jane Russell, whose pictures adorned "the walls of barracks, the bulkheads of ships, and the fuselages of planes on all fronts," is the most visible sign of the obsession with sex in World War II, albeit in suggestive and expurgated ways only.[4] The U.S. government—in close collaboration with the Hollywood movie industry—carefully orchestrated "the production and distribution of millions of photographs of Hollywood's leading ladies and rising starlets," in order to present American army men with images of why they were fighting, as Robert B. Westbrook has argued.[5] "Sexual deprivation and inordinate desire generally did not trouble men on the front line," Paul Fussell claims: "They were too scared, busy, hungry, tired, and demoralized to think about sex at all." Yet those soldiers who, like Shapiro, were not exposed to the actual fighting were "constantly seeking an outlet," which they "seldom satisfactorily found."[6]

In 1941 the military "advocated abstinence and self-control on the part of the servicemen," as Christina S. Jarvis has observed, but this idea was soon abandoned as unrealistic.[7] Later the military encouraged "healthy, heterosexual desire" in an attempt to prevent homosexuality among the troops.[8] One of the outlets to release sexual tension was through masturbation, which Kirstein described in "Load," a rare poem on this subject. There may be "numerous testimonies associating masturbation and exhibitionism with the fears and excitements of infantry fighting," as Paul Fussell claims, but it is uncommon to find examples of this in poetry. John D'Emilio and Estelle Freedman have claimed that the American military to a certain extent advocated autoeroticism—for instance, through disseminating pin-ups—as long as it did not become a habit.[9] Punning on words like load and shooting,

Kirstein's poem describes how soldiers masturbate at night in their cots out of pure nervousness while under attack from German missiles:

These thing-spray every fluent fear,
    Greasing its shudder, gag, and shock.
Wow! Here it comes! Just feel this floor
    Rise to the blast, bend, crack, and rock.
Well aimed from forty miles away
    Are steel-turned tubes the Jerries use,
But the most harm their banging does
    Is stiffen us to self-abuse.
Waiting the next note from their gun,
    A hot hand strokes an aching hard.
Nervousness exceeding fun
    Jacks a poor peter to its yard.[10]

As always, Kirstein's lines are chock-full of adjectives and images that are fired at his readers the way the shells are aimed at Kirstein's GIs. The quick tempo of these lines—with their exclamation marks and many rhymes—reflects the anxiousness that the soldiers must be feeling. "Load" suggests that the proximity to danger increases prurient urgings. Kirstein's poem shows "the disturbing relationship between intense physical fear and erotic desire," as Vernon Scannell has put it, or something even more primal: the body's automatic response to fear of death.[11]

Afraid that servicemen would contract venereal diseases, the authorities dissuaded soldiers from visiting prostitutes by means of posters and through disciplinary action. Not surprisingly, however, visiting prostitutes became one of the most common means to release sexual energy. One of the few poems on wartime prostitution by an American poet is Kirstein's brutally honest "Snatch." Its speaker indicates that the troops regarded prostitutes as "their rationed piece of ass," something they were entitled to. Although the soldiers are "exhausted," they "are still unrelieved" until they can unburden themselves.[12] It is in essence an instinctual, primal craving, equated by Kirstein with eating, drinking, and horsing around. If masculinity is sometimes seen as a performance, triggered by peer pressure and societal expectations, it does not seem to apply to Kirstein's soldiers in this poem. They are acting perfunctorily, Kirstein suggests with a stunning conceit, as if they are fixing a car:

Though he's no expert, still he can manage five-minute stiff routine
As skillfully as grease a jeep or service other mild machine.

Slips off his brakes; gives her the gas; dog tags and rosary entwine;

Moistures distilled from tenderness lubricates the kinky spine.
Well: up and at 'em[13]

Surprisingly, Richard Wilbur is another poet who published a brothel poem about World War II. Wilbur is often depicted as the most decorous and well-mannered poet of the postwar generation. Jarrell, for instance, criticized Wilbur in 1951, using a football metaphor, for always settling "for six or eight yards," and implored him to: "Come on, *take a chance*!"[14] Yet in "Place Pigalle" he took a chance, at least thematically. The atmosphere of the poem is immediately charged—building on Wilbur's conceit of electricity, which he maintains throughout the poem—as the soldiers enter the bars of this infamous Paris square. They are boys "with ancient faces," in Wilbur's paradoxical phrase, "seeking their ancient friends." Their respective professions cause both the soldiers and the prostitutes to wise up quickly. As Jarrell frequently does in his war poems, Wilbur compares the soldiers but also the prostitutes to animals. Both the prostitutes and the soldiers are described as hares because they are both hunted down by puppies and hounds, metaphors that could stand for randy boys or enemy soldiers.[15] Yet the "soldier and the whore" can temporarily "mark off their refuge with a gaudy door," shutting out the rest of the world where at least the soldiers will not be stalked.[16]

In "Snatch," Kirstein recounts the sexual act in the most unromantic terms. His bizarre but effective tropes and the ridiculous bounciness of his iambic octometer, combined with the sexually explicit slang, make the brothel scene seem like an outlandish spectacle: "To toss her tit and wink her twat and cense her scent of musky pores."[17] Kirstein is not just mocking the soldier, but takes an almost anthropological stance toward the lecherous soldiers. His speaker is an outsider who does not partake in the action himself. He is therefore ideally placed to describe how the other soldiers are transformed into animalistic predators, hunting for sex. As a closeted gay poet in the army, Kirstein had an exceptionally insightful vantage point from which to observe male heterosexual desire during the war.

Fussell has expressed his amazement that "the unique physical tenderness, the readiness to admit openly the bodily beauty of young men, the unapologetic recognition that men may be in love with each other" is so dominant in English poetry of the First World War but absent in the American poetry of the Second World War.[18] "Were writers of the Second War sexually and socially more self-conscious than those of the First? Were they more sensitive to the risks of shame and ridicule?" Fussell asks?[19] The World War II poets' awareness of Freudian theory about sexuality may have prevented them from sharing such feelings and insights publicly. When W. H. Auden wrote that Kirstein "in childhood was, or believed himself to be, a sissy," he makes a point of mentioning that "sissy" is "a term with no real European equivalent."[20] The fear of being considered effeminate or gay may have contributed to the American poets' silence about homosexual desire. This generation of war poets was generally so extraordinarily open and accepting about behavior that the dominant culture may have considered unmanly or un-American, however, that this explanation seems wanting.

Fussell himself provides another plausible explanation when he writes that "it was largely members of the upper and upper-middle classes who were prepared by public-school training to experience such [homoerotic] crushes."[21] American boys did not experience the gender-segregated schooling of their English counterparts, and they were thus socialized differently during their adolescence. English boys did not have much contact with girls and therefore geared their early adolescent sexuality more toward boys. Like Wilfred Owen and to some extent Walt Whitman, Jarrell was "the voice of inarticulate boys, he had to testify on their behalf," to quote Fussell again, but Jarrell never indulges in the kind of physical adoration that Owen and Whitman exhibit.[22] Only Dickey's celebration of the male body and homosocial bonding in *To the White Sea, Alnilam,* and "The Performance," and some of Kirstein's verse—for instance, his Whitmanesque "Bath"—may evince homosexual desire. Yet these poems are more sublimated, and there are fewer of them. The expression of heterosexual desire in the poetry of World War II was rare enough; the expression of homosexual desire was even more exceptional.

The war poems and novels that celebrate homosocial bonding or homosexual desire were significantly all published after the 1960s when sexual mores had become more liberal during later decades. An incident between Robert Duncan and John Crowe Ransom in 1945 shows this. Ransom had praised Robert Duncan's poem "Sections toward an African Elegy"—not a war poem incidentally—and had accepted it for publication by the *Kenyon Review.* When, later on, Ransom read Duncan's article "The Homosexual in Society" in *Politics,* he thought that the poem had "an obvious homosexual advertisement, and for that reason" it could not "be eligible for publication."[23] Despite Duncan's protests, Ransom refused to print the poem. Duncan would never publish in the *Kenyon Review.*

Wilbur's poem "Place Pigalle" was published in the 1940s, but is much less explicit about sexuality, and it is in any case about heterosexual desire rather than homosexual desire. Wilbur's speaker is equally aloof as Kirstein's in "Snatch," but in his case his reserve seems more related to Wilbur's poetic style than the particular perspective chosen for this poem. At the end of the poem, though, the soldier suddenly bursts out in an exaggerated exclamation, partly borrowing his rhetoric from Shakespeare's sonnet 29:[24]

"Girl, if I love thee not, then let me die;
Do I not scorn to change my state with kings?
Your muchtouched flesh, incalculable, which wrings
Me so, now shall I gently seize in my
Desperate soldier's hands which kill all things."[25]

The formal, antiquated diction makes the soldier seem contrived, but his "desperate" attachment to the girl nevertheless seems heartfelt. The soldier can be gentle as a puppy and murderous as a bloodhound, suggesting the same dialectic of "puppies" and "wolves" that Jarrell used to typify his airmen in "Eighth Air Force." Whereas Kirstein emphasizes the primal, animalistic need for sex in which women are little more than instruments that allow the soldiers to perform a routine action, Wilbur stresses the soldier's psychological need for temporary protection and shelter. The prostitutes in "Place Pigalle" become idealized saviors who can heal the soldiers' wounded souls.

Despite these incidental poems that touch upon wartime sexuality, other poets, such as Jarrell and Nemerov, are mostly silent about this subject. Nemerov lets on in a letter how much he missed "the society of women—merely even their talk & their attitudes."[26] Although Jarrell is widely praised for his representation of army life, he is "mute on wartime sexuality," as Lorrie Goldensohn has indicated, and his letters to Mackie Jarrell are more like "a boy's communications from sleep-away camp" than passionate love letters to his wife.[27] Jarrell did not generally indulge in typically male activities, however, and once admitted that he had a "semifeminine mind."[28] He did not "drink or smoke" and disapproved of "sexual innuendoes in conversation," which may explain why his poetry also lacks any reference to wartime sexuality.[29] Only in his aggressive poetry reviews and in his jibes at fellow poets does Jarrell show a fierce sense of competitiveness that is associated with hegemonic masculinity.

Yet there are also other, more general reasons that explain why the middle generation poets did not appear to readily commit their sexual desire to paper. First, as a group the middle generation poets did not seem particularly interested in exploring sexuality as a theme in the same way that following generations did, with the exception of Ciardi and Shapiro. In more than one sense, the middle generation poets were inheritors of the genteel generation who wrote elegant, refined, and mannered poetry, especially in the 1940s and 1950s, and which tended to preclude sexuality as an appropriate subject. Second, an open discussion of sexuality was still generally unthinkable in the literature of the 1940s. Publishers were not keen to publish racy poems during World War II, a fact that made self-censorship likely. Kirstein's poems, for instance, were only published in the mid-1960s when sexual morals in the United States were changing, and after the publishing industry had survived several censorship trials involving alleged obscenities.

After the war Kirstein had tried to find a publisher for his manuscript, "but the response of American publishers was uniformly negative," as Kirstein's biographer, Martin Duberman, has reported. While some publishers were taken aback by "the poem's vernacular" or uncertain about "the quality of the verse," Duberman suggests that the "several oblique references to homosexuality" contributed to why mainstream publishers were unwilling to commit to Kirstein's book.[30] Allen Tate, who passed on *Rhymes of a PFC* when he was poetry editor at Henry Holt in 1946, did recommend it to independent publishers. "The language here and there is a little obscene," Tate wrote to Harry Duncan at Cummington Press, who had also issued Lowell's *Land of Unlikeness,* "and it would be hard for a trade publisher to handle it."[31] Tate hoped Cummington Press would publish Kirstein's books, but Duncan never did. In 1954 Kirstein seemed to concede that he would never publish his war poems: "I don't think my war poems are of much interest to anyone, but me. They are dirty, and I don't want to clean them up, and the sentiments expressed are subversive."[32] Kirstein had sat on the poems of *Rhymes of a PFC* for almost twenty years when New Directions finally accepted it in 1964.

Even though many historians agree that World War II helped relinquish some sexual taboos and was a catalyst for dramatic changes in terms of gender, the official disposition was conservative, forcing the soldiers and soldier-poets to be more prudish and reticent than their successors. Sexuality was hardly represented in war poetry, and when it was, it was transmitted in coded terms, just as in wartime movies. There is a difference between how fiction and poetry treated wartime sex, however. Hemingway already openly discussed wartime prostitution in *A Farewell to Arms* (1929), and his successors during World War II—for instance, Norman Mailer in *The Naked and the Dead* (1948) and James Jones in *The Thin Red Line* (1962)—took the blunt treatment of sexuality to another level. Karl Shapiro was unique among the middle generation poets for his urge to express himself sexually during the war, somewhat like the characters in Mailer's and Jones's novels.

Some of the poems Shapiro published in the United States, especially in *V-Letter* (1944), communicate his libido through sexual innuendo, in love poems to his fiancée, Evalyn Katz. Yet the poems he published in *Place of Love* (1942), assisted by his Australian mistress, publisher, and editor, Cecily Crozier, are more unabashedly erotic. Most of them never made it to the United States, for even though Shapiro was gaining the reputation of being a "fine clean upstanding American" soldier-poet whose alliance with Katz made him the poet-darling of the popular press, his actions in Australia and New Guinea were not very respectable. Many soldiers overseas took advantage of the opportunities to gain "new sexual possibilities" that the war offered them, as John D'Emilio and Estelle B. Freedman have argued. It released them "from the social environments that inhibited erotic expression" in the United States.[33] Yet despite his affair in Australia, Shapiro also tried to build up a meaningful relationship with his American sweetheart back home. This liminal position makes Shapiro's poetry representative for the paradoxical, romantic, and prurient feelings that American World War II soldiers held, but, oddly enough, unrepresentative for the poets of that war.

Susan Schweik has called the title poem of *V-Letter* "influential" because it revamped and made popular the epistolary poetic form during World War II.[34] In her book *A Gulf So Deeply Cut,* Schweik cites more than a dozen examples of the epistolary war poem written in the mid-1940s and calls it a typically "masculine" form of writing. Not only were they mostly written by men, these V-letter poems are also "*virility* letters" in the sense that they "confirm the true centrality of men's position" and put women in a subordinate place.[35] V-letter—short for Victory-letter—referred to a new postal system that was started in June 1942 for letters to and from servicemen in the armed forces overseas. To save cargo space, a uniform single sheet was introduced, which would be reduced in size by microfilm equipment to a photograph of 4 by 5.25 inches. Once the V-mail had passed the office of censorship, it would be folded in an envelope and sent abroad, saving valuable cargo space. Like many other soldiers, Shapiro frequently used V-mail, which was free for servicemen. Roughly half of his letters to Katz were sent that way, including many that contained his poems for *V-Letter.*[36]

Schweik singles out Shapiro's autobiographical poem "V-Letter" as a prototypical example because even though Shapiro worships his addressee, Evalyn Katz, she is "confined to the position of silent but reassuring object."[37] A line such as "I love you first because you wait" certainly confirms this. What is peculiar about this line for a love poem is that it could refer to any woman back home, as long as she waits. Throughout the poem, "V-Letter" is unspecific in its details about the woman addressed, except in the first lines in which he says that he loves her "because your face is fair, / Because your eyes Jewish and blue, / Set sweetly with the touch of foreignness."[38] This pronouncement lets on that he admires her for what she looks like, foreign and a shiksa. This compliment is turned inside out, however, when Shapiro admits that her eyes remind him of a mischievous boy who "tortured his parents and compelled my hate," which makes her sound fickle and untrustworthy.[39] On a superficial level "V-Letter" is a straightforward love poem by an American soldier, but Shapiro undercuts it with his suspicions and patronizing generalizations of women.

A number of female stereotypes surface in Shapiro's *V-Letter.* Many traditional gender roles were (temporarily) abandoned during the war because of the Women Army Corps (WAC) and the many female employees in the war industry, but at the same time soldiers continued to look at women in age-old platitudinous categories of mother, housewife, girl-next-door, or sexpot. Like Kirstein's soldiers, Shapiro's speakers first view women as objects of sexual desire. Schweik would surely typify "Birthday Poem" as a "*virility* letter." For her birthday, along with the poem, Shapiro sends Katz a letter-opener, although in Shapiro's diction it becomes an obvious phallic symbol: "I send you, darling, a polished stick / To open letters, hold in your hand. / The lovely marking smooth and warm."[40] "The Gun" is charged with even more phallic imagery than "Birthday Poem," and the wonderfully evocative opening of "Troop Train" depicts soldiers eyeing and vying for local women, from the train, "with catcalls and with leers."[41]

In both "V-Letter" and "Troop Train" sexual desire is at least partly evoked by the fear of death that the soldier-speaker is experiencing, which they share with Kirstein's "Load." In the final stanza Shapiro writes how

> Trains lead to ships and ships to death or trains,
> And trains to death or trucks, and trucks to death,
> Or trucks lead to the march, the march to death,
> Or that survival which is all our hope;[42]

Shapiro's acquiescent tone, the repetitions of the common, monosyllabic nouns—like "trains," "ships," "trucks," and "march"—and the theme of being uncertain where the war or the army will take these soldiers are remarkably similar to both the style and content Jarrell's "The Lines." Standing in ubiquitous and meaningless lines becomes a trope in Jarrell's poem of being trapped in war. Yet Shapiro—and Kirstein—juxtapose the feeling of ennui and fear of death with sexual yearning. Sex can be seen as a "reward of combat," as Goldstein has argued, something the soldiers feel they are entitled to for possibly sacrificing their lives for the state; it is "their rationed piece of ass," as Kirstein described it brusquely. To these soldiers sex was an instinctual reaction to the fear of dying because procreation creates life and thus is the opposite of death.

Shapiro also looks at Katz in "V-Letter" for consolation and comfort, for a mother figure or a housewife. "You are my home," Shapiro writes, "and in your spacious love / I dream to march as under flaring flags."[43] Shapiro's soldier connects love not only with domesticity but also with tickertape parade–type patriotism. He loves his girlfriend not just because she waits for him, but also because she epitomizes the United States for him. In the last stanza of "V-Letter," Shapiro indulges in an unlikely Audenesque conceit in which he compares his relationship to foodstuff stacked in a pantry:

> As groceries in a pantry gleam and smile
> Because they are important weights
> Bought with the metal minutes of your pay,
> So do these hours stand in solid rows,
> The dowry for a use in common life.[44]

Again we encounter images of food and domestic life similar to those in Gwendolyn Brooks's "Gay Chaps at the Bar" and James Dickey's "The Firebombing," but Shapiro links these more directly to romance and sexuality. Kirstein did the same in "Snatch" when he suggests that what activates the "blackmail base for lust" is the "sullen dreams of luxury unspent for starveling months to come."[45] "Luxury" is etymologically linked to the Latin word *"luxuria,"* which not only implies abundance and comfort but also rankness or lust. When deprived of worldly goods as well as female company during a war, soldiers begin to equate them.

The yearning in "V-Letter" for an American girl back home is ultimately not a love poem addressed to one specific girl, but for a type of girl; the girl next door, the average American girl:

> I see you woman-size
> And this looms larger and more goddess-like
> Than silver goddesses on screens.
> I see you in the ugliness of light,
> Yet you are beautiful,
> And in the dark of absence your full length
> Is such as meets my body to the full
> Though I am starved and huge.[46]

It is was not uncommon for soldier-poets during World War II to express "hunger for women," as Lorrie Goldensohn writes, but few poets were so "starved" as Shapiro, whose addition "and huge" seems a straightforward admission of his erection.[47] Despite his lurking distrust earlier in the poem, he claims that his home-front girl is more desirable than the Hollywood stars that Shapiro and his fellow soldiers leered at in an open-air theater in Australia.

Yet even though these Hollywood stars and pin-up girls may have been objects of sexual fantasy for many soldiers, GIs were just as keen on "representative women, standing in for wives and sweethearts on the homefront," as Robert B. Westbrook has argued. Westbrook reminds us that the most popular pin-up girl was Betty Grable, who was "less an erotic 'sex-goddess' than a symbol of the kind of woman for whom American men—especially

American working-class men—were fighting."[48] Shapiro's ode is directed at exactly such an American girl (with a whiff of foreignness), Evalyn Katz, who reminds him of his Baltimore home and who waits for him. In a letter Shapiro called Katz his "fool-proof girl" whose perfections made him "a little moony."[49] Ironically, in the *World-Telegram* picture Katz did her best to pose like a Hollywood star, with cigarette in hand and "appearing in slacks and sweater to make a robust appearance," as the journalist of the article noted. Katz's appearance suggests, as Westbrook points out in general terms about the World War II era, that women on the home front began to "fashion themselves into pin-up girls worth fighting for.[50]

Shapiro's wartime infidelity with the Australian publisher Cecily Crozier may be surprising in view of his sentimental attachment to Katz in "V-Letter." Shapiro himself explained the affair in his autobiography with Kirsteinian candor: "Nobody said anything about love; love was in the photographs on the cotside box. Love was American. Banging sheilas was something else, a kind of raise in pay for being overseas, a duty to the flag, so to speak."[51]

Love is patriotic whereas sex abroad is a bonus. Crozier was a cosmopolitan English woman living in Melbourne who had lived in Egypt and who edited the little magazine *Comment.* Shapiro picked up one of the issues in a bookstore in 1942 and called the editor hoping to meet Australian poets. Confused by her first name, Shapiro expected to encounter a man, but quickly found out that she was a married woman who had filed for divorce from her husband who was fighting in northern Africa. Before Shapiro was shipped off to Sydney, a brief but intense love affair ensued between the two, resulting in *The Place of Love,* a book of poems, prose poems, and aphorisms that are more openly sexually explicit than the poems in *V-Letter.*

The title poem of *The Place of Love* closely resembles Walt Whitman's "Song of Myself" because of its free verse and its catalogs, but also because of its open celebration of sexuality. "Man only is ashamed to be seen to love and copulate," Shapiro says boldly.[52] Other poems, such as "The Egyptian Silk" and "Syllabus," prove that this shame does not bother him in the least, as he suggests how he slipped between Crozier's sheets. In the opening poem, "The New Ring," Shapiro also scoffs at marriage. A ring, the symbol of marriage "oppresses the finger, embarrasses the hand, encumbers the whole arm," Shapiro suggests in the poem's first line. The final image is even more extreme, as Shapiro likens marriage to a crucifixion: "the new ring is a new nail / driven through the hand upon the living wood, and / the boy hangs from the nail, and the nail holds."[53] These lines must have been upsetting to Katz, his fiancée, who was hoping to marry her GI after the war. Despite his obvious infidelity, however, Shapiro insensitively sent a copy of

The Place of Love to Katz, hoping that she could publish the book in the United States.

Neither Reynal & Hitchcock nor Katz was particularly keen to publish *The Place of Love* on the other side of the Pacific Ocean, though. Katz told Shapiro that his publisher had suggested in May 1943 that such an experiment was costly and that the poems were not in good taste. Shapiro reacted furiously and threatened to go look for another publisher: "This means that the publishing arbiters are above us in taste and purpose. I would rather abandon writing altogether than believe this. We have gone so far as to obtain the approval of librarians."[54] Although he was certainly right that the wartime publishing industry was conservative—as Kirstein also found out—Shapiro is overstressing his point here, as he was apt to do. His indignation expressed to Katz seems out of place. If anyone should have been angry at this point it should have been Katz, who was asked to place a volume of erotic verse by her fiancé in which he writes about his infidelities. Shapiro was aware of the "possible embarrassment" to Katz, but thought that the subject was "too delicate for discussion" and should "wait until [they] were together."[55] Shapiro apparently believed that Katz took it in good spirit and realized that he was just cashing in on his "raise in pay for being overseas" or performing his "duty to the flag."

Even though Katz was privately hurt by Shapiro's infidelities, she publicly clung to her role as a faithful Rosie the Riveter. She appeared on a radio show *We the Women* and gave many interviews with newspapers telling about her poetry-writing husband-to-be and how her editorial and managerial work advanced his career. The media were so enthralled with the couple that *Vogue* magazine even asked Katz to publish Shapiro's love letters. Shapiro was not amused by this free publicity. He lashed out against Katz in a letter dated May 13, 1944: "We have a reputation that we're going to have to love down—the far-off soldier who made good through his sweetheart. Don't you see that you're slipping in with the professionals, the bond-sellers, the pin-up magazines? How do we fit into that? Why do you want that, particularly when you know I detest it so much? What are you after?"[56]

Shapiro's letter is charged with the same kind of "vehement, sexualized ridicule" that Susan Schweik recognizes in acerbic male reviews of Edna St. Vincent Millay's *The Murder of Lidice* (1942) and Muriel Rukeyser's *Wake Island* (1942).[57] Shapiro began to see that he was being groomed into a patriotic poet, the kind of "fine clean upstanding American one" that Jarrell was poking fun at in his letter to Lowell. Shapiro blames Katz for this reputation, calling her "stage struck" and bent on "publicity madness," expressing the same creeping distrust of her honesty that also informs "V-Letter." Katz certainly seemed to relish the attention; yet Shapiro had also egged her on, encouraging her to publish his poems in light magazines, like *Good Housekeeping, Harper's,* and *Mademoiselle.* What Katz was after, to answer Shapiro's rhetorical question, was that Shapiro would be more like the public persona of him that she helped to create, and less like the distrustful and deceitful fiancé that he proved to be.

By November 1944, when Shapiro knew he would be shipped back to the United States soon, Shapiro began to realize the full extent of his duplicity while reading through Katz's correspondence to him: "When I was through I felt frozen with the pain I had caused and revolted with myself. What you write is all one beautiful flowing word; you are so clear, so explicit and right: I was the opposite; soiled, ambiguous, wrong. It wd be easiest to say that my confusion was necessary and inevitable during that first year, and the second which took a turn from emotional to psychic confusion—or were they the same things?"[58]

Katz is once again Shapiro's "fool-proof girl" as it turns out. Even though Shapiro's complete devotion and trust in her judgment is no longer entirely believable after his mistrust earlier on, his analysis of himself and how confused he was is accurate enough. Shapiro's sexual confusion can to a certain extent be related to the war, which also left many of his fellow poets confused. Yet it was clearly the result of his personality as well. Shapiro's love for and attachment to Katz was on one level genuine. He was truly grateful for the way she edited his volumes and advanced his career. Moreover, he also enjoyed the recognition he received, which gave him a sense of identity in the uniformed army. For a time he also did not mind being presented as a "fine clean upstanding American" patriotic poet, and even willingly contributed to this image. Yet he ultimately rebelled against it since he realized that societal pressures would force him into a straitjacket of correct behavior and pleasing, patriotic poetry. Suspecting that Katz wanted him to fit that public persona, he grew aggressive. The physical distance between them, the haphazard communication, and the time that had elapsed since they had last seen each other further fueled his suspicion and distrust.

Shapiro had also "fallen in love, in a Little Magazine kind of way, in an avant-garde kind of way," with Cecily Crozier, as he asserted in his autobiography.[59] This affair allowed Shapiro to explore a more bohemian side of himself, away from the more conservative morality in the United States. The consummation of that love affair was also prompted by the fear of death, loneliness, and peer pressure as well. It was a way to "shut out the army and the war."[60] His fellow soldiers "congratulated" Shapiro for moving in "on a dame if that was what he wanted."[61] Shapiro's confusion was triggered by the war, but exacerbated by two sides of his personality: his more rebellious, anti-authoritarian, and sexual side, and his desire to fit in and be respected, to be the bourgeois poet. Shapiro's war poems reflect these tensions perfectly. Morally dubious and hastily conceived and written, Shapiro's poems do not measure up to the most haunting war poems by Jarrell, Hecht, and Nemerov, but they do acutely reveal the anxieties felt by a generation of soldiers.

CHAPTER 12

Alternative Masculinities

It is not surprising, given the democratic spirit of the poets of World War II, that this generation was highly conscious of how other people experienced and suffered during the war. This is especially apparent for Randall Jarrell, who made it into his trademark of his war poetry. Lincoln Kirstein's "4F" and Karl Shapiro's "The Conscientious Objector" are especially emblematic of this broadmindedness. They focus on the anxieties of men who were different from them and who fell outside the perimeters of hegemonic masculinity during World War II. Most of the male poets of the middle generation were reluctantly inducted and obediently performed their wartime duties. Some of them, however, were declared unfit to fight—for instance, John Berryman, Weldon Kees, and Delmore Schwartz—while others refused to serve as soldiers. This latter group includes—besides Lowell—William Everson, Stanley Kunitz, and William Stafford.

The military historian Michael Howard has suggested that during the Second World War the "traditional distinction between soldier and civilian, which had been so clear in the eighteenth and nineteenth centuries and which had even survived the First World War, once again disappeared."[1] The whole economy of a nation was at the disposal of the war effort, so it did not matter much whether one contributed to the warring state in a civilian capacity or in uniform. "Those who were not called up," Howard concludes, were thus "left alone."[2] Yet this was not entirely the case, as the American poets of World War II knew. The nature of war may have changed from 1939 to 1945, but the expectations of men remained the same. Their collective poetry evinces the belief that society still demanded that a real man ought to wear a uniform.

"Some twelve thousand of us of draft age went into the alternative service program called Civilian Public Service," Stafford writes in *Down in My Heart*, his account of his experiences as a conscientious objector: "Some five thousand were sent to prison," which included Lowell for a time, while "some unspecified thousands went into noncombatant service with the armed forces."[3] Kunitz was drafted just after his thirty-eighth birthday "as a nonaffiliated pacifist, with moral scruples against bearing arms." He was supposed to fall in the third category that Stafford mentions, but things turned out differently, as Kunitz reported in an interview in which he remembered his dismal time in the army: "My understanding with the draft board was that I would be assigned to a service unit, such as the Medical Corps. Instead the papers on my status got lost or were never delivered, and I was shuttled for three years from camp to camp, doing KP duty most of the time or digging latrines. A combination of pneumonia, scarlet fever, and just downright humiliation almost did me in. While I was still in uniform, *Passport to a War,* my bleakest book was published, but I was scarcely aware of the event. It seemed to sink without a trace."[4] World War II was not only for the soldier-poets but also for noncombatants such as Kunitz and Stafford the most formidable and formative events of their lives, influencing their outlook on human behavior forever.

The title of Kirstein's "4F" refers to one of the most famous designations of American men during World War II. Draft boards divided males between the ages of eighteen and forty-five into four categories: Class 1 referred to draftees who were available for military service after examination; Class 2 indicated men who were fit for service but received a deferral of no longer than six months; Class 3 consisted of men with dependents; and Class 4 comprised "non-declarant aliens, conscientious objectors, men who had already completed military service, and those considered 'mentally, physically, or morally unfit,'" as Christina S. Jarvis has noted.[5] Classes 1A and 4F quickly caught on in the popular imagination as they reflected the prototype of the healthy and perfect American man and its opposite, the ill-adjusted, strange, and sickly kind of man who was either unable or unwilling to take up arms. In her hit song "He's 1-A in the Army and He's A-1 in My Heart," Betty Bonney celebrates her clean-cut American guy because she knows "he wants to do his part," while Ted Courtney's "Four-F Charlie" cleverly stigmatizes those who were not allowed to join the army by listing Charlie's physical deficiencies.[6] Even though Kirstein himself was classified as 1A, he does not feel any contempt for his imaginary protagonist. This 4F works for *Life* magazine during the war, "deep down the masthead of the Lucemachine," as Kirstein says referring to the publisher of that famous illustrated magazine.[7]

Kirstein's "4F" is much more respectful than "Four-F Charlie," and Kirstein invites his readers to empathize with this intellectual man who falls outside the norms of expected male wartime behavior:

So far, survived he had. Now, he needn't worry.
Secure on *Life,* his draft board knows the tale:
Orphan since three; years of neglect; TB;
Weak lungs still. Poor risk. How can we fail?

It's all true. He isn't strong; often, sleeps poorly.
Nightmares toss him back on battles' borders.
Far from raw life yet tapping global strife,
Hoards gobbets snatched from the secular orders.[8]

Punning on the name *Life,* Kirstein suggests that while this military reject has a stable enough job at the monthly, and his existence is not immediately in danger, he still has to follow his superior's commands, and he is also troubled by similar bad dreams. In the poem's climax he locks himself in the bathroom, and stares at a *Life* magazine spread of marines in the Pacific. He breaks down and cries, wistful for the action that the marines and *Life*'s star photographer W. Eugene Smith witness, and from which he is excluded.

The ending is downright sentimental, but "4F" is nevertheless remarkable because Kirstein does not feel disdain for this failed conscript, but identifies with him. The only people that Kirstein scoffs at are *Life*'s executives and a "manufacturer of Jet Jumbo Jems" whom the protagonist has to interview.[9] *Life*'s senior officials are contemptible specimens of their gender, in Kirstein's estimate. These men expect their employees to follow their instructions unquestionably, but they are only interested in how "Wall Street boosts our war potential."[10] The maker of war planes is like Arthur Miller's character Joe Keller in *All My Sons* (1947), "a smug thug jobber" who switches careers because he senses he can make a fortune selling war planes.[11] Miller was also declared 4F, and like Kirstein's protagonist he became a journalist of sorts during the war.

Weldon Kees did likewise. In 1943 Kees also worked in "the Lucemachine," as he was briefly part of the book review department of *Time* magazine. Like Kirstein's imaginary 4F, Kees slaved away in the Time and Life Building, which Kees facetiously called "the Grime and Strife Building," while others were sent to the European and Pacific theaters.[12] Kees did not have the same anxiety about not doing his part in the war effort as Kirstein's 4F. From the start Kees was opposed to America's involvement in the war, and he consistently expressed a desire not to be enlisted. Kees "joked about becoming a Jehovah's Witness or feigning an 'epileptic fit,'" as his biographer James Reidel has noted, "like the one in his novel *Fall Quarter* with a mouth full of soap flakes."[13] When he was summoned before the draft board, Kees was "lovingly placed in classification 4F," as he put it in a letter. It is not clear whether Kees used any of the tricks quoted above; Reidel assumes that he "was simply himself, a man with a slight build who said that he wrote poetry."[14]

If Kees did not share Kirstein's 4F's torment about his inability to join the army, he did consider himself an outsider in his own country. In "June 1940"—his most explicit poetic commentary on World War II and war in general—Kees indignantly reacts against the ostentatious nationalist warmongers in an American small town. They were until recently fervent isolationists, but are now trimming their sails to an "idiot wind."[15] "The beaters of drums, the flag-kissing men, whose eyes / Once saw the murder, are washing it clean, accusing: / 'You are cowards! All that we told you before was lies!'"[16] Kees finds the patriotic air sickening, even before Pearl Harbor, and he feels stigmatized and taunted as a yellow-belly. The hot weather seems to spawn the hot-tempered bellicose patriots, and it feels like a déjà vu of earlier wars:

> It is summer again, the evening is warm and silent.
> The windows are dark and the mountains are miles away.
> And the men who were haters of war are mounting the platforms.
> An idiot wind is blowing; the conscience dies.[17]

With his typically simple but suggestive imagery, Kees expresses his loneliness, isolation, and claustrophobia. He would rather flee into the faraway mountains, but he thinks there is no escaping once the patriots get on stage. Kees's moody alliteration and assonance—"I am alone in a worn-out town in wartime"—suggests that he feels like a pariah in small-town America, where he is regarded as an unmanly male.

The only people Kees senses a connection with in "June 1940" are writers and noncombatants like himself—Randolph Bourne, Gustav Flaubert, James Joyce, D. H. Lawrence, and Rainer Maria Rilke, who also became disgusted by war.[18] They were also all either exiled or misunderstood. They are "gun-shy, annoyers, sick of the kill, the watchers" who "suffered the same attack till it broke them or left its scars."[19] The poem's two epigraphs are taken from Wilfred Owen, once again confirming how much Kees's generation of poets was aware of the poets of the Great War. The first is culled from Owen's preface and states that "all a poet can do is warn." The second consists of the last two lines of Owen's famous poem "Dulce et Decorum Est," insinuating that Horace's epigraph that it is sweet and honorable to die for your country is a lie. None of the writers that Kees mentions in "June 1940" were alive when he wrote the poem, underlining his spiritual isolation in the middle of America and in the middle of the twentieth century.

John Berryman, who was declared 4F because of his poor eyesight, felt equally cut off from mainstream America during the war, and he began increasingly to identify with other outsiders, those who were vulnerable, persecuted, or victimized, as both his short story "The Imaginary Jew" and his poem "Boston Common" show. This poem, which is subtitled "Meditation upon the Hero," was the "most formidable and complex lyric" he had written until then, as his biographer Paul Mariani has written.[20] "Boston Common" centers on Augustus Saint-Gaudens's bronze bas relief sculpture of Union colonel Robert Gould Shaw and the Fifty-fourth Massachusetts Regiment. It features Shaw on horseback and surrounded by African American soldiers marching to Charleston, South Carolina, during the Civil War. The monument is situated opposite the Massachusetts State Capitol and pays tribute to the colonel and his men, most of whom—Shaw included—died at Fort Wagner. Berryman wonders what his feelings are about this Civil War hero who was considered to be worthy of a memorial, but whose character seems completely enigmatic to the noncombatant poet during World War II.

Berryman's "Boston Common" is similar to two poems by Lowell, "Christmas Eve under Hooker's Statue" and "For the Union Dead." Written more than a decade later, "For the Union Dead" is, in fact, about the same artwork by Saint-Gaudens. Like Lowell in "Christmas Eve under Hooker's Statue," the equestrian statue that is only fifty yards away from the Shaw memorial, Berryman also evokes Herman Melville's "The March into Virginia": "War is the / Congress of adolescents," Berryman writes: "love in a mask, / Bestial and easy, issueless, / Or gets a man of bronze."[21] Wars are fought by those who are no longer children, but not yet adults either, by those who act irrationally and immaturely. Berryman does not regard Shaw as a "Hero," and neither does Lowell in "For the Union Dead," who condescendingly refers to the colonel's "angry wrenlike vigilance."[22]

Yet Lowell is equally fascinated by Shaw, as he also recognizes the importance of civic duty. Both "Boston Common" and "For the Union Dead" dramatize once more the almost irresistible attraction of the military hero, but also the equally strong understanding that this model has severe risks. While Lowell is ambivalent about Shaw, Berryman would be satisfied if "the common man rather than the leader" becomes the "hero of our time," as Helen Vendler has argued.[23] Berryman seems just as intrigued by the hobo who sleeps underneath Saint-Gaudens's sculpture as by the historical figure of Shaw. "Slumped under the impressive genitals / Of the bronze charger," this vagrant is as much an impotent reject of wartime American masculinity as Berryman.[24]

Like Kirstein's "4F," Karl Shapiro's "The Conscientious Objector" pictures a man who does not fit the mold of hegemonic masculinity during World War II. Shapiro is, like Kirstein, not dismissive of the other and calls him as much a hero as the soldiers who fought in the war:

Yet you who saved neither yourselves nor us
Are equally with those who shed the blood
The heroes of our cause. Your conscience is
What we come back to in the armistice.[25]

Shapiro's acceptance of the conscientious objector who is praised for his steadfast conviction counters the much more negative appraisal of this group by mainstream America.

Shapiro applauds the conscientious objector because he acts on his principles, accepts the consequences, and suffers because of them, just like soldiers do in a war. The conscientious objector suffers, "not so physically," but he experiences "maltreatment, hunger, ennui of the mind" all the same. Shapiro expresses an awareness of how powerfully hostile a society that is at war can be to those who fall outside the norm. Reflecting the same aggressive and intimidating atmosphere that Kees pictures in "June 1940," Shapiro writes:

the flags that dripped
From every mother's windowpane, obscene
The bloodlust sweating from the public heart,
The dog authority slavering at your throat.[26]

Shapiro's violent and heavy-handed diction suggests that even if the outside world does not physically attack the conscientious objector, it does exert a strong mental pressure to conform. Being locked up in jail paradoxically feels like a release, like freedom to the conscientious objector, because "the hostile world" is "shut out."[27]

It has been assumed that Shapiro wrote "The Conscientious Objector" with Robert Lowell in mind.[28] The imagery in the second and third stanzas alluding to the principled Puritans who sailed to New England makes such an interpretation plausible because Lowell was a descendant from the *Mayflower* and also took the moral high ground during the war. Yet Shapiro's correspondence with the *New Yorker,* to which he offered the poem in 1946, shows that he actually wrote it with several religious conscientious objectors whom he met in New Guinea in mind. Shapiro suggested to the *New Yorker*'s poetry editor, Katharine White, that he did not "follow the suicidal logic of pacifists at all," but "merely tried to state their case."[29]

Despite his defense of conscientious objectors immediately after the war, Shapiro incongruously lashed out against Lowell in *The Old Horsefly,* the last book he published during his lifetime. In "Robert Lowell" Shapiro viciously charged that Lowell

Tried to get a Navy commission but failed,
Tried to joining the Army; they didn't want him either,

Joined the R.C.'s (temporarily) and then
Joined the Conscientious Objectors.
Sent to a nice prison but quickly released,
Because he was "a Lowell" the others said, and stayed.[30]

Shapiro's angry denunciation of Lowell contradicts his "The Conscientious Objector," in which he expressed compassion for those who thought and acted differently. It has never been proven that Lowell tried to get a commission in the navy, and the frustration and obvious unfairness of this poem tell more about Shapiro's paranoia and bitterness in his later years than about Lowell's wavering position during World War II.

The *New Yorker* did not accept "The Conscientious Objector." Some of the magazine's editors thought that it was "possibly a trifle overstated on the matter of the treatment of conscientious objectors in this war and that it would have been more applicable after the First World War," as White reported to Shapiro. White personally disagreed with this verdict but thought that Shapiro's final stanza was unsuccessful because the reader might "believe the poem could be taken as a vindication of their position." Several editors at the *New Yorker* also thought the two middle stanzas were "a bit hard to follow," which is true.[31] Yet it seems as if Shapiro's—for that time—dicey content rather than the poem's style made the *New Yorker* decide not to publish this much-anthologized poem by the recent Pulitzer Prize–winning poet.

Shapiro's "The Conscientious Objector" was not intended to represent either of the two, but it is more applicable to William Stafford than to Lowell. Stafford, who was briefly Shapiro's student at the University of Iowa Writers' Workshop in the early 1950s, spent four years in camps for conscientious objectors because he refused to be inducted into the army. His master thesis at the University of Kansas, a nonfictional account of those years, was published as a book, *Down in My Heart,* and shows that Shapiro's imaginary testimony of "the treatment of conscientious objectors in this war" was not "a trifle overstated," as the *New Yorker* made it out to be. In the first chapter of *Down in My Heart,* for instance, titled "The Mob Scene at McNeil," Stafford relates how he and two other conscientious objectors were cornered in a small Arkansas community by an angry crowd when they discovered that the three men refused to fight in the war. Like Kees, Stafford felt like a foreigner in his own country: "Those of us who objected openly found our country conquered overnight—conquered by aliens who could shout on any corner or in any building and bring down on us wrath and hate more intense than any foreigner. . . . It was unnerving to wake up in a barracks and find ourselves almost alien, proscribed, lost, tagged, orphaned, outlawed."[32]

Down in My Heart offers a generally unsentimental account of how the conscientious objectors lived and worked, building in the meantime an alternative, pacifist community in the midst of a warring nation. Yet Stafford's nonfiction book also sometimes reads as an instruction guide on how not to engage in violence and seek the conciliatory solution. In the aptly titled chapter "The Battle of Anapamu Creek," for instance, Stafford recounts how the pacifists clash with a U.S. Forest Service foreman, "a big, rough, tough hater of Germans, Japanese and CO's."[33] The foreman's attitude turns out to be fairly typical of the Forest Service men's prejudices against the noncombatants: "At first some of the Forest Service men had talked largely, among themselves when some of our men had happened to overhear, about their enmity for CO's; and I myself had overheard one man, later our friend, say in the ranger station, 'I wish I was superintendent of that camp; I'd line 'em up and uh-uh-uh-uh'—he made the sound of a machine gun. I went ahead with my clerical work, and regaled the boys with the story that night."[34]

When about a dozen conscientious objectors have to accompany the redneck Forest Service foreman on a spike camp to cut down southwestern chaparral, the conscientious objectors send their "first team" for their "first, and crucial battle."[35] The foreman tries to bully the conscientious objectors, including the appointed cook, Ken, in a typically military fashion. Ken does not accept this unfair treatment, however, and draws up a list of demands that have to be fulfilled before he starts cooking. The foreman is furious and threatens Ken, and orders other conscientious objectors to take his place. None of them budges, and they reach an impasse. The Forest Service man is then asked which of Ken's terms are unacceptable to him and how he would like to change them. This is how they come to an understanding that is agreeable to everyone. The conscientious objectors teach the foreman a nonviolent, democratic lesson that changes the foreman's bigoted ways.

Stafford's poetry is clearly influenced by his years in the Civilian Public Service projects as well as by his interaction with other pacifists. His best poems that allude to war are less overtly didactic than *Down in My Heart,* but curiously enough more instructive. These poems are similar in subject matter to Berryman's "Boston Common" since they are meditations on heroes, although Berryman's poem is decidedly more "stately" and "Yeatsian," as Vendler has argued.[36] Like Kees's "June 1940," Stafford also seeks to expose the danger and hollowness of patriotism. What distinguishes Stafford from Berryman and Kees is that he is much more positive than these archpessimists, and seeks conciliation with those who hold opposing views. In doing so, Stafford establishes an alternative model of masculinity. Rather than emphasize negative masculine qualities such as "toughness, dominance, repression of empathy, [and] extreme competitiveness," to use definitions that Dan Kindlon and Michael Thomson introduce, Stafford emphasizes positive ones, such as "unusual courage, curiosity, sense of adventure, and independence from societal pressures."[37]

Many of Stafford's poems revolve around issues of masculinity, but "Men" most explicitly addresses how traditional Western conceptions of masculinity and femininity create a vicious cycle that continually breeds warriors:

After a war come the memorials—
tanks, cutlasses, men with cigars.
If women are there they adore
and are saved, shielding their children.

For a long time people rehearse
just how it happened, and you have to learn
how important all that armament was—
and it really could happen again.

So the women and children can wait, whatever
their importance might have been, and they
come to stand around the memorials
and listen some more and be grateful, and smell the cigars.[38]

The understated conversational tone and uncomplicated diction are typical of Stafford's style. Yet, as Philip Metres has argued, "Stafford presents a deceptively simple narrative in deceptively plain language as a way of addressing the reader and creating, through parable, a way of living that has been 'forgotten by everyone alive.'"[39] By the same token he also presents alternative ways of being a man. Memorials—like Saint-Gaudens's Shaw bas relief sculpture that Berryman wrote about—and memorabilia from previous wars reflect normative and desired behavior for males to model themselves on. The notion of the man as warrior also "depends on an 'other' constructed as feminine," as Joshua S. Goldstein has argued, and women therefore consciously or unconsciously "take on the 'specific nonwarrior roles.'"[40] In the case of Stafford's poem the women (and children) are there to "adore," to be "saved," to "listen some more and be grateful, and to smell the cigars." Stafford uses hyperbolic and stereotypical images of cigar-smoking men and obedient women, but he does so to make a general point about war and gender.

Men and women tend to accept the traditional gender roles that are assigned to them, especially during times of war. These roles are neither natural nor desirable, but part of a culturally determined "system" that is dangerous because it perpetuates a cycle of violence, Stafford suggests. Stafford's tone throughout the poem is that of the weary observer who has seen it all before. It almost seems as if Stafford has accepted this type of memorializing that glorifies a previous war and paves the way for new wars. The fact that Stafford has written and published this poem, however, reveals that he has not given up yet. He keeps on trying to convince people that the masculine war cycle can be broken, and that wars are neither necessary nor inevitable. Stafford wants to shake people out of their complacency and urges them to think about how they can prevent wars before they occur. This requires a radically different mindset.

In "Allegiances" Stafford dismisses the traditional hero type as Berryman does in "Boston Common." Yet he also provides more concrete, alternative ways of living and being:

> It is time for all the heroes to go home
> if they have any, time for all of us common ones
> to locate ourselves by the real things
> we live by.[41]

Stafford's style is much prosier and unadorned than Berryman's more formal early verse, but it fits with his argument that he wants to side with ordinary people rather than with heroes who are always in the spotlight. He takes the "common ones" on an imaginary trip to nature where "strange mountains and creatures have always lurked."[42] Stafford utters a similar plea as Kees does in "June 1940," for he also wants to escape to the mountains rather than be stuck in small-town America. Nature can offer solace and shelter to people, as Stafford confirms.

Stafford's title is ironically more formal than the casual and colloquial rest of the poem. The title conjures up the Pledge of Allegiance or other signs of (wartime) loyalty and support to the state. Yet Stafford suggests in "Allegiances" that people should be faithful to the land and earth rather than to a nation. Stafford is not preachy in "Allegiances." He reasons with his readers, trying to coax them into taking an alternative route, without forcing anything on them or raising his voice. In the final stanza Stafford alludes to war when he asks us to "suppose an insane wind holds all the hills / while strange beliefs whine at the traveler's ears."[43] Stafford "insane wind" consciously or unconsciously echoes Kees's "idiot wind" to describe the hostile climate that was setting in. Stafford uses a similar trope to depict the temporary madness that takes hold of the majority of a country when at war. Yet unlike Kees, who is the most skeptical or even cynical of the middle generation poets, Stafford sends off a positive message at the end. There is always another way: "we ordinary beings can cling to the earth and love / where we are, sturdy for common things," as Stafford says in his typically homely idiom.[44]

In "At the Un-National Monument along the Canadian Border" and "A Ritual to Read to Each Other," two of his most anthologized poems, Stafford expresses most perfectly this affirmative and alternative way of being, and of manhood. "At the Un-National Monument" can be regarded as a pacifist revision of Abraham Lincoln's famous Gettysburg Address. Like Lincoln, Stafford calls a field "hallowed." Yet the field is not consecrated by the men who died on that field as Lincoln had said about Gettysburg. The area around the Canadian border is a sacred place because "the unknown soldier did not die." It is a site where "only grass joined hands," where "no monument stands / and the only heroic thing is the sky."[45] Whereas in traditional eulogies like Lincoln's Gettysburg Address dead soldiers are honored for giving their lives, Stafford gives tribute to mankind because "no people killed—or were killed—on this ground."[46] This is as much if not more of an achievement, Stafford suggests, as it requires not only determination and perseverance but also restraint and acts of conciliation. In most of his war poems one can sense sarcasm and anger hiding underneath his civilized diction, but in "At the Un-National Monument" he uses a constructive example to show people how to live alternatively, to live peacefully.

In "Men" Stafford had also touched on the influence of monuments, deploring how they are used conventionally to glorify wars, but in "At the Un-National Monument" he goes a step further by ironically applauding the absence of a monument at the border where two nations have been at peace with each other for several centuries. Stafford wrote and published "At the Un-National Monument" in 1977, shortly after the U.S. Bicentennial, which celebrated the violent birth of Stafford's nation, replete with many festivities and much merriment. In his poem Stafford commemorates quietly and alone a battle and war that were not fought.

In his most compelling poems—such as "Allegiances" and "At the Un-National Monument"—Stafford makes a convincing case that alternative masculinities are possible and that a nonviolent future for our planet is feasible, even if he sometimes loses patience, as "Men" shows. When asked in an interview during the last year of his life whether he ever got angry, he admitted that irritation and annoyance were certainly part of his temperament: "Oh, yes, yes, you get angry; yes, yes, we're animals. But it's not my best self. What I'm voicing is not so much an achieved position as a desired position."[47] As Jarrell also knew, man could be "a wolf to man," to quote his phrase from "Eighth Air Force."[48]

Yet rather than accept this depressing lesson from World War II and the twentieth century, which many of his contemporaries did, Stafford sought to emphasize men's tremendous capacity for tenderness. Stafford would have disagreed with Kees and agreed with Shapiro. No matter how many idiot or insane winds are blowing, conscience does not die. It is to Stafford's peace-making conscience that the poets of World War II returned "in the armistice." Despite their inspirational content, however, Stafford's miniature narratives about war resistance are sometimes a bit thin as aesthetic achievements. The sound and form contribute little to their overall effect. Multiple readings of a poem will yield few new insights as opposed to, for instance, Lowell's war resistance poem "Memories of West Street and Lepke," which continues to intrigue readers. Moreover, since "a collection of his poems rarely builds from poem to poem," as Metres writes, Stafford's message can sound repetitive and staid.[49]

Stafford's importance as a war poet resides foremost in his advocacy for alternative ways of being masculine. No matter how entranced the World War II poets had been by the hypermasculine, military male during their boyish years, they steadily searched for alternative ways to assert their manhood in the postwar years. Only James Dickey kept fantasizing about the male warrior type until he reached old age. Yet Dickey's reaction reads as a compensation for the kind of vulnerability that the other poets of World War II owned up to more readily, and which he chose to hide except in some telling poems. Quietly rejecting the soldier as a masculine ideal, the World War II poets de-emphasized the qualities that are usually associated with it, such as roughness, domination, loudness, repression of empathy, and being fiercely rivalrous. These qualities were replaced by characteristics that can be equally manly and which also rhymed with their professions of poets—for instance, their intellectual curiosity, their broadmindedness, and their independence from social pressure. Gradually during their afterlives of the war they embraced other ways of being masculine, while they sought to subtly correct the way in which their war was being remembered and memorialized.

PART
[4]

TROUBLED AFTERLIVES

CHAPTER 13

"Ought I to regret my seedtime?"

The only rhetorical question in Robert Lowell's much-anthologized poem "Memories of West Street and Lepke"—in which he reminisces in his comfortable home on Boston's Marlborough Street about being sent to jail for refusing to enter military service a decade earlier—is: "Ought I to regret my seedtime?"[1] It is a curious question in remarkably formal diction in an otherwise colloquial poem. The question signifies Lowell's uneasiness about his sudden move to declare himself a conscientious objector, a decision analyzed earlier in this book. Lowell has lost the certainty of judgment that characterized his war years, and has come instead to question his own mind and memory, a feature that is typical of other poets of his generation as well.

Alan Williamson is probably correct in assuming that Lowell borrowed the word "seedtime" from one of William Blake's Proverbs of Hell: "In seedtime learn, in harvest teach, in winter enjoy."[2] In the first line of "Memories of West Street and Lepke" Lowell had mentioned that he was "only teaching on Tuesdays," which might indicate that Lowell had indeed reached the autumn of his life. An earlier title of Lowell's poem was "My Season in Hell," a reference to Arthur Rimbaud's *Une saison en enfer.* It confirms how preoccupied Lowell was with the seasons of life. Like Lowell, nearly all the poets of World War II had by the "tranquilized *Fifties*" become instructors, and they were spending their "harvest" years teaching poetry at colleges and universities throughout the United States.[3]

Unlike several major English poets of World War II, including Keith Douglas, Sidney Keyes, and Alun Lewis, all of the major American poets of that war survived it. Like Lowell, many of them "built later careers on the foundations of their early war poems," as Paul Fussell has claimed, and spent the decades following the war pondering about those decisive war years.[4] Lowell was not alone in feeling disturbed and remorseful about his actions (or lack thereof) during World War II, even though his refusal to enlist was not representative of his generation. Many poets who joined the military shared Lowell's nagging doubts about their formative years during the 1940s and wondered what had motivated them to take up arms, or contemplated whether their involvement in World War II was morally justified. For some, including John Ciardi, Anthony Hecht, and Louis Simpson, their participation in this global conflict led to a series of traumatic memories, but for all others, too, World War II remained a constant preoccupation that they never got rid of. Lowell's question sums up the collective, brooding, and doubting mind of the poets of World War II. Although they were relieved when the war was over, they did not partake in the ticker-tape-parade atmosphere of their compatriots. While the collective American memory transformed World War II into a mythological "Good War," their poetry steadfastly but quietly expresses their general unease about what the war meant about themselves, their country, and humankind.

Ranging from Richard Hugo—a bombardier who dropped his incendiaries on civilian populations—to Randall Jarrell—a celestial navigation instructor who never left the United States—all of them tried to come to terms in their verse with feelings of guilt in the afterlife of the war. In a notebook now held at the Berg Collection of the New York Public Library, Jarrell scribbled:

> I was sorry for them. I would have saved them if I
> could.
> ~~I would even have saved the others that you killed.~~
> I sat alone in the darkness and *moved the stars over your head.*
> I helped you on your way, the way
> I guided you to them
> ~~I would have saved the people that they killed~~[5]

Teaching young men the position of the stars would under normal circumstances not have created feelings of contrition, but Jarrell knows that he cannot escape some responsibility for the atrocities that happened during the war. Even if he is sitting alone in the dark by himself in his home country, performing the most poetic-sounding job in the military, he is among the nightmare fighters. Jarrell realizes that he has indirectly "guided" American airmen to their targets in Europe and Southeast Asia, and that many people died because of those raids. Yet he also knows that he could not have stopped those deaths either, and the sense of powerlessness that this awareness creates is as equally strong as his feelings of culpability. It is important that Jarrell does not deal directly with his own sense of guilt in his published poems. It becomes palpable in his unpublished writings, which helps us recognize remnants of those troubled feelings in the published poems as well.

Published two years after the war, "Eighth Air Force" is Jarrell's fullest expression of how to "behold" himself and the aircrew he trained.[6] Growing flowers, playing pitch, and frolicking with young dogs on their day off, these air force men—who are like puppies themselves—seem the antithesis of evil. Still, these innocent-looking boys and men were responsible for many thousands of civilian casualties as they bombed German cities, such as Dresden and Hamburg, in the latter days of the war. "Eighth Air Force" hinges on the speaker's unnerving realization that the air force men are murderers, but also saviors as many of them died in an effort to rid the world of nazism and to preserve liberty and democracy. Jarrell himself "did as these have done, but did not die," and ultimately appears to absolve himself and them from blame. Yet he also calls this remission a "lie."[7] His troubled verse fragment shows that he has not resolved this quandary for himself, and he probably never did.

As a bombardier in the Fifteenth Air Force stationed in the Mediterranean, Hugo's life was not unlike the airmen that Jarrell describes in "Eighth Air Force." Yet Hugo did not yet have the broad moral vision that Jarrell's narrator could muster immediately after the war. "The more missions you flew," Hugo later recalled, "the narrower became your concerns until finally all you really cared about was your own survival."[8] His view on what he had done during World War II widened considerably in the decades following the war. A chance meeting with fellow-poet Charles Simic in San Francisco, for instance, forced him to observe the bombings from a radically different perspective. Simic, who had emigrated to the United States when he was fifteen, had been born in Belgrade in 1938. Hugo and Simic discovered during their encounter that Hugo had bombed Simic's hometown in 1944 when Simic was a five-year-old child in the war-torn capital of Yugoslavia. Simic recalled that Hugo "became very upset" and "was deeply shaken" by his newly found knowledge. Even after Simic assured him that "he bore no grudges," Hugo "continued to plead for forgiveness and explain himself."[9]

With a mixture of comedy and contrition, Hugo wrote an epistolary poem about it, "Letter to Simic from Boulder," a kind of belated and distressed V-letter. The poem was part of his confessional *31 Letters and 13 Dreams* (1977) in which he loosened his structures and became more radically autobiographical, as Lowell had done before him in *Life Studies* (1959). Hugo does not "apologize for the war, or what I was" in his revealing and public letter to Simic. This may sound arrogant, but the opposite is true:

> I was
> willingly confused by the times. I think I even believed
> in heroics (for others, not for me). I even believed the necessity

of that suffering world, hoping it would learn not to do
it again. But I was young. The world never learns. History
has a way of making the past palatable, the dead
a dream.[10]

Hugo's letter is a humbling testimony of what his life in the air corps was like and who he was, but he does not want to find excuses for what he did when he was his younger self. Hugo only wants to explain himself and testify how grateful he is that Simic was not killed. In order to survive himself, both physically and mentally, Hugo "willingly" chose to forget "the target" and ignore "the enemy."[11] Back then Hugo tried not to think of the people down below and clung to the abstract idea that some people had to suffer for a higher cause. Even though he came to believe later that World War II was "as close to being 'justified'" as any war ever was, he also knows that war entails gratuitous and unjustified suffering for many.[12] A simple apology would be disingenuous, but Hugo is genuinely sorry.

Hugo's "Letter to Simic from Boulder" is not merely an account about himself, however, but also a genuine effort to get to know and reach out to Simic. Asking Simic what happened to his mind when he heard "the terrible howl of bombs" and what the Serb word for "fear" is, Hugo longs to hear how the Other, the victim, had experienced this moment of history from down below.[13] Like Wilfred Owen's "Strange Meeting"—which would also have been an apt title for Hugo's poem—"Letter to Simic from Boulder" describes a haunting encounter of the self with someone who is supposed to be faceless, but turns out to be frighteningly similar to the speaker. Hugo's poem is the opposite of hypermasculine boasting. In fact Hugo paints a picture of himself as a hopelessly incompetent bombardier who could not hit his "ass" if he "sat on a Norden or ride a bomb down singing / The Star Spangled Banner."[14] With self-deprecatory humor Hugo says that if there would ever be a next time, Simic should "sit on the bridge I'm trying to hit and wave." This time his "bombs are candy," and he has "lost the lead plane."[15] The jokey last lines of his poem show Hugo's attempt at atonement, but they are also a halfhearted attempt to make light of a situation that he finds terribly painful and confrontational.

Whereas Hugo used Simic as an addressee to examine the moral anguish that his actions during World War II generated, "The Firebombing" by Hugo's friend James Dickey is a sprawling interior monologue voiced by an anxious former airman who by himself agonizes over his contribution in the destruction of Japanese cities. Dickey has stated in an interview with Ernest Suarez that "The Firebombing" verbalizes "the guilt at the inability to feel guilty."[16] There are scattered clues all over Dickey's poem to prove this, from Günter Eich's epigraph that after all destruction every man will want to prove that he is not guilty, to the final lines of the poem: "Absolution? Sentence? No matter; / The thing itself is in that."[17] The question about the airman's guilt or innocence is irrelevant, according to the speaker, because his actions and his life contain both forgiveness and punishment. His life in his affluent suburb is—like Lowell's on Boston's Marlborough Street—comfortable enough, and as a returning veteran he must have received a hero's welcome. His country and his neighbors will have gladly forgiven him for his actions, if they are even aware of them.

Yet Dickey's bombardier is also sentenced to a life of nightmares and numbness, despite his seemingly tranquil life in suburbia. When he looks into mirrors at bars, his face "dilates in a cloud like Japan."[18] He is also curiously disconnected from his family and his home, as Dickey's characteristic "split line"[19] technique—the distinct white space in between the lines of some of his later poems, which works like an extended caesura—also suggests: "I cannot say / Where the screwdriver is   where the children / Get off the bus."[20] Like Shapiro in "V-Letter," Dickey presents myriad images connoting domesticity and material comfort. The wartime past of the airman is juxtaposed to the suburban present, and war is presented as the opposite of home life.

Domesticity implies safety as well as civilization, although in a total war even civilians' houses are not protected from warfare. The "well-stocked" pantry has caused the speaker to become overweight, but his hunger is still not satisfied:

> All this, and I am still hungry
> Still twenty years overweight, still unable
> To get down there or see
> What really happened.[21]

The hunger is not physical, but emotional and spiritual. Dickey's speaker wills himself to consider what it would be like to have his house bombed, to have his "enemies and their children / For all time burned / Alive," as Dickey wrote in a draft for this poem.[22] Yet such feelings of contrition do not come naturally to him anymore. His sense of empathy seems to have been eroded by the war. "The others try to feel / For them. Some can, it is often said."[23] Although the speaker voices the general claim that people can empathize, it is clear that he cannot and shows disbelief that others can.

What makes "The Firebombing" exceptional among the poems of World War II—besides its voluminous size—is that Dickey discloses not only the bombardier's struggle with his conscience but also his acceptance that the war was the highlight of his life. In his long, chaotic, and mysterious tour-de-force Dickey tries to recapture the exhilaration of being an airman in World War II, while Ciardi, Jarrell, and Nemerov, to name just three, focus almost exclusively on the danger and disaster that were always looming. The boyish delight that Dickey's middle-aged speaker still takes in the details of aerial flight—the instruments, the angles, the sheer power of the plane—has disappeared in the poems of the other three, although those were exactly the aspects of flying that made them want to join the air corps.

Besides "The Firebombing," only Dickey's own equally lengthy "Reunioning Dialogue" (the second part of "Two Poems of Flight Sleep") and a short, offhand poem by Karl Shapiro called "Human Nature" also voice the veteran's nostalgia for the war. Driving behind "a Diesel-stinking bus / On the way to the university to teach / Stevens and Pound and Mallarmé" Shapiro recollects riding "the battle-grey Diesel-stinking ships / Among the brilliantly advertised Pacific Islands." Like Lowell, Shapiro appears to experience his teaching job as unexciting compared to the rocky years during "a forgotten war," even though the war was for him also full of boredom and hatred. Considering the unappealing images that he conjures up about the war, Shapiro's conclusion that he is "homesick for war" comes as a shock. It elicits curiosity in the reader as to what this nostalgia reveals about human nature, but Shapiro leaves this open.[24]

The "Reunioning Dialogue" that a former Black Widow pilot and a radar operator share in the bar of the St. Moritz hotel in New York in 1972 conveys more fully and wholeheartedly the homesickness that Shapiro addresses. Dickey had originally set the poem somewhere in Cleveland. Yet the atmosphere of wealth of this bar overlooking Central Park reflects more perfectly the contrast between the prosperous, tranquil postwar years and the nervous war years.[25] While becoming inebriated, the two airmen muse over why they got lost in the Pacific on a mission covering a convoy of navy ships. Entranced by the "Southern Cross," which had "the most delicious lungs / For me" and the smooth run of their brand-new P-61, the navigator falls asleep.[26] The pilot meanwhile fears that they will meet a similar grim fate to that of five men from their squadron who were decapitated by Japanese enemies, a fear that fascinated Dickey as "The Performance" confirms. When the navigator wakes up, however, they find their way to their base safely, and nearly three decades later this scary event has become an enthralling memory. "Reunioning Dialogue," which at times borders on sentimentality, is the only poem by a member of this generation of war poets that celebrates this type of camaraderie among former servicemen; most of the poets of the middle generation were usually wary of this type of male bonding.

Another poem that expresses yearning for the war years is, surprisingly, William Stafford's "In Camp." Stafford realizes in this poem, like the other poets of his generation, that the war years were the most momentous and decisive years of his life. Yet ironically this conscientious objector turns out to be much more wistful about his four years in the Civilian Public Service camps than even the soldier-poets about the army. The other poets did not reminisce about, or perhaps never experienced, the sense of brotherhood that Stafford relates in "In Camp." "That winter of the war, every day sprang outward," Stafford opens the poem, expressing how every day was special and unique, even though they were the darkest days of the twentieth century. "No task I do today has justice / at the end," Stafford adds revealingly a stanza later.[27]

Stafford's son Kim has written how after the war his father longed for the solidarity and comradeship he had found in the camp, despite the diversity that existed among the conscientious objectors: "I sense that my father was lonely the rest of his life for the intensity of purpose he felt with others in camp," Kim Stafford writes before comparing it to "the experience soldiers can have, no matter how horrific their combat: nothing at home can ever match the vitality of war, and this is the greatest secret they must keep from those they love at home."[28] Judging from their poetry, however, the soldier-poets of World War II experienced fewer pangs of nostalgia than Stafford did. Unlike Lowell, the other conscientious objector poet, Stafford has no regrets about his decision to become a conscientious objector, even though the consequences were tough and temporarily tore his family apart. Stafford was also spared the nightmares that plagued his friend Hugo. In his poem "Some Remarks When Richard Hugo Came," Stafford writes how Hugo had imparted to Stafford that "the bodies I had killed began to scream."[29]

Hugo seems as traumatized by the war as Dickey's speaker in "The Firebombing." Yet Dickey's airman also cherishes delightful memories of aerial flight like the pilot and radar operator in "Reunioning Dialogue," even though he has no one to share his memories with. Using words like "spooled," "wire thread," and "quilt," Dickey's speaker in "The Firebombing" equates flying with the work of a weaver whose labor also requires speed and dexterity. The physical beauty of flying, combined with the sense of control and power he could exert in his younger years, makes his current life in the suburbs little more than a prosaic afterlife, just as Shapiro's "Human Nature" suggested. Dickey's poem is reminiscent of what J. Glenn Gray's describes in his chapter "The Enduring Appeals of Battle" in his book *The Warriors*. Gray probed the psychological underpinnings of "the fascination that manifestations of power and magnitude hold for the human spirit."[30] Dickey tries to tap into this basic emotion of how men long for the awe-inspiring experience of war decades after the event, which is nevertheless not often explored in contemporary war poetry.

Yet Dickey's middle-aged speaker's homesickness for war in "The Firebombing" takes on sinister and possibly even pathological dimensions that are absent in "Human Nature" and "Reunioning Dialogue." In fact, the bombardier secretly wishes he had the sense of strength, supremacy, and destructive power he used to have:

> I still have charge—secret charge—
> Of the fire developed to cling
> To everything: to golf carts and fingernail
> Scissors as yet unborn   tennis shoes
> Grocery baskets   toy fire engines
> New Buicks stalled by the half-moon
> Shining at midnight on crossroads   green paint
> Of jolly garden tools   red Christmas ribbons:[31]

Dickey's airman has violent fantasies to set ablaze the suburb from which he feels so disconnected. In his article "The Collapse of James Dickey," Robert Bly famously attacked Dickey's poem for allegedly celebrating the annihilation of cities and the mass murder of civilian populations: "In its easy acceptance of brutality, the poem is deeply middle class. Dickey appears to be embarrassing the military establishment for its Japanese air raids, but he is actually performing a function for the establishment. He is teaching us that our way of dealing with military brutality is right: do it, later talk about it, and take two teaspoonfuls of remorse every seventh year. In short, if we read this poem right, we can go on living with napalm."[32] Yet "The Firebombing" is more complex and profound than Bly sketches. Dickey's poem explores the conflicting emotions of a veteran who is both glad that he is so well-off in the suburbs and regretful that his prime is over, and who is both proud of and disgusted by what he has done in the war. This liminal, ambiguous position is emblematic for how the poets of World War II underwent the afterlives of the war.

When describing the first of a series of flashbacks that takes his middle-aged speaker back to memories of the war in one of the fair copies for "The Firebombing," Dickey changed the neutral word "someone" to "some technical-minded stranger with my hands," as it occurs in the published version. The noun phrase aptly reveals the machinelike quality of his wartime profession, which unnerved so many World War II poets in the afterlives of the war, including Hugo and Nemerov. They did not see their victims down below, which made their actions feel so unreal. The change also articulates how foreign his younger, well-trained self feels to the overweight veteran of now. Dickey, Hugo, and Lowell present men who are all bewildered when trying to understand the motives and rationales of their earlier selves. Hugo, for instance, goes to great length to explain to Simic how different he has become from when he was a flyboy, without completely dismissing what he stood for back then. Not only do they consider World War II a life-changing experience, they feel as if that war produced or spawned a different kind of man who seems vaguely unfamiliar or even alien to the men they have become after the war.

This was most strongly felt by Lowell, who also had the most extreme response to the war of all the poets of World War II. More specifically than even the published poems themselves, the drafts of "Memories of West Street and Lepke" and "Our Afterlife I" show the intense unease that the memories of the war conjured up later in Lowell's life. Hiding beneath the question "Ought I to regret my seedtime?" the drafts reveal how Lowell agonized for years over the motives of his sudden move to become a conscientious objector, why his "head rang with the glory / Of my refusal to serve in the army," and what this reveals about his character now and during the war. In one of his many drafts of the poem Lowell admits he was "as if levitated to transcendence" when he told off "the state and president."[33]

"Our Afterlife I," which was published in *Day By Day* (1977) in the year of his death, shows that Lowell did not really enjoy the winter season of his life, as one of Blake's Proverbs of Hell had promised. A Proustian madeleine in the form of two Tennessee cardinals in his English garden transports Lowell back to his "boyish years" when he met the aspiring novelist Peter Taylor, who would become a good friend and to whom "Our Afterlife" is dedicated. Like the cardinals, Taylor is also from Tennessee, and, like Jarrell, he followed John Crowe Ransom to Kenyon College, where they met the young Lowell. The two birds are still as "young as they want to be" and celebrate their youth by spending their winter in warmer climes, down south. "We're not," Lowell glumly states, in the shortest line of the poem. His "second fatherhood" and his stay in England have made it clear that he is now "a generation older." He also notes sorrowfully that the year that he writes this poem, in 1973, has "killed / Pound, Wilson, Auden . . . ," some of Lowell's principal predecessors and literary fathers.[34]

"Our Afterlife I" is in its published version not a war poem, but more a poem in which Lowell reminisces about the prewar South with an old friend. The drafts, however, make clear that Lowell was thinking about the war years when he wrote his poem:

We drink in the central heat
To keep the cold wave out—
The War we shared
Was shared by everybody;
I shan't write you again
Of the Messiah, Leviathan,
The field of Armageddon, lost
By my faith not made for use.[35]

Lowell clearly feels embarrassed and uncomfortable remembering his earlier, apocalyptic wartime self, as is also indirectly noticeable in "Memories." Yet why did Lowell remove these lines from the finished poem? It is possible that Lowell thought that the poem would be less coherent if it was both about the 1930s and about World War II. It is also possible, however, that these memories were too personal and painful to share with the reading public. "Memories" is "the poet's only published work directly dealing with his objection," as Philip Metres notes, and perhaps Lowell did not want to open old wounds.[36] Like Jarrell, who did not openly share his feelings of remorse and unease about his role in the war effort but hid them from sight in a draft, Lowell also may not have been prepared to impart some of his most innermost feelings about a confused time in his life.

Lowell is highly aware of his "face and profile" in "Our Afterlife I." He does not know what to make of his past and his present and his different selves during half a century of life. Yet in the final image of the poem, in a coda of three lines, he gives it a try anyway. Using again the image of birds, he asserts that human beings are like birds that are released and become "alive in flight." People take on "the color of the chameleon," Lowell suggests.[37] Like the lizard that changes color to match that of its surroundings, human beings also change because their environment and the times change. Like the other poets of the middle generation, Lowell believes he has multiple selves. The reddish-brown hue that Lowell has now assumed is that of the cardinal, but also the color of rust, the color of tarnish, corrosion, and age.

The poetic style of "Memories of West Street and Lepke" as compared to Lowell's earlier war poems, such as "On the Eve of the Feast of the Immaculate Conception: 1942" and "The Bomber," already reflected the shift in Lowell's personality. The poems of the 1940s were more schematic, contrived, artificial, and political, whereas "Memories" is more personal, musing, and reflective. Even though "Memories" is more loosely organized than his previous war poems, this poem is structured in four distinct stanzas of about equal size. The first one paints a picture of Lowell's comfortable life in Boston's Marlborough Street in the 1950s; the second is dominated by the rhetorical question cited above; the third paints a picture of his exotic fellow jailbirds; while the fourth focuses on the disconcerting image of a "lobotomized" Lepke among his luxury goods in prison.

As many critics have argued, the world inside the West Street jail is inhabited by all sorts of outcasts whom a college-educated Boston Brahmin like Lowell had never encountered in his life. The prison includes an African American boy who has sold or used marijuana, the gentle vegetarian Abramowitz, Jehovah's Witnesses, "Hollywood Pimps," and finally the narcotics ringleader Louis Buchalter, aka "Czar Lepke." Abramowitz, who wears only "rope shoes" and only eats "fallen fruit" because he cannot hurt animals or other organisms, gets beaten up for trying to convert two Chicago mafiosi to his vegetarian and pacifist convictions.[38] By exposing Abramowitz's strong but unusual convictions, Lowell is half poking fun at his own views: he is an eccentric and nonconformist among more extreme cases. These characters that Lowell marks out are strange and colorful, and they have all defied the homogenized army culture that would have swooped up Lowell had he enlisted.

By writing "Memories" Lowell had vindicated Jarrell's critique a decade earlier that Lowell was "not putting enough about people in the poems" since Lowell now fully empathizes with other people radically unlike himself in this late war poem.[39] In fact, "Memories" is a very Jarrellian poem in tone and subject matter, as Lowell realized when dedicating to his old friend an unpublished addition to this poem. The sequel starts where the narrative of "Memories" left off, when Lowell is driven in a police car or van from the West Street jail in New York ninety miles north to the federal penitentiary at Danbury, Connecticut. Even though the typescript follows the events of "Memories" in time, it might have been written earlier; it is not possible to give an exact date of when the typescript was written. Yet instead of the free verse of "Memories," the sequel is written in rhyming pentameters, similar to those of "The Mills of the Kavenaughs," which Lowell published in 1951. Provisionally called "From the Tombs to Danbury," the typescript opens as follows:

> Randall, no one knows better how the poor
> And stunted strangers enter the front-door
> To hold this fine house of wonders that the State
> Holds open for our good: to reinstate
> Us in the graces of the honest, open mind
> Whose target-practice atomized its kind.
> These Porto Rican heroes are no worse
> Than those unholy innocents, your verse
> Shows us for mirrors of ourselves: the child,
> The Jew, the kenneled German and that mild
> And open-handed bomber in his void
> Of vision—the destroyer, the destroyed.[40]

Lowell did not exactly write with the same kindness and compassion about the derelicts in the West Street jail as Jarrell did in his war poems when sketching the war-torn lives of children, women, and young soldiers. Yet there is a similarity in the way that they both focus on the Other. After the 1940s Lowell had made the same transformation that Jarrell had made during the war, and he embraced a perspective on the world that had materialized into a dominant theme of midcentury poetry. As Edward Hirsch has remarked, Jarrell, Lowell, and company shared an "overwhelming and overwhelmed reverence . . . for whatever is wounded or broken, flawed, vulnerable, lost."[41]

This adjective "lost" is the penultimate word of "Memories of West Street and Lepke," and contributes to form the all-important noun phrase "lost connections . . . ."[42] These two final words of the poem sum up the compulsive but hopeless task of trying to relive one's former self's life, which the poets of World War II all tried to do in the afterlife of the war. Lowell utters this phrase when referring to Lepke, who is "flabby, bald, lobotomized" and thus flows "in a sheepish calm, / where no agonizing reappraisal / jarred his concentration on the electric chair."[43] Pacified by society, Lepke is awaiting his capital punishment, but fortunately for the mobster the lobotomy saves him from having to reexamine his nefarious actions in the previous decades. Lowell probably took the phrase "agonizing reappraisal" from a speech that John Foster Dulles, the secretary of state, made in 1953, thereby further emphasizing the Cold War mood that hangs over "Memories of West Street and Lepke" and *Life Studies.* In this speech Dulles threatened France that it should ratify plans to establish the European Defense Community (EDC) because otherwise the United States would have to reconsider its relationship with the former world power.[44]

Yet the political reference covers up the personal allusion that Lowell had intended to make earlier. In a draft of "Memories of West Street and Lepke" at the Berg Collection of the New York Public Library, Lowell describes Lepke as: "Flabby, bald, lobotomized, / Where no cruel traumas of self-analysis / Jarred his concentration on the electric chair."[45] In another earlier version Lowell points out that Lepke "looked like myself."[46] Both drafts establish more poignantly than the published version does that Lowell recognizes himself in the convicted murderer Lepke. Even though Lowell's refusal to serve in the war cannot compare with Lepke's crimes, Lowell nevertheless senses a connection. Like Lepke, Lowell was forced to undergo psychiatric treatments because of his aberrant behavior, and both inmates have to bear the brunt of their actions in the past. Lepke's lobotomy, however, prevents him from undergoing the "cruel traumas of self-analysis" that Lowell has undertaken regarding his youth and war years in *Life Studies,* agonizing over whether he "ought to regret" his "seed-time."

One of the most remarkable discoveries that Lowell's self-analysis yields, but which he decided to keep from the world, revolves once again around his sense of masculinity. In a typescript called "Death and the Maiden,"[47] which is related to "Memories of West Street and Lepke," Lowell declared that he was essentially "two people." This is an extraordinary confession characterizing Lowell's divided nature and also in a sense his bipolar disease, but what is even more astonishing is that he views his two personalities as divided along gender lines:

One is this boy too hept [*sic*] to mess
With masochistic gallantries;
His bearing, all periphrasis,
Is single-angled to appear
Simple, sensuous and sincere
And he glories in his stock
Allied with mine since Plymouth Rock.[48]

Here is the Robert Lowell of the 1940s, the mischievous "boy" who tortured his parents by refusing to enter military service, and telling the *New York Times* all about it; the Robert Lowell who bragged about his family history to President Roosevelt while breaking with his inheritance all the same; the Robert Lowell who wrote verbose war poems in which he wanted to appear honest and peace loving, but in which he mostly displayed his pent-up anger and violent disposition.

Lowell's gentler side and superior self, the Lowell of the 1950s, however, is female:

Thank God my better self is woman:
All night she screams, "*Nihil humanum*—
I'm alien to no alien thing;
The thousand thousand languishing,
Poisoned devils of conscience drouse [*sic*]
Outside my open floodgate house,
Throbbing, glowing, reddened, whole,
We burn together, one live coal.[49]

Nothing human is alien to her, Lowell suggests, quoting from the Roman dramatist's Terence's comedy *Heauton Timorumenous,* or *The Self-Tormentor,* written around 163 B.C.[50] Like Jarrell, Lowell has a "semifeminine mind" that feels a natural compassion, a nurturing kindness for the underprivileged and victimized people of this world.[51] The final image that Lowell presents in this draft is reminiscent of "The Dead in Europe" where Lowell imagined that the bombers and the bombed were "buried together."[52] Even though Lowell's female identity is less self-centered and aggressive than Lowell's boyish self, she is not less problematic to Lowell. She is represented as a hysterical woman who is plagued by nightmares and who identifies with others so wholeheartedly that it could destroy her.

Lowell's emotions are more extreme than those of other World War II poets, but he is not idiosyncratic. More poets felt uneasy about their violent past, as this chapter has shown, even if it was sanctioned by their country.

Like Lowell, Dickey did not believe that there was one true self, but that every person consists of different and sometimes opposing characters, in his case "a saint, a murderer, a pervert, a monster, a good husband, a scoutmaster, a provider, a businessman, a shrewd horse trader, a hopeless aesthete."[53] Dickey's review of Jarrell's *Selected Poems* in two voices—one negative, antagonistic, and aggressive, and the other positive, considerate, and kindhearted—reflects similar contradictory emotions that Lowell displayed. Dickey held the middle between "his father's violent passions" and "his mother's refinements," as Henry Hart has suggested.[54] He was competitive "like the gamecocks" his father "spent his life raising," as he admitted in a letter to James Wright, which made him behave like one of the "Roosters" in Elizabeth Bishop's war poem:[55] "Deep from protruding chests / in green-gold medals dressed, / planned to command and terrorize the rest."[56] Yet the sentimental letters Dickey sent to his mother evidence that other side of him.

It is significant that Jarrell and Lowell associate these diverse selves along the gender lines of male versus female. "Cultures produce male warriors by toughening up boys from an early age," as Joshua S. Goldstein has argued: "We pass along authorized forms of masculinity suited to the war system." Yet even though "boys on average are more prone to more rough-and-tumble play, they are not innately 'tougher' than girls," Goldstein continues: "They do not have fewer emotions or attachments, or feel less pain."[57] The poets of World War II nearly all responded to the challenge to be "tough" during World War II, but in the afterlife they also testified to having another, more vulnerable, side to their personality.

CHAPTER 14

"Lucky" John Ciardi's Trauma of War

The legacy of World War II was for a number of poets more troublesome than Lowell's occasional nagging doubts. Anthony Hecht and Louis Simpson, who were among the infantry troops in Europe, have both testified that they experienced serious psychological problems when they returned home. Both were diagnosed with "what in those primitive days was called a 'nervous breakdown,' and which today would be styled a 'post-traumatic shock syndrome'" or post-traumatic stress disorder (PTSD), as Hecht remembered.[1] Simpson exhibited nearly all of the symptoms of PTSD, including "hyperarousal": "I suffered from the condition described by Robert Graves and familiar to many an ex-infantryman: at every street corner, and when I passed an open place, I would look for a machine-gun position; at any whistling sound or bang my whole body would convulse."[2] Yet Simpson also suffered from sleep deficiency, emotional numbing, and violent hallucinations, to name a few of the other symptoms.[3] Dickey's speaker in "The Firebombing" exhibits all these symptoms as well, but he is also prone to "substance abuse," as his heavy drinking suggests.[4] "The Firebombing" is consequently the most detailed poetic portrait of a traumatized World War II veteran.

The poems in which Dickey, Hecht, and Simpson address such symptoms, however, are rare. While there are many poems by the poets of World War II that hint at the traumatic effect of war, there are only half a dozen that concentrate on trauma or that openly acknowledge how trauma affects the soldier's life after the war. John Ciardi wrote most extensively about the trauma of his war experience, albeit in veiled terms. Other poets—Dickey, Hecht, Nemerov, Simpson, and Brooks—wrote incidental poems about the traumatic effect of war. The arresting single image at the end of Simpson's "On The Ledge" where the ex-infantry soldier feels as if life has passed him by and he is still standing on a ridge "watching an ant / climb a blade of grass and climb back down" is as powerful as "The Firebombing" in expressing that the shock of war has never left this man.[5] The dazed imagery of "Lazarus Convalescent" bespeaks Simpson's miraculous survival and illustrates his slow road to recovery after being committed to a mental hospital when he had suffered a nervous breakdown. "For weeks I hardly slept at all," Simpson remarked about his mental collapse immediately after the war: "I read furiously, making my brains feverish with metaphysics," not unlike Lowell during the war. "I was perplexed by religion; I worried about Jesus; at the same time I was conscious of being a Jew," Simpson goes on, echoing similar anxieties that also troubled Karl Shapiro.[6] "Lazarus Convalescent," which incidentally nowhere refers to the war explicitly, shows Simpson's determination to fit back into normal society, "to learn," once again, "to use a knife and fork."[7]

The images in "Lazarus Convalescent" are less powerful in evoking postwar trauma than those in Howard Nemerov's "Redeployment," which is, alongside Dickey's "The Firebombing" and Simpson's own "On the Ledge," one of the most perfectly realized poetic portraits of the troubling effects of war on veterans and their slow reintegration back into society. The diction and tone may seem cool and distant, but they betray the speaker's sense of isolation:

> They say the war is over. But water still
> Comes bloody from the taps, and my pet cat
> In his disorder vomits worms which crawl
> Swiftly away. Maybe they leave the house.
> These worms are white, and flecked with the cat's blood.[8]

The thrust of Nemerov's powerful opening lines is repeated in the poem's subsequent images. Each of the four stanzas contains one or more carefully chosen tropes, which are all different yet connected and suggestive of the postwar ruins in which people have to live. The cat throwing up blood-speckled worms, a veteran fondling a dead soldier's eyeballs in his pocket, and the cockroaches crawling in the speaker's house all point to the same despair. "Redeployment" revolves around the binary oppositions of inside and outside, invisible and visible, dirt and cleanliness, and war and peace. A superficial glance may suggest that "the war is over," but upon closer inspection individual people are still disturbed by it.

In "It Out-Herods Herod. Pray You, Avoid It" Hecht also attends to how his memories of World War II continually created anxieties, even decades after the event. Hecht's peculiar title is culled from *Hamlet* (III, ii, 13) when the title character in Shakespeare's play chides his actors that they are exaggerating emotions. Hecht's title seems initially unrelated to the narrative of his poem. "It Out-Herods Herod" features a father—presumably Hecht himself—who is watching a feel-good movie on television with his children.

The father muses about how his children's outlook on life is determined by the westerns, fairy tales, and children's stories that they consume:

And in their fairy tales
The warty giant and witch
Get sealed in doorless jails
And the match-girl strikes it rich.[9]

Borrowing the stanzaic form and simple rhyme and rhythm of a lullaby, Hecht sketches that in such narratives the bad guys are easily distinguished from the good guys by their bad looks and ugly demeanor, and that the good are rewarded, as in Horatio Alger's upbeat morality tale *The Little Match Girl* (1846). Nothing is frightening in their perception; even the evildoers are not punished severely but put in "doorless jails."[10]

As soon as the children go to bed, though, the speaker grabs the bottle to make himself a drink, which is intended to ease his troubled soul. It marks a change in the poem. The tone of the poem immediately turns darker and the imagery more impenetrable, indicating that there is a great discrepancy between Hecht's and his children's worldviews. To his children, Hecht is "half God, half Santa Claus," partly because of his beard perhaps, but more important because he gave life to them, provides for them, and punishes them when necessary.[11] They are unaware how distressed their father is, or how cruel real life can be. Like Job, his children believe that the "poorman, beggarman, thief" will all be rewarded by some benign force if they are virtuous. The children still hold the cherished illusion that it is possible to "put an end to grief," something their father can no longer believe.[12] The stories that occupy the speaker are not the affirmative stories his children consume, but the Old Testament story of Job. Even though Job is a paragon of piety and virtue, the events he has witnessed make him question the fairness of God, as Hecht does as well.

In the poem's powerful but shocking denouement, Hecht says a prayer for his children:

And that their sleep be sound
I say this childermas
Who could not, at one time,
Have saved them from the gas.[13]

What started off as an inconspicuous anecdotal narrative about a family watching television ends devastatingly with Hecht's cynical comment about humanity. The word "childermas" refers to the memorial mass celebrated on December 28, the feast of the Holy Innocents who were slaughtered by Herod, the king of Judea. Afraid that his throne was in jeopardy when Christ was born, Herod ordered all children younger than two years old to be killed.

"In my poem," Hecht has explained, "the Holocaust is something which, in a very literal way, 'out-Herods Herod.' It out-does the terrible acts of Herod in a way that is scarcely measurable."[14] The final line in this outstanding poem disturbingly expresses more intense emotions than typical parental concerns fathers have about the safety of their children. The memory of the Holocaust, which Hecht personally witnessed at the Flossenbürg concentration camp that he and his regiment discovered, keeps coming back to him even during a seemingly innocent evening of watching television with his children.

While Ciardi, Dickey, Hecht, Nemerov, and Simpson address their own sense of trauma in their autobiographical poetry, Brooks's sonnets "piano after war" and "mentors" from "Gay Chaps at the Bar" are about traumatic experiences she did not witness herself. Reworked from "the stuff of letters," as she euphemistically called the material she used in these poems, Brooks presents a speaker who feels guilty about his own survival while so many around him have died and who barely knows how to continue with life.[15] Brooks's poem "mentors" could stand as an epigraph to Ciardi's traumatic poems. In the postwar era Ciardi presented himself to the world as an affluent and successful man. Similar to Brooks's "Gay Chaps at the Bar," he was outwardly happy, but inwardly "crying and trembling."[16] His aircrew died while he survived, as we will see, and this uncomfortable fact haunted him for the rest of his life:

For I am rightful fellow of their band.
My best allegiances are to the dead.
I swear to keep the dead upon my mind,
Disdain for all time to be overglad.
Among spring flowers, under summer trees,
By chilling autumn waters, in the frosts
Of supercilious winter—all my days
I'll have as mentors those reproving ghosts.[17]

For Ciardi, surviving implied a sense of duty and obligation to the dead to live as well and prosperously as possible. The understated tragedy of that belief is palpable when considering his war poems as an accumulating account of his trauma.

The extensive body of Ciardi's World War II poetry shows more completely than the more sporadic poems by Dickey, Hecht, Nemerov, Simpson, and Brooks the traumatizing effects of their war experiences, offering an unprecedented poetic record of mental trauma incurred during World War II. Ciardi published roughly fifty poems about the war but wrote another two dozen, which have been left unfinished, uncollected, and unseen in his archive at the Library of Congress. Even though Ciardi was never hospitalized like Hecht and Simpson, many of these poems address traumatic events, which he revisits in his poems. They are "poems of reflexive self-examination," as Janis P. Stout has argued, but they also analyze the unlucky ones who never made it home.[18]

Ciardi's war diary—transcribed by the poet's biographer, Edward M. Cifelli, and published posthumously as *Saipan*—also provides an intimate account of the disturbing sights he experienced as a gunner on a B-29 as part of the Strategic Bombing Offensive launched to destroy Japanese factories and later cities. This journal makes it possible to analyze Ciardi's trauma as it evolved. Ciardi kept his diary from November 5, 1944, when he and his crew had received orders to redeploy to Saipan from the Midwest, to March 10, 1945, the day that the infamous Tokyo firebombing started, which Dickey describes so vividly and grandiosely in his novel *To the White Sea*.

Ciardi's mounting fear and insecurity, which gradually becomes apparent in *Saipan,* makes him distinctly different from Dickey's intrepid hypermasculine hero Muldrow. With the same bravado that characterizes Dickey, Ciardi had boasted in November 1944 that "nothing happens to the brave," but in a few weeks he had revised this view.[19] Citing in his diary that he was plagued by "one of those sudden chemical anxieties," Ciardi began to suffer sleepless nights and could only with great difficulty muster the selfless courage that is required of men in battle.[20] When General Curtis LeMay ordered American bombers to fly thousands of feet lower than they normally would to bomb the Japanese cities more accurately, Ciardi "made some sort of peace with the near-certainty that [he] would never leave that flowering rock alive."[21] The giant Superfortresses had become easy targets for flak and Japanese fighter planes, but LeMay's low-level and flying-formation tactical plan went ahead as planned. "Our bombers were built for altitude," Ciardi wrote indignantly in his diary in March 1945: "At 36,000 feet attacking fighters were reduced in efficiency to the point where we could laugh them off, and the flak was that much less accurate."[22]

Ciardi ultimately comes to this reproachful conclusion in one of the final entries of his war journal: "We were on the Island to destroy Japanese factories and Japanese factories had a price tag attached. We were the price and neither longing nor the will to live mattered in the final balance. The General was our bargainer; he bid for those factories at the asking price, and he signed to pay for them in the universal currency that in the end is the currency that buys all of the world—human life. . . . I am reminded of Melville's observation in *Moby Dick,* that not a gallon of sperm oil came ashore to light the lamps of America but a drop of human blood went with it."[23] Ciardi cannot view World War II as the struggle for freedom and democracy, as the collective American memory would remember this war. In fact, Ciardi's vision here is closer to that of Karl Marx, who saw the struggle between nations as economically motivated, one in which common people were mere pawns, or that of Wilfred Owen and Siegfried Sassoon, who explored in their war poetry their increasing disdain for military authorities. The reference to Melville—which has proven to be representative of the well-educated literary minds of the middle generation poets—is also Ciardi's first attempt to understand the firebombings in which he took part as reflective of a violent and destructive side of the American character that the nineteenth-century writer explored in *Moby Dick.*

Yet Ciardi miraculously survived the Pacific war without shedding a drop of blood in the process, unlike most of the aircrew with whom he had trained and flown. As Ciardi writes in his memoir, "About Being Born and Surviving It," poetry and luck had caused him to stay alive against all odds. Survival became the leitmotif of his life. Earlier in the war, in March 1943, Ciardi had been eliminated from the squadron he had been training with under mysterious circumstances, just one day before graduation. "Ciardi's accumulated demerits," "FBI files with reports of his communist leanings," and the presence of a girlfriend near the air corps base probably explain Ciardi's sudden demotion, as Cifelli has argued.[24] Whatever the reasons, however, this military decision saved Ciardi's life: "I did not know it then, but I was once more Lucky John. Everyone I had trained with went to the Eighth Air Force in England to be ground up in the daylight B-17 raids against Germany. General Curtis (Iron Pants) LeMay ran the meat grinder. 'I can't save these boys,' he was once reported as saying, 'but if I spend them wisely, I won't have to kill off their kid brothers in a year or two.'"[25] A year later Ciardi heard through a friend that every man he had trained with was at that time "listed as KIA (Killed in Action) or MIA (Missing in Action)."[26]

Ciardi had unwittingly escaped from LeMay's clutches in 1943; exactly two years later history repeated itself. This time Ciardi was suddenly ordered to report to headquarters after a completed sortie over Japan. It appeared that the "colonel in charge of personnel needed what he called a grammarian" who would write letters about awards and decorations as well as letters of condolence bearing the signature of General Rosie O'Donnell, who "meant to pose as a close buddy of every man in his command."[27] A recent poem by Ciardi in the *Atlantic Monthly* convinced the colonel that the poet Ciardi would do just fine as a "grammarian," and he got the job. As fate would have it, three missions after Ciardi accepted his new job, a B-29 carrying most of the crew members that Ciardi had been flying with "took a direct hit over Tokyo Bay, the plane exploded in midair, and all hands were reported lost."[28]

The letters of condolence that Ciardi was writing included letters to family members of the men with whom he had flown and whom he regarded as friends. Ciardi was no longer religiously inclined during the war years, having renounced his strict Catholic upbringing since adolescence. He instead attributed his survival to chance: "I am a lucky survivor of forces usually beyond my control."[29] Ciardi realized, like the other poets of his generation, that he survived the total war of World War II not because he was a better, braver, and more courageous warrior than the others. The catastrophe that hit the other members of his crew made the big man from Boston see the hollowness of such ancient military myths, and made him "perceive himself as a very wee thing," to quote Stephen Crane in his Civil War novella *The Red Badge of Courage* (1895).[30]

After the war "Lucky" John became a "successful man of the world, a poor boy who rode the American dream all the way to millionaire status," as Cifelli puts it. Ciardi made it big not only in poetry but especially in "television, radio, lecture halls, political campaigns, college classrooms."[31] Ciardi bragged in his memoir how as a veteran he "hit the street with over $8000," most of which he had won playing craps, and he quickly multiplied this amount because of his shrewd business sense.[32] Yet underneath the veneer of boisterous "Lucky" John, who claimed in the 1950s that he was "the richest poet in America," was a vulnerable and traumatized man. "Sgt. Ciardi," as he called his military self, never got rid of what he had seen on Saipan and over Japan.[33] Cathy Caruth asks in *Unclaimed Experience*: "Is the trauma the encounter with death, or the ongoing experience of having survived it? At the core of . . . stories [of trauma], I would suggest, is thus a kind of double telling, the oscillation between a *crisis of death* and the correlative *crisis of life*: between the story of the unbearable nature of an event and the story of the unbearable nature of its survival." Ciardi's war poetry written in the aftermath of his narrow escape from death shows both a "*crisis of death*" and a "*crisis of life*."[34]

This is most impressively apparent in "Bashing the Babies." Written during Easter 1968, the year in which the war in Vietnam reached a crisis point and the United States was shocked by the assassinations of Martin Luther King Jr. and Robert Kennedy and by mass demonstrations against the war on the home front, "Bashing the Babies" is remarkably irregular and unadorned for a Ciardi poem.[35] Like "The Firebombing," it involves an affluent, middle-aged, and overweight man who seems troubled by his comfortable life. Like Hecht's "It Out-Herods Herod," Ciardi's poem evokes the story of Herod's order to kill all babies in Judea after hearing that Jesus Christ was born, and Ciardi compares that gruesome, biblical tale to how his own children were born and raised in luxury. Even his dog lives a life of plenty:

It is Easter. I rise fat, rich
hand out chocolate eggs, later drink coffee,

smoke. My dog gulps the poverty
of India heaped in an aluminum dish:
meat, egg, milk, cereal, bone meal,
cod liver oil.
                How shall we not feel
something for the babies who could not leave town?
who were not German Shepherds? who were hit
by their eggs and burned?[36]

Ciardi defied death during World War II, and he can thus "rise" at Easter, as Jesus Christ did before him. Even his dog eats better than most people in India, Ciardi remarks apologetically. Unlike Dickey's firebomber, Ciardi finds that his feelings of guilt have not eroded. Even his dog eats better than most people in India, Ciardi remarks apologetically.

Jesus's parents were warned by an angel to flee to Egypt, but many people cannot escape the disasters of their time, Ciardi knows. The recurring image of eggs is important in "Bashing the Babies," and not just because they suggest both fragility and fertility. Ciardi metaphorically juxtaposes the chocolate eggs that are hidden in his garden for his children with the egg-shaped bombs that are landing on other children. In the final stanza Ciardi describes himself as "an easy man" who can play with his dog on the lawn of his impressive New Jersey mansion. His children are, like Ciardi himself, "chocolate-lucky" as they are left unscathed by history's fate. They are "happy together and got away / without being bashed."[37] Ciardi survived his childhood and adulthood without a scratch, but "Bashing the Babies" shows that his survival was accompanied by perpetual feelings of unease about what he had seen and done.

Even though "Bashing the Babies" addresses Ciardi's crisis of survival in general terms, there are two specific traumatic tales that he keeps returning to and which are related in his mind. The first one is the imagined sight of Ciardi's fellow crew members who were blown out of the sky; the second one is the cave full of bones that he discovered and which to him represented "all the dead I ever saw / that dying year," as he wrote in his autobiographical poem *Lives of X*.[38] It is striking that a considerable number of Ciardi's poems in which he directly or indirectly evokes the fate of his crew members are occasional poems. National holidays, remembrances, or birthdays prompted the unpleasant memories of the war for Ciardi, and he kept a faithful and almost compulsive record of his thoughts and feelings especially on those days. "Poem for My Twenty-Ninth Birthday," "V-J Day," "First Summer after a War," "First Autumn after a War," "The Formalities," "Memorial Day," and "On a Photo of Sgt. Ciardi a Year Later" are some of the most notable examples.[39] While it is understandable that Ciardi wrote poems on such days of remembrance, they are also a bit similar and therefore predictable, and perhaps more intriguing as psychological testimonies than as poems.

Ciardi turned twenty-nine on June 24, 1945, some three months after being taken off the B-29 to be a "grammarian" and three months before being sent home. Yet in "Poem for My Twenty-Ninth Birthday" (1946), Ciardi already looks back at the war and to the future. The poem's central motif is the jungle, which Ciardi uses at various points in the poem, including in the opening and closing stanzas. The jungle also reflects the chaotic and jumbled order of the poem, which is at odds with the neat delineation of fourteen stanzas of six lines with an intricate rhyme scheme. Ciardi states that the "native" is "in his jungle, I in mine," using the conventional use of the word—denoting the Pacific's tropical forest—but also a more metaphorical meaning.[40] The jungle that Ciardi finds himself in is an internal jungle. Even though he cannot yet see the forest for the trees, he still tries to see the bigger picture of what this war means for humankind. The title "Poem for My Twenty-Ninth Birthday" suggests that this poem will focus on Ciardi himself, but the opposite is true as he affirms: "Now I have named another year of time / Learning to count not mine but a world's age."[41]

When reviewing *Other Skies* (1947) for the *Nation*, Randall Jarrell was not much enamored. He called Ciardi's collection "Karl Shapiro second hand," and he charged acerbically that "it is extremely disappointing that a B-29 gunner shouldn't get more of the feel of what happened to him into what he writes."[42] It was not the only time that Jarrell made a comment like this about poets of his generation who had had more experience at the front than he. Jarrell's critique perhaps contains an element of defensiveness that he did not have similar experiences. Yet Jarrell was certainly right to point out that Ciardi's early war poetry—like that of Shapiro—was often uneven; powerful and moving lines alternated with trite phrases. Jarrell judged correctly that "the quoted sentences of interphone conversations" in "V-J Day" "have a thousand times the reality of 'await the rose / Blossoming in the fire upon the town,'" from "Poem for My Twenty-Ninth Birthday."

What is remarkable, though, is that some of the more appealing images that Ciardi uses in "Poem for My Twenty-Ninth Birthday" are strikingly similar to Jarrell's poetry, although he could not have read Jarrell's war poems when he was writing this poem in Saipan. In a line such as "our innocence shall haunt our murderous end," Ciardi uses the same paradoxical notion that Jarrell used to typify American bombers in "Eighth Air Force."[43] Ciardi also presents a bomber plane as a "metal womb," using the same image that Jarrell would make famous in "The Death of the Ball Turret Gunner." Moreover Ciardi focuses on dreams, "necessity"—that concept about the inevitability of fate that Jarrell borrowed from Auden or Spinoza—and compassion for all of war's victims: dead American bombers, the Japanese, the indigenous Saipanese, and a girl on the home front. Despite his more limited exposure to warfare, however, Jarrell was ultimately more successful in molding vivid and memorable poems out of the same material. Ciardi (but also Shapiro) wrote memorable lines about the war, but not poems such as "The Death of the Ball Turret Gunner" and "Eighth Air Force," which, with their perfect precision and frightening vision, can shake up and haunt readers.

The poems in which Ciardi focuses most explicitly on his dead fellow crew members are "V-J Day" and "The Formalities," which both address the official end of the war. Ciardi did not indulge in exuberant celebrations, as both poems show. The day on which the Allies announced the surrender of Japanese forces, August 15, 1945, gave rise to jubilant reactions back home, but Ciardi can only think of his crew members who died and who now come, in the imagery of poem, flying back to his mind. Ciardi compares V-J Day to the Apocalypse, as it is the day when "the dead came back," as well as to the millennium. According to Ciardi, the postwar era is not the period of a thousand years of great happiness or human perfection, as predicted in Revelation, but rather "a blank millennium."[44]

The most ingenuous touch of "V-J Day" is Ciardi's use of the crew's metaphorical intercom messages on a B-29 Superfortress for dramatic effect. Jarrell had called his collection *Little Friend, Little Friend* (1945) after such communications, but Ciardi uses it more elaborately in "V-J Day":

> The interphone was talking
> Abracadabra to the cumulus tops:
>
> *Dreamboat three-one to Yearsend—loud and clear,*
> *Angels one-two, on course at one-six-nine.*
> *Megallan to Bilboa. Propwash to Century.*
> *How do you read me? Bombay to Valentine.*
>
> Fading and out. And all the dead were homing.
> (*Wisecrack to Halfmast. Doom to Memory.*)
> On the tallest day in time we saw them coming,
> Wheels jammed and flaming on a metal sea.[45]

Some of the references, such as "Dreamboat three-one," "Angels one-two," "Magellan," and "Balboa," refer to the actual "coded language of flight operations," as David K. Vaughan has pointed out.[46] Yet other nouns sound like magical incantations or meaningless gibber. Gradually the words spoken become more meaningful, however, without becoming completely intelligible or unambiguous. The phrase "How do you read me?" for instance, is a realistically sounding radio message expressing the angst of an airman to be heard. Yet this question can also be perceived as Ciardi's anxious attempt to reach out to his readers. In the last stanza the words "*Halfmast*," "*Doom*," and "*Memory*" are no longer actual intercom messages, but words that merely connote the dire fate of the dead air crew.

"The Formalities" further demonstrates the rift that Ciardi believes exists between the political history of World War II and the personal history of that war. "The Formalities" zooms in on another important official day signaling the end of the war in the Pacific, namely September 2, 1945. On that day Japanese officials signed the formal surrender of their country on board the USS *Missouri*. "The Formalities" is an ekphrastic poem, as it describes two famous photographs of this carefully scripted event. The first one displays half a dozen uniformed Japanese officers representing the imperial armed forces along with three officials representing the imperial government. The second photograph is more crucial. It features Douglas MacArthur, the brilliant but controversial American general who, according to Ciardi and other critics, acted as if he were God.

What went on aboard the *USS Missouri* on September 2, 1945, was "a great morality play," as historian John W. Dower has suggested.[47] Ciardi knew this full well, as is evident from the simile that the *Missouri* was "flagged like a parade" in the first stanza. The way the "native and allied brass" in "open-collar" with "suntans" are positioned for the cameras and the way the Japanese officials are literally surrounded by their enemies are heavily symbolic.[48] Ciardi's disdain for MacArthur is almost as great as the grudge he has against General LeMay. It is more personal than the general distaste the poets of World War II had for hard-edged masculine military leaders.

Exactly halfway through "The Formalities" Ciardi shifts perspective and contrasts this ceremonial spectacle to the essentials, a detailed description of the crew members who flew in Ciardi's B-29 that crashed in the Pacific some two months earlier. In "V-J Day" and several other poems Ciardi alludes to these airmen, but in "The Formalities" he addresses them most specifically and personally. Ciardi uses their proper names or nicknames—"Chico," "Coxie," "Frankie," "Hewie," "O'Dell," "T.J."—and mentions whatever idiosyncratic, physical characteristics he can remember.[49] In his war journal *Saipan* Ciardi writes as tenderly about these men who were all a few years younger than him, despite the irritations that also frequently surface. He describes how he visits Guam with Chico, for instance, and how he had an argument with Coxie about how the latter did not clean the turret properly.[50]

The silly nicknames and trite abbreviations "are names of nothing, to be sure," Ciardi wrote in a manuscript draft for this poem, but mentioning them anyway underlines that Ciardi wants to showcase their unique individualities.[51] This is remarkably different from the anonymous aircrew that

Jarrell describes in his war poems. Yet mentioning their names serves another purpose: Ciardi needs to give his crewmates a name and a face to rescue them from oblivion. MacArthur may be shining in the spotlight, but Ciardi feels compelled to show that Chico, Coxie, Frankie, Hewie, O'Dell, and T.J. deserve it infinitely more. His awareness of the unfairness of fate and fame leads him to imagine chillingly what must have happened to the remains of the crew members. Ciardi reasons that after the crash fish had about "two months / to pick clean Coxie's little go-to-hell / moustache" as well as "Chico's tattoo and the mole on / Frankie's chin and the scapular from / O'Dell's neck."[52] This part of "The Formalities" is similar to Thomas Hardy's "The Convergence of the Twain" about the sinking of the *Titanic*. In Hardy's poem, which oozes the same odd mixture of pathos and sarcasm, the speaker imagines how a "grotesque, slimed, dumb, indifferent" sea worm creeps around the wreckage of that once powerful ship at the bottom of the ocean.[53] Yet even pessimistic Hardy did not go as far as Ciardi in visualizing how fish eat the flesh off the victims' faces.

Macabre and shocking images are a trademark of Ciardi's other World War II poems. No other poet gave free rein to their most abject fantasies about what happens to a human body when people die. Ciardi's best-known war poem, "Elegy Just in Case," in which he both quasi-comically but also deadly seriously envisions his own death, is similarly replete with images of decomposing corpses:

Here lie Ciardi's pearly bones
In their ripe organic mess.
Jungle blown, his chromosomes
Breed to a new address.

Was it bullets or a wind
Or a rip cord fouled on chance?
Artifacts the natives find
Decorate them when they dance.

Here lies the sgt.'s mortal wreck
Lily spiked and termite kissed,
Spiders pendant from his neck
And a beetle on his wrist.

Bring the tick and southern flies
Where the land crabs run unmourning
Through a night of jungle skies
To a climeless morning.[54]

Like Rupert Brooke's World War I poem "The Soldier" and Keith Douglas's World War II poem "Simplify Me When I'm Dead," Ciardi's poem is a self-elegy.[55] Ciardi's poem is a "wry mock-elegy or mock-epitaph," as Paul Fussell has pointed out, which he considers "a new kind of poem indigenous to the Second World War."[56] Yet whereas the English poems are solemn, "Elegy Just in Case" is not.

The title alone exemplifies Ciardi's tonal complexity. The first word suggests the seriousness of his lament, while the three words that follow indicate the absurdity of the enterprise to write an elegy in the event that Ciardi dies. The poem's first stanza could stand alone as an epitaph, a genre often practiced by Ciardi when writing about war. Ciardi's epitaphs are reminiscent of and possibly inspired by Rudyard Kipling's *Epitaphs of the War* (1918), even though Ciardi is often more witty and less openly bitter. In the first three stanzas Ciardi evokes the language of funeral rites, but the simple rhyme scheme, tetrameter, and alternating rhyme undercut the traditional solemnity of those rites.

The idea that he might be devoured by flora and fauna, as happened to his dead crew members at the bottom of the Pacific Ocean, haunts him. Several animals—"tick," "southern flies," and "crabs"—adorn Ciardi's poem and add *couleur locale* of Southeast Asia while all connoting death and decay. All these animals are—like the crab—"unmourning," in Ciardi's ungrammatical but effective word. Lilies impale him, the white ants seal the kiss of death, and spiders spin their web around the dead sergeant's neck like a necklace. This conceit of courtship is linked to the speaker's girlfriend on the home front, whom he addresses later in the poem. In a poem that is so much centered on flesh, bone, and body parts, the speaker appropriately bids farewell by saying "your flesh was sweet to learn."[57]

The central poem to understand Ciardi's second traumatic memory is "Elegy for a Cave Full of Bones." Discovered by Cifelli alongside Ciardi's war journal, this poem was published posthumously in *Poetry* in March 1988. Like "Elegy Just in Case," "Elegy for a Cave Full of Bones" starts off in epigraphic style. The trochaic rhythm makes it sound like an amusing nursery rhyme, but the imagery is revolting because of its graphic detail:

> Tibia, tarsal, skull and shin:
> Bones come out where the guns go in.
> Hermit crabs like fleas in armor
> Crawl the coral-pock, a tremor
> Moves the sea, and surf falls cold
> On caves where glutton rats grow bold.[58]

The rhythm and the rhyme are again as simple and innocent as any children's rhyme, like Hecht's "It Out-Herods Herod" and Ciardi's own "Elegy Just in Case," but what Ciardi is imparting is anything but innocuous. Ciardi was obsessed by bones and body parts during the war. The rhyming couplets give the poem once again a jaunty edge, a high-spirited energy and movement, but the subject matter is austere and portentous. Ciardi's war poems—like many war poems by Nemerov—have a veneer of humor, but they only mask the poet's desperate and despondent mood.

It is estimated that about ten thousand civilians and thirty thousand Japanese soldiers died on Saipan after American army and marine units stormed its beaches in June 1944; American casualties were roughly 10 percent of the number of Japanese deaths.[59] When Ciardi arrived six months later the stench and sight of death had not disappeared on this small island, measuring just twelve and a half by five and a half miles. On November 26, 1944, Ciardi mentions in his diary that he hopes he will be back in the United States within a year, or otherwise he "will probably be very dead and wrapped in about as much soul as those caves full of Jap bones."[60] About a week later he notes casually that the caves where he "found the dead Japs" have now been occupied by American officers who had them "sandbagged, furnished and fixed for living as a super air raid shelter."[61]

Even though Ciardi does not dwell in his diary on this incident of discovering caves with Japanese bones and is almost cavalier about it, these bones had a belated impact on him. They came to make visible and symbolize the deaths that surrounded him everywhere, but that he could not see. In his poetic autobiography *Lives of X* (1971), Ciardi recalls the shocking sight in sobering blank verse, devoid of the bouncy rhymes he had used in "Elegy Just in Case" and "Elegy for a Cave Full of Bones":

I pick a cave,
bottle in hand, flashlight in the other
—and there were all the dead I ever saw
that dying year, where the flamethrowers had left them
blown back to the inner wall and toppled over
on one another, sizzled to dry to rot
or so I guessed (and maybe sea-air salted).
Which pocket of Hell was that? Drink to them all.[62]

The poet who would become famous and rich for translating Dante's *The Divine Comedy* stumbled upon his own version of hell in these caves. The ghastly sight, which is as surreal and terrifying as the paintings of Hieronymus Bosch, to whom he refers a little later on, allows Ciardi to reify his own mortality and that of his dead crewmates.

It was "a saving grace, we didn't see our dead, / Who rarely bothered coming home to die," Nemerov would claim in "The War in the Air" with his distinct deadpan humor. They "simply stayed away out there / In the clean war, the war in the air."[63] The cave full of bones that Ciardi found, however, made tangible and visible that World War II was not a clean war, and that people are in the end reduced to matter. The "caves of fear," as Ciardi called the caves full of bones in "The Pilot in the Jungle," were a portal that made him visualize and comprehend mortality, which he could ignore up to then.[64] Once he had seen death in his mind's eye, his imagination could not stop imagining his own death. "Lucky" John Ciardi survived the jungle of the Pacific theater, but he never left his interior jungle in the afterlife of the war.

CHAPTER 15

"Aftersight and foresight"

THE VIETNAM WAR

While the memories of World War II were a constant presence in the lives of the middle generation poets, they were awakened more than ever during the Vietnam War. Nearly all of them wrote poems about that war, and nearly all of them positioned themselves unambiguously against the war as it dragged on and escalated in the mid-1960s and early 1970s. World War II had been a nightmare, too, but it had been, if not a good war, at least a defensible or necessary war. Or so they told themselves, even if they were not entirely convinced. The Vietnam War was clearly none of these things, according to the poets of World War II. Louis Simpson spoke for his entire generation of war poets when he wrote "Vietnam was the wrong place for Americans to be, and this was a war they could not win—unless they were willing to start World War III."[1]

Even though their protest was less aggressive and voluble than Robert Bly's and Allen Ginsberg's tirades against the war, many of them showed their disapproval by taking part in marches and poetry readings, expressing sorrow about the new war. Their antiwar poems during the Vietnam era are remarkably different from their poems about World War II, however, in that they are less diverse and complex, and are predominantly political and satirical in tone. This last fact is surprising because—with the exception of Robert Lowell—none of the middle generation poets had written any satirical verses about World War II when it happened.[2] War poets on both sides of the Atlantic seemed to agree with Jarrell—when chiding Allen Tate for writing his sardonic "Ode to Our Young Pro-Consuls of the Air"—that "the evil of the universe is a poor thing to be ironic about."[3] Poems like Howard Nemerov's "To the Rulers" and "The Language of the Tribe" and Richard Wilbur's "A Miltonic Sonnet for Mr. Johnson on His Refusal of Peter Hurd's Official Portrait" show that this verdict apparently did not pertain to the Vietnam War era. Aimed at exposing the supposedly dangerous ignorance of politicians and world leaders that would ruin the United States and the rest of the world, these poems are distinct from the generally graver poems they wrote about the Second World War. Yet their Vietnam War poetry was also markedly different from that of the veteran poets of the Vietnam War and the protest poetry written by younger antiwar poets like Bly and Ginsberg.

The sardonic poems that Nemerov wrote about Vietnam were not a big leap from several of the poems he had written about World War II. The humorless irony of "A Memory of the War," for instance—relating how on a troop ship to the United States he was handed "a whopping great / Blue automatic" and was ordered to shoot all enlisted men who wanted to escape if the ship should sink—evinces the same kind of scorn that characterizes many of his Vietnam War poems. Yet like his peers, in the late 1960s and early 1970s Nemerov aimed at politicians instead of military authorities. In "To the Rulers," which is illustrative for the type of poem the middle generation poets were wont to write during this time, Nemerov addresses the war casually, as the final three tercets, with their sarcastic end rhymes, show:

O Conscripts Fathers, sponsors of the draft,
Prospective survivors on the little raft
That when the world sinks will be what is left,

I hear you praying, as your fingers trill
Unnervingly at night beside the pill,
The button, the hot line to the Other Will,

Your prayer, that used to be Caligula's too
If they all only had one neck . . . It's so
Unnecessary and out of date. We do.[4]

Only in one single line does he refer explicitly to the war. The advocates of the contentious draft and the successors of the more inspirational Pilgrim Fathers and Founding Fathers will be responsible if—as happened in the story of Noah's ark—only a small portion of humankind will survive the destruction of the earth. Most likely "the rulers" will be those who survive and everyone else will die, Nemerov implies.

The doom of nuclear holocaust looms large in "To the Rulers." This apocalyptic theme is representative of the way in which "Vietnam was imaged" by the "anti-war movement," although Nemerov was never part of any organized protest.[5] Nemerov compares the anxious atmosphere of the Cold War with the belief among Christians that the world would come to an end in the year 2000. Nemerov predicts pessimistically that the world leaders may not "wait two dozen years to round the sum" and could annihilate the planet immediately.[6] A phone line that connects the world leaders is the mere thread on which the future of the world hangs. Caligula wished that the collective Roman people had just one neck, so he could strike it and kill them all with one blow, as Nemerov muses in the poem's final image. Technological progress entails that the world leaders can now kill the world's population instantly. It was the culmination of a revolutionary change of warfare that occurred in the twentieth century and that ran parallel to the lives of the middle generation poets. The air of heroism still clung to warfare when they grew up, but the emergence of highly destructive weapons like the nuclear bomb made notions such as courage and valor void and obsolete. The modern world has in the postwar era one neck, metaphorically speaking, and the leaders of the world have more power of destruction than the fierce and feared Roman emperor imagined.[7]

"The Language of the Tribe" zeroes in on the way in which one of them—the American secretary of defense—manipulates language to further his plans. Nemerov's poem is in a sense a poetic rendition of the argument George Orwell makes in his famous essay "Politics and the English Language." The butt of Nemerov's mockery is Melvin R. Laird, secretary of defense under President Richard Nixon from 1969 to 1973, and the only one during the Vietnam era who had a "bald dome," as Nemerov says irreverently.[8] Laird, who was responsible for the withdrawal of American troops and of the "Vietnamization" process during his days in office, is not mentioned by name; neither is this policy criticized directly. Not specifying his name but referring only to Laird's position suggests that Nemerov is more bent at exposing the officialese language of his kind rather than targeting Laird personally.

Carefully camouflaging his language, Laird uses euphemisms to cover up the messy message that he is bringing the American public. When asked about the goals of dropping bombs, Laird says in loose iambic pentameter that they "might have / Deprived the enemy's facilities // Of access to logistic and supply / Facilities in close proximity."[9] At the end of the poem Nemerov puts Laird's lingo in "plain American which cats and dogs can read," to borrow Marianne Moore's famous phrase: "The bastards kept the bullets near the guns."[10] Nemerov's poem suggests that politicians obfuscate their speeches to try and ensure that journalists and the public at large do not look too closely at their policies. "The Language of the Tribe" is, as Nemerov's title indicates, a reflection on a famous phrase by another modernist poet. In the fourth part of *Four Quartets,* "Little Gidding"—his World War II poem about spiritual renewal—T. S. Eliot argued that the poet's task is purifying the tribe's language and urging "the mind to aftersight and foresight."[11] Yet Nemerov's poem exemplifies that during the war in Vietnam politicians did exactly the opposite as they wanted to make both "aftersight and foresight" impossible.

Nemerov's political satires during the Vietnam era came as no surprise as he had already developed a sharply ironic tone as a central feature of his poetics. Richard Wilbur's "A Miltonic Sonnet for Mr. Johnson" and William Meredith's "A Mild-Spoken Citizen Finally Writes to the White House" are much more astonishing. Wilbur and Meredith were both exponents of what Jarrell had called "the poet in the Grey Flannel Suit." Unfortunately Jarrell was not alive to see how Wilbur and Meredith shook off their air of politeness when they believed the political climate forced them to do so.[12] Jarrell died in 1965 before Vietnam became a national obsession. Yet Jarrell's "somber fatalism," to use Nelson Hathcock's phrase, is similar to Nemerov's pessimism. The atomic bomb was very much a part of "Jarrell's postwar, post-Hiroshima state of mind."[13] Still, he would have been astounded by especially Wilbur's "A Miltonic Sonnet for Mr. Johnson," which may be the angriest and most powerful denunciation of an American politician by a middle generation poet.

In the poem's sestet Wilbur explains what occasioned his anger and his sonnet. The day that Wilbur wrote his poem the news had just broken that Johnson had refused Peter Hurd's official portrait of the thirty-seventh president of the United States, which the White House Historical Association had commissioned. In fact, Johnson, who had sat for Hurd when he was painting the portrait, called it "the ugliest thing" he had ever seen. Much to the painter's chagrin, Johnson made it known to Hurd that he had wanted something closer to the style of the famous illustrator Norman Rockwell, who had painted so many patriotic covers for the *Saturday Evening Post* as well as the Four Freedoms during World War II. According to the First Lady's press secretary, Hurd's painting had been rejected because the painting was "too big for an official White House portrait," because the "'brilliantly lighted'" Capitol building was deemed "inappropriate for this kind of portrait," and because the "positioning of the figure and the general style was not 'consistent' with other White House portraits."[14]

Wilbur sarcastically comments on these justifications of Johnson's rejection by inserting the adverbs "rightly" and "justly" before paraphrasing the reasons of "the picture" as being "too large" and the Capitol being "too bright":

> Rightly you say the picture is too large
> Which Peter Hurd by your appointment drew,
> And justly call the Capitol too bright
> Which signifies our people in your charge;[15]

Johnson objected to the painting's size and the colors used, but Wilbur cleverly twists the meaning of the press secretary's words to indicate that

Johnson thinks of himself as too big a man to give Congress, as the representative body of the American people, a prominent place in his image of America. Wilbur reads Johnson's rejection of Hurd's painting not only as snubbing artists in general but also as an insult to all American citizens. "I'm really angry at him, of course, because of the Vietnam war," Wilbur later explained in an interview, "but the poem presumes to be attacking him because he refused Peter Hurd's commissioned portrait."[16]

This underlying motive becomes apparent in Wilbur's octave where he compares Johnson unfavorably to one of his most illustrious predecessors. Without actually naming him explicitly, Wilbur presents Thomas Jefferson as superior to Johnson for three reasons. First, striking below the belt, Wilbur indicates that Jefferson was elected to office rather than "heir to the office of a man" who had died.[17] Johnson of course became president only because John F. Kennedy was assassinated in 1963. Second, Wilbur presents Jefferson as a cultured man who not only had the vocabulary and the intellectual capacity to draw "our Declaration up" but also was a gifted architect Third, during Jefferson's days in office, "no army's blood was shed," Wilbur states significantly in the final line of his octave. Rather than invade a postcolonial nation that wanted to vote for "self-rule" as Johnson did with Vietnam, Jefferson theoretically paved the way for all nations of the world who chose to become independent by drafting the Declaration of Independence.[18]

It is revealing about Wilbur as a poet that he is able to contain his anger within the strict form of a sonnet. Wilbur addresses the president as "Sir" and remains polite throughout his poem. "I'm all for institutions," Wilbur remarked in an interview in 1968, in an attempt to differentiate himself from Allen Ginsberg's more insubordinate criticism of the presidency.[19] This more traditional and conservative view is embodied in his sonnet, as James Longenbach has noted, "both thematically, in its meditation on the office of the president, and formally, in its rejuvenation of Milton's trumpet for political poetry."[20] Even though few poets of his generation remained as formal (both poetically and politically) as Wilbur at this point in their careers, the respectful tone of Wilbur's sonnet (despite the evident sarcasm) marks a clear contrast between the polite and quiet middle generation and the more volatile Beat generation.

Like Wilbur's "A Miltonic Sonnet for Mr. Johnson," Meredith's "A Mild-Spoken Citizen" directly addresses an American president who got embroiled in the war in Vietnam. As is apparent from the title, Meredith reluctantly and belatedly has his say. Neither Wilbur nor Meredith is the kind of person who frequently jumps on the political bandwagon, so their protests are expressions of deep-seated resentment of citizens who cannot be silent anymore. First published in the November 27, 1971, issue of the *Saturday Review,* the poetry section of which was edited by John Ciardi, "A Mild-Spoken Citizen" must have been addressed to President Richard Nixon. The direct occasion of Meredith's letter to the president is not disclosed, but it can be guessed at since Meredith refers to the "criminal folly" that the president committed "last spring." The incident that Meredith refers to is probably Nixon's decision to invade Cambodia. In April 1970 Nixon had stunned Americans by announcing that he had sent troops to that country thereby further escalating the war, even though he had promised (and won his presidential campaign on the pledge) to bring troops home and end the war.[21]

Throughout the poem Meredith presents himself as a model and modest citizen—for instance, by adding parenthetically "in my eyes" or "if I may lecture you" and acknowledging that, similar to Wilbur, he "respect[s] the office." Like Wilbur too, Meredith can no longer be meek and polite. Neither sparing Nixon nor himself, Meredith argues:

> A man's mistakes (if I may lecture you), his worst acts,
> aren't out of character, as he'd like to think,
> are not put on him by power or stress or too much to drink,
>
> but are simply a worse self he consents to be. Thus
> there is no mistaking you. I marvel that there's
> so much disrespect for a man just being himself, being his errors.
>
> 'I never met a worse man than myself,'
> Thoreau said. When we're our best selves, we can all
> afford to say that. Self-respect is best when marginal.
>
> And when the office of the presidency will again
> accommodate that remark, it may be held by better men
> than you or me.[22]

Meredith's regular tercets and loose end-rhymes are striking. They suggest that Meredith, again like Wilbur, is able to contain his anger within bounds, even if Meredith's rhymes become more sporadic toward the end of his poem. Like Wilbur, Meredith is struggling to stay reasonable and not to lose himself in rage. As if speaking for his entire generation, Meredith admits that he has acted out his "worst self" and hints that this occurred during World War II and during the Korean War when he was a naval aviator. Meredith tries to be his better self because he no "longer pretend[s] that I don't swindle or kill / When there is swindling and killing on my nation's part."

Meredith's "A Mild-Spoken Citizen" is essentially a meditation on what sort of person should inhabit the White House. Like Wilbur, Meredith suspects that the president he addresses is arrogant, made so by the deference of the people who surround him. He is not asking the president to be infallible, but that he be modest and that he own up to his mistakes; in other words, that Nixon accepts that he has a "worse self" that has committed terrible acts. Even though Meredith admits that he is not a religious man, he prays to God that the current crisis will be resolved quickly.[23] Unlike most other people, Meredith does not ask God to "bless the presidency," but asks God to "cause the President to change."[24] What makes Meredith's poem stand out from the political satires discussed above is that it reflects more complex emotions than anger alone. Meredith's "A Mild-Spoken Citizen" is an expression of his own military history that he finds troubling, and a rational although farfetched appeal to the president to experience the same transformation to a nonviolent self that Meredith went through himself.

Politicians were not the only ones who were singled out for the middle generation poets' denigration. In "An Overview," Anthony Hecht aims not only at the president and the general staff but also at the "mission-happy Air Force boys" whom he presents as arrogant, carefree, and Icarus-like youths who consider bombs and war planes as toys for boys.[25] None of the other poets of the middle generation aimed at members of the armed forces in their poems about Vietnam. In fact, soldiers, marines, and air force crew are conspicuously absent from their poetry about Vietnam, as opposed to their own poetry about World War II and the soldier-poetry of Doug Anderson, W. D. Ehrhart, Yusef Komunyakaa, Jim Nye, Bruce Weigl, and others about "their" war in Vietnam. It is unclear whether this omission is out of respect for the young men who—like themselves two or three decades earlier—were forced to fight a foreign war, or because they feel uncomfortable writing about experiences they did not witness firsthand. Yet it underlines the fact that the poets of World War II had become stateside poets. This fact dramatically changed their focal point on war. They were writing not about the Second World War, but about the third major war they lived through, to paraphrase Jarrell's critique of Tate's "Ode to the Young Pro-Consuls of the Air," which is "a very different thing" altogether.[26]

Like Allen Tate's surprisingly similar "Ode to the Young Pro-Consuls of the Air" and Robert Lowell's more religiously apocalyptic "The Bomber," "An Overview" evokes a one-sided image of the overconfidence of youth, without the correcting sympathy that Jarrell could muster for these young men who were not only aggressors but also victims of history, their culture, and their own naïveté at the time. The happy-go-lucky bombardiers—who drop bombs like unloading "eggs on what appear / The perfect patchwork squares of chess" or on "F.A.O. Schwartz"–size "highways, trees and ports"—are convenient targets for the superior poet, but these airmen may well have been—just like Hecht in 1944—sucked into a war without fully comprehending what was happening.[27] Hecht's point that he was exposing "the impersonal, technological warfare of modern times" is correct, but for that insight readers are better served by Nemerov's "Models" and "The Air Force

Museum at Dayton,"[28] which use the same metaphors and drive home the same point. Yet Nemerov's poems are more effective because they are not merely aimed at derision and do more justice to lived experience.

"An Overview" thus exposes a potential weakness in the sarcastic Vietnam War poetry of the middle generation poets. Whereas their poems about World War II, taken together, offer a more comprehensive and ambiguous view of war, their sardonic poems about Vietnam offer—even collectively—a limited view of the war that is sometimes fueled by only one basic emotion: anger. Their active participation in World War II, which may have enabled them to bear witness in more credible and convincing testimonies, partially explains this discrepancy, but poets such as Hecht and Jarrell also dared to go beyond their own selves to imagine how World War II impacted people unlike themselves. This ability to evoke poignant realities and make them come alive for readers who have not personally witnessed these events makes Hecht's "The Book of Yolek" and Jarrell's "Eighth Air Force" superior war poems and "An Overview" or "Ode to the Young Pro-Consuls of the Air" less so.

The more successful Vietnam War poems that members of the middle generation wrote espouse more ambiguous emotions. They lament the war, but also reflect their own political helplessness and impotence. They indirectly admit that "poetry makes nothing happen," as W. H. Auden noted three decades earlier.[29] Despite this sobering knowledge they nevertheless wrote their poems because of their innate desire or compulsion to comprehend or communicate their "isolation" and "griefs," to cite Auden again.[30] These subdued emotions often obliquely refer to World War II. The most powerful Vietnam War poems by the World War II generation poets are all hesitant attempts to speak to the poets' own military past, without making large moral claims.

Hayden Carruth's "The Birds of Vietnam" is a good example of this subtler kind of Vietnam war poetry. Philip Metres has argued that a major problem facing war resistance poets during the war in Vietnam was how to render "visible again the invisible battle and its connections to the homefront." Carruth's approach to escape this problem could be categorized as "a visionary mode," a technique also used by Robert Bly, Robert Duncan, W. S. Merwin, and Adrienne Rich. It makes the war visible "through associate leaps," through the imagination.[31] In "Birds of Vietnam" Carruth mourns the demise of Vietnam's flora and fauna because of the defoliation raids by the American air force. The resentment that characterizes so many protest poems are also clearly present in "The Birds of Vietnam," and Carruth also idealizes Vietnam as a pastoral landscape, as anti–Vietnam War poets were apt to do. Carruth charges that Vietnam's nature is being destroyed by American colonial barbarians who act like "the Appointed Avengers, the Destroyers, the Wrathful Ones." Carruth indicates in his irregular, free verse poem that the United States has its fair share of "endangered species," including "the road runner and the golden eagle, / the great white heron and the Kirtland's warbler," and its extinct animals, "whooping cranes, condors, white-tailed kites, / and the ivory-bills." Yet they are also "certainly gone, all gone!" Carruth exclaims emphatically albeit parenthetically.[32]

"The Birds in Vietnam" is exceptional among the many protest poems that appeared during the Vietnam War era because it sustains diverse and sometimes contradictory emotions. Despite the sincerity of his resentment of the American authorities who are responsible for the carnage, Carruth also undercuts these feelings by openly questioning what he actually knows about the war, something other "visionary" poets did not frequently do. This is especially apparent in the first stanza that starts off in the apostrophic style of Romantic poetry in praise of nature, but lasts only two lines:

O bright, o swift and bright,
you flashing among pandanus boughs
        (is that right? pandanus?)
under the great banyan, in and out
the dusky delicate bamboo groves
        (yes? banyan, bamboo?)
low, wide-winged, gliding
over the wetlands and drylands
        (but I have not seen you
        I do not know your names,
        I do not know
        what I am talking about).[33]

Immediately after evoking the colorful birds in his euphonious lines, Carruth questions whether "pandanus"—which refers to a genus of flowering shrubs and plants indigenous to Southeast Asia—is the right word to use to conjure up a Vietnamese landscape. A little farther down Carruth again interrupts his pastoral rhetoric with similar questions about "banyan," a species of tropical figs, and "bamboo." At the end of the quoted stanza Carruth admits to his own ignorance about nature in that part of the world. By doing so he also questions his own authority to speak about the subject and by implication the war in Vietnam, a war in which he is not directly involved, and in a country that he has never visited.

Yet his vulnerable admission of his limited viewpoint in writing about the war ironically gives Carruth's words a sense of honesty, integrity, and power that many of the more assertive and self-righteous protest poems do not have. When, in the third stanza, Carruth imagines what the "cindered country" of Vietnam must look like with its "crusted kids" and with its birds "poisoned in your nests," we accept the emotion as genuine sorrow for all lives lost. Whether by empathetic imagination or from bygone experiences from World War II when he served in the air force in Italy, Carruth knows that "flesh" does not "turn to dust," as the phrase goes, but that "a man-corpse or woman-corpse is a bloody pulp," evoking a similar image as Jarrell's shot ball turret gunner. A dead bird retains its colors to "remind us what the earth has been," Carruth states movingly.[34]

Lowell's "The March 1" and "The March 2"—which both depict a demonstration at the Pentagon in October 1967 in which he participated—also look like straightforward protest poems, but they are similarly undercut by the poet's skepticism about his own protest. Whereas Carruth doubts his legitimacy in addressing a war in a country that he does not really know, Lowell reflects on how uncomfortable and awkward the act of public protest makes him feel. Like the Lincoln Memorial, which is "too white," and the "marmoreal Washington Obelisk," which is "too tall," everything seems a little bit off, awkward, or out of place during the march on the Pentagon.[35] Interlocking arms with fellow protesters feels ridiculous to Lowell, and he even seems irritated by ranting speeches that are shouted through megaphones and that seem to go on forever. At the end of "The March 2" Lowell is more than ready to "flee" the scene.[36] As Ernest J. Smith has claimed, the speaker "is more witness and commentator than activist."[37]

Throughout the two poems Lowell complains about his health and about how physically weak his fellow marchers and he are. Those who take part in the demonstration are not like the vigorous students at Columbia University, the French bourgeoisie who stormed the Bastille on July 14 in 1789, or "the green Union Army recruits" who boarded trains "for the first Bull Run" during the Civil War. It is possible that Lowell again had Herman Melville's "The March into Virginia" in mind as that poem focuses on soldiers moving toward the First Battle of Manassas, as the First Battle of Bull Run is also called. Lowell and his fellow demonstrators are not "boyish."[38] On the contrary, those who march on "our Bastille, the Pentagon" are "mostly white-haired, or bald, or women" who are all nursing various cramps and other ailments.

Philip Metres has charged that this poem is an "ad hominem attack" on those who protested the war since Lowell appears to present "war resistance simply as the strivings of the weak."[39] Such a reading is certainly plausible, but Lowell also seems to make another point. Despite his reservations and discomfiture, he is there, but not to tell off "the state and president" this time, as the righteous conviction that had characterized Lowell during World War II is gone. He is there because he feels he ought to be there. Like the writing of the poem, protesting the war is a symbolic act, Lowell knows. It will not have an immediate political effect, but it is an important gesture to make. At this point in his life, Lowell would have concurred with Nemerov who claimed in his poem "To the Poets" that "it's a pretty humble business, singing songs."[40] Yet it is the nature of birds and poets to sing.

Nemerov's "On Being Asked for a Peace Poem," whose title—though not its tone and length—echoes W. B. Yeats's "On Being Asked for a War Poem," demonstrates the same self-effacing conviction that poetry has limited political power. It is the only satirical poem among the group of Vietnam War poems written by the middle generation poets that is also profound. Despite its tongue-in-cheek humor, it ultimately has a long-lasting message. Nemerov conjures up a poetic persona for this occasional poem by the name of Joe Blow. This average poet person imagines what glory will be bestowed on him if he can pull off writing a great poem about the war in Vietnam. He owes the world a poem, Blow reasons, as he senses it can stop "this senseless war" in the same way that "Homer stopped that dreadful thing at Troy" and "Wordsworth stopped the Revolution when / He felt that Robespierre had gone too far." Homer never stopped the Trojan War of course, and neither did Wordsworth stop the massacre of the French Revolution. Still, these alternative realities allow Blow to dream what it would be like to hold a speech before the "General Assembly" and the "Security Council" of the United Nations. His wishful thinking even allows him to imagine that a "bright producer" may want to present his poem "on TV." Blow does not have a "good first line," however, although he considers the sound "O" an appropriate beginning for such a weighty subject.[41]

Nemerov is clearly ridiculing the pretentiousness of poets who think they can change the world by writing a poem, just as Hecht does in a recently dug up epitaph from the 1970s:

> Here lies fierce Strephon, whose poetic rage,
> Lashed out on Viet Nam from page and stage
> Whereby from basements of Bohemia, he
> Rose to the lofts of sweet celebrity.[42]

Both Hecht and Nemerov caricature the kind of poets who during the Vietnam era donned what Chattarji has called "the prophetic mantle" and saw themselves as "truthteller."[43] Hecht also frequently lashed out against the loudmouthed protest poetry that was "composed and read aloud from forum and platform during the Vietnam era." He found such events "ridiculous spectacle[s]."[44] Even William Stafford, a middle generation poet who participated in many of the rallies, was not an advocate of the vociferous approach:

"I have always felt that a raised voice was a mistake," Stafford said during an interview, "in the sixties or anytime."[45]

Nemerov's "On Being Asked for a Peace Poem" could be a sneering comment at overtly political poets, but it is more effectively an expression of his sense of powerlessness in the face of another war. It is an expression of a "hopeless hope" that it might be different, to borrow a phrase that Helen Vendler has used to characterize Nemerov's poetry.[46] Nemerov could have decided to decline the invitation to write a peace poem. Instead he wrote this ambivalent peace poem that shows the dilemma of writing poems about war in the postmodern world. You have to be foolish to think that your poem will matter politically, but being silent could signify that you are apathetic. Nemerov may come across as cynical in the poems of *The Western Approaches* (1975) and *Sentences* (1980), but his pessimism masks his deep sense of commitment about the world and its people.

Carruth's "On Being Asked to Write a Poem against the War in Vietnam" shares almost the same title as Nemerov's poem, but it also presents a similar outlook on poetry. Like Nemerov's poem, it is essentially a poem about despair as well as the lack of conviction that poetry can change even one iota of all the wars that took place in the twentieth century. Carruth's method of sharing this sad wisdom is entirely different, though. He lists a few of the wars he wrote poems against. Carruth's spelling and syntax break down toward the end of the poem, and his poem gradually descends into an emotional stammer when considering all the twentieth-century deaths caused by war. Carruth's, Lowell's, and Nemerov's view on war poetry was commonly shared by the middle generation poets, and it separates them from activist poets like Bly, Ginsberg, and Levertov. The World War II poets no longer believed that poems and protest can change the policies of governments. Yet their poetic responses show that while they are wary of protests, they are not indifferent. They had simply witnessed so many wars that they felt and knew that the world would not change. "All wars are boyish," Lowell quoted from Melville's "The March into Virginia" in 1945 before adding "but we are old."[47] By the 1970s they had grown even older.

These ideas merge in Anthony Hecht's "The Odds," perhaps the most moving and powerful American poem about the Vietnam War. "The Odds" celebrates the birth of Anthony Hecht's son Evan, to whom the poem is also dedicated. Evan Hecht's birth occurred in the "eleventh year of war" in Vietnam, but the Hechts seem at first unaffected by that conflict thousands of miles away. In his typically richly ornate diction—so unlike Carruth's equally effective emotional stammering—Hecht paints a harmonious scene of winter (even though it is April) as if he is describing a Norman Rockwell painting or revisiting Robert Frost:

Three new and matching loaves,
Each set upon a motionless swing seat,
Straight from some elemental stoves
And winter bakeries of unearthly wheat,
In diamonded, smooth, pillowings of white
Have risen out of nothing overnight.

And all the woods for miles,
Stooped by these clean endowments of the north
Flaunt the same candle-dripping styles
In poured combers of pumice and the froth
Of heady steins. Upon the railings lodge
The fat shapes of a nineteen-thirties Dodge.[48]

Hecht paints a picture of warmth, comfort, and luxury, as the "fat shapes of a nineteen-thirties Dodge" symbolize. In a draft of the poem Hecht had written "bulging shapes," but the adjective "fat" emphasizes more aptly the image of plenty that Hecht wants to emphasize.[49] Yet the snow-made bread that has "risen out of nothing overnight" also has religious connotations, as the meticulous poet surely realized. When the children of Israel were led from Egypt to the Promised Land, they did not have time to wait until their bread rose, so they baked it before it had a chance to rise, resulting in matzo, unleavened bread. The fact that Hecht and his wife can let (imaginary) bread rise is a sign of calm and serenity.

From the fourth stanza onward, however, there is a sudden change in tone, as Hecht starts to bewail the spectacle of nature outside his kitchen window. It is

A sort of stagy show
Put on by a spoiled, eccentric millionaire.
Lacking the craft and choice that go
With weighed precision, meditated care,
Into a work of art, these are the spent,
Loose, aimless squanderings of the discontent.

Like the blind, headlong cells,
Crowding toward dreams of life, only to die
In dark fallopian canals,
Or that wild strew of bodies at My Lai.
Thick drifts, huddled embankments at our door
Pile up in this eleventh year of war.[50]

Hecht's "spoiled, eccentric millionaire" is the incarnation of the American nation itself. Aggressive, conceited, and unable to appreciate the gifts he has been given, he wastes his money on resentment and bitterness, as is apparent during the war in Vietnam. He is the opposite of Hecht himself who, with "weighed precision" and "meditated care," tries to understand the world by producing a "work of art" as he does in this poem. The prodigal and wasteful manner of Americans is being compared in two unlikely yet effective Homeric similes: first, to the sperm seeds that are "crowding toward dreams of life" when a penis ejaculates in a vagina "only to die / In dark fallopian canals," and second, the scattering of Vietnamese bodies after the My Lai massacre. Some five hundred people died during that infamous incident, mostly innocent women and children, when an American platoon shot them in search of Viet Cong sympathizers. Seeing, reading, or hearing about the atrocities at My Lai must have been a nauseating déjà-vu for Hecht, who witnessed how members of his own regiment during World War II killed two innocent German women and children when they were ready to surrender. The widely divergent images that Hecht yokes together are unusual and extreme, but they fit the theme of Hecht's poem perfectly as Hecht is "vaguely stunned" by the birth of his son and contemplates the randomness of birth and death, "those incalculable odds." He is troubled by questions—"who died for him? Who gave him place?"—but of course he gets no answers.[51]

Hecht is troubled by the aftersight of World War II and the foresight of new wars to come, in his young son's life. Hecht's distressed reflections contrast sharply with the blissful happiness of his wife whose joy knows no bounds. She is oblivious that "the whole war and winter" exist outside their cozy home. Hecht's final images are beautifully fitting as he compares the winter wonderland and his son's birth to "those crystal balls / With Christmas storms and manageable size." It presents a happy, self-contained image of an ideal community, a "tiny settlement" that can "shape our world, but that is never ours."[52] By the 1970s, when a new generation of boys was growing up and being dragged into a war, Hecht and the other middle generation poets understood that the world is not "manageable." These poets shared a sense of befuddled helplessness when confronted with yet another war. They had felt like bit players in World War II, but had even less control over this war. And yet they were not silent or apathetic. Their poems are faint and sometimes reluctant protests by a generation of poets who were old enough to know that their poems would not change the world. They felt compelled to write their protests, even though they were convinced that their messages would probably not be heard.

CHAPTER 16

Howard Nemerov and the "Good War" Myth

Of all the American poets who were involved in World War II, Howard Nemerov debunked the "Good War" myth most consistently and assertively. Made popular by Studs Terkel's Pulitzer Prize–winning oral history, the term the "Good War" was often used by former American servicemen to denote World War II as distinct from other wars, such as the Korean War and the Vietnam War, where the enemy and the goal of the military conflict seemed less distinct and morally more ambiguous. Terkel consciously put the "Good War" in quotation marks, realizing that "the adjective 'good' mated to the noun 'war' is so incongruous."[1] With the passing of time, however, the "Good War" has lost its quotation marks and has become a pervasive myth in the United States. As Michael C. C. Adams has asserted in his ironically titled book *The Best War Ever: America and World War II,* this war "has been converted over time from a complex, problematic event, full of nuance and debatable meaning, to a simple, shining legend of the Good War. For many, including a majority of survivors from the era, the war years have become America's golden age, a peak in the life of society when everything worked out and the good guys definitely got a happy ending. It was a great war. For Americans, it was the best war ever."[2]

Since the publication of Adams's book in 1994, the celebration and even glorification of America's involvement in World War II has increased rather than waned, culminating in the dedication of the World War II memorial in Washington, D.C. on Memorial Weekend 2004. The National World War II reunion that took place concurrently was entitled "America Celebrates the Greatest Generation." It was named after Tom Brokaw's best-selling book about World War II, *The Greatest Generation* (1998). Both the titles of the reunion and the book appeared, significantly, without quotation marks.

Other poets than Nemerov also tried to expose the cheerful myth that the American memory of World War II had become. William Stafford comes close to falling out of his conciliatory mode in "Explaining the Big One," his most sarcastic war poem. Assuming the casual and colloquial voice of a redneck who holds opposite views from himself, Stafford shows how many Americans remembered World War II as a huge, adventurous spectacle that everyone wanted to be a part of. This enthusiastic embrace of World War II is already shown in the euphemistic title in which that war is metaphorically referred to as "the Big One." Typical of the historical amnesia of Stafford's boorish speaker is that he cannot remember the names or nationalities of two dictators, so he refers to them as "the leader with the funny mustache" (Adolf Hitler) and "the one with the big mustache" (Josef Stalin).[3] He also does not recall whether Stalin was part of the Allied or Axis forces: "He was our friend, I think."[4] The fact that Stalin "eliminated malcontents / by the millions" does not bother Stafford's coarse speaker. His reasoning may awaken the uncomfortable question in the reader of how such a tyrant could also earlier have been "our friend."[5]

Stafford makes a mockery of the ever-more popular notion of the "Good War" by simply quoting verbatim how many veterans and Americans from the 1940s onward chose to remember World War II. Women partook in as much of the "fun" as the men since "they danced and sang for the soldiers or volunteered / their help."[6] Whereas Hitler was "jolly, sometimes" and Stalin "always jovial / for the camera," Roosevelt had a "jaunty cigarette holder" and a fascination for "pearl-handled revolvers," while Eisenhower "played golf."[7] It is distressing that Stafford's inane speaker remembers only the most trivial details from "the Big One." It makes us question whether the war was as simple as he puts it: "It was us / against the bad guys, then. You should have been there."[8] Stafford "should have been there" in a slightly different meaning of that phrase, but he chose not to, in part because he did not believe in the cliché-ridden and hollow rhetoric of the warring nation.

Stafford's exposure of the American World War II myth may not be surprising given that he was opposed to the war from the outset. As a member of the "greatest generation" and a war hero in the conventional sense of the word, Nemerov, however, did not feel the urge to glorify the war or his contribution to it. On the contrary, hidden behind the diffuse and elusive nature of his poetry are constant warnings against the perennial masculine appeal of war, and how quickly people forget the horror of previous wars. Shortly after graduating from Harvard in 1941 and just before Pearl Harbor, Nemerov had signed up for the American air corps, attempting to fulfill his childhood dream of becoming a pilot. As a child, Nemerov played with model airplanes he himself constructed, as his poem "Models" shows. His childhood hero had been Charles Lindbergh, the first aviator to fly solo across the Atlantic Ocean in 1927. (Lindbergh became a hardcore isolationist in the late 1930s and early 1940s, with pro-fascist and anti-Semitic sentiments, but as a child Nemerov was still unaware of these characteristics.) Like many inductees in the air force, Nemerov failed the rigorous training and was dismissed. Undaunted, he enlisted in the Royal Canadian Air Force (RCAF), qualified as a fighter pilot, and went overseas in June 1943. Asked in an interview about his move to become a pilot in Canada, Nemerov replied that his answer would involve "a long, rather stupid tedious story." When relating the gist of the story anyway, Nemerov could not resist making an ironic stab at his laconic, "boyish" earlier self: "When the United States Air Force kicked me out before Pearl Harbor because they could not teach me to fly, they said: 'If we wash you out will you go to Canada?' And I thought of those powder blue uniforms and how beautiful I would look, and said: 'Oh sure.' So I went."[9]

Nemerov flew with the RCAF until January 1944 when he was transferred to the American air force. He had completed his tour in April 1945, was shipped back to the United States, and was honorably discharged in August 1945 at Fort Dix, New Jersey, just at the time when World War II ended after the explosions of the two nuclear bombs over Hiroshima and Nagasaki. He completed the RCAF tour of duty, which consisted of thirty operations, followed by a period of training and a second tour of an additional twenty missions.[10] He then flew another fifty-seven missions for the U.S. Army Air Force (USAAF), much more than a USAAF crew ordinarily flew, mostly involving anti-shipping patrol over the North Sea and attacking the German coastal defense lines.[11] Nemerov's record shows that he also flew missions in the aerial campaign over Normandy, northern France, and the Rhineland, contributing to the heavy bombardments of German military targets and cities.[12] Nemerov was honored with a Ribbon-Air Medal with Four Oak Leaf Clusters. For a long time, however, he did not feel the need to share the details of his military career publicly.

Nemerov may have been physically unharmed by the war, but not unaffected mentally. Like Ciardi and many other surviving airmen, Nemerov suffered from nightmares, which continued off and on for the rest of his life. Considering the ordeal he and others had to deal with, this was not abnormal.[13] Only 50 percent of the crew that flew the RCAF tour of duty survived the total of fifty missions, and Nemerov flew many more hazardous flights than that. Alexander Nemerov, the poet's son, has recorded how, during World War II, his father was invited to be part of an all-American squadron of de Havillard Mosquitoes instead of the slower RCAF plane, the Bristol Beaufighter, he was then flying. Nemerov declined the offer, and shortly afterward the Mosquitoes were destroyed, killing all the pilots. Like "Lucky" John Ciardi, Nemerov beat the odds and survived. Nemerov also related to his son that at one point a single bullet went through the windscreen of his cockpit, narrowly missing the pilot-poet. Alexander Nemerov has suggested that the title (rather than the subject) of the poem "I Only Am Escaped to Tell Thee" is "strongly autobiographical, redolent of his own catastrophe recently survived."[14] The title of Nemerov's poem refers not only to the book of Job but also to the epilogue of Herman Melville's *Moby-Dick* where Ishmael tries to make sense of the wreckage around him.[15]

Allied aircrew lived bizarre lives, as historians have pointed out. They lived a deceptively comfortable life in eastern England until they had to fly their dangerous missions, during which they were shot at by enemy planes, by flak, and occasionally by friendly fire. While the majority of the surviving aircrew were able to cope with the mental pressures, a sizable minority were not, and snapped. Judging from the many sorties he completed, Nemerov was better equipped than most to handle the mental pressures. The fact that he was squadron leader confirms this. "Leadership was crucial, leadership within the squadron," Ben Shephard has asserted: "Much of it had a talismanic quality: someone who had survived hitherto obviously had luck on his side; the more operations a squadron commander . . . went on, the more extraordinary the fact of his survival became, the more his authority was enhanced."[16]

The sheer danger, destruction, and death that surrounded him at an early age stayed with Nemerov. After the war Nemerov did not much talk about the war with his wife, Margaret, whom he had met during the war in Bournemouth, England. They were so "pleased and surprised" that they "came out of the war alive" that they "never discussed" it, she has admitted.[17] Yet "the war never really went away in our house," Alexander Nemerov remembered, "even as it became a thing of the distant past."[18] It was through writing poetry that Nemerov spoke up about the war. Yet "poetry is about the silence," he related to his friend Reed Whittemore in 1961, "about trying to say the silence."[19] Even though veterans, especially fighter pilots, received a herolike status after the war and many were able to function like normal citizens, many continued to be troubled by what they had seen. "The flyer who returns to his home and is lionized for heroic exploits may still torture himself with the feeling of unworthiness and guilt," said Willard Waller, a World War I veteran in his book *Veteran Comes Back,* and this seems true of Nemerov as well.[20] Following in the wake of modernism, the New Criticism, and what T. S. Eliot called the "objective correlative," many of Nemerov's early poems seem at first detached, impersonal, obscure, and pessimistic observations about human nature.[21] Yet Nemerov's unemotional, ironic tone cannot hide that his war poems are deeply personal, emotional, and autobiographical accounts of a mind troubled by guilt and trauma. As the quotation from *Moby-Dick* and Job hints at, Nemerov seems to have been troubled by the kind of survivor's guilt that also affected Ciardi, although he never addresses these topics explicitly in his poetry.

Nemerov wrote consistently about the war, from his first volume, *The Image and the Law* (1947), to his almost final poetic statement, *War Stories: Poems about Long Ago and Now* (1987). With the exception of two volumes, the ten books of poetry in between contain at least one poem about World War II. Later than all of his contemporaries, however, Nemerov—always a traditionalist poet—embraced a plainer statement of feeling when trying to come to terms with his war record in *War Stories*. His childhood dream had become an adult nightmare. When, in the 1980s, America's involvement in World War II began to be celebrated as the "Good War," Nemerov voiced his experiences more directly and passionately.

His early war poem "Redeployment," his most anthologized poem, is still representative of Nemerov's modernist leanings during the 1940s and 1950s. The poem hints at the discrepancy between how the veteran perceives the war and how the public at large does, as is reflected in the first two lines: "They say the war is over. But water still / Comes bloody from the taps."[22] The platitude that "the war is over" is voiced by those who are not acquainted with the horrors, and they are contemptuously referred to in the plural pronoun. In real life Nemerov was also frustrated by the smugness and complacency of people back home, which, together with the images of horror that he had seen, infuriated him. To Patricia Bosworth, the biographer of Nemerov's sister, photographer Diane Arbus, he reported how this clash between him and his family soured his homecoming party: "Everyone around me was complaining about gas rationing and not getting enough steak to eat. I'd seen blood and crushed bones—death. I clammed up and refused to talk. Mommy was furious."[23]

The emotion in "Redeployment" is not expressed personally, but rather through morose and evocative images, as the modernists had done. The poem ends disconcertingly and more personally than the opening stanzas and Nemerov's other war poems from the 1940s:

> The end of the war. I took it quietly
> Enough. I tried to wash the dirt out of
> My hair and from under my fingernails,
> I dressed in clean white clothes and went to bed.
> I heard the dust falling between the walls.[24]

Even though the speaker focuses on himself in this final stanza in blank verse, his identity is not disclosed, and "Redeployment" ultimately does not seem a personal poem. The title, as well as the reference to a veteran with the obsessive habit of clicking a dead soldier's eyeballs, indicates that the speaker is a soldier himself who has also suffered from war trauma, as these last lines could imply.

The protagonist's obsession with washing himself reveals the speaker's urge to wash away the foulness of war, or perhaps his sins and his feelings of guilt. Jarrell used a similar reference to Pontius Pilate in another exceptional World War II poem, "Eighth Air Force," about combat pilots like Nemerov, whom he described simultaneously as saviors and murderers: "Men wash their hands, in blood, as best they can: / I find no fault in this just man."[25] Nemerov is careful not to reveal the speaker's age or history, and thus "Redeployment" stands as testimony to its modernist and New Critical time. Nemerov's speaker is consciously universalized, an impersonal persona who could be anyone in the postwar era. As T. S. Eliot suggested in "Tradition and the Individual Talent," "poetry is not a turning loose of emotion, but an escape from emotion; it is not the expression of personality, but an escape from personality." Nemerov was faithful to this adage, at least early on in his career.[26] Yet despite these efforts to hide private emotions, it is a supremely personal poem in which Nemerov is "trying to say the silence." It makes "Redeployment" not only one of the best but also an exemplary poem of World War II.

Written more than a decade after the war, "An Old Warplane" from *Mirrors and Windows* (1958) is a precursor of the type of aerial warfare poem that Nemerov would perfect late in life. Following in Jarrell's footsteps, who wrote most prolifically about airmen, Nemerov would develop this genre in the next three decades. More personal and written in a looser, more relaxed style than "Redeployment," "An Old Warplane" shows traces of the poet's youthful infatuation with aircraft, but at the end of the poem he warns against the romantic images that planes awaken in him and other men. The sheer joy of detail when describing the beaten-up and personified aircraft taking to the sky reveals Nemerov's love for the visual beauty of flight, much like Dickey in "The Firebombing" and "Two Poems of Flight-Sleep." Nemerov renders the warplane as a grand old lady who is proud despite her physical ailments: "Even a thing like this takes pathos / After the years," the first two lines casually read. Following this initial reference to the aircraft as a "thing," Nemerov switches to the feminine pronouns "she" and "her"—as aircrew were apt to do—showing that the plane is no longer just an inanimate object to him.[27] The pity and compassion she arouses in the speaker stem from the rust showing underneath the paint, the oil stains, the burned spots on the chrome, and her brave attempt to stay in the air, regardless of her old age.

Yet the old warplane is also a temptress who can lure men into war with her "old / Inflexible will and devious wile," a point of view that is absent in Dickey's poetry.[28] Many young men lost their hearts and subsequently their lives trying to tame her, enamored as they were by the alluring colors and aerodynamic speed. The camouflage colors are only a thin layer of veneer, however, a facade that hides the rust and grime of war. Nemerov's speaker is also almost taken in by the old aircraft once again. Yet the thunderous, roaring sounds wake him from the enchanting dream and evoke other images, of the dangerous nightmare of war:

We heard again
The empty thunder of the war
By engines drummed on the stretched sky;

Burnt patches on the cannon ports
And under the exhaust pipes flared
Like danger and experience,
And all that dirty camouflage,

Of mackerel-back and belly of
The hanging rain-cloud on the sea,
Ran past, reminding of the old
Inflexible will and devious wile.[29]

As in all good poems, the syntax as well as the sounds of the words contribute almost as much to the meaning of the poem as the denotation of the words themselves. The cacophony of these lines, especially "stretched sky" and the plosives of "Burnt patches" and "cannon parts," echo the noise of the plane's engines. It offers a discordant contrast with the previous, more melodious lines in which Nemerov's speaker seemed spellbound by the plane flying to the horizon.

The crux of Nemerov's poem is contained in the last three stanzas in which he asserts that this old warplane still threatens us. Even if one has lived through the horrors of World War II, as Nemerov has, the grace and glamour of a warplane can still lure us to the next war. It can easily break through that frightful memory, which is "inadequately armed" and only "camouflaged" against the lure of the warplane, as Nemerov's clever puns suggest. "The Old Warplane" is thus a slight variation on fellow Harvardian George Santayana's famous quote that "those who cannot remember the past are condemned to repeat it."[30] Even those who learned more from the war than they ever bargained for can be tempted to feel the war's beckoning call all over again. As we will see again, Nemerov's history lessons were becoming increasingly personal and subtler than those that were winding up in the history books.

Nemerov's poignant poem "The Air Force Museum at Dayton" from *Inside the Onion* (1984) is also a variation on Santayana's saying and a precursor of *War Stories*. The visit to the Dayton air force museum constitutes a time-lapse spanning one hundred years of aviation and triggers his memories of World War II that seemed dead and buried. From the start of the poem the tone and mood are glum, mimicking the atmosphere of the museum, since the aerial museum pieces are displayed in "solemn gloom." Even the roof, which is shaped like a gun's "barrel," is suggestive of the violent nature of the museum's holdings. Nemerov's use of personification in "the pictures dead in period costumes" makes the past look dead, remote, and unreachable. Yet in 1984 there were still people around who were alive when the Wright brothers took to the sky at Kitty Hawk, North Carolina, on December 17, 1903, in the first powered, heavier-than-air machine to achieve controlled, sustained flight with a pilot aboard. Those members of Nemerov's generation who had survived the war also had witnessed the miraculous transformation from these primitive flying objects to the advanced rockets that landed on the moon only sixty-six years later. These planes, which propelled young boys' fantasies about air travel, are now grounded for good. After the first two stanzas, the mood becomes even more oppressive:

> After the pterodactyl and the Wright
> Brothers every kite carries a gun
> As it was meant to do, for right and might
> Are properly understood by everyone.[31]

The euphemistic metonymy "kite" underlines the notion that aviation and warfare became the domain of boys' fantasies. Yet Nemerov's ultimate message is more pressing, that aviation has been completely appropriated by the armed forces. The internal rhyme of the third stanza, connecting "Wright," "kite," "right and might," makes these lines sound sarcastic.[32] While science has been used to reach other planets, it has also been used to wipe out communities with one big bang, as happened with the nuclear bombs dropped over Hiroshima and Nagasaki. Nemerov's word choice—"cancelled cities in a single flare"—is especially clinical, but drive his point home that the business of war is anything but child's play.[33]

In the concluding two stanzas Nemerov muses that all artifacts of history are eventually sanctified. They are put in museums for people to stare and gloat at, irrespective of whether the instruments displayed were used for atrocious acts:

> When anything's over, it turns into art,
> Religion, history; what's come to pass
> Bows down the mind and presses upon the heart:
> The ancient bombsight here enshrined in glass

Is the relic left us of a robot saint
With a passion for accuracy, who long ago
Saw towns as targets miniature and quaint,
Townfolk invisible that far below.[34]

The mechanical analog computer that made up the much-coveted Norden bombsight is encased in glass, confirming its status as a precious museum piece. During World War II, this top-secret apparatus was used to drop bombs more accurately from aircraft such as the B-17, and thereby contributed to the American war effort but also to the destruction of numerous German, Italian, and Japanese towns and cities, and many thousands of their inhabitants. Nemerov's religious diction culminates in the ironic juxtaposition of "robot saint," a phrase that denotes the warplane but by implication also its crew. Revered for making the world safe for democracy, these seemingly blameless members of the "Greatest Generation" and their mechanical warplanes caused more harm to the "townfolk invisible" than would ever have seemed imaginable to Nemerov's speaker when he was young and enamored of the Wright brothers and their aerial experiments. It is a point that Richard Hugo was making in "Letter to Simic from Boulder" and Dickey in "The Firebombing." Oblivious to the consequences of their actions because they could not be seen from high above, the bomber squads are able to do their killing automatically and emotionlessly.

The steady but sporadic publication of Nemerov's war poems after 1950 could not have predicted the sudden outburst of World War II poems he wrote in the mid-1980s. *War Stories* (1987) contains a dozen poems that directly address Nemerov's own involvement in World War II. They are collected in the second and middle section of that volume, "The War in the Air." Some of the other poems in the first and third sections, "The War in the Streets" and "The War in the Heavens," respectively, refer to World War II and other wars in more indirect ways. The incentives behind Nemerov's sudden and intense focus on his personal past during World War II seem threefold.

First, the political and social climate in the United States in the mid-1980s seems to have played a part: "The reason we do not learn from history is / Because we are not the people who learned last time," is the pessimistic opening of Nemerov's "Ultima Ratio Reagan," yet again echoing Santayana.[35] Ronald Reagan is not mentioned or referred to in the text of "Ultima Ratio Reagan," except in the title. Nemerov's odd title is a pun on the Latin saying "Ultima Ratio Regum" and a reference to Stephen Spender's war poem of that name. Nemerov's poem thus adds another intertextual war poem to the long list of World War II poems of his generation. The reason Nemerov alludes to Reagan is because he is the kind of president who will send people off to a foreign war, as he did in Granada in 1983, or get enmeshed in yet another international scandal, the Iran-Contra Affair in 1986. Yet even when such invasions and scandals occur, "history will not blame us if once again / The light at the end of the tunnel is the train," Nemerov writes, subverting a familiar cliché that politicians frequently use to promise that a war is really nearly over.[36] Robert Lowell had made the same joke at the end of his less jocose poem "Since 1939" from *Day By Day* (1977), that poem in which he invoked Auden:

> We feel the machine slipping from our hands,
> as if someone else were steering;
> if we see a light at the end of the tunnel,
> it's the light of an oncoming train.[37]

Nemerov warns of new stupid wars to come in "Ultima Ratio Reagan," but like the other poets of his generation he does not have much faith that he will be heard or can do much about it.

Despite his criticism of Reagan, Nemerov received the National Medal of Arts, the highest prize given to artists and arts patrons by the U.S. government, from President Reagan on June 19, 1987—right at the time when *War Stories* came out. Nemerov would have realized that this quirk of fate was a result of his friendly demeanor, which allowed him to tell the most devastating truths that nobody would take seriously. In his autobiography of sorts, *Journal of the Fictive Life* (1965), Nemerov had described himself as basically "the Nice Guy type": "I grin at people, I tell them funny things, I am almost utterly non-controversial, even nonpolitical. If you behave in this manner publicly, I've found, it is possible to say the most shocking and even subversive, things, equally certain that they will have no effect and that people won't challenge them, for they are stubbornly persuaded of one's harmlessness, as well as, maybe of a certain innocuous unreality in the whole subject and situation."[38] "Ultima Ratio Reagan" is a highly political poem, "most shocking and even subversive," but the joke at the end ensures that people will probably not take offense. Yet it is a wry joke that also exposes how new generations of leaders and voters persist in a superior innocence that ignored the reality of history.

The second incentive that may have prompted Nemerov to write *War Stories* was the fortieth anniversary of the end of World War II, which was often discussed in the media. The publication of Studs Terkel's *"The Good War,"* for instance, provoked many other veterans to break the silence about their own war experiences. Third, approaching retirement and old age, Nemerov may have felt that this was the right and possibly the last time to set the record straight and have his say. With Paul Fussell, the literary historian and veteran who penned his and other soldiers' war experiences in his 1989 best seller *Wartime,* Nemerov seems to say: "There has been so much talk about 'The Good War,' the Justified War, the Necessary War, and the like, that the young and innocent could get the impression that it was really not such a bad thing after all. It's thus necessary to observe that it was a war and nothing else, and thus stupid and sadistic."[39]

In the title poem of the section on his World War II memories, "The War in the Air," Nemerov voices more directly and lucidly than before his distaste of how that war is being remembered and memorialized in the United States:

> That was the good war, the war we won
> As if there were no death, for goodness' sake,
> With the help of the losers we left out there
> In the air, in the empty air.[40]

Nemerov clearly despises the phrase "the good war." His atypically direct and impatient exclamation "for goodness' sake" is indicative of how much this prevalent misconception of the war offends him. "The War in the Air" elegizes the bomber crews who did not survive the war without heroicizing them. Those who died could never tell their war stories and lacked graves because their bodies were rarely found; they had vanished into thin air. Instead of "graves," they therefore got "epitaphs," from, for instance, Winston Churchill, who said about the Royal Air Force during the Battle of Britain that "never in the field of human conflict was so much owed by so many to so few."[41] Nemerov cynically twists Churchill's famous words to "never so many spoke for never so few" to emphasize how many people spent many winged words on those who died.

Another epitaph that Nemerov undercuts in "The War in the Air" is the Royal Air Force motto "per ardua ad astra," meaning "through adversity to the stars." By inserting the phrase "said the partisans of Mars" between the two parts of this Latin phrase, Nemerov links the Royal Air Force to the bellicose Roman god of war. Nemerov implies that these romantic epitaphs, as does the aesthetic beauty of planes, lure young people into war. In a sense "The War in the Air" serves as yet another epitaph commemorating the dead in the air war over Europe. Yet because Nemerov is a survivor and refuses to cry up the dead, his epitaph sounds more genuine than the officious (but effective) rhetoric of Churchill and the Royal Air Force.

Part of the "Good War" myth is the belief that the American army and their Allies formed a well-oiled machine, that the United States "outproduced and outfought everyone else," and that soldiers of all ranks harmoniously worked together to fight nazism and the belligerent Japanese.[42] In "IFF," aptly named after a signaling device on board an aircraft to identify friend or foe, Nemerov counteracts one of these in his first, colloquial line:

"Hate Hitler? No, I spared him hardly a thought."[43] Nemerov's more annoying, immediate enemies in his day-to-day life were his superiors with their power trips, and basically everyone who did not fly with them, as the last line of this poem indicates: "All above were friends. And then the foe."[44] There was no band of brothers in his war recollections. Nemerov was "not one of the good old boys," as Margaret Nemerov remembered.[45] The crew at the air force base hardly interacted with each other, Nemerov's speaker asserts in "IFF," and the racist slurs of the anti-Semitic navigator did not particularly contribute to morale either. Nemerov recounts how his British crew member Bert: "shyly explained to me that the Jews / Were ruining England and Hitler might be wrong / But he had the right idea . . . ."[46] Post-war generations came to believe that the Allied forces fought Nazi Germany because of its anti-Semitic and racist policies, but Nemerov shows in "IFF" how erroneous such a belief is. If during World War II, as Fussell asserts, the view was developed that the Allies "were by nature, by instinct really, morally superior," Nemerov's poem certainly challenges that notion.[47] Life as an air force officer was all about identifying friend or foe, but this task was less easily accomplished than would seem apparent.

"Night Operations, Coastal Command RAF" does away with the myth that all those who perished in the war in the air died an honorable, heroic death. Like "IFF," it starts off deadpan, stating that the Royal Air Force hardly needed the Luftwaffe to have so many losses. With their German counterparts, the "encounters were confused and few" and over in a heartbeat.[48] In a multitude of tragic errors, however, many of the airmen lost their lives because of human blunders, such as hitting power lines or forgetting to put the wheels out before landing. "Night Operations, Coastal Command RAF" is reminiscent of James Dickey's "Joel Cahill Dead" with its unfortunate training accident, or of Randall Jarrell's "Losses," which cited similar "routine crashes" with pilots "scattered on mountains" or "blazed up on the lines" they never saw.[49]

Yet whereas Dickey's and Jarrell's poems are empathetic, Nemerov's poem is satiric in order to challenge the heroism that is associated with the war in the air. In both "IFF" and "Night Operations, Coastal Command RAF" Nemerov is closer to the absurd tradition of *Catch-22* and *Slaughterhouse Five,* whose authors, Joseph Heller and Kurt Vonnegut, respectively, perceived in "blunders, errors, and accidents something very close to the essence of the Second World War."[50] The conversational, anecdotal, and witty style of these two poems and others in *War Stories* is distinctly different from the stiffer and more detached images Nemerov presented early on in his career. They work superbly to negate common myths about World War II.

Nemerov's take on World War II is remarkably consistent, although his poetic style changed dramatically. The difference between how he as a veteran experienced the bygone war and how people in the United States collectively remembered it remained a dominant theme from *The Image of the Law* (1947) to *War Stories* (1987). In nearly all of his war poems Nemerov is also concerned with drawing lessons from the past, and he frequently hints at how insidious historical memory is. It is true that the poems from *War Stories* address Nemerov's past more directly, personally, and autobiographically than he did in his early poetry. Yet in retrospect and in the context of his later poetry, even a seemingly impersonal poem like "Redeployment" acquires a personal intimacy that reflects, as we can now see, Nemerov's private grief. What Randall Jarrell once said of T. S. Eliot rings also true for Nemerov. Imagining how future generations of readers would evaluate Eliot's poetry, Jarrell spoke in the guise of such a reader and exclaimed: "But did you actually believe that all those things about objective correlatives, classicism, the tradition, applied to *his* poetry? Surely you must have seen that he was one of the most subjective and daemonic poets who ever lived, the victim and helpless beneficiary of his own inexorable compulsions, obsessions? From a psychoanalytical point of view he was far and away the most interesting poet of your century."[51]

Zooming in on Nemerov's war experiences and juxtaposing "Redeployment" to his later war poems have revealed that Nemerov is a more daemonic, haunting, and lyrical poet than has been previously understood. In "The Afterlife" of his life as a combat pilot, he tried desperately to comprehend through his poetry how his childhood dream had turned into an adulthood nightmare. Despite the intricate and carefully constructed metaphors, the pervasive ironic voice, the impersonal persona, the studious allusions, and the generally intellectual nature of his poetry, Nemerov is, like many other poets of his generation, at heart a subjective and emotional poet whose traumatic experiences during World War II formed an inescapable obsession about which he was compelled to write. He did so gradually throughout the war's afterlife, amassing an impressive oeuvre of war poems that only Anthony Hecht and Randall Jarrell can match.

Conclusion

"ALL WARS ARE BOYISH, . . . BUT WE ARE OLD"

Herman Melville's notorious line "All wars are boyish, and are fought by boys" from his Civil War poem "The March into Virginia" has resonated throughout this book.[1] It encapsulates key themes for the poets of World War II. Randall Jarrell once approvingly quoted Melville's line at a poetry reading at Pfeiffer College to indicate "that soldiers in an army kind of behave like junior high school students. They push each other and shove around in lines and act pretty childish."[2] Jarrell's own war poems, especially his air corps poems, point to a more significant correlation between Melville's words and the war poetry of the middle generation. Jarrell's war poems frequently feature young and not fully formed airmen who are oblivious of the havoc they wreak and the impact that their actions will have on others and on themselves. "The Death of the Ball Turret Gunner" dramatizes most concisely and poignantly the soldier's youthful naïveté, his doom, and the wisdom he gathers, paradoxically only at the moment when he dies.

Melville's "The March into Virginia" revolves around some of the same themes as "The Death of the Ball Turret Gunner," even though Jarrell's imagery, combining air power and Freudian theory, belongs unmistakably to the twentieth century. The First Battle of Bull Run, also known as the First Battle of Manassas, which Melville evokes in his poem, presents a more classic battlefield. The Union and Confederate armies that met on that Virginian ground in the first major land battle of the Civil War consisted of many rookie soldiers. The Confederate army, which had been waiting for the Union army on that fateful day in July 1861, won convincingly, forcing the surviving Union soldiers to flee ignobly back to Washington, D.C. The retreat of the Union army caused considerable chaos, in part because civilians from the capital had come to watch the battle while going on a "picnic party," a fact to which Melville's poem alludes.[3]

Nearly three thousand Union soldiers and almost two thousand Confederate soldiers were killed in the First Battle of Bull Run. The casualties were low compared to the numbers of men who died in later battles, but since this one occurred so early in the Civil War it shook Americans out of their smugness. "Wars are all alike in beginning complacently," as Paul Fussell has said sagely: "The reason is psychological and compensatory: no one wants to foresee or contemplate the horror, the inevitable ruin of civilized usages, which war will entail. Hence the defensive exercise of the optimistic imagination."[4] This cheerful disposition can be found especially among the soldiers themselves, Melville suggests. They are so excited to discover "battle's unknown mystery" that they cannot be easily discouraged:

All they feel is this: 'tis glory,
A rapture sharp, though transitory.
Yet lasting in belaureled story.
So they gaily go to fight,
Chatting left and laughing right.[5]

Melville knows, however, that these soldiers who volunteer to fight in this war will be sacrificed in the way that in the past children were offered to Moloch, the ancient Canaanite fire god. In the most famous lines of his poem, Melville suggests that the eagerness of young men to fight is nearly unstoppable:

All wars are boyish, and are fought by boys,
The champions and enthusiasts of the state:
Turbid ardors and vain joys
Not barrenly abate—
Stimulants to the power mature,
Preparatives of fate.[6]

Melville counters the cheerful ecstasy of the soldiers marching into Virginia with sobering predictions later on in his poem. Within three days many of the soldiers will have died, and the rapturous innocence of those who have survived will have given way to a hardened experience. They will feel only remorse and the deplorable knowledge that the First Manassas only leads to the Second Manassas, the equally bloody battle that was fought almost a year later, in 1862. "Age finds place in the rear," Melville knows, but few listen to the "warnings of the wise."[7]

Robert Lowell must have considered himself wise beyond his years when he modified Melville's phrase in the final stanza of "Christmas Eve under Hooker's Statue":

His stocking is full of stones. Santa in red
Is crowned with wizened berries. Man of war,
Where is the summer's garden? In its bed
The ancient speckled serpent will appear,
And black-eyed susan with her frizzled head.
When Chancellorsville mowed down the volunteer,
"All wars are boyish," Herman Melville said;
But we are old, our fields are running wild:
Till Christ again turn wanderer and child.[8]

Lowell was twenty-nine when "Christmas Eve under Hooker's Statue" was published in *Lord Weary's Castle* (1946). He had been tinkering with the concept of this poem for almost the entire duration of the war, and it had appeared before in two different versions and under different titles, in *Partisan Review* (1943) and *Land of Unlikeness* (1944). The idea to quote Melville occurs only in Lowell's final published version, and his drafts at Harvard's Houghton Library show that it was one of the very last changes he made. When he had nearly completed the final version of "Christmas Eve under Hooker's Statue," Lowell sent it to Jarrell, though it still lacked the intertextual allusion to Melville as the climax of his poem.

Jarrell was impressed by Lowell's improvements, but still did not warm to the ending that Lowell had sent in typescript:

His stocking is full of stones. Fragile and red,
The Statehouse stares at Hooker. Man of war,
Where is the garish pathos of your bed,
Flaring poinsettia, sweet william, larkspur
And black-eyed susan with her frizzled head:
The victims dead upon the field of honor?
"I bring no peace but swords," the elder said,
"My nakedness was handled and defiled,
But woe unto Jerusalem got with child." the city?[9]

Jarrell encircled the phrase "I bring no peace but swords," and added in holograph remarks in the margins that it "seems awkward when you remember the real quotation." In Matthew 10:34 Jesus had stated: "Think not that I am come to send peace on earth: I came not to send peace, but a sword." This declaration has most commonly been interpreted as either a plea for a violent propagation of Jesus's message or as his realization that if a person accepts the gospel, he or she should expect that life will be a struggle. Jarrell also suggested that the noun phrase "the elder" was less successful than the word "Christ," which Lowell had previously used. Jarrell did prefer "the city" to "Jerusalem" in the final line, which Lowell had hesitantly proposed in a holograph annotation. Jarrell's overall comment indicates that he was not completely satisfied yet with the poem's conclusion: "much better; but I don't much like this end."[10]

It was only after Jarrell's critique that Lowell decided to bring Melville into his poem. We do not know how Jarrell reacted to Lowell's final version, although he appreciated Melville's line enough to use it later on when reading his poems at Pfeiffer College. We may also surmise that the colloquial quotation appealed to him more than the verbose religious rhetoric of the earlier version. "Christmas Eve under Hooker's Statue" is not Lowell's best poem as it still contains many obscure allusions and awkward verbiage. Yet it nevertheless contains at least four aspects that in retrospect appear as typical for the (war) poetry of the middle generation.

First, "Christmas Eve under Hooker's Statue" is intensely personal and autobiographical, as the opening stanza of the final printed version establishes:

Tonight a blackout. Twenty years ago
I hung my stocking on the tree, and hell's
Serpent entwined the apple in the toe
To sting the child with knowledge. Hooker's heels
Kicking at nothing in the shifting snow,
Rusting before the blackened Statehouse, know
How the long horn of plenty broke like glass
In Hooker's gauntlets. Once I came from Mass;

Now storm-clouds shelter Christmas[11]

Lowell contrasts his childhood when Christmas was a time of peace and quiet to the present, which is dominated by Mars, the Roman god of war. Lowell uses the alliteration of "Mass" and "Mars" to illustrate what is wrong with the modern world. The god of war is being centralized instead of God, and the pathetic Civil War general Hooker—with all of his name's connotations of vice—is put on a pedestal instead of Christ.

Lowell's poem shares the Christian backdrop of Allen Tate's "More Sonnets at Christmas" and T. S. Eliot's *Four Quartets.* It is similar to Tate's sequence not only because it is set at the holiday to celebrate the birth of Christ but also because of Lowell's assertion that Christmas has become a feast to celebrate "the long horn of plenty" rather than a time of inner reflection and contemplation. What distinguishes Lowell's poem from Eliot's *Four Quartets* and Tate's Christmas sonnets is that it is marked by several revealing autobiographical details. Whereas Eliot's and Tate's poems shy away from the personal, Lowell's includes comments about his childhood and his uneasy relationship with his father: "I ask for bread, my father gives me mould."[12] The ambiguity of "father" in this line—referring to his biological as well as to his heavenly father—is an early instance in which Lowell weaves several narratives together: a personal story and a more public, religious musing.

Combining such multiple narratives was also a trademark of Auden's poetry at the time, as "September 1, 1939" and *For the Time Being* testify. When Auden evaluated Lincoln Kirstein's achievement as a war poet, he called him, significantly, a "Private Poet," and considered this personal aspect of his poetry quintessentially American. With some degree of generalization, Auden wrote: "Lacking a common mythological past, every American artist has, in weaving his pattern, to make use of a personal mythology which means that, in order to make this intelligible to others, he has to provide many more autobiographical facts than a European would need to."[13] Auden's explanation of why American (war) poets are more autobiographical and personal than their European counterparts is not entirely satisfactory, in part because the World War II poets were extremely conscious of the past and of a tradition. Yet his comment on the war poets' "personal mythology" rings true. Their quietly stubborn emphasis on their individualist take on World War II, thereby rescuing fragments or snippets of personal experiences, feels distinctly American, as does the uncompromising tone that Kirstein, Lowell, and others take. Their war poetry is certainly not written in the "'high' style" in which so much of the classic European war poetry was written.[14]

A second characteristic that is emblematic for this generation of war poets (and links them to Auden) is that Lowell questions militarized masculinity as a desirable ideal of manhood. "Christmas Eve under Hooker's Statue" is an "ironic critique of romantic myths of war," as Thomas Travisano has claimed.[15] Auden wrote in "Private Poet" that in traditional war poetry "the Warrior is a Hero, that is to say, a numinous being."[16] Yet the figure of Fighting Joe Hooker, who was known for his relentless violence, is hardly awe-inspiring in Lowell's poem. Even though his likeness features in an equestrian statue next to Charles Bulfinch's impressive Massachusetts State House, the historical figure is entirely unimpressive to Lowell. Hooker is remembered best for his loss of the Battle of Chancellorsville in 1863 to Generals Lee and Jackson, even though Hooker's troops outnumbered the Confederates two to one. Hooker's volunteer army was "mowed down" unceremoniously, and Lowell wonders why American society elevates this "blundering butcher" to the rank of hero, why it holds Hooker up as a model for boys to emulate.[17]

As children, the poets of World War II were fascinated by masculine heroes and strong male role models, but as adults they had reservations about the traditional military man whose spitting image was likely to end up as a statue in public parks. In August 1945 Jarrell planned to write about George Patton, the gutsy and violent general, and "the three soldiers he kicked and slapped," which Jarrell felt was "a sort of archetypal event."[18] Around the same time Lincoln Kirstein met and served under Patton. While Jarrell in the end never wrote an exposé of the controversial field commander, Kirstein wrote an ambivalent ode about Patton. Kirstein's moving portrayal "Patton" deconstructs the carefully constructed masculine image that Patton created for himself and others. Patton is "unshaken obviously" when "inspecting cots of amputees," for instance, but has to hide "in th' enlisted men's latrine so he can quietly / Have one good hearty cry."[19] In spite of the slapping incident, Patton is presented not as a hard-bitten, cynical soldier but as a vulnerable man who occasionally breaks.

As a boy Lowell had a "heroic figure obsession" for military men like Napoleon, as Blair Clark mentioned in an interview, and this fascination would return during his manic phases.[20] By the time he wrote "Christmas Eve under Hooker's Statue," however, he had grown weary of them. More intriguing to Lowell became those characters who, as he had, had fallen by the wayside during or because of the war, like Czar Lepke or those Puerto Rican kids whom he remembered from West Street prison and Danbury, Connecticut. Or Claude Eatherly, the now mostly forgotten air corps pilot who flew weather reconnaissance over Hiroshima just before the first nuclear bomb was dropped over that Japanese city. Lowell contemplated writing a play about Eatherley, who had allegedly become so remorseful about "what he had done, or maybe it was in his character anyway," that he got into petty crimes and also twice tried to commit suicide, as Lowell wrote to Elizabeth Bishop in 1963: "I would want to write a tragedy, not a piece of peace propaganda—not at all that for I don't think it could be done in a way that would do any good. Part of the poor man's tragedy is that although he exploded as one should and as practically no one else did, yet he has little to say, and is condemned to an almost monomaniac whittling down of his life to this one subject. Well, we'll see."[21]

It is no coincidence that Karl Shapiro left extensive handwritten notes in his archive for a poem about Eatherley as well. He conceived of the poem as a belated V-letter, either "a letter to Major Claude Eatherly [*sic*] the first atomic pilot in the world" or "maybe it's a letter to Compton & Fermi," or "a memo to Mortimer Adler," the latter two apparently from Eatherley's perspective.[22] Arthur Holly Compton and Enrico Fermi were physicists who contributed to the development of the nuclear bomb, while Adler was a philosopher and author of *How to Think About War and Peace* (1944). Neither work on Eatherley was ever published, but the interest in exploring this troubled pilot's psyche establishes once again this generation's "passionate involvement and deep identification with the sufferings of others," and their "apparently simple commitment to the humanly flawed," as Edward Hirsch has put it.[23] The poets of World War II tried to expose the masculine war hero as Lowell does with Hooker or show the surprising soft side of tough military men as Kirstein shows with Patton; or they ignored this type of male altogether to focus instead on giving voice to the ordinarily inconspicuous victims that war created. Jarrell's war poems—with their focus on women, children, and youthful airmen—demonstrate this most intrinsically.

Lowell's curiosity about the historical figures of Eatherley, Lepke, Hooker, and Napoleon was also an indirect way in which he examined his own masculinity and different selves. "I am two people I confess," Lowell wrote in that unpublished draft of "Memories of West Street and Lepke," quoted earlier in this book. "One is this boy too hept [*sic*] to mess / With masochistic gallantries," but Lowell's "better self is woman."[24] All the poets of World War II—Dickey chief among them—had such a feral, aggressive boy in them. Even William Stafford, the staunchest pacifist among the World War II poets, admitted he had an aggressive side. This was not his "best self," though.[25] Meredith admitted in "A Mild-Spoken Citizen Finally Writes to the White House" that he also had "a worse self" that caused him to "swindle or kill / When there is swindling and killing on my nation's part."[26] Yet Meredith also speaks of the human capacity to change, to discover another, more compassionate side of one's self. Whether this should be considered a female side, as Lowell does, depends on whether a society allows men to have the emotions that are perfectly natural to any human being, or to gender those feelings as female.

The third feature that makes Lowell's "Christmas Eve under Hooker's Statue" such a characteristic World War II poem is that the poet is so self-consciously historical, and wonders somewhat oddly how he should place himself within a tradition of war poetry in English. Within his own World War II poem Lowell invokes a war poem and war poet from the past, as did so many of his peers. The poets of World War II were truly obsessed by earlier war poems. "All wars are boyish, and are fought by boys," Melville had written in "The March into Virginia," but Lowell modifies Melville's line by adding "but we are old." Lowell's adjustment in the final stanza of "Christmas Eve under Hooker's Statue" has clear religious connotations,[27] but the phrase also carries generational significance, whether intended or not.

The American poets of World War II were young back then, but already old spiritually. They were "a race of young animals to whom pessimism has become a natural and constant condition of mind," as Richard Wilbur claimed in 1941.[28] This bleak temper contradicted with the more general national mood of "optimistic imagination" that Paul Fussell discerned in the United States at the beginning of the war.[29] Karl Shapiro believed that the poets' inclination to fatalism was caused by the tremendous turmoil they witnessed early on in their lives, which caused them to be acutely aware of history: "Our generation—the generation of Jarrell, Wilbur, myself, Roethke, Lowell, Schwartz, Bishop, Ciardi, Berryman, Kunitz, Nemerov, Whittemore—one is almost inclined to add Merrill Lynch, Pierce, Fenner and Smith—our generation lived through more history than most or maybe any. We lived through more history even than Stendhal, who fell, as he says, with Napoleon. We were reared as intellectuals and fought World War II before it happened and then again when it did happen."[30]

Growing up during World War I or immediately after, becoming young intellectuals during the Great Depression and at a time when a new global war seemed imminent, how could this generation be anything but historically savvy? The poets of World War II were extremely knowledgeable about the past, but they realized that they lived in a culture often focused on the present and occasionally lapsing into a kind of historical amnesia. "Most Americans pretend there isn't a past at all," Alan Dugan claimed in an interview when explaining why so many of his war poems refer to earlier, ancient wars.[31] Shapiro's surprising sentence at the end of his quotation suggests that the poets of World War II had already imagined how bloody, brutal, and senseless all wars are. They therefore experienced World War II as a déjà-vu. The American veteran-poets of the war in Vietnam show "a progression from innocence to experience," as Subarno Chattarji has argued, and this is equally true of he English poets of World War I.[32] Yet such a clear line of development is less germane for the poets of World War II. Jarrell, Lowell, and Shapiro were "old" as Lowell said, and "age finds place in the rear," as Melville had written in "The March into Virginia." "We inherited a historical perspective which was denied our fathers," Shapiro wrote revealingly in his eulogy for Jarrell.[33] This is the reason why, according to Shapiro, so many poets of his generation did not distinguish themselves as soldiers: "There is a salient difference between our war poetry such as Jarrell's and that first great war poetry written in our fathers' war by Wilfred Owen and Sassoon and Rosenberg and Blunden and so on. The British war poets who showed everyone how to write antiwar poetry were themselves all outstanding warriors and heroes. They cried out against war but were as conversant with blood as Lawrence of Arabia. None of my generation was a war hero, that I remember, or even an outstanding soldier."[34] Shapiro's reasoning is not entirely accurate. Several American poets of World War II—most notably Nemerov—had excellent military records.

Yet there is a kernel of truth to his words, which becomes apparent when juxtaposing the American war poets to their British peers. Not only were the English war poets of the First World War more heroically inclined than the American poets of the Second World War, so were several of the well-known English poets who fought between 1939 and 1945. Keith Douglas saw war "as a male rite of passage," as Simon Featherstone has written.[35] Douglas famously described the Battle of Alamein "as an important test, which I was interested in passing."[36] According to Linda M. Shires, Sidney Keyes also saw battle "as a test of personal courage."[37] Compared to these two boyish British war poets who both died in the war, the American poets sounded more prudent and mature.[38] Jarrell, for instance, wrote about many airmen who experienced the progression of innocence to experience, but the war itself held few surprises for him. Jarrell had no desire to see combat to showcase his manliness the way Brooke, Blunden, Owen, Rosenberg, Sassoon, or indeed Douglas and Keyes had. "Our poor wits" are "sharpened with their blood," Jarrell had written in "The Soldier," speaking for his generation of war poets. Jarrell's poem was a response to Rupert Brooke's "The Soldier," and Jarrell did not intend to follow Brooke's fate. Like Shapiro, Jarrell took a "place in the rear." Even though he did not see battle, however, Jarrell experienced a transformation in the army that is both similar to and different from the conventional rite of passage that makes men out of boys in times of war. World War II allowed Jarrell to mature as a poet and person by overcoming literary influences like Auden and Tate. It is more than a joke when he remarked to his wife, Mackie, that reading Tate during the war made Jarrell feel "old and responsible."[39]

This emphasis on maturity and its opposite, childhood, is a fourth characteristic that makes Lowell's poem representative for his generation's war poetry. Like many World War II poems, "Christmas Eve under Hooker's Statue" contains allusions to childhood, growing up, and reaching maturity. Powerful World War II poems, such as Jarrell's "The Death of the Ball Turret Gunner" and Nemerov's "Models," explore the same trajectories "from innocence to experience" that characterize many World War I and Vietnam War poems. Yet American World War II poems are more steeped in boyhood memory. The child stung with knowledge that Lowell presents so prominently in "Christmas Eve under Hooker's Statue" is the archetypal image of the poet of World War II. War was the apple that the poets all found in their Christmas stockings, providing an unpleasant epiphany about humanity that lasted a lifetime.

The uncomfortable gift of knowledge that war provided is equally applicable to the World War II poets who were in the army as to those who were not, as William Meredith's "John and Anne" indicates. As in "Talking Back (To W. H. Auden)," Meredith speaks in this poem directly to a deceased poet and friend, trying to resolve the conundrums that were facing his poet-friend in life and work. Meredith was a naval aviator during the war, but when trying to come to grips with the life and works of his dead colleague

John Berryman, he comes to understand that Berryman became the kind of man he was because of the same war, which Berryman had missed out on as a 4F. The Anne in the title is not Anne Bradstreet of Berryman's well-known poem *Homage to Mistress Bradstreet* (1953) to which Meredith also alludes, but another Anne whom he admired and was inspired by: Anne Frank.

Meredith's epigraph to "John and Anne" is taken from Berryman's article on Frank. Berryman writes that Frank's diary is "even more mysterious than St. Augustine's" because it traces "the conversion of a child into a person." Anne Frank "was *forced* to mature."[40] Meredith lets on that Berryman—who often turned to Meredith to read and critique his poetry before he sent it on for publication—was a childish man at times. Berryman frequently threw "tantrums," Meredith indicates: "*—Nobody listens to me,* the child would shout— / because we ourselves remain shrill little folk: / there must be somewhere we'll hear each other out."[41] Through reading Anne Frank, who cried "for the naked gypsy girls gassed" at Auschwitz, Berryman reached adulthood. "Dying at Belsen, she helped you grow up," Meredith concludes somewhat simplistically.[42] What Meredith says about Berryman, however, is essentially true for their entire generation. The war not just helped them artistically; it forced them to mature.

World War II did not make this generation silent, but it did make them quiet and somber. They struggled with large heroic stories, whether religious or national myths, such as that of the "Good War." They could only depict life around them, the small details, write the "unimportant poems" that Ciardi talked about, or write about the miniature world that Nemerov had seen from up above.[43] Following Auden, who had claimed in "In Memory of W. B. Yeats" (1939) that "poetry makes nothing happen," the poets of World War II did not have much faith that their poetry could change the world.[44] "It's a pretty humble business, singing songs," Nemerov had written modestly in "To the Poets," which could serve as an anthem for his entire generation of poets.[45] It would not be farfetched to suggest that this kind of humility stems at least partly from the war itself. It taught them how vulnerable human beings are when "the uncontrolled, traditional cries" rise again, to quote Elizabeth Bishop's "Roosters."[46]

The celebration of World War II as the "Good War" in the United States was anathema to them, as Nemerov's poem "The War in the Air" shows most explicitly: "That was the good war, the war we won / As if there were no death, for goodness' sake."[47] The epitaph of "the Greatest Generation" that Tom Brokaw chose to define the war generation would not have set well with them either. Brokaw's book pays homage to the members of the so-called greatest generation who "answered the call to help save the world from the two most powerful and ruthless machines ever assembled, instruments of conquest in the hands of fascist maniacs."[48] Yet Steven Gould Axelrod has pleaded that Americans should "stop listening so intently and exclusively to a single 'war story' that can be boiled down to a paragraph," or, in Brokaw's case, to one phrase.[49] This "single 'war story'" is a simplified version of reality and therefore misleading and potentially dangerous.

The Greatest Generation is somewhat akin to a hagiography as it venerates the American participants of World War II, glances over painful and horrific incidents of that war, and simplifies a complex war into a rather one-sided storyline. Brokaw does not focus on the victims of the saturation bombings of civilian populations in Germany and Japan, and is silent about the slow American response to the Holocaust, issues that the poets of World War II all bring to the fore. Brokaw does mention the Japanese internment camps, but ironically focuses on Nao Takasugi, who was offered a getaway from the camps and was allowed to take a business degree at Temple University during the war. Instead of embracing Brokaw's reductive World War II narrative, Axelrod asks us "to attend to the myriad of smaller stories told about World War II, in all their contradiction and specificity," because "their mixed messages, their nuances and indeterminacies, have more use value today than the one, by now over-told, story of defeat leading to triumph."[50]

The poems of World War II provide myriad shades of differences, complexities, and uncertainties about the American victory narrative. The fifth, final, and perhaps most important representative feature of Lowell's "Christmas Eve under Hooker's Statue" as a World War II poem is that it counters the accepted version of World War II that has been "perpetuated and reinforced by a set of remarkably complex and durable popular-culture representations of the war," as Philip D. Beidler remarks in his *The Good War's Greatest Hits*.[51] Lowell's scornful suggestion that the American people are experiencing a "blackout" and are being led by the belligerent god of war negates Brokaw's upbeat view that those who participated in the war effort on the European, Pacific, and home front should be honored for their "lives of sacrifice and achievement, duty and honor."[52]

The importance of the middle generation's war poems collectively is paradoxically that they are "unimportant poems" which, first, subtly or overtly contradict the American victory narrative, and, second, provide stories about the war on a more human scale.[53] These poetic stories will not replace the dominant storyline about World War II that rightfully honors the men and women who worked hard or gave their lives so that others could be free. Yet a little Kirstein to counteract John Wayne's masculine performance as Sergeant John Stryker in *Sands of Iwo Jima* (1949), some Ciardi and Nemerov to offset *Thirty Seconds over Tokyo* (1944), or Lowell's "Christmas Eve under

Hooker's Statue" and Stafford's "At the Un-National Monument along the Canadian Border" to demonstrate the power and danger of memorials, such as the recent World War II one on the National Mall, would be enriching for anyone who wants to gain a deeper understanding of that war.

Brokaw writes about the entire World War II generation: "There is a common theme of pride in all that they've accomplished for themselves, their families, and their country, and so little clamor for attention, given all they've done."[54] The pride and sense of achievement, Brokaw argues, stem from having given "the succeeding generations the opportunity to accumulate great economic wealth, political muscle, and the freedom from foreign oppression to make whatever choices they like."[55] The "silent" or quiet generation of poets of the Second World War certainly did not make much noise, but pride, too, is almost completely absent from their war poetry. The poets of World War II saw the world in pessimistic terms and themselves in tragic terms, as Shapiro suggested in his tribute to Jarrell:

> When we came home there was grass growing on all the highways of the forty-eight states, but not for long. Our army went from demobilization to college or television school; our poets became the university poets. But the tragedy of our generation—and I believe it is the tragedy—was that our army never melted away. It remained, it grew bigger, it was more and more all over the world. It became the way of life, the state—if not the garrison state itself, then something resembling it mightily. The war never came to a stop; only the protocols of armistice were suspended. Our poetry, from the forties on, records the helplessness we felt in the face of the impersonal character of the age—the Impersonal itself, which is always death to poetry.[56]

Shapiro's melancholic words contrast sharply with Brokaw's more buoyant message of triumph, and they might begin to explain why the poets of World War II led such rough and troubled lives in the postwar era. Despite the seemingly easy, bourgeois lives they all had, many were plagued with the same problems, ranging from alcoholism to bouts of severe psychological depression. Like Shapiro, Lowell also blamed these on the unpropitious age, as this excerpt from a letter from 1959 to Berryman—who had recently been hospitalized—shows: "I am just back from Greensboro, where Randall and [I] enjoyed (?) ourselves lamenting the times. It seems there's been something curious twisted and against the grain about the world poets of our generation have had to live in. What troubles you and I, Ted Roethke, Elizabeth Bishop, Delmore, Randall—even Karl Shapiro—have had. I hope your exhaustion is nothing very drastic; these knocks are almost a proof of intelligence and valor in us. However, all in all, each year grows better and gayer and more serious."[57]

Helen Vendler's phrase "hopeless hope" (which she used to characterize Nemerov's poetry) springs to mind when reading Lowell's sympathetic words to his friend, and when remembering the sad ending of Berryman's life by suicide some fifteen years later. Underneath the veneer of happiness that the war's triumph and the luxury of the postwar occasioned, there is a sadness and grief that connects all of the poets of World War II. The intense sorrow of the war had swallowed them all up—the sorrowful knowledge that the war had to happen, that the war happened, that wars keep happening, and their belief that as vulnerable human beings they are incapable of stopping them.

While they were growing old, they had learned that "the world never learns," as Richard Hugo wrote ruefully to Charles Simic.[58] Or, as Nemerov argued even more precisely in "Ultima Ratio Reagan": "The reason we do not learn from history is / Because we are not the people who learned last time."[59] Living through a more intense history than any other generation, the poets of World War II were convinced that every generation will spawn new soldiers, but that "traditional heroism" has become an illusory, boyish notion that belongs irrevocably to "the past," as Anthony Hecht has suggested.[60] Until well into the nineteenth century war had been "pre-eminently the sphere of public deeds of heroism by individual persons," as Auden claimed.[61] But that time was long gone. After the clash of the revolutionary ironclads the *Merrimack* and the *Monitor* during the Civil War, Melville—another model for the World War II poets—suggested in "A Utilitarian View of the Monitor's Fight" that heroic warfare had vanished from the earth: "War yet shall be, but warriors / Are now but operatives."[62]

Yet World War II was even more a war of technologists than Melville could have imagined. It transformed not only the people on those naval ships but all soldiers into cogs trapped in a gigantic industrial machine. They were trapped by the war like Jarrell's ball turret gunner in the womb of a powerful warplane, or like flies in amber, to use another image employed by Jarrell in "A Lullaby." The poets' response to World War II was not noiseless like the flies transfixed forever in time, but faint and muffled like the fleeting words of the dead ball turret gunner that reach us from the other side. Americans were not eager to listen to these troubled and troubling poems in the postwar years. Americans did not build many cenotaphs and obelisks for those who fought and died in the Second World War as they had done after the First World War. Instead they constructed bridges, parks, auditoriums, and highways that looked to the future and that increased the welfare and well-being of the living, as Kristin Ann Hass has pointed out.[63]

The poets' messages went largely unheard in an amnesiac American victory culture that celebrated the war's outcome, and in a postwar society that wanted to look forward rather than back. There was not much room for mournful reflection, and the American poets of World War II must have sensed their compatriots' indifference to or impatience with their solemn lyrics. "I don't think my war poems are of much interest to anyone, but me," Kirstein once admitted in the privacy of a letter.[64] Nemerov was convinced that "no one will find them, no one will read / Them," as he mentioned in "D Day plus 20 Years," the poem he left unpublished among his papers.[65] Yet their tales of human frailty and sorrow are not lost and can still be heard by anyone who is willing to listen carefully.

NOTES

Introduction

1. Nemerov, "D Day plus 20 years," typescript, Howard Nemerov Papers, Special Collection, Washington University Libraries, St. Louis.

2. Ibid.

3. Allen, *Eisenhower and the Mass Media,* 193.

4. Stout, *Coming Out of War,* 142.

5. Brinkley, "Commentary."

6. Winn, *Poetry of War,* 212.

7. See, for instance, Axelrod's "Middle Generation and WWII" (1999), Gubar's *Poetry after Auschwitz* (2003), and Stout's *Coming Out of War* (2005). Scannell's *Not without Glory* (1976), Walsh's *American War Literature* (1982), and Fussell's *Wartime* (1989) appeared earlier and also contain discussions of key American poets of World War II. Vaughan's *Words to Measure a War* (2009) has appeared most recently and briefly discusses the poetry of nine American war poets in their biographical context.

8. Leon Stokesbury's anthology *Articles of War* (1990) was just as comprehensive as Shapiro's anthology and preceded it by more than a decade, but generated much less attention.

9. Shapiro, introduction, xx.

10. Norris, "War Poetry in the USA," 43.

11. Van Wienen, introduction, 7.

12. See Schweik's *A Gulf So Deeply Cut* for a more elaborate discussion of how World War II affected female American poets.

13. For African American war poetry, see James's *A Freedom Bought with Blood,* and for Japanese internment camp poetry, see Nakano and Yokoyama's *Poets behind Barbed Wire.*

14. Van Wienen, *Partisans and Poets,* 2.

15. Haralson, introduction, 1.

16. Ferguson, preface, xi.

17. Shapiro, *Bourgeois Poet,* 112.

18. Simpson, *Owner of the House,* 167.

19. Act 3, Scene 3, lines 347–57, in Shakespeare, *Othello, the Moor of Venice.*

20. Auden, "Private Poet," 317.

21. Watson, "'Death's Proletariat,'" 318.

22. Notable exceptions are the expansive poems "Route" by George Oppen and "The Runner" by Louis Simpson.

23. See also Edward Brunner's discussion of Richard Wilbur's "The Death of a Toad" in his *Cold War Poetry.* Brunner argues convincingly that this ostensibly straightforward poem of the amphibian's death can retrospectively be read as an indirect comment on a soldier dying in a mechanized war. Yet postwar readers, including Randall Jarrell, did not pick up on such cues, because they were "disinclined to mourn openly," as Brunner suggests. As in Nemerov's poem discussed in this introduction, the "elegiac moment" in Wilbur's "The Death of a Toad" is "distinctly private" (20).

24. Axelrod, "Counter-Memory in American Poetry," 20.

25. Wittgenstein, *Philosophical Investigations,* 32.

26. Vaughan, *Words to Measure a War,* 4.

27. Travisano, *Midcentury Quartet,* 9.

28. Ciardi, *Collected Poems,* 61.

29. Höbling, "Second World War," 212.

30. Cordray, foreword, xxiv.

31. Fussell, *The Great War and Modern Memory,* 272. There were some gay war poets who served during World War II, including Lincoln Kirstein, William Meredith, and Frank O'Hara. Meredith's war poems—for instance, "Notes for an Elegy" and "June: Dutch Harbor"—come closest to expressing the kind of physical companionship that was more common in the English poets of World War I, but Meredith's poems are even more sublimated. O'Hara's poems only sporadically refer to World War II, and Kirstein for the most part shielded his homosexuality in his poems.

32. Nemerov, *War Stories,* 39.

33. "Interview with James Dickey," 12.

Chapter 1: "Im no Wilfred Owen, darling"

1. Lowell, *Collected Poems,* 21.

2. Goldensohn, *Dismantling Glory,* 22.

3. Winn, *Poetry of War,* 1–2.

4. Bellamy, "'Others Have Come before You,'" 313.

5. See Anderson's section "Raids on Homer" in *The Moon Reflected Fire* (1994), which consists of eight poems in which he takes on Homer, and Komunyakaa's *Warhorses* (2009).

6. Ryan, "Interview with Alan Dugan," 96.

7. Dugan, *Poems Seven,* 266.

8. Ibid.

9. Ibid.

10. Winn, *Poetry of War,* 33.

11. Homer, *Iliad,* 128.

12. Dugan, *Poems Seven,* 236.

13. Ibid., 236, 237.

14. Ibid., 268.

15. The name may also allude to the World War I poet and memoirist, Siegfried Sassoon.

16. Travisano, *Midcentury Quartet,* 176.

17. Jarrell, *Complete Poems,* 149. For a more in-depth analogy of the Germanic hero and Jarrell's Siegfried, see Ferguson, *Poetry of Randall Jarrell,* 43–46; and Travisano, *Midcentury Quartet,* 175–81.

18. Hitler admired Wagner's operas and music dramas, and some of his political ideas were derived from Wagner's works, as Dugan's fellow poet Peter Viereck explored in 1941 in a historical book. See chapter 5, "Siegfried: The Metapolitics of Richard Wagner," and chapter 6, "Hitler and Wagner," in Viereck, *Metapolitics.*

19. Dugan, *Poems Seven,* 268

20. Ciardi was not the first to parody Lovelace's poem; see, for instance, Robert Graves's "To Lucasta, On Going to the Wars—For the Fourth Time" (1917) and Rudyard Kipling's "The Bridegroom" (1919).

21. Richard Lovelace, "To Lucasta, Going to the Wars," in Stallworthy, *Oxford Book of War Poetry,* 50.

22. Ciardi, *Collected Poems,* 222. Fussell writes in *Wartime* that "the expectation of the boredom, the knowledge that there is no escaping it" is characteristic of the American soldier's experience during World War II (76).

23. Ciardi to Frederick Panzer, October 28, 1961, John Ciardi Papers, Library of Congress, Washington, D.C.

24. Ciardi, *Collected Poems,* 222.

25. Lovelace, "To Lucasta, Going to the Wars," 50.

26. Ciardi, *Collected Poems,* 223.

27. Cifelli, *John Ciardi,* 70.

28. Alfred, Lord Tennyson, "The Charge of the Light Brigade," in Stallworthy, *Oxford Book of War Poetry,* 115.

29. Jarrell, draft of "The Charge of the Light Brigade, converted," Randall Jarrell Papers, Berg Collection, New York Public Library.

30. Tennyson, "Charge of the Light Brigade," 116.

31. Jarrell to Mackie Jarrell, May 25, 1943, quoted in Wright, *Randall Jarrell,* 247.

32. Brooke, "The Soldier," in Stallworthy, *Oxford Book of War Poetry,* 163.

33. Jarrell, *Complete Poems,* 402.

34. Cowley to Randall Jarrell, June 15, 1943, Randall Jarrell Papers, Berg Collection, New York Public Library.

35. Jarrell, *Complete Poems,* 402.

36. Fussell, introduction, xxiv.

37. Shapiro, *Younger Son,* 199.

38. Shapiro, *Coda,* 48.

39. Dickey did not write any poems about other war poets or parodies on war poems, but he was just as fascinated to compare his own war experiences with his poetic ancestors and peers, as is evident from his *Classes on Modern Poets and the Art of Poetry,* which contains comments on the war poetry of Keith Douglas, Sidney Keyes, Alun Lewis, Thomas Hardy, Wilfred Owen, and others.

40. Dickey, *Whole Motion,* 117.

41. Ibid., 116.

42. Jarrell, draft of "The Charge of the Light Brigade, converted."

43. Roosevelt was the subject of many poems and also elegies, as Whisenhunt's *Poetry of the People* shows, but they appeared mostly in the popular press and were not written by middle generation poets.

44. Morris, *Better Angel,* 243. It is unlikely that Simpson echoed Whitman consciously, however. In *The King My Father's Wreck,* Simpson claims that "the poem took the form of a ballad" because he "had been reading [Heinrich] Heine's ballads" (57).

45. Simpson, *Owner of the House,* 104.

46. Whitman, *Complete Poetry and Collected Prose,* 467.

47. Jarrell, *Complete Poems,* 144.

48. Fussell, *The Great War and Modern Memory,* 231.

49. Dostoyevsky, *Crime and Punishment,* 191.

50. Stout, *Coming Out of War,* 160.

51. Simpson, "On the Ledge," in Shapiro, *Poets of World War II,* 189.

52. Howard, *War in European History,* 127–28.

53. Robinson, "'Down in the Terraces,'" 509. A notable exception is W. B. Yeats's "An Irish Airman Foresees His Death," as Robinson mentions.

54. See chapter 7 of Howard's *War in European History,* 116–35.

55. Cox, "Richard Wilbur," 10.

56. Gubar, *Poetry after Auschwitz.*

57. Dugan, *Poems Seven,* 66.

58. Tennyson, "Charge of the Light Brigade," 115.

59. Larkin, "MCMXIV," in Stallworthy, *Oxford Book of War Poetry,* 222. British poets of World War II were similar to their American colleagues in this respect, as Linda M. Shires has stated: "There was no development from initial optimism about war to rejection of it, a development clearly evident in the poetry of the First World War"; see her book *British Poetry of the Second World War,* 53.

60. Dugan, *Poems Seven,* 66.

61. Ibid.

62. Shapiro to Evalyn Katz, February 9, 1944, Karl Shapiro Papers, University of Maryland Library, College Park.

63. Auden, "Private Poet," 318.

64. Fussell, *The Great War and Modern Memory,* 21.

65. Shapiro, "Poet as Hero."

66. This is again similar to the British poets of World War II, as Shires has indicated: "When poets of the second generation recalled the first, they did so not to join a tradition, but to differentiate themselves"; see *British Poetry of the Second World War,* 53.

67. Höbling, "Second World War," 212–13.

Chapter 2: A Little Disagreement with Some Modernists

1. Eliot, *Collected Poems,* 62.

2. Ibid., 74.

3. Ibid., 64.
4. Hecht, *Collected Earlier Poems,* 42.
5. Travisano, *Midcentury Quartet,* 73.
6. Keller, *Re-making It New,* 7. Keller pairs up Wallace Stevens and John Ashbery, Marianne Moore and Elizabeth Bishop, William Carlos Williams and Robert Creeley, and W. H. Auden and James Merrill in her book to show both the continuity and divergence between the modernist and postmodernist poets. Shires argues that the British poets of World War II were similar: "Though Auden, Eliot, Yeats and Dylan Thomas stimulated the young," they also "sought their own subjects and voices" (*British Poetry of the Second World War,* 62).
7. Keller, *Re-making It New,* 6.
8. Jarrell, *Kipling, Auden & Co.,* 81.
9. Jarrell, "Note on Poetry," 50.
10. Ibid., 51.
11. Travisano, *Midcentury Quartet,* 176.
12. Longenbach, *Modern Poetry after Modernism,* 177.
13. Jarrell, *Poetry and the Age,* 194.
14. Boyers, "Interview with Howard Nemerov," 118.
15. Ibid., 119.
16. Nemerov, *Collected Poems,* 61.
17. Lowell, *Letters of Robert Lowell,* 3.
18. Bartlett and Witemeyer, "Ezra Pound and James Dickey," 310, 302.
19. Hecht, *Anthony Hecht in Conversation with Philip Hoy,* 93.
20. Ibid., 98.
21. Hecht, *Collected Earlier Poems,* 40.
22. Ibid.
23. Hecht, draft of "Rites and Ceremonies," Anthony Hecht Papers, Emory University.
24. Hecht, *Collected Earlier Poems,* 40, 41.
25. Ibid., 41.
26. Bell, *Sacred Communities,* 115–16; Foa, *Jews of Europe after the Black Death,* 15.
27. The influence of these events on Hecht's life and poetry are discussed more elaborately in the next chapter.
28. Hecht, *Collected Earlier Poems,* 41–42.
29. Ibid., 42.
30. Foa suggests that about one hundred Jews were in fact saved because they converted to Christianity; see Foa, *Jews of Europe after the Black Death,* 15.
31. Hecht, *Anthony Hecht in Conversation with Philip Hoy,* 98.
32. Eliot, *Collected Poems,* 29.
33. Quoted in Julius, *T. S. Eliot, Anti-Semitism, and Literary Form,* 1.
34. Quoted in Levy and Scherle, *Affectionately, T. S. Eliot,* 81.
35. Hecht, *Anthony Hecht in Conversation with Philip Hoy,* 96.
36. Nemerov, "Jewish Writer," 216.
37. Hecht, *Anthony Hecht in Conversation with Philip Hoy,* 95.
38. Eliot, *After Strange Gods,* 16.

39. Shapiro, *Selected Poems,* 17.

40. Shapiro, *Younger Son,* 226.

41. Ibid., 227.

42. Kirstein, *Rhymes and More Rhymes,* 81.

43. See, for instance, the title poem of Hughes's pamphlet *Jim Crow's Last Stand* (New York: Negro Publication Society of America, 1943), "Will V-Day Be Me-Day Too?" and "Message to the President," all of which are included in *The Collected Poems of Langston Hughes.*

44. Burt, *Randall Jarrell and His Age,* 86. Burt's chapter titled "Psychology and Psychoanalysis" is particularly relevant for the influence of these fields on Jarrell.

45. Jarrell, *Complete Poems,* 149.

46. Quoted in Michael Di Capua to Hannah Arendt, September 28, 1966, Farrar, Straus & Giroux Inc. Records, New York Public Library.

47. Hirsch, "One Life, One Writing!" 10.

48. Shapiro, "Death of Randall Jarrell," 220.

49. Eliot, *For Lancelot Andrews,* ix.

50. Costello, "1930–1934," 254.

51. Williams, *Selected Poems,* 53.

52. Axelrod's essay "Gwendolyn Brooks and the Middle Generation" raises the issue of Elizabeth Bishop's subtle and perhaps subconscious racism (26–28). Henry Hart details the origins and manifestations of James Dickey's anti-Semitism in *James Dickey.*

53. Julius, *T. S. Eliot,* 35.

54. Flory, "Pound and Antisemitism," 292.

55. Schwartz, *Letters of Delmore Schwartz,* 68. The letter is dated March 5, 193.

56. Berryman, *Recovery,* 246.

57. Ibid., 252.

58. See Berryman, "Development of Anne Frank," 76–80.

59. Ciardi, "Sarko," holograph manuscript, John Ciardi Papers, Library of Congress.

60. Ciardi to Ezra Pound, July 13, 1956, Ezra Pound Collection, Beinecke Library, Yale University, New Haven, Conn.

61. Hecht, *Collected Earlier Poems,* 42.

62. Hecht, draft of "Rites and Ceremonies."

63. Hecht, *Collected Earlier Poems,* 47.

64. Ibid.

Chapter 3: "Childish" Allen Tate, the New Critics, and Reaching Poetic Maturity

1. Reidel, *Vanished Act,* 81.

2. Ransom to Howard Nemerov, December 26, 1939, Howard Nemerov Papers, Washington University.

3. Hecht, "Few Green Leaves," 569.

4. Tate, *Collected Essays,* 91.

5. Hecht, "Few Green Leaves," 569.

6. Tate, *Collected Essays,* 94.

7. Ibid., 100.

8. Ibid., 75, 65.

9. Tate to Robert Lowell, December 3, 1957, quoted in Doreski, *Years of Our Friendship,* 120.

10. See also Beck, "Beyond the Anxiety of Influence," 71–83. Beck's essay addresses some similar issues as this chapter does, but she is more concerned with the personal friendship of Tate and Jarrell and less with poetic concerns and how their relationship is representative for the entire generation of war poets.

11. Ferguson, *Poetry of Randall Jarrell,* 36.

12. Jarrell to Allen Tate, December 1941, Allen Tate Papers, Princeton University Library, Princeton, N.J.

13. Pritchard, *Randall Jarrell,* 82.

14. Jarrell, *Kipling, Auden & Co.,* 65.

15. Jarrell, "Levels and Opposites," 697.

16. Ibid., 712. Even though much of this lecture was an implicit attack on Tate and the New Critics, Jarrell did praise "Ode to the Confederate Dead" as one of "the two best of all graveyard poems" (704).

17. Ransom, "Criticism Inc.," 229.

18. Jarrell, "Contemporary Poetry Criticism," 61.

19. Travisano, *Midcentury Quartet,* 173.

20. The other three were "Eclogue of the Liberal and the Poet" (1938), "False Nightmare" (1941), and "Jubilo" (1942).

21. Tate, *Collected Poems,* 108.

22. Doreski, *Years of Our Friendship,* 63.

23. MacLeish, *Irresponsibles,* 14.

24. Brooks, *Opinions of Oliver Allston,* 243.

25. Ibid., 228.

26. Tate, *Collected Poems,* 109. Tate's attack was rather mild compared to some of the more vituperative reactions to MacLeish's politics at the time; see Donaldson, *Archibald MacLeish,* 333–40.

27. Tate, draft of "Ode to Our Young Pro-Consuls of the Air," Allen Tate Papers, Princeton University Library.

28. Tate, *Collected Poems,* 109.

29. Ibid., 110.

30. Drafts of "Ode to Our Young Pro-Consuls of the Air," Allen Tate Papers, Princeton University Library.

31. Jarrell, *Randall Jarrell's Letters,* 81.

32. Ibid., 133.

33. Lowell to Karl Shapiro, n.d. [circa 1947], Karl Shapiro Papers, Harry Ransom Humanities Research Center, University of Texas, Austin.

34. Shapiro, *Younger Son,* 118; Doreski, *Years of Our Friendship,* 62.

35. Shapiro, *Selected Poems,* 10.

36. Tate, "Karl Shapiro," 208.

37. Ibid., 209.

38. Tate to Karl Shapiro, April 29, 1943, Karl Shapiro Papers, University of Maryland Library, College Park.

39. Shapiro to Allen Tate, May 14, 1943, Karl Shapiro Papers, University of Maryland Library, College Park.

40. Jarrell, *Randall Jarrell's Letters,* 30.

41. Ibid., 37.

42. Ibid., 167; Jarrell to Allen Tate, n.d. [circa 1944]. Allen Tate Papers, Princeton University Library.

43. Jarrell, *Randall Jarrell's Letters,* 81.

44. Ibid.

45. Ibid.

46. Ibid, 132.

47. This appropriation of identities will be explored in chapter 8 of this book.

48. Jarrell, *Randall Jarrell's Letters,* 124.

49. Randall Jarrell, "An analysis of why 'particulars' should seem so much more effective than 'universals,'" holograph notes and draft of essay, Berg Collection, New York Public Library.

50. Hecht, "Few Green Leaves," 570.

51. Tate, *Collected Poems,* 85.

52. Underwood, *Allen Tate,* 184.

53. Tate, *Lytle-Tate Letters,* 61

54. Tate, *Collected Poems,* 86.

55. Tate, "Young Randall," 232.

56. Ibid., 231.

Chapter 4: Talking Back to W. H. Auden

1. Auden, *Collected Poems,* 248

2. Meredith, *Effort at Speech,* 204.

3. Ibid.

4. Ibid.

5. Ibid.

6. Ibid., 205.

7. Jarrell, *Third Book of Criticism,* 142.

8. For a more elaborate analysis of Auden's influence on postwar American poets in general, especially John Ashbery, James Merrill, and Adrienne Rich, see Aidan Wasley's *The Age of Auden.* Linda M. Shires has written about Auden's general importance to British poets of the 1940s in *British Poetry of the Second World War,* but she is not specific about which war poets were influenced by what aspect of Auden's poetry at the time.

9. Jarrell, *Kipling, Auden & Co.,* 82–83.

10. Dickey, unpublished review of Auden's *Collected Poems,* ca. 1978, James Dickey Papers, Emory University.

11. Quoted in Simpson, *Poets in Their Youth,* 110.

12. Sansom, "'Flouting Papa,'" 273.

13. Jarrell, *On W. H. Auden,* 71.

14. Dickey, lecture notes, notes for planned poems, and reflections on poetry, ca. early 1950s, James Dickey Papers, Emory University.

15. Dickey, unpublished review of Auden's *Collected Poems,* James Dickey Papers, Emory University.
16. Dickey "*Alnilam,* early notes, ca. 1981," James Dickey Papers, Emory University.
17. Mendelson, *Early Auden,* 96.
18. Lowell, *Collected Poems,* 740.
19. Lowell, typescript "1938–1975," Robert Lowell Papers, University of Texas at Austin.
20. Hecht to Melvyn and Dorothea Hecht, September 28, 1944, Anthony Hecht Papers, Emory University.
21. Auden, *Ascent of F6,* 16.
22. Jarrell, *Pictures from an Institution,* 243.
23. Hecht, *Hidden Law,* 1.
24. Spargo, *Ethics of Mourning,* 210. For a more detailed discussion of the poem, see Spargo, "Ethical Uselessness of Grief," 49–65.
25. Jarrell, *Complete Poems,* 392.
26. Hecht, *Hidden Law,* 82.
27. Shapiro to Evalyn Katz, May 14, 1943, Karl Shapiro Papers, University of Maryland Library, College Park.
28. Jarrell to Robert Lowell, n.d. [ca. 1947], Houghton Library, Harvard University, Cambridge, Mass.
29. Jarrell, *Third Book of Criticism,* 115.
30. Ibid., 153, 156, 158.
31. Burt, introduction, 5.
32. Boly, *Reading Auden,* 40.
33. Jarrell, *Third Book of Criticism,* 186, 187.
34. Ibid., 186.
35. Sansom, "'Flouting Papa,'" 276.
36. Jarrell, *On Auden,* 68.
37. Jarrell, *Third Book of Criticism,* 124.
38. Ibid., 116.
39. Jarrell, *Complete Poems,* 149.
40. Ibid., 150.
41. Ibid., 151. Jarrell's "Siegfried" also seems similar to Wilfred Owen's "Disabled," in which Owen also speaks to a wounded soldier who has returned home. A key difference between these poems is that Owen uses a third-person speaker, which creates a distance between the wounded veteran and the audience, while Jarrell lets Siegfried talk directly to the reader. Jarrell's wondering, impersonal, and aureate diction is also distancing, however.
42. Jarrell, *Third Book of Criticism,* 162.
43. Jarrell, *Complete Poems,* 151.
44. Ibid., 150.
45. Mendelson, *Early Auden,* 176.
46. Jarrell, *Complete Poems,* 150.
47. Jarrell, *Third Book of Criticism,* 187.

48. Hecht, *Hidden Law,* 8.
49. Ibid., 9.
50. Ibid., 9–10.
51. Ibid., 152, 127, 128, 131.
52. Ibid., 152.
53. Ibid.
54. Hecht, *Collected Earlier Poems,* 152.
55. Ibid., 153.
56. Hecht, *Hidden Law,* 441.
57. Ibid., 442.
58. Ibid., 438.
59. Ibid,, 428.
60. Auden, *Collected Poems,* 598.
61. Hecht, *Hidden Law,* 435.
62. Howard, *War in European History,* 120.
63. Hecht, *Hidden Law,* 437.
64. Ibid., 441.
65. For Dugan's indebtedness to Auden, see also his poem "Speech for Auden" in his *Poems Seven,* 358.
66. Kirstein, *Poems of Lincoln Kirstein,* 247.
67. Ibid.
68. Ibid., 246.
69. Ibid., 247.
70. Ibid., 246.
71. Kirstein, "Auden in America," unpublished typescript, Lincoln Kirstein Papers, Jerome Robbins Dance Division, New York Public Library.
72. Kirstein, *Poems of Lincoln Kirstein,* 249.
73. Ibid., 250.
74. Ibid., 249.
75. Ibid.
76. Owen, *Collected Poems,* 31.
77. Shapiro, *In Defense of Ignorance,* 139.
78. Jarrell, "Analysis of why 'particulars' should seem so much more effective than 'universals.'"

Chapter 5: Caught in Amber

1. Hirsch, "One Life, One Writing!" 7, 6.
2. Linderman, *World within War,* 186.
3. This does not mean that war poets of other countries were unaffected by such threats to their sense of identity. The English poet Terence Tiller's *The Inward Animal* shows a similar obsession with the self; see, for instance, Roger Bowen's chapter "Terence Tiller and the 'Customary Self'" in his *"Many Histories Deep."* Yet this anxiety about the self seems to be expressed more consistently by American war poets.
4. Ciardi, *Collected Poems,* 26.
5. Eliot, *Collected Poems,* 5.

6. Ciardi, *Collected Poems,* 26.

7. Ciardi, *Saipan,* 3.

8. Goldensohn, *Dismantling Glory,* 24.

9. Shapiro, *Selected Poems,* 44. Shapiro's poem is very similar to war poems by the Anglo-Welsh poet Alun Lewis—for instance, "All Day It Has Rained." Not only do they both express the boredom and homesickness of a soldier's life, they also both use the same casual rhymes and detailed descriptiveness.

10. Fussell, *The Great War and Modern Memory,* 231.

11. Brooks, *Selected Poems,* 23.

12. Dickey, *Whole Motion,* 195, 198.

13. Ibid., 199.

14. Fussell, *Wartime,* 66.

15. Meredith, *Effort at Speech,* 16.

16. Jarrell to Mackie Jarrell, February 21, 1943, Berg Collection, New York Public Library.

17. Nemerov to Howard Turner, November 18, 1941, Nemerov Papers, Correspondence, Alexander Nemerov, New Haven, Conn. For an elaborate discussion of the phenomenon of "chickenshit," see chapter 7, "Chickenshit, An Anatomy," in Fussell, *Wartime,* 79–95.

18. Shapiro, *Younger Son,* 171.

19. Jarrell to Mackie Jarrell, March 17, 1943, Berg Collection, New York Public Library.

20. Shapiro, *Younger Son,* 160, 187.

21. Tate to Karl Shapiro, April 29, 1943, Karl Shapiro Papers, University of Maryland Library, College Park.

22. Shapiro, *V-Letter and Other Poems,* vi.

23. Lowell to Harry Duncan, June 11, 1944, Harry Duncan Papers, Emory University. See also Robert Dana's *Against the Grain* on how pressure from Wells College Press, with which Duncan collaborated, prevented him from publishing Lowell's poem (66–67).

24. Dickey, *Crux,* 20–22; Hart, *James Dickey,* 103.

25. Hecht to Melvyn and Dorothea Hecht, April 26, 1945, Anthony Hecht Papers, Emory University.

26. Jarrell, *Randall Jarrell's Letters,* 84.

27. Jarrell to Mackie Jarrell, June 24, 1943, Randall Jarrell Papers, New York Public Library.

28. Mary Jarrell, "Sheppard Field, Wichita Falls, Texas: February–April 1943," in *Randall Jarrell's Letters,* 72.

29. Jarrell, *Randall Jarrell's Letters,* 99.

30. Jarrell to Parker Tyler, n.d. [probably 1941], Parker Tyler Papers, University of Texas at Austin.

31. Ibid.; Jarrell, "Sheppard Field, Wichita Falls, Texas."

32. Shapiro, introduction, xxi.

33. Quoted in Pritchard, *Randall Jarrell,* 99.

34. Jarrell, *Randall Jarrell's Letters,* 140.

35. Jarrell, *Complete Poems,* 198.

36. Dickey, *Babel to Byzantium,* 21.

37. Jarrell, *Complete Poems,* 169.

38. Fussell, *Wartime,* 92.

39. Jarrell, *Complete Poems,* 169.

40. Jarrell, *Randall Jarrell Reads and Discusses His Poems against War.*

41. Jarrell to Mackie Jarrell, March 3, 1943, Randall Jarrell Papers, New York Public Library.

42. Simpson, *Selected Prose,* 96.

43. Jarrell, *Complete Poems,* 170.

44. Shapiro, *V-Letter,* vi. There are a number of exceptions, though—for instance, some poems by Alan Dugan, Lincoln Kirstein, and Howard Nemerov. These poems, however, were written many years after the war when these poets were mentally and physically removed from their army years.

45. Jarrell, *Randall Jarrell's Letters,* 143. One other war poem that can be qualified as humorous is his uncharacteristically aphoristic war poem "A War": "There set out, slowly, for a Different World / At four, on winter mornings, different legs . . . / *You can't break eggs without making an omelette* / —That's what they tell the eggs" (*Complete Poems,* 208). Jarrell's comparison of soldiers to eggs confirms how vulnerable Jarrell perceived the soldiers to be in a modern technological war such as World War II.

46. Jarrell, *Complete Poems,* 161.

47. Jarrell, *Randall Jarrell's Letters,* 103. Burt's chapter "Institutions, Professions, Criticism" in *Randall Jarrell and His Age* explores how this preoccupation with institutions developed after the war.

48. Nemerov's later war poetry forms an exception. His sometimes satirical war poems from *War Stories* (1987) will be discussed in chapter 16.

49. Jarrell, *Randall Jarrell's Letters,* 81.

50. Ibid., 139.

51. Pritchard, *Randall Jarrell,* 100.

52. Doherty, *Projections of War,* 184.

53. Ibid., 186.

54. Pritchard, *Randall Jarrell,* 100.

55. Jarrell to Mackie Jarrell, February 21, 1943, Randall Jarrell Papers, New York Public Library.

56. Ibid.

57. Nemerov, *Oak in the Acorn,* xi.

58. Hecht to Melvyn and Dorothea Hecht, October 12, 1944, Anthony Hecht Papers, Emory University.

59. Hecht, untitled and unpublished radio script, November 1945, Anthony Hecht Papers, Emory University.

60. Hirsch, "Comedy and Hardship," 53–61.

61. Hecht, *Anthony Hecht in Conversation with Philip Hoy,* 26.

62. Snodgrass, *Not for Specialists,* 16.

63. Shapiro, *Younger Son,* 267.

64. Ibid., 268.

65. Carruth, *Selected Essays & Reviews,* 96.

66. Hirsch, "One Life, One Writing!" 10.

67. Shires, *British Poets of the Second World War,* 86.

Chapter 6: "To be a Jew in the twentieth century"

1. Rukeyser, *Collected Poems,* 243.

2. Kaufman, "'But not the study,'" 45.

3. Rukeyser, *Collected Poems,* 243.

4. Hecht, *Anthony Hecht in Conversation with Philip Hoy,* 27.

5. Lindsay, "Anthony Hecht," 1. Lindsay gives a detailed biographical account of Hecht's army experiences.

6. Rukeyser, *Collected Poems,* 243.

7. Caruth, *Unclaimed Experience,* 4, 7.

8. Hecht, *Anthony Hecht in Conversation with Philip Hoy,* 36, 37.

9. Gubar, *Poetry after Auschwitz,* 3.

10. Flanzbaum, "Imaginary Jew," 19.

11. Jarrell, *Complete Poems,* 167.

12. Ibid., 168.

13. Ibid., 10.

14. Ibid., 167.

15. Jarrell, draft of "A Camp in the Prussian Forest," Randall Jarrell Papers, University of North Carolina at Greensboro.

16. Flanzbaum, "Imaginary Jew," 21, 23.

17. Gubar, *Poetry after Auschwitz,* 8.

18. Novick, *Holocaust in American Life,* 32.

19. Shapiro to Evalyn Katz, June 20, 1943, Karl Shapiro Papers, University of Maryland Library, College Park.

20. Shapiro, *Selected Poems,* 50, 51, 52.

21. Nemerov, *Journal of the Fictive Life,* 122.

22. Shapiro to Evalyn Katz, March 26, 1944, Karl Shapiro Papers, University of Maryland Library, College Park.

23. Shapiro, *Younger Son,* 247–48.

24. Shapiro, *V-Letter,* 27.

25. Shapiro to Evalyn Katz, April 10, 1944, Karl Shapiro Papers, University of Maryland Library, College Park.

26. Shapiro, *V-Letter,* 28.

27. Shapiro to Evalyn Katz, June 20, 1943, Karl Shapiro Papers, University of Maryland Library, College Park.

28. Hecht to Melvyn and Dorothea Hecht, March 5, 1945. Anthony Hecht Papers, Emory University.

29. Hecht, *Obbligati,* 214.

30. Ibid., 219.

31. Hecht, *Collected Earlier Poems,* 38.

32. Hecht, "Introduction to Reading of 'Rites and Ceremonies' on Yom Kippur," Anthony Hecht Papers, Emory University.

33. Hecht, *Collected Earlier Poems,* 39.

34. Ibid.

35. Ibid.
36. Ibid.
37. Ibid., 38.
38. Hecht, *Anthony Hecht in Conversation with Philip Hoy,* 59. Hecht refers to Matheson's *The Third Reich and the Christian Churches* to refute the claim of the Catholic Church.
39. See Jonathan F. S. Post's "The Genesis of Venice in Anthony Hecht's 'Venetian Vespers,'" especially 174–76, for a more extensive discussion how the war is palpable in Hecht's postwar poems about Austria, Germany, and Italy.
40. Gubar, *Poetry after Auschwitz,* 145.
41. Hecht, *Collected Earlier Poems,* 64.
42. Goethe, "On German Architecture," 103.
43. Hecht, draft of "Rites and Ceremonies."
44. Hecht, *Obbligati,* 147.
45. Gubar, *Poetry after Auschwitz,* 20.
46. Hecht, "Introduction to Reading of 'Rites and Ceremonies' on Yom Kippur."
47. In his article "Anthony Hecht, Private First Class," Geoffrey Lindsay points out that Hecht's "Persistences" also addresses Hecht's experiences at Flossenbürg (24).
48. Shapiro, *Younger Son,* 249.
49. Shapiro, *Essay on Rime with Trial of a Poet,* 112.
50. Tate said so in a letter to Karl Shapiro, April 22, 1949, Allen Tate Papers, Princeton University. In "Poetry's New Priesthood," Robert Hillyer called Shapiro "an interesting example of how an honest mind may be confused by the miasmas of estheticism" (8).

Chapter 7: Robert Lowell's Ideological Vacillations

1. Lowell, "War," 158.
2. Lowell, *Letters of Robert Lowell,* 36.
3. Stafford, "Some Letters to Peter and Eleanor Taylor," 43.
4. Lowell, *Collected Prose,* 370.
5. Eller, *Conscientious Objectors,* 49.
6. Ibid., 58.
7. See, for instance, Mariani, *Lost Puritan,* 90, 130.
8. Stafford, *Early Morning,* 40.
9. Ibid., 48.
10. Metres, *Behind the Lines,* 30.
11. Mariani, *Lost Puritan,* 93.
12. Lowell, *Collected Poems,* 187.
13. Lowell, "Typescript version of 'Memories of West Street and Lepke'" Robert Lowell Papers, Houghton Library, Harvard University.
14. Cox, "Richard Wilbur," 8.
15. Nemerov to Howard Turner, n.d., Nemerov Papers, Correspondence, Alexander Nemerov, New Haven, Conn..
16. The same can be said of the Anglo-Welsh poet Alun Lewis, whose "ideological commitments" also "altered dramatically from the late thirties when he was a

pacifist, to 1944 when he died on duty in Burma. He flirted with becoming a conscientious objector before volunteering for a non-combative unit in the Royal Engineers" (Shires, *British Poets of the Second World War,* 90).

17. Mariani, *Lost Puritan,* 99–101, 112.

18. *Land of Unlikeness* was out of print almost immediately after its publication. Robert Lowell described the collection to Karl Shapiro in 1946 as "almost nonexistent. . . . I am reprinting a good bit of Land of Unl. in my new book [*Lord Weary's Castle*] and will send you a copy when it comes out. I made $ 4.81 on Land of Unl. And am sure I could have made ten if I hadn't been underprinted. The poor people at Cummington [Press] had to give up smoking to stay alive and in business" (Lowell to Karl Shapiro, December 22, 1946, Karl Shapiro Papers, University of Texas at Austin). Lowell chose none of the poems of *Land of Unlikeness* for his *Selected Poems* (1976) and fifteen from *Lord Weary's Castle.*

19. Axelrod, *Robert Lowell,* 44.

20. Lowell, *Letters of Robert Lowell,* 145.

21. Norris, "War Poetry in the USA," 52.

22. Lowell, *Collected Poems,* 866.

23. Hamilton, *Robert Lowell,* 82.

24. Lowell, *Collected Poems,* 866.

25. Lowell, "To the President of the United States Who, on the Verge of War Desires the Blessings of the Churches," Robert Lowell Papers, Houghton Library, Harvard University.

26. Jarrell, *Randall Jarrell's Letters,* 128. For a more general and extensive overview of Jarrell's influence on Lowell during this time, see Michelson, "Randall Jarrell and Robert Lowell," 402–25.

27. Jarrell, *Randall Jarrell's Letters,* 139.

28. Ibid., 136.

29. Lowell, "The Bomber," Robert Lowell Papers, Houghton Library, Harvard University.

30. Lowell, *Collected Poems,* 870.

31. Ibid.

32. Burt, *Randall Jarrell and His Age,* 159.

33. Jarrell, *Complete Poems,* 143.

34. Lowell, *Collected Poems,* 870. While Jarrell accused Lowell of not representing "the 'actions of men,'" James Dickey ironically accused Jarrell of something similar: "I don't think there are really any *people* in the war poems. There are only The Ball Turret Gunner, A Pilot from the Carrier, The Wingman, and assorted faceless types in uniform. They are just collective Objects, or Attitudes, or Killable Puppets. You care very little what happens to them, and that is terrible" (Dickey, *Babel to Byzantium,* 22). This critique will be explored further in chapter 8.

35. Lowell, *Collected Poems,* 870.

36. The first printed version of this poem was called "The Capitalist's Meditation by the Civil War Monument, Christmas, 1942" and appeared in *Partisan Review* in 1943. It is reprinted by Frank Bidart and David Gewanter in the notes of Robert Lowell's *Collected Poems,* 881–887. A second printed version, entitled

"Christmas Eve in the Time of War," appeared in *Land of Unlikeness,* and is also reprinted in *Collected Poems,* 887–888.

37. Lowell, *Collected Poems,* 21, 1153.

38. Lowell, "Christmas Eve under Hooker's Statue," Robert Lowell Papers, Houghton Library, Harvard University.

39. Lowell, "The Dead in Europe," Robert Lowell Papers, Houghton Library, Harvard University.

40. Lowell, *Collected Poems,* 68.

41. Ibid.

42. Jarrell, *Complete Poems,* 145.

43. Lowell, "The Dead in Europe."

44. Robert Lowell, *Letters of Robert Lowell,* 339.

Chapter 8: Randall Jarrell's Secondhand Reality

1. Auden, "The Public v. the Late Mr. William Butler Yeats," 3–7.

2. Dickey, *Babel to Byzantium,* 22.

3. Jarrell, *Randall Jarrell's Letters,* 139.

4. Eberhart, "The Fury of Aerial Bombardment," in Shapiro, *Poets of World War II,* 31.

5. Dickey, *Babel to Byzantium,* 22. Fussell agrees with A and argues that the "new anonymity . . . imposed upon characters in poems who earlier might have been carefully named and singled out as heroes" in poems such as "The Death of the Ball Turret Gunner" and "A Field Hospital" shows how these military men represent "one of the ten million identical units from the production line, indistinguishable in their olive drab." See his introduction in *Articles of War,* xxv.

6. Dickey, *Babel to Byzantium,* 22.

7. Auden, "Private Poet," 318.

8. Whitman, *Complete Poetry and Collected Prose,* 466.

9. Jarrell, "Answers to Questions," 183.

10. Spargo judges in *The Ethics of Mourning* that Jarrell is unsuccessful is realistically presenting his speaker as an American soldier because of "Jarrell's anachronistic inclusion of information readily available to his audience a year subsequent to but not necessarily during the liberation of the camps" (221).

11. Hecht, *Obbligati,* 204.

12. Jarrell, *Blood for a Stranger,* 18.

13. Jarrell, *Complete Poems,* 389.

14. Jarrell, *Blood for a Stranger,* 19.

15. Ibid., 21.

16. Ibid., 22.

17. Spargo, *Ethics of Mourning,* 215, 234.

18. Jarrell wrote two poems called "To the New World." The poem I refer to is subtitled "(For an emigrant of 1939)" and can be found in *Complete Poems,* 80–81.

19. Tobin, *Ernie Pyle's War,* 21.

20. Jarrell, *Kipling, Auden & Co.,* 113, 120.

21. Quoted in Tobin, *Ernie Pyle's War,* 24.

22. See, for instance, Zertal, *Israel's Holocaust,* 45.

23. Jarrell, draft of "Jews at Haifa," Randall Jarrell Papers, University of North Carolina at Greensboro.

24. Jarrell, *Complete Poems,* 163.

25. Ibid.

26. Jarrell, draft of "Jews at Haifa."

27. Jarrell, "Analysis of why 'particulars' should seem so much more effective than 'universals.'"

28. Gubar, *Poetry after Auschwitz,* 23.

29. Ibid., 146.

30. Ibid., 145.

31. Hecht, *Collected Earlier Poems,* 64.

32. Jarrell, *On W. H. Auden,* 71.

33. Hecht, "Commentary," 82.

34. Hecht, *Collected Later Poems,* 80.

35. "The Book of Yolek" is, for instance, not included in Stallworthy's *The Oxford Book of War Poetry* (1984), Stokesbury's *Articles of War* (1990), Shapiro's *Poets of World War II* (2003), or Goldensohn's *American War Poetry* (2006).

36. Hecht, "Letters to the Editor," 105–6.

37. Ciardi published his only other poem about the Holocaust, which is called "The Gift"; see his *Collected Poems,* 225.

38. Ciardi, "Sarko."

39. Howard, *War in European History,* 110.

40. Jarrell, *Randall Jarrell's Letters,* 19. See also Longenbach's chapter "Randall Jarrell's Semifeminine Mind" in his *Modern Poetry after Modernism,* 49–64.

41. Burt, *Randall Jarrell and His Age,* 40.

42. Jarrell, *Complete Poems,* 158.

43. See, for instance, Whitman's "First O Songs for a Prelude" and "Pensive on Her Dead Gazing, I Heard the Mother of All."

44. Schweik, *Gulf So Deeply Cut,* 109.

45. Taylor, "Gwendolyn Brooks," 260.

46. See Fussell's chapters "Type-Casting" in *Wartime* and "Adversary Proceedings" in *The Great War and Modern Memory.*

47. Jarrell, *Kipling, Auden & Co.,* 118.

48. Carruth, *Selected Essays & Reviews,* 96.

49. Dickey, *Babel to Byzantium,* 25.

50. Carruth, *Selected Essays & Reviews,* 96.

51. Lowell, "From the Tombs to Danbury," Robert Lowell Papers, Houghton Library, Harvard University.

52. These are quotations from Alan Seeger's "The Aisne" about the First World War and Edwin Rolfe's "First Love" about the Spanish Civil War in Goldensohn, *American War Poetry,* 165, 187.

53. Melville, "The March into Virginia, Ending in the First Manassas," in Goldensohn, *American War Poetry,* 65; Lowell, *Collected Poems,* 21.

54. Nemerov, *Collected Poems,* 237.

Chapter 9: James Dickey's Hypermasculinity

1. Dickey, *Crux,* 7.

2. Hart, *James Dickey,* 672.

3. Dickey, draft of "Joel Cahill Dead," James Dickey Papers, Washington University.

4. Hart, *James Dickey,* 41.

5. Dickey also wrote another war novel, "Crux"—a sequel to *Alnilam*—which he never finished. An excerpt from "Crux" was included in *The James Dickey Reader,* 211–28.

6. Dickey, "*Thallassa* [variant title for *To the White Sea*], early notes," James Dickey Papers, Emory University.

7. Dickey, *To the White Sea,* 7.

8. Ibid., 6.

9. Dickey, "*Thallassa.*"

10. Ibid.

11. Goldstein, *War and Gender,* 266.

12. Hathcock, "No Further Claim to Innocence," 33–34.

13. Ibid., 26.

14. Hecht, *Hidden Law,* 435.

15. Dickey, *Alnilam,* 304.

16. Ibid., 108–9.

17. Ibid., 401.

18. Suarez, "Interview with James Dickey," 130.

19. Dickey, "Alnilam aphorisms," James Dickey Papers, Emory University.

20. Dickey, *Alnilam,* 428.

21. Clabough, *Elements,* 75.

22. Suarez, "Interview with James Dickey," 128.

23. Quoted in Terkel, *"The Good War,"* 198.

24. Margaret Nemerov, telephone interview by author, March 1, 2007.

25. Nemerov, Memo, Correspondence 1986–1987, August 4, 1987, Howard Nemerov Papers, Washington University.

26. Shapiro, "He-Man," 42.

27. Goldstein, *War and Gender,* 282.

28. Dickey, *Alnilam,* 154.

29. Goldstein, *War and Gender,* 282.

30. Dickey, typescript draft of "Joel Cahill Dead," James Dickey Papers, Washington University.

31. Dickey, typescript fair copy with holograph annotations of "Three Poems Flight-Sleep," James Dickey Papers, Emory University. Dickey only finished and published two parts of the poem. The second part, "Reunioning Dialogue," was published in the *Atlantic Monthly* in 1973 and reprinted in *The Strength of Fields* (1979).

32. Dickey, *Whole Motion,* 385.

33. Ibid.

34. Ibid.

35. Ibid., 386.
36. Ibid.
37. Baughman, *Understanding James Dickey,* 132; Hart, *James Dickey,* 73.
38. Goldstein, *War and Gender,* 253.
39. Dickey, *Whole Motion,* 59.
40. Ibid., 59, 60.
41. Ibid., 60.
42. Ibid.
43. Ibid., 3.
44. Ibid.
45. Ibid., 4.
46. Ibid.
47. Goldensohn, *Dismantling Glory,* 8.
48. Ibid.
49. Goldensohn, "War Poetry of James Dickey," 151.
50. Hart, *James Dickey,* 97.
51. Ibid., 100.
52. Ibid.
53. Dickey, *Whole Motion,* 59.
54. Ibid.
55. Jarvis, *Male Body at War,* 5.
56. In *Alnilam,* Frank Cahill's amusement park in Atlanta is also home to a great number of bodybuilders. James Dickey, "Body Exchange" [variant title for "Two Poems on the Survival of the Male Body"], James Dickey Papers, Emory University.
57. Hart, *World as a Lie,* 91.
58. Dickey, "Two Poems on the Survival of the Male Body."
59. Jarvis, *Male Body at War,* 52.
60. Ciardi, *Saipan,* 92.
61. Quoted in Kalstone, *Becoming a Poet,* 157.
62. Dickey, "Alnilam aphorisms," James Dickey Papers, Emory University.

Chapter 10: "All wars are boyish"

1. Travisano, *Midcentury Quartet,* 78.
2. Quoted in Young, *Gentleman in a Dustcoat,* 23.
3. Travisano, *Midcentury Quartet,* 78.
4. Flynn, "'Infant Sight,'" 110.
5. Flynn, *Randall Jarrell,* x.
6. Flynn, "Infant Sight," 124.
7. Travisano makes this point as well, but in a more general way for Berryman, Bishop, Jarrell, and Lowell; see Travisano, *Midcentury Quartet,* 77–78.
8. Bishop, *Complete Poems,* 59.
9. Flynn, "Infant Sight," 105. See also Travisano, *Elizabeth Bishop,* 120–24.
10. Bishop, *Complete Poems,* 161.
11. Ibid., 160.
12. Barry, "Elizabeth Bishop and World War I," 97.

13. Bishop, *Collected Prose,* 17.

14. Ibid., 251.

15. Travisano, *Midcentury Quartet,* 73.

16. Jarrell, *Complete Poems,* 289.

17. Ibid.

18. Smith, *Army Brat,* 35.

19. Bishop, *Collected Prose,* 253.

20. Brooks, *Selected Poems,* 20.

21. James, *Freedom Bought with Blood,* 168.

22. Brooks, *Selected Poems,* 20.

23. Schweik, *Gulf So Deeply Cut,* 118–19.

24. Hart, *James Dickey,* 27.

25. Shapiro, *Bourgeois Poet,* 31, 32.

26. Lowell, *Collected Prose,* 312.

27. Goldstein, *War and Gender,* 298.

28. Lowell, *Collected Prose,* 312.

29. Mariani, *Lost Puritan,* 37.

30. Lowell, *Collected Prose,* 344.

31. Ibid., 330.

32. Ibid., 329.

33. Nemerov, *Sentences,* 79.

34. Nemerov, *War Stories,* 25.

35. Furbank, *E. M. Forster,* 254.

36. Nemerov, *War Stories,* 26.

37. Nemerov, *Inside the Onion,* 55.

38. Nemerov, Memo, Correspondence 1986–1987, August 4, 1987, Washington University.

39. Carlsson-Paige and Levin, *War Play Dilemma,* 21.

40. Nemerov, *War Stories,* 26.

41. Bosworth, *Diane Arbus,* 25, 11.

42. Ibid., 61.

43. Ibid., 57.

44. Nemerov, "Memorial to Archibald MacLeish at the American Academy of Arts and Letters," December 3, 1982, Howard Nemerov Papers, Washington University.

45. Auden, "Private Poet," 319.

46. Kirstein, "World War I Scrapbook," Lincoln Kirstein Papers, Jerome Robbins Dance Division, New York Public Library.

47. Kirstein, *Rhymes and More Rhymes,* 3.

48. Ibid., 4.

49. Goldstein, *War and Gender,* 269.

50. Nemerov, *Collected Poems,* 238.

51. Ibid., 237.

52. Nemerov's poem was almost certainly a reaction to or comment on W. H. Auden's "Homage to Clio" (1955), which became the title poem of a volume that Auden published in 1960. Auden likens Clio to the Virgin Mary, who is equally

mysterious and serenely silent, and the saint we turn to "when we have lost control" (*Collected Poems* 612). Nemerov's poem is more overtly personal and less abstract than Auden's, and he is less deferential to the muse of history, and even suggests that she led him astray.

53. See, for instance, Ferguson's chapter on Jarrell's *The Lost World* in *The Poetry of Randall Jarrell,* 187–223, and Burt's *Randall Jarrell and His Age,* 125–27, 215–16. Nemerov began reading Proust during the war, and collected his later Brandeis lectures on Proust in *The Oak in the Acorn.*

54. Dickey, *Striking In,* 259–60.

55. Goldstein, *War and Gender,* 252.

56. A carbon copy of Nemerov's letter was enclosed in Nemerov to Stanley Edgar Hyman, November 29, 1968, Stanley Edgar Hymen Papers, Library of Congress. Nemerov added in a note to Hyman: "Seems unlikely now that the N.Y. Times will print the enclosed; and inasmuch as your file on me is far completer than mine, things will naturally gravitate thither."

57. David Nemerov's lottery number had been called two weeks before his graduation from college, but did not have to serve when Secretary of Defense Melvin R. Laird announced on January 27, 1973, that the draft would be suspended. David Nemerov, telephone interview by author, March 4, 2007.

58. Lowell, *Collected Poems,* 780.

59. Lowell to Stanley Kunitz, April 24, 1972, quoted in Mariani, *Lost Puritan,* 412.

60. Lowell, *Collected Poems,* 779.

61. Lowell, typescript of "Sheridan," Robert Lowell Papers, Harry Ransom Humanities Research Center, University of Texas, Austin.

62. Melville, "March into Virginia."

63. Fussell, *Wartime,* 52.

64. Stafford, *The Way It Is,* 9.

65. Lowell, *Collected Poems,* 21.

66. Jarrell, *Complete Poems,* 144.

Chapter 11: Karl Shapiro's Sexual Appetite

1. Jarrell, *Randall Jarrell's Letters,* 144.

2. See, for instance, "The Puritan," which depicts the dark and evil-spirited side of the Pilgrim fathers; "Jefferson" and "Franklin," which debunk two Founding Fathers; and "Red Indian" and "Nigger," which zoom in on two of the victims of the quest for American nationhood, all of which were published in *V-Letter.* While he was less disparaging than Lowell in *Land of Unlikeness* (1944) and *Lord Weary's Castle* (1946), Shapiro shared Lowell's interest in American history and how it could be linked to World War II.

3. Goldstein, *War and Gender,* 333.

4. Westbrook, "'I Want a Girl,'" 595.

5. Ibid., 594–595.

6. Fussell, *Wartime,* 108.

7. Jarvis, *Male Body at War,* 82

8. Westbrook, "'I Want a Girl,'" 595.

9. D'Emilio and Freedman, *Intimate Matters,* 274.

10. Kirstein, *Rhymes and More Rhymes,* 147–48.

11. Scannell, *Not without Glory,* 182

12. Kirstein, *Rhymes and More Rhymes,* 126.

13. Ibid., 127.

14. Jarrell, *Poetry and the Age,* 225, 226. Jarrell was more positive about Wilbur in his long article "Fifty Years of American Poetry," singling "A Baroque Wall-Fountain in the Villa Sciarra" as "one of the most marvelously beautiful, one of the most nearly perfect poems any American has written" (Jarrell, *Third Book of Criticism,* 331). Still, Jarrell continued to bemoan Wilbur's lack of range.

15. The characterization of soldiers as both "puppies" and "hounds" seems similar to Jarrell's poem "Eighth Air Force," where he described the airmen as both "puppies" and "wolves," *Complete Poems,* 143.

16. Wilbur, *Collected Poems,* 420.

17. Kirstein, *Rhymes and More Rhymes,* 126.

18. Fussell, *Great War and Modern Memory,* 279–80.

19. Ibid., 280.

20. Auden, "Private Poet," 319.

21. Fussell, *Great War and Modern Memory,* 273.

22. Ibid., 290.

23. Quoted in Janssen, *Kenyon Review,* 140.

24. Like a seventeenth-century metaphysical poem, it seems to have one overriding metaphor, electricity, which is introduced in the first stanza and elaborated in the later stanzas.

25. Wilbur, *Collected Poems,* 420.

26. Nemerov to Howard Turner, November 18, 1941, Nemerov Papers, Correspondence, Alexander Nemerov, New Haven, Conn.

27. Goldensohn, *Dismantling Glory,* 179, 214.

28. Jarrell, *Randall Jarrell's Letters,* 19. See also James Longenbach's essay "Randall Jarrell's Semifeminine Mind" in his *Modern Poetry after Modernism,* 49–64.

29. Simpson, *Poets in Their Youth,* 111.

30. Duberman, *Worlds of Lincoln Kirstein,* 554.

31. Tate to Harry Duncan, July 31, 1946, Harry Duncan Papers, Emory University.

32. Kirstein to Harry Duncan, October 12, 1954, Harry Duncan Papers, Emory University.

33. D'Emilio and Freedman, *Intimate Matters,* 260.

34. Schweik, *Gulf So Deeply Cut,* 88. Schweik traces the genre back to early modern times and cites Cavalier poet Richard Lovelace's "To Lucasta, Going to the Wars" as an early example.

35. Ibid., 108, 86.

36. To be safe, Shapiro kept carbon copies of his poems until they reached Katz and also sent duplicates to his mother in Baltimore. All his V-mail and some of Shapiro's regular letters passed the military censor since they bear the censor's stamp, but there is no proof that Shapiro's letters were tampered with or withheld.

In fact, none of Shapiro's or Katz's letters seemed to have gotten lost, although many were delayed for weeks and months.

37. Schweik, *Gulf So Deeply Cut,* 108, 90.

38. Shapiro, *Selected Poems,* 69.

39. Ibid.

40. Ibid., 54.

41. Ibid., 41.

42. Ibid., 42.

43. Ibid., 70.

44. Ibid., 71.

45. Kirstein, *Rhymes and More Rhymes,* 127.

46. Shapiro, *Selected Poems,* 69–70. Agata Lisiak pointed out to me that "V-Letter" seems inspired by Charles Baudelaire's poem "La Géante" ("Giantess"), which Shapiro translated en route to the Pacific theater. Shapiro's translation is included in *The Flowers of Evil,* which Marthiel Matthews and Jackson Matthews edited for New Directions in 1955.

47. Goldensohn, *Dismantling Glory,* 24.

48. Westbrook, "I Want a Girl,'" 596.

49. Shapiro to Evalyn Katz, May 16, 1943, Karl Shapiro Papers, University of Maryland Library, College Park.

50. "Soldier's Girl Keeps Busy Making His Poems Famous," *New York World-Telegram,* November 23, 1942; Westbrook, "I Want a Girl,'" 603.

51. Shapiro, *Younger Son,* 206.

52. Shapiro, *Place of Love,* 37. A few of the poems of this volume have been reprinted—for instance, "The New Ring" and "The Dirty Word" in *Trial of a Poet* (1947)—but most have never been published in the United States.

53. Shapiro, *Place of Love,* 9.

54. Shapiro to Evalyn Katz, May 16, 1943, Karl Shapiro Papers, University of Maryland Library, College Park.

55. Ibid.

56. Shapiro to Evalyn Katz, May 13, 1943, Karl Shapiro Papers, University of Maryland Library, College Park.

57. Schweik, *Gulf So Deeply Cut,* 66.

58. Shapiro to Evalyn Katz, November 29, 1943, Karl Shapiro Papers, University of Maryland Library, College Park.

59. Shapiro, *Younger Son,* 206.

60. Ibid.

61. Ibid.

Chapter 12: Alternative Masculinities

1. Howard, *War in European History,* 134.

2. Ibid.

3. Stafford, *Down in My Heart,* 7.

4. Kunitz, *Interviews and Encounters,* 75.

5. Jarvis, *Male Body at War,* 58.

6. Betty Bonney, "He's 1-A in the Army and He's A-1 in My Heart," recorded October 15, 1941, Valiant Music Company.

7. Kirstein, *Rhymes and More Rhymes,* 25.

8. Ibid., 26.

9. Ibid., 25.

10. Ibid.

11. Ibid.

12. Reidel, *Vanished Act,* 125.

13. Ibid., 128.

14. Ibid., 129.

15. The phrase "idiot wind" was also used by Bob Dylan as the title of one of his songs on the album *Blood on the Tracks* (1975). It is unclear whether Dylan knew that Kees had used it before. Dylan's song is not about war, but it is as bitter as Kees's poem.

16. Kees, *Collected Poems,* 17.

17. Ibid.

18. Rainier Maria Rilke did not always denounce war, however. Early in his life he heroized a soldier's death in his lyrical tale *Die Weise von Liebe und Tod des Cornets Christoph Rilke* (1899/1904). Much to Rilke's dismay, this poem became popular during the First World War. Typical of his generation's desire to de-emphasize heroism in warfare by writing back to their literary elders, Howard Nemerov wrote a response to Rilke's poem, "On Reading 'The Love and Death of Cornet Christopher Rilke.'" In this early war poem from *The Image and the Law* (1947), Nemerov deplored how "the ancestors" tried to "intervene" during his war with their "celebration of death" (*Collected Poems,* 43).

19. Kees, *Collected Poems,* 17.

20. Mariani, *Dream Song,* 122.

21. Berryman, *Collected Poems,* 42.

22. Lowell, *Collected Poems,* 377.

23. Vendler, "Art, Heroism, and Poetry," 211.

24. Berryman, *Collected Poems,* 41.

25. Shapiro, *Selected Poems,* 80.

26. Ibid., 79.

27. Ibid.

28. Hilene Flanzbaum writes in "The Imaginary Jew and the American Poet" that "there is ample reason to believe that Shapiro had Robert Lowell in mind when he wrote this poem" (31). She assumes that Steven Gould Axelrod agreed with her because "he begins his section on Lowell's conscientious-objector status in *Robert Lowell: Life and Art* with a quotation from Shapiro's poem" (288), but Axelrod never actually claims that Shapiro wrote about Lowell in "The Conscientious Objector."

29. Shapiro to Katharine White, January 24, 1946, the *New Yorker* Papers, New York Public Library.

30. Shapiro, *Old Horsefly,* 43.

31. White to Karl Shapiro, January 23, 1946, the *New Yorker* Papers, New York Public Library.

32. Stafford, *Down in My Heart,* 7–8.
33. Ibid., 28.
34. Ibid.
35. Ibid., 30.
36. Vendler, "Art, Heroism, and Poetry," 211.
37. Kindlon and Thomson with Baker, *Raising Cain,* xiv.
38. Stafford, *The Way It Is,* 171.
39. Metres, *Behind the Lines,* 66.
40. Goldstein, *War and Gender,* 251.
41. Stafford, *The Way It Is,* 128.
42. Ibid., 129.
43. Ibid.
44. Ibid.
45. Ibid., 56.
46. Ibid.
47. Stafford. *Every War Has Two Losers,* 145.
48. Jarrell, *Complete Poems,* 143.
49. Metres, *Behind the Lines,* 70.

Chapter 13: "Ought I to regret my seedtime?"

1. Lowell, *Collected Poems,* 187.
2. Williamson, *Pity the Monsters,* 80. Frank Bidart and David Gewanter note that William Wordsworth also uses the phrase "fair seed-time had my soul" in *The Prelude,* I; see Lowell, *Collected Poems,* 1041.
3. Lowell, *Collected Poems,* 187.
4. Fussell, introduction, xxiv.
5. Jarrell, "[Poems] Holograph notebook, unsigned [ca. 1939–1945?]," Berg Collection, New York Public Library.
6. Jarrell, *Complete Poems,* 143.
7. Ibid.
8. Hugo, *Real West,* 98.
9. Simic, *Fly in the Soup,* 12, 13.
10. Hugo, *Making Certain It Goes On,* 279.
11. Ibid., 280.
12. Hugo, *Real West,* 95.
13. Hugo, *Making Certain It Goes On,* 279.
14. Ibid., 280.
15. Ibid.
16. Suarez, "Interview with James Dickey," 122.
17. Dickey, *Whole Motion,* 200.
18. Ibid., 197.
19. Dickey, *Self-Interviews,* 184.
20. Dickey, *Whole Motion,* 195.
21. Ibid., 199.
22. Dickey, draft of "The Firebombing," James Dickey Papers, Washington University.

23. Dickey, *Whole Motion,* 193.
24. Shapiro, *Selected Poems,* 143.
25. Dickey, draft of "Reunioning Dialogue," James Dickey Papers, Emory University.
26. Dickey, *Whole Motion,* 389.
27. Stafford, *The Way It Is,* 250.
28. Stafford, *Early Morning,* 49.
29. Stafford, *The Way It Is,* 164.
30. Gray, *Warriors,* 33.
31. Dickey, *Whole Motion,* 195–96.
32. Bly, "Collapse of James Dickey," 36.
33. Lowell, *Collected Poems,* 1042.
34. Ibid., 731.
35. Lowell, draft of "Our Afterlife I," Robert Lowell Papers, Harry Ransom Humanities Center, University of Texas, Austin.
36. Metres, *Behind the Lines,* 35.
37. Lowell, *Collected Poems,* 732.
38. Ibid., 187, 188.
39. Jarrell, *Randall Jarrell's Letters,* 139.
40. Lowell, "From the Tombs to Danbury," Robert Lowell Papers, Houghton Library, Harvard University.
41. Hirsch, "One Life, One Writing!" 10.
42. Lowell, *Collected Poems,* 188.
43. Ibid.
44. See Bidart and Gewanter's endnote, 4.15, in Lowell, *Collected Poems,* 1042.
45. Lowell, draft of "Memories of West Street and Lepke," Robert Lowell Papers, Berg Collection, New York Public Library.
46. Lowell, *Collected Poems,* 1042.
47. The title of the typescript refers to Franz Schubert's "Der Tod und das Mädchen," but the content of the typescript does not seem directly related to the two poems of the same name, "Death and the Maiden," which appeared in Lowell's *The Dolphin* (1973) and *History* (1973).
48. Lowell, "Death and the Maiden," Robert Lowell Papers, Houghton Library, Harvard University.
49. Ibid.
50. Terence, *Comedies,* 76. The original Latin phrase is: "Homo sum; humani nil a me alienum puto." Lowell studied the classics at Kenyon College, so it is possible he knew the original. Since Lowell uses it in a slightly different wording, it is more likely that he copied it or remembered it from another source—for instance, from Ezra Pound, who quotes "nihil humanum alienum" in Canto LXIV. See Pound, *Cantos,* 360.
51. Jarrell, *Randall Jarrell's Letters,* 19.
52. Lowell, *Collected Poems,* 68.
53. Quoted in Hart, *James Dickey,* xvii.
54. Hart, *James Dickey,* 14.

55. Dickey to James Wright, August 30, 1961, quoted in Hart, *James Dickey,* 14.
56. Bishop, *Collected Poems,* 35.
57. Goldstein, *War and Gender,* 288.

Chapter 14: Lucky John Ciardi's Trauma of War

1. Hecht, *Anthony Hecht in Conversation with Philip Hoy,* 36.
2. Simpson, *Air with Armed Men,* 131.
3. Goldstein, *War and Gender,* 258, 261.
4. Ibid., 261.
5. Simpson, "On the Ledge."
6. Simpson, *Air with Armed Men,* 134.
7. Simpson, *Owner of the House,* 100.
8. Nemerov, *Collected Poems,* 61.
9. Hecht, *Collected Earlier Poems,* 67.
10. Ibid.
11. Ibid.
12. Ibid., 68.
13. Ibid.
14. Baer, "'It Out-Herods Herod,'" 62.
15. Stavros, "Interview with Gwendolyn Brooks," 45.
16. Brooks, *Selected Poems,* 22.
17. Ibid., 25.
18. Stout, *Coming Out of War,* 153.
19. Ciardi, *Saipan,* 26.
20. Ibid., 58.
21. Ciardi, "About Being Born," 11.
22. Ciardi, *Saipan,* 100.
23. Ibid., 101.
24. Cifelli, *John Ciardi,* 75.
25. Ciardi, "About Being Born," 12.
26. Ibid.
27. Ibid., 14, 15.
28. Ibid., 15.
29. Ibid., 3.
30. Crane, *Red Badge of Courage and Other Stories,* 148.
31. Cifelli, *John Ciardi,* xv.
32. Ciardi, "About Being Born," 16.
33. Cifelli, *John Ciardi,* 181.
34. Caruth, *Unclaimed Experience,* 7.
35. It is probably a coincidence that Ciardi wrote this poem a month after the My Lai massacre because the news about the mass murder by Charlie Company was not known until 1969 when Seymour Hersh reported about it in the *New York Times.*
36. Ibid., 492.
37. Ciardi, *Collected Poems,* 491.
38. Ciardi, *Lives of X,* 98.

39. Nemerov also has a number of such occasional poems; see, for instance, "D-Day Plus All the Years, "D-Day plus Twenty Years," and "Thirtieth Anniversary Report of the Class of '41."

40. Ciardi, *Collected Poems,* 50.

41. Ibid.

42. Jarrell, *Kipling, Auden & Co.,* 148–49.

43. Ciardi, *Collected Poems,* 52.

44. Ibid., 57.

45. Ibid.

46. Vaughan, *Words to Measure a War,* 60.

47. Dower, *Embracing Defeat,* 41.

48. Ciardi, *Collected Poems,* 371.

49. See the appendix "People and Nicknames" in Ciardi's *Saipan* for the rank and proper identification of these air crew (125-28). "O'Dell" was the navigator O'Hara, whose name Ciardi had used in the working sheets, but Ciardi must have changed his name to "O'Dell" because he is poking fun of O'Hara's religion. Ciardi describes him as "probably blubbering a prayer" (*Collected Poems,* 372).

50. In his drafts Ciardi had used the name "Tiger" instead of "Coxie," the nickname for Richard G. Johnson, a gunner on the same flight crew and barracks mate of Ciardi.

51. Ciardi, draft of "The Formalities," John Ciardi Papers, Library of Congress.

52. Ciardi, *Collected Poems,* 371.

53. Hardy, *Selected Poems,* 71.

54. Ciardi, *Collected Poems,* 45.

55. See chapter 9, "Self-Elegy: Keith Douglas and Sidney Keyes," of Tim Kendall's *Modern English War Poetry* for an insightful analysis of this subgenre in English war poetry. It appears that the self-elegy was less rife in American World War II poetry, with the exception of Ciardi.

56. Fussell, introduction, xxvi.

57. Ciardi, *Collected Poems,* 46.

58. Ciardi, *Saipan,* 120.

59. Dower, *War without Mercy,* 298, 299.

60. Ciardi, *Saipan,* 22.

61. Ibid., 33.

62. Ciardi, *Lives of X,* 98.

63. Nemerov, *War Stories,* 31.

64. Ciardi, *Collected Poems,* 70.

Chapter 15: "Aftersight and foresight"

1. Simpson, *The King My Father's Wreck,* 73.

2. Lincoln Kirstein, in *Rhymes and More Rhymes of a PFC,* and Howard Nemerov, in *War Stories,* did write and publish satirical poems about World War II, but only decades later. Neither had their British peers for that matter; as Linda M. Shires points out in *British Poetry of the Second World War,* the British war poets did not favor this tone or mode of writing either: "Forced into a war they did not want, these poets rarely resorted to outright satire" (69).

3. Jarrell, *Randall Jarrell's Letters,* 81.
4. Nemerov, *Collected Poems,* 465.
5. Chattarji, *Memories of a Lost War,* 38.
6. Nemerov, *Collected Poems,* 465.
7. Nemerov was not the only or first one to write poems that refer to the atomic bomb. John Frederick Nims, Robert Lowell, and Richard Wilbur preceded him. See chapter 7, "Poems about the Bomb: Noir Poetics," and chapter 8, "Poems about the Bomb: Nuclear Family," of Edward Brunner's *Cold War Poetry.*
8. Nemerov, *Sentences,* 18.
9. Ibid.
10. Moore, *Complete Poems,* 46; Nemerov, *Sentences,* 18.
11. Eliot, *Collected Poems,* 204. Morag Shiach notes that Eliot took the phrase from the French poet Stéphane Mallarmé, but it is also a tribute to Edgar Allan Poe; see Shiach, "'To Purify the dialect of the tribe,'" 26.
12. Jarrell, *Randall Jarrell's Letters,* 413. Meredith told Edward Hirsch that he was afraid that when Jarrell asserted in 1962 that there was a large group of "poets, who, so to speak, came from under Richard Wilbur's overcoat," he also alluded to Meredith. Meredith, "The Art of Poetry XXXIV," *Paris Review* 95 (1985): 46.
13. Hathcock, "'Standardizing Catastrophe,'" 113.
14. Quoted in Robertson, "Johnson Dislikes His Likeness," 35.
15. Wilbur, *Collected Poems,* 221.
16. Broughton, "Interview with Richard Wilbur," 136–37.
17. Johnson, as vice president, inherited the presidency when John F. Kennedy was assassinated on November 22, 1963.
18. Wilbur's reasons for preferring Jefferson over Johnson are not entirely convincing in these lines. While "no *army*'s blood was shed" during Jefferson's presidency, the United States was involved in the First Barbary War (1801–1805). Jefferson also sought to block Haiti from becoming an independent nation, so it is unlikely that he "would have wept to see small nations dread / The imposition of our cattle-brand," as Wilbur suggests (*Collected Poems,* 221). See R. B. Bernstein's *Thomas Jefferson* for an account of Jefferson's foreign policy during his presidency (176–78).
19. Hutton, "Interview with Richard Wilbur," 49.
20. Longenbach, *Modern Poetry after Modernism,* 80.
21. "A Mild-Spoken Citizen" cannot be about the Watergate scandal because that occurred a few years later, even if some of Meredith's critique of Nixon may seem to comment on Nixon's reaction to and role in that scandal.
22. Meredith, *Effort at Speech,* 153.
23. Ibid.
24. Ibid., 154.
25. Hecht, *Collected Earlier Poems,* 209.
26. Jarrell, *Randall Jarrell's Letters,* 132.
27. Hecht, *Collected Earlier Poems,* 209.
28. Hecht, *Anthony Hecht in Conversation with Philip Hoy,* 78.
29. Auden, *Collected Poems,* 248.
30. Ibid.

31. Metres, *Behind the Lines,* 112–13.
32. Carruth, *Collected Shorter Poems,* 94.
33. Ibid., 93.
34. Ibid., 94.
35. Lowell, *Collected Poems,* 545.
36. Ibid., 546.
37. Smith, "'Approaching Our Maturity,'" 289.
38. Melville, "March into Virginia."
39. Metres, *Behind the Lines,* 48.
40. Nemerov, *Collected Poems,* 424.
41. Ibid., 428.
42. Quoted in *Anthony Hecht in Conversation with Philip Hoy,* 78. See also Tim Kendall's reading of this poem in *Modern English War Poetry.* He suggests that Hecht's attack on antiwar poets may also be applied to those who quickly seized the opportunity to bring out anthologies when the war in Iraq broke out (238–40).
43. Chattarji, *Memories of a Lost War,* 51, 57.
44. Hecht, *Hidden Law,* 145.
45. Quoted in Stafford, *Early Morning,* 50.
46. Vendler, *Part of Nature,* 177.
47. Lowell, *Collected Poems,* 21.
48. Hecht, *Collected Earlier Poems,* 152.
49. Hecht, draft of "The Odds," Anthony Hecht Papers, Emory University.
50. Hecht, *Collected Earlier Poems,* 152.
51. Ibid., 153.
52. Ibid.

Chapter 16: Howard Nemerov and the "Good War" Myth

1. Terkel, *"The Good War,"* iv.
2. Adams, *Best War Ever,* 2.
3. Stafford, *The Way It Is,* 14, 15.
4. Ibid., 15.
5. Ibid.
6. Ibid.
7. Ibid.
8. Ibid.
9. Press, "Interview with Howard Nemerov."
10. Bosworth, *Diane Arbus,* 57.
11. Shephard, *War of Nerves,* 283.
12. Nemerov's Army Separation Qualification Record and Military Record are held at Special Collections of the John M. Olin Library of Washington University.
13. Bosworth, *Diane Arbus,* 90.
14. Nemerov, "Modeling My Father," 557.
15. Dickey has noted that Wilfred Owen's poems reminded him of the same words from the Bible and *Moby Dick;* see Dickey, *Classes on Modern Poets,* 244.
16. Shephard, *War of Nerves,* 285.
17. Margaret Nemerov, telephone interview by author, February 19, 2007.

18. Alexander Nemerov, e-mail message to author, February 20, 2007.

19. Nemerov to Reed Whittemore, June 22, 1961, Reed Whittemore Papers, University of Maryland Library, College Park.

20. Waller, *Veteran Comes Back,* 54.

21. Eliot, *Selected Essays,* 145.

22. Nemerov, *Collected Poems,* 61.

23. Bosworth, *Diane Arbus,* 61.

24. Ibid.

25. Jarrell, *Complete Poems,* 143.

26. Eliot, *Selected Essays,* 21.

27. Nemerov, *Collected Poems,* 151.

28. Ibid.

29. Ibid.

30. Santayana, *Life of Reason,* 82.

31. Nemerov, *Inside the Onion,* 54.

32. Ibid.

33. Ibid.

34. Ibid.

35. Ibid., 54–55.

36. Nemerov, *War Stories,* 6.

37. Ibid.

38. Lowell, *Collected Poems,* 741.

39. Nemerov, *Journal of the Fictive Life,* 18.

40. Fussell, *Wartime,* 142.

41. Nemerov, *War Stories,* 31.

42. Winston Churchill, House of Commons, August 20, 1940.

43. Adams, *Best War Ever,* 69.

44. Nemerov, *War Stories,* 29.

45. Ibid., 30.

46. Margaret Nemerov interview.

47. Nemerov, *War Stories,* 29.

48. Fussell, *Wartime,* 165.

49. Ibid., 28.

50. Jarrell, *Complete Poems,* 145.

51. Fussell, *Wartime,* 26.

52. Jarrell, "Fifty Years of American Poetry," 314.

Conclusion

1. Melville, "March into Virginia."

2. *Randall Jarrell Reads and Discusses His Poems against War.* In *Wartime,* Paul Fussell devotes a chapter, "School of the Soldier," to the notion that the army was a continuation of high school (52–65).

3. Melville, "March into Virginia," 66.

4. Fussell, *Wartime,* 10.

5. Melville, "March into Virginia," 66.

6. Ibid., 65–66.

7. Ibid., 65, 66.

8. Lowell, *Collected Poems,* 21.

9. Lowell, typescript draft of "Christmas Eve under Hooker's Statue," Robert Lowell Papers, Houghton Library, Harvard University.

10. Jarrell, holograph remarks on Robert Lowell, typescript draft of "Christmas Eve under Hooker's Statue," Robert Lowell Papers, Houghton Library, Harvard University.

11. Lowell, *Collected Poems,* 21.

12. Ibid.

13. Auden, "Private Poet," 319.

14. Ibid., 317.

15. Travisano, *Midcentury Quartet,* 119.

16. Auden, "Private Poet," 317.

17. Lowell, *Collected Poems,* 21.

18. Jarrell, *Randall Jarrell's Letters,* 128.

19. Kirstein, *Rhymes and More Rhymes,* 106.

20. Clark, interview by Ian Hamilton, November 1979, Blair Clark Papers, University of Texas at Austin.

21. Lowell, *Letters of Robert Lowell,* 427.

22. Shapiro, holograph notes in "Black leatherette ring binder," Karl Shapiro Papers, University of Texas at Austin.

23. Hirsch, "One Life, One Writing!" 10.

24. Lowell, "Death and the Maiden" Robert Lowell Papers, Houghton Library, Harvard University.

25. Stafford, *Every War Has Two Losers,* 145.

26. Meredith, *Effort at Speech,* 153.

27. As Bell argues in *Robert Lowell,* "man in time is old, and therefore responsible, but doomed by his nature to continue to despoil his original Eden" (22).

28. Wilbur made this statement in an editorial called "For the Record" in the *Amherst Student,* May 22, 1941. Quoted in Lancaster and Hagstrom, "Richard Wilbur's Early Writing," 27.

29. Fussell, *Wartime,* 10.

30. Shapiro, "Death of Randall Jarrell," 203.

31. Ryan, "Interview with Alan Dugan," 96.

32. Chattarji, *Memories of a Lost War,* 109.

33. Shapiro, "Death of Randall Jarrell," 222.

34. Ibid., 221–22.

35. Featherstone, *War Poetry,* 110.

36. Douglas, *Alamein to Zem Zem,* 15.

37. Shires, *British Poetry of the Second World War,* 110.

38. Even Dickey, who of his generation of poets wanted to become a military hero the most, seemed to be taken aback that Douglas was such "a superlatively good soldier" and was so "interested in any and all kinds of experiences, even when it involved his own terrible pain." Dickey considered himself "typical" and Douglas a "curiosity." See Dickey *Classes on Modern Poets,* 81

39. Jarrell, *Randall Jarrell's Letters,* 81.

40. Meredith, *Effort at Speech,* 176.

41. Ibid.

42. Ibid. Travisano analyzes in *Midcentury Quartet* the importance of Anne Frank to Berryman and shows how her diary offered a model for Berryman's own exploration of childhood (80–83).

43. Lovill, "At Home with Words," 47.

44. Auden, *Collected Poems,* 248.

45. Nemerov, *Collected Poems,* 424.

46. Bishop, *Collected Poems,* 35.

47. Nemerov, *War Stories,* 31.

48. Brokaw, *Greatest Generation,* xix.

49. Axelrod, "Counter-Memory in American Poetry," 20.

50. Ibid., 20–21. Thomas Travisano agrees and, referring to Jean-François Lyotard's *The Postmodern Condition,* links such a preference in postwar American poets for "pluralistic or multivalent" narratives rather than a "single 'master narrative'" or a "single 'totalizing perspective'" to the postmodern condition (*Midcentury Quartet,* 25).

51. Beidler, *The Good War's Greatest Hits,* 3.

52. Brokaw, *Greatest Generation,* 390.

53. Lovill, "At Home with Words," 47.

54. Brokaw, *Greatest Generation,* 388.

55. Ibid.

56. Shapiro, "Death of Randall Jarrell," 222.

57. Lowell, *Letters of Robert Lowell,* 338.

58. Hugo, *Making Certain It Goes On,* 279.

59. Nemerov, *War Stories,* 6.

60. Hecht, *Hidden Law,* 437.

61. Auden, "Private Poet," 317.

62. Melville, "A Utilitarian View of the Monitor's Fight," in Goldensohn, *American War Poetry,* 68.

63. Hass, *Carried to the Wall,* 60.

64. Kirstein to Harry Duncan, October 12, 1954, Harry Duncan Papers, Emory University.

65. Nemerov, "D Day plus 20 years."

BIBLIOGRAPHY

Adams, Michael C. C. *The Best War Ever: America and World War II.* Baltimore: Johns Hopkins University Press, 1994.

Allen, Craig. *Eisenhower and the Mass Media: Peace, Prosperity, & Prime-Time TV.* Chapel Hill: University of North Carolina Press, 1993.

Anderson, Doug. *The Moon Reflected Fire.* Cambridge, Mass.: Alice James Books, 1994.

Auden, W. H. *The Ascent of F6.* London: Faber and Faber, 1936.

———. *Collected Poems.* 1976. Reprint, New York: Random House, 1991.

———. "Private Poet." In *The Poems of Lincoln Kirstein,* edited by Lincoln Kirstein, 317–20. New York: Atheneum, 1987.

———. "The Public v. the Late Mr. William Butler Yeats." In *The Complete Works of W. H. Auden.* Vol. 2, *1939–1948,* edited by Edward Mendelson, 3–7. Princeton, N.J.: Princeton University Press, 2002.

Axelrod, Steven Gould. "Counter-Memory in American Poetry." In *Tales of the Great American Victory: World War II in Politics and Poetics,* edited by Diederik Oostdijk and Markha G. Valenta, 19–35. Amsterdam: VU University Press, 2006.

———. "Gwendolyn Brooks and the Middle Generation." In *Jarrell, Bishop, Lowell & Co.: Middle-Generation Poets in Context,* edited by Suzanne Ferguson, 26–40. Knoxville: University of Tennessee Press, 2003.

———. "The Middle Generation and WWII: Jarrell, Shapiro, Brooks, Bishop, Lowell." *War, Literature & the Arts* 11, no. 1 (1999): 1–41.

———. *Robert Lowell: Life and Art.* Princeton, N.J.: Princeton University Press, 1978.

Baer, William. "'It Out-Herods Herod. Pray You, Avoid It.': An Interview with Anthony Hecht." *Formalist* 15, no. 1 (2004): 57–68.

Bartlett, Lee, and Hugh Witemeyer. "Ezra Pound and James Dickey: A Correspondence and a Kinship." *Paideuma* 11, no. 2 (1982): 290–312.

Barry, Sandra. "Elizabeth Bishop and World War I." *War, Literature and the Arts* 11, no. 1 (1999): 93–110.

Baughman, Ronald. *Understanding James Dickey.* Columbia: University of South Carolina Press, 1985.

Beck, Charlotte H. "Beyond the Anxiety of Influence: Randall Jarrell and Allen Tate." In *The Vanderbilt Tradition: Essays in Honor of Thomas Daniel Young,* edited by Mark Royden Winchell, 71–83. Baton Rouge: Louisiana State University Press, 1991.

Beidler, Philip D. *The Good War's Greatest Hits.* Athens: University of Georgia Press, 1998.

Bell, Dean Philip. *Sacred Communities: Jewish and Christian Identities in Fifteenth-Century Europe.* Leiden: Brill, 2001.

Bell, Vereen M. *Robert Lowell: Nihilist as Hero.* Cambridge, Mass.: Harvard University Press, 1983.

Bellamy, Dawn. "'Others Have Come Before You': The Influence of Great War Poetry on Second World War Poets." In *The Oxford Handbook of British & Irish War Poetry,* edited by Tim Kendall, 299–314. Oxford: Oxford University Press, 2007.

Bernstein, R. B. *Thomas Jefferson: The Revolution of Ideas.* New York: Oxford University Press, 2004.

Berryman, John. *Collected Poems: 1937–1971.* New York: Farrar, Straus & Giroux, 1991.

———. "The Development of Anne Frank." In *Anne Frank: Reflections on Her Life and Legacy,* edited by Hyman A. Enzer and Sandra Solotaroff-Enzer, 76–80. Urbana: University of Illinois Press, 2000.

———. *Recovery.* New York: Thunder's Mouth, 1993.

Bishop, Elizabeth. *Collected Poems, 1927–1979.* New York: Farrar, Straus & Giroux, 1983.

———. *The Collected Prose.* New York: Farrar, Straus & Giroux, 1984.

Bly, Robert. "The Collapse of James Dickey." In *Critical Essays on James Dickey,* edited by Robert Kirschten, 33–38. New York: G. K. Hall, 1994.

Boly, John R. *Reading Auden: The Returns of Caliban.* Ithaca, N.Y.: Cornell University Press, 1991.

Bosworth, Patricia. *Diane Arbus: A Biography.* New York: Alfred A. Knopf, 1984.

Bowen, Roger. *"Many Histories Deep": The Personal Landscape Poets in Egypt, 1940–45.* Madison, N.J.: Fairleigh Dickinson University Press, 1995.

Boyers, Robert. "An Interview with Howard Nemerov." *Salmagundi* 31–32 (1975–1976): 109–19.

Brinkley, Douglas. "Commentary: Lack of More Great Battlefield Poetry from the World War II Era." *Weekend Edition Sunday,* National Public Radio, November 28, 1999.

Brokaw, Tom. *The Greatest Generation.* New York: Random House, 1998.

Brooks, Gwendolyn. *Selected Poems.* New York: Perennial Classics, 1999.

Brooks, Van Wyck. *Opinions of Oliver Allston.* New York: E. P. Dutton, 1941.

Broughton, Irv. "An Interview with Richard Wilbur." In *Conversations with Richard Wilbur,* edited by William Butts, 125–45. Jackson: University Press of Mississippi, 1990.

Brunner, Edward. *Cold War Poetry.* Urbana: University of Illinois Press, 2001.

Burt, Stephen. "Introduction." In *Randall Jarrell on W. H. Auden,* edited by Stephen Burt with Hannah Brooks-Motl, 1–17. New York: Columbia University Press, 2005.

———. *Randall Jarrell and His Age.* New York: Columbia University Press, 2002.

Carlsson-Paige, Nancy, and Diane E. Levin. *The War Play Dilemma: Balancing Needs and Values in the Early Childhood Classroom.* New York: Teachers College Press, 1987.

Carruth, Hayden. *Collected Shorter Poems.* Port Townsend, Wash.: Copper Canyon Press, 1991.

———. *Selected Essays & Reviews.* Port Townsend, Wash.: Copper Canyon Press, 1996.

Caruth, Cathy. *Unclaimed Experience: Trauma, Narrative, and History.* Baltimore: Johns Hopkins University Press, 1996.

Chattarji, Subarno. *Memories of a Lost War: American Poetic Responses to the Vietnam War.* New York: Oxford University Press, 2001.

Ciardi, John. "About Being Born, and Surviving It." In *John Ciardi: Measure of the Man,* edited by Vince Clemente, 3–19. Fayetteville: University of Arkansas Press, 1987.

———. Ciardi Papers. Correspondence, drafts, unpublished papers. Library of Congress, Washington, D.C.

———. *The Collected Poems of John Ciardi.* Edited by Edward M. Cifelli. Fayetteville: University of Arkansas Press, 1997.

———. *Lives of X.* New Brunswick, N.J.: Rutgers University Press, 1971.

———, ed. *Mid-Century American Poets.* New York: Twayne, 1950.

———. *Saipan: The War Diary of John Ciardi.* Edited by Edward M. Cifelli. Fayetteville: University of Arkansas Press, 1988.

Cifelli, Edward M. *John Ciardi: A Biography.* Fayetteville: University of Arkansas Press, 1997.

Clabough, Casey, *Elements: The Novels of James Dickey.* Macon, Ga.: Mercer University Press, 2002.

Clark, Blair. Clark Papers. Unpublished papers. Harry Ransom Humanities Center, University of Texas at Austin.

Cordray, Robert M. Foreword. In *Saipan: The War Diary of John Ciardi,* edited by Edward M. Cifelli, xxiii–xxiv. Fayetteville: University of Arkansas Press, 1988.

Costello, Bonnie. "1930–1934: The Poet in Brooklyn." In *The Selected Letters of Marianne Moore,* edited by Bonnie Costello, 251–55. New York: Penguin Books, 1997.

Cox, Joseph T. "Richard Wilbur: An Interview." *War, Literature & the Arts* 10, no. 1 (1998): 7–21.

Crane, Stephen. *The Red Badge of Courage and Other Stories.* New York: Penguin Books, 1991.

Dana, Robert. *Against the Grain: Interviews with Maverick American Publishers.* Iowa City: University of Iowa Press, 1986.

D'Emilio, John, and Estelle B. Freedman. *Intimate Matters: A History of Sexuality in America.* New York: Harper & Row, 1988.

Dickey, James. *Alnilam.* New York: Doubleday, 1987.

———. *Babel to Byzantium: Poets & Poetry Now.* New York: Grosset & Dunlap, 1971.

———. *Classes on Modern Poets and the Art of Poetry.* Edited by Donald J. Greiner. Columbia: University of South Carolina Press, 2004.

———. *Crux: The Letters of James Dickey.* Edited by Mathew J. Bruccoli and Judith S. Baughman. New York: Alfred A. Knopf, 1999.

———. Dickey Papers. Correspondence, drafts, unpublished papers. Department of Special Collections, Washington University Libraries, St. Louis.

———. Dickey Papers. Correspondence, drafts, unpublished papers. Manuscript, Archives, and Rare Book Library, Emory University, Atlanta.

———. *The James Dickey Reader.* Edited by Henry Hart. New York: Touchstone, 1999.

———. "Joel Cahill Dead." *Beloit Poetry Journal* 8, no. 4 (1958): 18–19.

———. *Self-Interviews.* Edited by Barbara and James Reiss. New York: Doubleday, 1970.

———. *Striking In: The Early Notebooks.* Edited by Gordon Van Ness. Columbia: University of Missouri Press, 1996.

———. *To the White Sea.* Boston: Houghton Mifflin, 1993.

———. *The Whole Motion: Collected Poems, 1945–1992.* Hanover, N.H.: Wesleyan University Press, 1992.

Doherty, Thomas. *Projections of War: Hollywood, American Culture, and World War II.* New York: Columbia University Press, 1993.

Donaldson, Scott. *Archibald MacLeish: An American Life.* Boston: Houghton Mifflin, 1991.

Doreski, William. *The Years of Our Friendship: Robert Lowell and Allen Tate.* Jackson: University Press of Mississippi, 1990.

Dostoyevsky, Fyodor. *Crime and Punishment.* Translated by David McDuff. New York: Penguin Classics, 2003.

Douglas, Keith. *Alamein to Zem Zem.* Oxford: Oxford University Press, 1979.

Dower, John W. *Embracing Defeat: Japan in the Wake of World War II.* New York: Norton / The New Press, 1999.

———. *War without Mercy: Race & Power in the Pacific War.* New York: Pantheon Books, 1986.

Duberman, Martin. *The Worlds of Lincoln Kirstein.* New York: Alfred A. Knopf, 2007.

Dugan, Alan. *Poems Seven: New and Complete Poetry.* New York: Seven Stories Press, 2001.

Duncan, Harry. Duncan Papers. Correspondence. Department of Special Collections, Washington University Libraries, St. Louis.

Eliot, T. S. *After Strange Gods.* London: Faber and Faber, 1934.

———. *Collected Poems: 1909–1962.* New York: Harcourt Brace, 1963.

———. *For Lancelot Andrews: Essays on Style and Order.* London: Faber & Gwyer, 1928.

———. *Selected Essays.* London: Faber and Faber, 1949.

Eller, Cynthia. *Conscientious Objectors and the Second World War: Moral and Religious Arguments in Support of Pacifism.* Westport, Conn.: Praeger, 1991.

Emerson, Ralph Waldo. "Ode, Inscribed to W. H. Channing." In *American War Poetry: An Anthology,* edited by Lorrie Goldensohn, 42–45. New York: Columbia University Press, 2006.

Featherstone, Simon. *War Poetry: An Introductory Reader.* New York: Routledge, 1995.

Ferguson, Suzanne. *The Poetry of Randall Jarrell.* Baton Rouge: Louisiana State University Press, 1971.

———. "Preface." In *Jarrell, Bishop, Lowell & Co.: Middle-Generation Poets in*

Context, edited by Suzanne Ferguson, ix–xxxi. Knoxville: University of Tennessee Press, 2003.

Flanzbaum, Hilene. "The Imaginary Jew and the American Poet." In *The Americanization of the Holocaust,* edited by Hilene Flanzbaum, 18–32. Baltimore: Johns Hopkins University Press, 1999.

Flory, Wendy Stallard. "Pound and Antisemitism." In *The Cambridge Companion to Ezra Pound,* edited by Ira B. Nadel, 284–300. Cambridge: Cambridge University Press, 1999.

Flynn, Richard. "'Infant Sight': Romanticism, Childhood, and Postmodern Poetry." In *Literature and the Child: Romantic Continuations, Postmodern Contestations,* edited by James Holt McGavran, 105–29. Iowa City: University of Iowa Press, 1999.

———. *Randall Jarrell and the Lost World of Childhood.* Athens: University of Georgia Press, 1990.

Foa, Anna. *The Jews of Europe after the Black Death.* Translated by Andrea Grover. Berkeley: University of California Press, 2000.

Furbank, P. N. *E. M. Forster: A Life.* Vol. 2. London: Secker and Warburg, 1978.

Fussell, Paul. *The Great War and Modern Memory.* New York: Oxford University Press, 1975.

———. "Introduction." In *Articles of War: A Collection of Poetry about World War II,* edited by Leon Stokesbury, xxiii–xxix. Fayetteville: University of Arkansas Press, 1990.

———. *Wartime: Understanding and Behavior in the Second World War.* New York: Oxford University Press, 1989.

Ginsberg, Allen. *Collected Poems: 1947–1980.* New York: Harper & Row, 1984.

Goethe, Johann Wolfgang von. "On German Architecture (1772)." Translated by John Gage. In *Goethe on Art,* edited by John Gage, 103–12. London: Scolar Press, 1980.

Goldensohn, Lorrie, ed. *American War Poetry: An Anthology.* New York: Columbia University Press, 2006.

———. *Dismantling Glory: Twentieth-Century Soldier Poetry.* New York: Columbia University Press, 2003.

———. "The War Poetry of James Dickey." In *The Way We Read James Dickey: Critical Approaches for the Twenty-first Century,* edited by William B. Thesing and Theda Wrede, 151–61. Columbia: University of South Carolina Press, 2009.

Goldstein, Joshua S. *War and Gender: How Gender Shapes the War System and Vice Versa.* Cambridge: Cambridge University Press, 2001.

Gray, J. Glenn. *The Warriors: Reflections on Men in Battle.* Lincoln: University of Nebraska Press, 1998.

Gubar, Susan. *Poetry after Auschwitz: Remembering What One Never Knew.* Bloomington: Indiana University Press, 2003.

Hamilton, Ian. *Robert Lowell: A Biography.* New York: Random House, 1982.

Haralson, Eric. "Introduction." In *Reading the Middle Generation Anew: Culture, Community, and Form in Twentieth-Century American Poetry,* edited by Eric Haralson, 1–11. Iowa City: University of Iowa Press, 2006.

Hardy, Thomas. *Selected Poems.* New York: Penguin Books, 1998.

Hart, Henry. *James Dickey: The World as a Lie.* New York: Picador USA, 2000.

Hathcock, Nelson. "No Further Claim to Innocence: James Dickey's Revision of the American War Story." *Texas Review* 17, nos. 3–4 (1996/1997): 26–42.

———. "'Standardizing Catastrophe': Randall Jarrell and the Bomb." In *Jarrell, Bishop, Lowell & Co.: Middle-Generation Poets in Context,* edited by Suzanne Ferguson, 113–25. Knoxville: University of Tennessee Press, 2003.

Haughton, Hugh. "Anthologizing War." In *The Oxford Handbook of British & Irish War Poetry,* edited by Tim Kendall, 421–44. Oxford: Oxford University Press, 2007.

Hecht, Anthony. *Collected Earlier Poems.* New York: Alfred A. Knopf, 1990.

———. *Collected Later Poems.* New York: Alfred A. Knopf, 2003.

———. "Commentary." In *Jewish American Poetry: Poems, Commentary, and Reflections,* edited by Jonathan N. Barron and Eric Murphy Selinger, 80–83. Hanover, N.H.: Brandeis University Press, 2000.

———. "Dear Editor." *Poetry: A Magazine of Verse* 183, no. 2 (2003): 105–6.

———. "A Few Green Leaves." *Sewanee Review* 47, no. 1 (1960): 568–571.

———. Hecht Papers. Correspondence, drafts, unpublished papers. Manuscript, Archives, and Rare Book Library, Emory University, Atlanta.

———. *The Hidden Law: The Poetry of W. H. Auden.* Cambridge, Mass.: Harvard University Press, 1993.

———. *Obbligati: Essays in Criticism.* New York: Atheneum, 1986.

Hillyer, Robert. "Poetry's New Priesthood." *Saturday Review of Literature* 32 (June 18, 1949): 8–10, 38.

Hirsch, Edward. "Comedy and Hardship." In *The Burdens of Formality: Essays on the Poetry of Anthony Hecht,* edited by Sydney Lea, 53–61. Athens: University of Georgia Press, 1989.

———. "One Life, One Writing! The Middle Generation." In *Jarrell, Bishop, Lowell & Co.: Middle-Generation Poets in Context,* edited by Suzanne Ferguson, 3–25. Knoxville: University of Tennessee Press, 2003.

Hölbling, Walter. "The Second World War: American Writing." In *The Cambridge Companion to War Writing,* edited by Kate McLoughlin, 212–24. Cambridge: Cambridge University Press, 2009.

Homer. *The Iliad.* Translated by Robert Fitzgerald. New York: Farrar, Straus & Giroux, 1975.

Howard, Michael. *War in European History.* Oxford: Oxford University Press, 2001.

Hoy, Philip. *Anthony Hecht in Conversation.* London: Between the Lines, 1999.

Hughes, Langston. *The Collected Poems of Langston Hughes.* New York: Vintage, 1995.

Hugo, Richard. *Making Certain It Goes On: The Collected Poems.* New York: Norton, 1984.

———. *The Real West Marginal Way: A Poet's Autobiography.* New York: Norton, 1986.

Hutton, Joan. "Interview with Richard Wilbur." In *Conversations with Richard Wilbur,* edited by William Butts, 46–55. Jackson: University Press of Mississippi, 1990.

"An Interview with James Dickey." In *The Voiced Connections of James Dickey: Interviews and Connections,* edited by Ronald Baughman, 12–27. Columbia: University of South Carolina Press, 1989.

James, Jennifer C. *A Freedom Bought with Blood: African American Literature from the Civil War to World War II.* Chapel Hill: University of North Carolina Press, 2007.

Janssen, Marian. *The Kenyon Review, 1939–1970: A Critical History.* Baton Rouge: Louisiana State University Press, 1990.

Jarrell, Randall. "Answers to Questions." In *Mid-Century American Poets,* edited by John Ciardi, 182–84. New York: Twayne, 1950.

———. *Blood for a Stranger.* New York: Harcourt Brace, 1942.

———. *The Complete Poems.* New York: Farrar, Straus & Giroux, 1969.

———. Jarrell Papers. Correspondence, drafts, unpublished papers. Berg Collection, New York Public Library.

———. Jarrell Papers. Drafts, unpublished papers. Special Collections & University Archives, University Libraries, University of North Carolina at Greensboro.

———. *Kipling, Auden & Co.: Essays and Reviews, 1935–1964.* New York: Farrar, Straus & Giroux, 1980.

———. "Levels and Opposites: Structure in Poetry." *Georgia Review* 50, no. 4 (1996): 697–713.

———. *On W. H. Auden.* Edited by Stephen Burt with Hannah Brooks-Motl. New York: Columbia University Press, 2005.

———. *Pictures from an Institution.* New York: Alfred A. Knopf, 1954.

———. *Poetry and the Age.* New York: Farrar, Straus & Giroux, 1953.

———. *Randall Jarrell Reads and Discusses His Poems against War.* Recorded April 30, 1961. Caedmon SWC1363, 1972. Audiocassette.

———. *Randall Jarrell's Letters.* Edited by Mary Jarrell. Boston: Houghton Mifflin, 1985.

———. *The Third Book of Criticism.* New York: Farrar, Straus & Giroux, 1969.

Jarvis, Christina S. *The Male Body at War: American Masculinity during World War II.* De Kalb: Northern Illinois University Press, 2004.

Julius, Anthony. *T. S. Eliot, Anti-Semitism, and Literary Form.* Cambridge: Cambridge University Press, 1995.

Kalstone, David. *Becoming a Poet: Elizabeth Bishop with Marianne Moore and Robert Lowell.* New York: Farrar Straus Giroux, 1989.

Kaufman, Janet. "'But not the study': Writing as a Jew." In *"How Shall We Tell Each Other of the Poet?": The Life and Writing of Muriel Rukeyser,* edited by Anne F. Herzog and Janet E. Kaufman, 45–61. New York: St. Martin's Press, 1999.

Keller, Lynn. *Re-making It New: Contemporary American Poetry and the Modernist Tradition.* Cambridge: Cambridge University Press, 1987.

Kendall, Tim. *Modern English War Poetry.* New York: Oxford University Press, 2006.

Kirstein, Lincoln. Kirstein Papers. Unpublished papers. Jerome Robbins Dance Division, New York Public Library.

———. *The Poems of Lincoln Kirstein.* New York: Atheneum, 1987.

———. *Rhymes and More Rhymes of a PFC.* New York: New Directions, 1966.

Komunyakaa, Yusef. *Warhorses.* New York: Farrar, Straus & Giroux, 2009.

Kunitz, Stanley. *Interviews and Encounters with Stanley Kunitz.* Edited by Stanley Moss. River-on-Hudson, N.Y.: Sheep Meadow Press, 1993.

Lancaster, John, and Jack W. C. Hagstrom. "Richard Wilbur's Early Writing: Amherst College and World War II." *War, Literature & the Arts* 10, no. 1 (1998): 24–36.

Levy, William Turner, and Victor Scherle. *Affectionately, T. S. Eliot.* London: J. M. Dent, 1969.

Lewis, C. Day. *The Complete Poems.* Stanford, Calif.: Stanford University Press, 1992.

Linderman, Gerald F. *The World within War: America's Combat Experience in World War II.* Cambridge, Mass.: Harvard University Press, 1997.

Lindsay, Geoffrey. "Anthony Hecht, Private First Class." *Yale Review* 96, no. 3 (2008): 1–26.

Longenbach, James. *Modern Poetry after Modernism.* New York: Oxford University Press, 1997.

Lovill, Jeff. "At Home with Words: An Interview with John Ciardi." *New Letters* 54, no. 1 (1987): 46–63.

Lowell, Robert. *Collected Poems.* New York: Farrar, Straus & Giroux, 2003.

———. *Collected Prose.* New York: Farrar, Straus & Giroux, 1987.

———. *The Letters of Robert Lowell.* Edited by Saskia Hamilton. New York: Farrar, Straus & Giroux, 2005.

———. Lowell Papers. Correspondence, drafts, unpublished papers. Houghton Library, Harvard University, Cambridge, Mass.

———. Lowell Papers. Drafts, unpublished papers, Harry Ransom Humanities Center, Austin, Tex.

———. "War: A Justification." *Vindex* 59, no. 6 (1935): 156–58.

MacLeish, Archibald. *The Irresponsibles: A Declaration.* New York: Duell, Sloan and Pearce, 1940.

Mariani, Paul. *Dream Song: The Life of John Berryman.* Amherst: University of Massachusetts Press, 1990.

———. *Lost Puritan: A Life of Robert Lowell.* New York: Norton, 1994.

Matheson, Peter. *The Third Reich and the Christian Churches.* Edinburgh: T. & T. Clark, 1981.

Mendelson, Edward. *Early Auden.* New York: Farrar, Straus & Giroux, 1981.

———. *Later Auden.* New York: Farrar, Straus & Giroux, 1999.

Meredith, William. *Effort at Speech: New and Selected Poems.* Evanston, Ill.: Triquarterly Books / Northwestern University Press, 1997.

Metres Philip. *Behind the Lines: War Resistance Poetry on the American Homefront since 1941.* Iowa City: University of Iowa Press, 2007.

Michelson, Bruce. "Randall Jarrell and Robert Lowell: The Making of *Lord Weary's Castle.*" *Contemporary Literature* 26, no. 4 (1985): 402–25.

Moore, Marianne. *The Complete Poems of Marianne Moore.* New York: Macmillan, 1981.

———. *The Selected Letters of Marianne Moore.* Edited by Bonnie Costello. New York: Knopf, 1997.

Morris, Roy, Jr. *The Better Angel: Walt Whitman in the Civil War.* New York: Oxford University Press, 2000.

Nakano, Jiro, and Kay (Nakano) Yokoyama, eds. and trans. *Poets behind Barbed Wire.* Honolulu: Bamboo Ridge Press, 1983.

Nemerov, Alexander. "Modeling My Father." *American Scholar* 62, no. 4 (1993): 551–61.

Nemerov, Howard. *The Collected Poems of Howard Nemerov.* Chicago: University of Chicago Press, 1977.

———. *Inside the Onion.* Chicago: University of Chicago Press, 1984.

———. "The Jewish Writer and the English Literary Tradition." *Commentary* 8, no. 3 (1949): 216.

———. *Journal of the Fictive Life.* New Brunswick, N.J.: Rutgers University Press, 1965.

———. Nemerov Papers. Correspondence. Alexander Nemerov, New Haven, Conn.

———. Nemerov Papers. Correspondence, drafts, unpublished papers. Department of Special Collections, Washington University Libraries, St. Louis.

———. *The Oak in the Acorn: On Remembrance of Things Past and on Teaching Proust, Who Will Never Learn.* Baton Rouge: Louisiana State University Press, 1987.

———. *Sentences.* Chicago: University of Chicago Press, 1980.

———. *War Stories: Poems about Long Ago and Now.* Chicago: University of Chicago Press, 1987.

Norris, Margot. "War Poetry in the USA." In *The Cambridge Companion to the Literature of World War II,* edited by Marina Mackay, 43–55. Cambridge: Cambridge University Press, 2009.

Novick, Peter. *The Holocaust in American Life.* Boston: Houghton Mifflin, 1999.

Owen, Wilfred. *The Collected Poems.* New York: New Directions, 1963.

Post, Jonathan F. S. "The Genesis of Venice in Anthony Hecht's 'Venetian Vespers.'" *Hopkins Review* 3, no. 2 (2010): 166–87.

Pound, Ezra. *The Cantos.* New York: New Directions, 1970.

———. Pound Papers. Correspondence. Beinecke Library, Yale University, New Haven, Conn.

Press, Rebecca. "Interview with Howard Nemerov." *New Letters on the Air.* Kansas City, Mo., 1990. Audiocassette.

Pritchard, William H. *Randall Jarrell: A Literary Life.* New York: Farrar, Straus & Giroux, 1990.

Ransom, John Crowe. "Criticism Inc." In *20th Century Literary Criticism: A Reader,* edited by David Lodge, 228–39. New York: Longman, 1996.

Reidel, James. *Vanished Act: The Life and Art of Weldon Kees.* Lincoln: University of Nebraska Press, 2003.

Robertson, Nan. "Johnson Dislikes His Likeness: Terms Portrait 'Ugliest Thing I Ever Saw.'" *New York Times,* January 6, 1967.

Robinson, Peter. "'Down in the Terraces between the Targets': Civilians." In *The Oxford Handbook of British & Irish War Poetry,* edited by Tim Kendall, 504–23. Oxford: Oxford University Press, 2007.

Rukeyser, Muriel. *The Collected Poems.* Pittsburgh: University of Pittsburgh Press, 2005.

Ryan, Michael. "An Interview with Alan Dugan." *Iowa Review* 4, no. 3 (1973): 90–97.

Sansom, Ian. "'Flouting Papa': Randall Jarrell and W. H. Auden." In *"In Solitude, for Company": W. H. Auden after 1940,* edited by Katharine Bucknell and Nicholas Jenkins, 273–87. Oxford: Clarendon Press, 1995.

Santayana, George. *The Life of Reason: Or, the Phases of Human Progress.* New York: Charles Scribner's Sons, 1953.

Scannell, Vernon. *Not without Glory: Poets of the Second World War.* London: Woburn Press, 1976.

Schwartz, Delmore. *Letters of Delmore Schwartz.* Edited by Robert Phillips. Princeton, N.J.: Ontario Review Press, 1984.

Schweik, Susan. *A Gulf So Deeply Cut: American Women Poets and the Second World War.* Madison: University of Wisconsin Press, 1991.

Shapiro, Harvey. "Introduction." In *Poets of World War II,* edited by Harvey Shapiro, xix–xxxii. New York: Library of America, 2003.

———, ed. *Poets of World War II.* New York: Library of America, 2003.

Shapiro, Karl. *The Bourgeois Poet.* New York: Random House, 1964.

———. *Coda: Last Poems.* Huntsville: Texas Review Press, 2008.

———. "The Death of Randall Jarrell." In *Randall Jarrell: 1914–1965,* edited by Robert Lowell, Peter Taylor, and Robert Penn Warren, 195–229. New York: Farrar, Straus & Giroux, 1967.

———. *Essay on Rime with Trial of a Poet.* Ann Arbor: University of Michigan Press, 2004.

———. "He-Man." *New Yorker,* December 1, 1945, 42.

———. *In Defense of Ignorance.* New York: Random House, 1960.

———. *Person, Place, and Thing.* New York: Reynal & Hitchcock, 1942.

———. *The Place of Love.* Malvern, Victoria: Bradley Printers, 1942.

———. "The Poet as Hero." *Chicago Daily News, Panorama,* March 18, 1967, 7.

———. *Selected Poems.* Edited by John Updike. New York: Library of America, 2003.

———. Shapiro Papers. Correspondence. Special Collections, University of Maryland Library, College Park.

———. Shapiro Papers. Correspondence, drafts, unpublished papers. Harry Ransom Humanities Center, Austin, Tex.

———. *V-Letter and Other Poems.* New York: Reynal & Hitchcock, 1944.

———. *The Younger Son.* Chapel Hill, N.C.: Algonquin Books, 1988.

Shephard, Ben. *A War of Nerves: Soldiers and Psychiatry, 1914–1994.* London: Pimlico, 2000.

Shiach, Morag. "'To Purify the dialect of the tribe': Modernism and Language Reform." *Modernism/modernity* 14, no. 1 (2007): 21–34.

Shires, Linda M. *British Poetry of the Second World War.* New York: St. Martin's Press, 1985.

Simic, Charles. *A Fly in the Soup: Memoirs.* Ann Arbor: University of Michigan Press, 2000.

Simpson, Eileen. *Poets in Their Youth.* London: Faber and Faber, 1982.

Simpson, Louis. *Air with Armed Men.* London: London Magazine Editions, 1972.

———. *The King My Father's Wreck.* Brownsville, Ore.: Story Line Press, 1995.

———. *The Owner of the House: New Collected Poems, 1940–2001.* Rochester, N.Y.: BOA Editions, 2003.

———. *Selected Prose.* New York: Paragon House, 1989.

Smith, Ernest J. "'Approaching Our Maturity'": The Dialectic of Engagement and Withdrawal in the Political Poetry of Berryman and Lowell." In *Jarrell, Bishop, Lowell & Co.: Middle-Generation Poets in Context,* edited by Suzanne Ferguson, 287–302. Knoxville: University of Tennessee Press, 2003.

Smith, William Jay. *Army Brat: A Memoir.* New York: Persea Books, 1980.

Snodgrass, W. D. *The Fuehrer Bunker: The Complete Cycle.* Brockport, N.Y.: BOA Editions, 1995.

———. *Not for Specialists: New and Selected Poems.* Rochester, N.Y.: BOA Editions, 2006.

Spargo, R. Clifton. "The Ethical Uselessness of Grief: Randall Jarrell's 'The Refugees.'" *PMLA* 120, no. 1 (2005): 49–65.

———. *The Ethics of Mourning: Grief and Responsibility in Elegiac Literature.* Baltimore: John Hopkins University Press, 2004.

Stafford, Jean. "Some Letters to Peter and Eleanor Taylor." *Shenandoah* 30, no. 3 (1979): 27–55.

Stafford, Kim, *Early Morning: Remembering My Father, William Stafford.* St. Paul, Minn.: Graywolf Press, 2002.

Stafford, William. *Down in My Heart: Peace Witness in War Time.* Corvallis: Oregon State University Press, 2006.

———. *Every War Has Two Losers: On Peace and War.* Edited by Kim Stafford. Minneapolis, Minn.: Milkweed, 2003.

———. *The Way It Is: New & Selected Poems.* St. Paul, Minn.: Graywolf Press, 1998.

Stallworthy, Jon, ed. *The Oxford Book of War Poetry.* New York: Oxford University Press, 1984.

Stavros, George. "An Interview with Gwendolyn Brooks." In *Conversations with Gwendolyn Brooks,* edited by Gloria Wade Gayles, 37–53. Jackson: University Press of Mississippi, 2003.

Stokesbury, Leon, ed. *Articles of War: A Collection of Poetry about World War II.* Fayetteville: University of Arkansas Press, 1990.

Stout, Janis P. *Coming Out of War: Poetry, Grieving, and the Culture of the World Wars.* Tuscaloosa: University of Alabama Press, 2005.

Suarez, Ernest. "An Interview with James Dickey." *Contemporary Literature* 31, no. 2 (1990): 117–32.

Tate, Allen. Allen Tate Papers. Correspondence, drafts, unpublished papers. Manuscript Division, Department of Rare Books and Special Collections, Princeton University Library, Princeton, N.J.

———. *Collected Essays.* Denver: Alan Swallow, 1959.

———. *Collected Poems: 1919–1976.* New York: Farrar, Straus & Giroux, 1977.

———. *The Lytle-Tate Letters: The Correspondence of Andrew Lytle and Allen Tate.* Edited by Thomas Daniel Young and Elizabeth Sarcone. Jackson: University Press of Mississippi, 1987.

———. *The Poetry Reviews of Allen Tate: 1924–1944.* Edited by Ashley Brown and Frances Neel Cheney. Baton Rouge: Louisiana State University Press, 1983.

———. "Young Randall." In *Randall Jarrell: 1914–1965,* edited by Robert Lowell, Peter Taylor, and Robert Penn Warren, 230–32. New York: Straus & Giroux, 1967.

Taylor, Henry. "Gwendolyn Brooks: An Essential Sanity." In *On Gwendolyn Brooks: Reliant Contemplation,* edited by Stephen Caldwell Wright, 254–76. Ann Arbor: University of Michigan Press, 2001.

Terence. *The Comedies.* Translated by Betty Radice. New York: Penguin Classics, 1976.

Terkel, Studs. *"The Good War": An American Oral History of World War II.* New York: Pantheon Books, 1984.

Tobin, James. *Ernie Pyle's War: America's Eyewitness to World War II.* Lawrence: University Press of Kansas, 1997.

Travisano, Thomas. *Elizabeth Bishop: Her Artistic Development.* Charlottesville: University Press of Virginia, 1988.

———. *Midcentury Quartet: Bishop, Lowell, Jarrell, Berryman and the Making of a Postmodern Aesthetic.* Charlottesville: University Press of Virginia, 1999.

Tyler, Parker. Tyler Papers. Correspondence. Harry Ransom Humanities Center, Austin, Tex.

Underwood, Thomas A. *Allen Tate: Orphan of the South.* Princeton, N.J.: Princeton University Press, 2000.

Van Wienen, Mark W. "Introduction." In *Rendezvous with Death: American Poems of the Great War,* edited by Mark Van Wienen, 1–36. Urbana: University of Illinois Press, 2002.

———. *Partisans and Poets: The Political Work of American Poetry in the Great War.* Cambridge: Cambridge University Press, 1997.

Vaughan, David K. *Words to Measure a War: Nine American Poets of World War II.* Jefferson, N.C.: McFarland, 2009.

Vendler, Helen. "Art, Heroism, and Poetry: The Shaw Memorial, Lowell's 'For the Union Dead,' and Berryman's 'Boston Common: A Meditation upon the Hero.'" In *Hope & Glory: Essays on the Legacy of the Fifty-fourth Massachusetts Regiment,* edited by Martin H. Blatt, Thomas J. Brown, and Donald Yacovone, 202–14. Amherst: University of Massachusetts Press, 2001.

———. *Part of Nature, Part of Us: Modern American Poets.* Cambridge, Mass.: Harvard University Press, 1980.

Viereck, Peter. *Metapolitics: From Wagner and the German Romantics to Hitler.* New Brunswick, N.J.: Transaction, 2004.

Waller, Willard. *The Veteran Comes Back.* New York: Dryden Press, 1944.

Walsh, Jeffrey. *American War Literature: 1914 to Vietnam.* New York: St. Martin's Press, 1982.

Wasley, Aidan. *The Age of Auden: Postwar American Poetry and the Scene.* Princeton: Princeton University Press, 2011.

Watson, Roderick. "'Death's Proletariat': Scottish Poets of the Second World War." In *The Oxford Handbook of British & Irish War Poetry*, edited by Tim Kendall, 315–39. Oxford: Oxford University Press, 2007.

Westbrook, Robert B. "'I Want a Girl, Just Like the Girl That Married Harry James': American Women and the Problem of Political Obligation in World War II." *American Quarterly* 42, no. 4 (1990): 587–614.

Whisenhunt, Donald W. *Poetry of the People: Poems to the President, 1929–1945*. Bowling Green, Ohio: Bowling Green State Popular Press, 1996.

Whitman, Walt. *Complete Poetry and Collected Prose*. New York: Library of America, 1982.

Whittemore, Reed. Whittemore Papers. Correspondence. Special Collections, University of Maryland Library, College Park.

Wilbur, Richard. *Collected Poems: 1943–2004*. New York: Harcourt, 2004.

———. "Richard Wilbur on Writing." In *Operation Homecoming: Writing the Wartime Experience*. National Endowment for the Arts NEA8270–CD, 2004.

Williams, William Carlos. *Selected Poems*. New York: New Directions, 1985.

Williamson, Alan. *Pity the Monsters: The Political Vision of Robert Lowell*. New Haven, Conn.: Yale University Press, 1974.

Winn, James Anderson. *The Poetry of War*. Cambridge: Cambridge University Press, 2008.

Wittgenstein, Ludwig. *Philosophical Investigations*. New York: Macmillan, 1958.

Wright, Stuart, ed. *Randall Jarrell: A Descriptive Bibliography, 1929–1983*. Charlottesville: University Press of Virginia, 1986.

Young, Thomas Daniel. *Gentleman in a Dustcoat: A Biography of John Crowe Ransom*. Baton Rouge: Louisiana State University Press, 1976.

Zertal, Idith. *Israel's Holocaust and the Politics of Nationhood*. Cambridge: Cambridge University Press, 2005.

INDEX

ABOUT THE AUTHOR

Diederik Oostdijk is an associate professor at the VU University in Amsterdam. He is the coeditor of *Tales of the Great American Victory: World War II in Politics and Poetics,* based on an international conference, "The Stories of World War II," that he organized in Amsterdam in 2004. He has published more than a dozen journal articles and book chapters on American poetry and culture.